12-18          3-

*The Warsaw Diary of Adam Czerniakow*

# The Warsaw Diary of Adam Czerniakow

## PRELUDE TO DOOM

EDITED BY

Raul Hilberg, Stanislaw Staron, and Josef Kermisz

TRANSLATED BY

Stanislaw Staron and the staff of Yad Vashem

STEIN AND DAY/*Publishers*/New York

First English language edition published 1979.
Copyright 1968 by Yad Vashem, Jerusalem
Copyright © 1979 by Raul Hilberg, Stanislaw Staron,
and Yad Vashem Martyrs' and Heroes' Remembrance Authority
All rights reserved.
Designed by Ed Kaplin
Printed in the United States of America
Stein and Day/*Publishers*/Scarborough House,
Briarcliff Manor, N.Y. 10510

SECOND PRINTING, 1979


*Library of Congress Cataloging in Publication Data*

Czerniakow, Adam, 1880-1942.
    The Warsaw diary of Adam Czerniakow.

    Translation of Dziennik getta warszawskiego.
    Includes index.
    1. Jews in Warsaw—Persecutions.    2. Holocaust,
Jewish (1939-1945)—Poland—Warsaw.    3. Czerniakow,
Adam, 1880-1942.    4. Jews in Warsaw—Biography.
5. Warsaw—History.    I. Hilberg, Raul, 1926-
II. Staron, Stanislaw.    III. Kermisz, Josef.
DS135.P62W2613          943.8'4          78-9272
ISBN 0-8128-2523-3 ·

# Contents

Map öf Warsaw Ghetto on page x-xi

Notebook Five has never been recovered.

# Foreword

The first edition of the Czerniakow diary appeared in a Hebrew translation, with a facsimile of the original, in 1968. The Jewish Historical Institute in Warsaw brought out the Polish text in 1972.

Now, after several years of preparation, we present the diary to the English-speaking public. Stanislaw Staron was the principal translator of the Polish manuscript into English; Raul Hilberg translated the German material. The staff of Yad Vashem sent us a draft of an English translation for comparison with our effort. Raul Hilberg, Stanislaw Staron, and Josef Kermisz are co-editors of this volume. The notes in their final form are the distilled product of our own research and the work of Yad Vashem.

The translating and editing of the diary called for making the text meaningful to a reader who is not familiar with the scene of the drama. The diary depicts events in another society, with its own ways and mores and its own institutions, and in another time. There was a problem of rendering into English the multiplicity of the Jewish, Polish, and German administrative offices, positions, ranks, and practices, which have no counterpart in American society. Czerniakow himself faced this problem in making clear in Polish the instructions of his German overlords; the result was not always satisfactory. Above all, we have had to reproduce the bizarre world of the ghetto under Nazi rule; a world where the irrational, the absurd, and the unexpected were the order of the day; an existence unknown here and now.

In our efforts to bring the diary to the English-speaking reader, we were torn between conflicting considerations. A set of priorities was eventually decided upon. Our paramount concern has been to render the original faithfully. The translator's license has only been invoked when close rendition, literal or otherwise, led to distortion of the intended meaning. Czerniakow occasionally spelled names phonetically, he wrote Polish endings into German words, and he used old as well as modern forms for German *Umlaut* sounds. So far as possible, we have incorporated these errors and inconsistencies in the belief that they too reflected his state of mind. The temptation to polish Czerniakow's often awkward style was also deliberately resisted except where considerations of intelligibility made it imperative.

We have made every effort to identify names, offices, places and circumstances. For this task we have exploited the explanatory material produced by the Jewish Historical Institute in Warsaw and the unpublished annotations by Hanns von Krannhals deposited at the Zentrale Stelle der Landesjustizverwaltungen in Ludwigsburg. Yet we are still not in possession of all the information we need. As a consequence, gaps inevitably remain in our explanations of the text.

We wish to thank Dr. Henry Fenigstein, a survivor of the Warsaw ghetto, where he served as a physician, for the long interview he granted S. Staron in Toronto. Dr. Adalbert Rückerl, director of the Zentrale Stelle, was most helpful to Raul Hilberg in Ludwigsburg. The staff of Yad Vashem cordially received R. Hilberg in Jerusalem. We will gratefully remember the many acts of kindness extended to us by Dr. Yitzhak Arad, director of Yad Vashem, and his colleagues Dr. Israel Gutman and Dr. Kermisz. Mrs. Bronia Klibanski of Yad Vashem stood by us for a long time, helping us with her irreplaceable knowledge and insights. Dr. Lucjan Dobroszycki of the YIVO Institute shared with us his invaluable knowledge of sources. To Herman Wouk, always interested in the history of the Holocaust, we owe a special note of gratitude for his friendly intervention in support of our work during its formative period. Benton Arnovitz, our editor at Stein and Day, built a bridge between the United States and Israel in order that we might succeed.

Helen Stephenson, our secretary, worked on the manuscript with an uncommon understanding of its contents. She assisted us, encouraged us, and inspired us during our most difficult moments. No one can own this diary, but to the extent that it is ours, it is also hers.

*—Stanislaw Staron and Raul Hilberg*

*The Warsaw Diary of Adam Czerniakow*

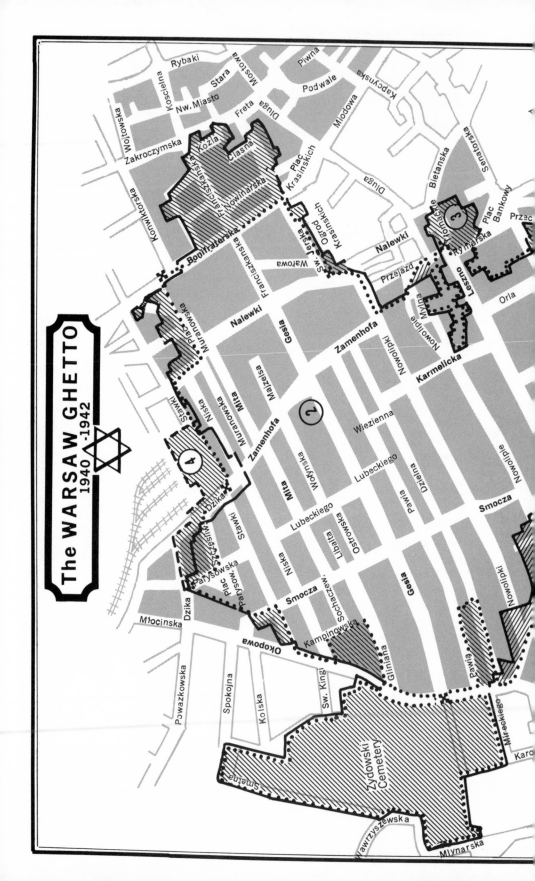

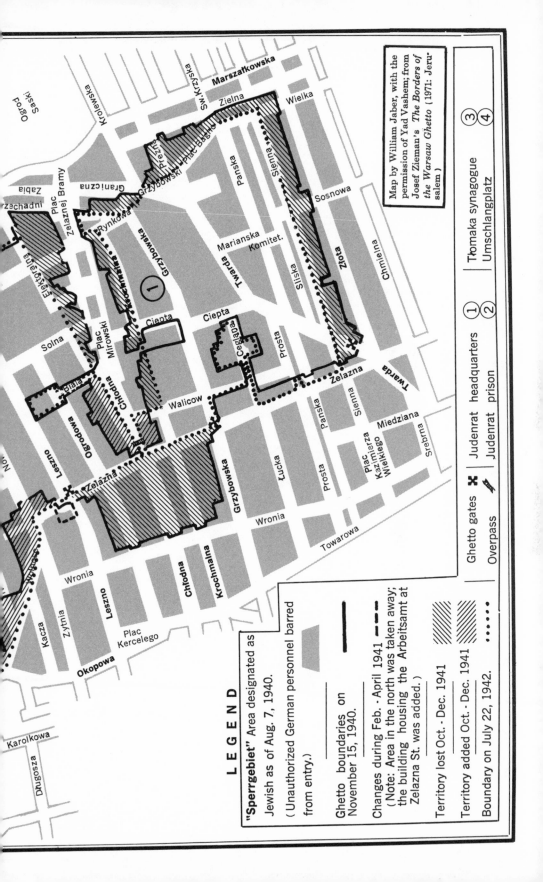

**LEGEND**

**"Sperrgebiet"** Area designated as Jewish as of Aug. 7, 1940.

(Unauthorized German personnel barred from entry.)

Ghetto boundaries on November 15, 1940.

Changes during Feb. - April 1941 (Note: Area in the north was taken away; the building housing the Arbeitsamt at Zelazna St. was added.)

Territory lost Oct. - Dec. 1941

Territory added Oct. - Dec. 1941

Boundary on July 22, 1942.

Ghetto gates

Overpass

① Judenrat headquarters
② Judenrat prison
③ Tłomacka synagogue
④ Umschlangplatz

Map by William Jaber, with the permission of Yad Vashem; from Josef Zieman's *The Borders of the Warsaw Ghetto* (1971: Jerusalem.)

# Introduction

## Josef Kermisz

Adam Czerniakow, one of the most tragic of Jewish community leaders during the Holocaust, was born in 1880 in Warsaw. After completing his studies in chemistry at the Warsaw Polytechnic, he went on to study industrial engineering in Dresden.

As a young man, he struggled against assimilation to find his way back to Judaism. Shortly before World War I he became involved in Jewish public life. He dedicated himself to defending and promoting the interests of Jewish craftsmen, and he published extensively on subjects concerning Jewish artisans, many of his articles appearing in *Hantverker-Zeitung,* the publication of the General Association of Jewish Craftsmen. In the 1924 yearbook of that association, published on the tenth anniversary of its founding, Czerniakow published a long article outlining a comprehensive program for vocational training and technical schools. He taught for many years in the Warsaw Jewish community's vocational schools.

Czerniakow took a stand against compulsory unionization of craftsmen in a lecture delivered to the First Congress of Jewish Artisans on October 5, 1925; the address was later published as a booklet. He was active in the struggle against the 1927 Guild Law, which in effect ousted Jewish workers from their jobs and shops.

For nearly 30 years he was a central figure among Polish Jewish craftsmen at a time when those workers supported one-third of

Polish Jewry. Fifty percent of all artisans in Poland were Jewish; in some trades they were even a majority.

Czerniakow was a member of the Engineers Association, known for its assimilationist stand. On the other hand, he joined the Jewish Nationalist camp of the Nationalist Minority Block, established to counteract attempts of Polish reactionary elements to squeeze minority representation out of Parliament. From 1927 until 1934, Czerniakow was the elected representative of Jewish artisans, on the National Jewish list, in the Warsaw Municipal Council. He was also a member of the municipal development committee.

Czerniakow played an active part in the 1928 Sejm and Senate elections and participated in the campaign for Jewish minority rights led by Yitzhak Gruenbaum. He spoke out against government discrimination and persecution. In the 1931 by-elections he won a place in the Senate, but the Pilsudski government dissolved the Senate and Sejm before the first sitting.

Czerniakow played an active role in all aspects of public, social, and economic life. Before the outbreak of World War II, he was nominated to the appointed Executive Council of the Warsaw Jewish Community as a representative of the Jewish craftsmen. He also chaired that council's education department. Together with Maurycy Mayzel, M. Lichtenbaum, and Łabędź, he was a member of the Warsaw delegation to the 1939 General Congress of Polish Jewry for Eretz Israel.

On September 23, 1939, during the siege of Warsaw, Czerniakow was appointed Chairman of the Jewish Council by the mayor and head of civil defense, Stefan Starzynski. The previous chairman, Maurycy Mayzel, fled Warsaw at the outbreak of the war. On that day, Czerniakow wrote in his diary of the historic task facing him and his determination to meet the challenge.

The early chapters of the diary deal with personal details, but when the Germans enter Warsaw, the pages fill with historic events and evaluations of the situation. Almost every day, from September 6, 1939 until his last hours on July 23, 1942, Czerniakow wrote in his diary regularly and systematically. In his final role, as Chairman of the Community and *Judenrat*—he was appointed to the *Judenrat*, or Jewish council, by the Germans on October 3, 1939—he showed the best of his character, his moral strength, and his devotion to his people.

Few knew of the existence of Czerniakow's diary. Professors

Hilel Seidman and Ludwik Hirszfeld mentioned it in their memoirs. With the discovery of the second part of the underground archives of the Warsaw ghetto, further details of the diary were revealed. Dr. Emanuel Ringelblum, the founder of the underground archives, a tireless worker who struggled to find and preserve Jewish writings and documents for further generations, noted in his essay "Oneg Shabat": "Czerniakow used to write everything that happened in the Ghetto during his term as chairman."

The diary, or, to be exact, the collection of notebooks, is of utmost interest because Czerniakow came into daily contact with various German authorities and Polish municipal officials and, as chairman of the community, held all the threads of Jewish public life in his hands.

Rosalia Pietkiewicz, a Warsaw ghetto survivor, bought the diary from an unknown source in the first half of 1959. After lengthy negotiations, through the kind offices of Mr. Gershon Avner, the Israeli Ambassador to Canada, and Mr. Mordechai Dagan, Embassy Advisor, Yad Vashem, the Israeli Martyrs' and Heroes' Remembrance Authority, received the diary on August 28, 1964.

The diary consists of several notebooks, each of different length, altogether 1009 pages. One notebook is missing, Notebook Five, from December 14, 1940 to April 22, 1941. The sizes are uniform, 9.8 cm × 15.6 cm. Many pages have corrections, and the additions in the margins, crossed out lines, and the often cramped handwriting also make the diary difficult to read.

In a collective effort made by our editorial staff, the diary was deciphered except for a few words, initials, abbreviations, names, and allusions. It was often necessary to clarify in the notes what Czerniakow only hinted at and to explain things that were common knowledge in his day.

The diary does record the major events outside the ghetto, Czerniakow's impressions, experiences, and important commands. Czerniakow wrote briefly every day until his death, sometimes several times a day, to fix events firmly in his memory. There is no doubt that he prepared these notes for his own use, planning to elaborate after the war. Addenda such as orders, letters, and the like were affixed to the text or incorporated into it by Czerniakow.

Czerniakow wrote in Polish, in a style that is simple, unadorned, and to the point. Concealment was another reason for his brevity.

The importance of the diary lies in its accuracy. The facts given are exact and well presented and, in general, cannot be disputed. Events are dated and precise figures are given.

Much of the information in the diary is not to be found in other sources. Though he did not dwell on the suffering in the ghetto and camps where the Warsaw Jews worked, major happenings are recorded—the evil decrees, the terror, forced labor, work camps, starvation, epidemics, mass expulsion from provincial towns to the Warsaw ghetto, and the evictions from streets and houses within the ghetto. Of special value are figures given for refugees entering Warsaw from provincial towns and foreign countries, confiscation of property, the extent of starvation, epidemics, and death.

Invaluable information is given on the Jewish Council and its activities and organizations, social aid, intensified social conflicts, budgetary matters, tax policy, interrelationships between Jews, the economic and cultural struggle, and on Jewish reactions, behavior, and endurance in the ghetto.

All aspects of the German policy of exploitation are reflected in the diary. They placed a heavy burden on the shoulders of the Jews, primarily through the Jewish Council. In helpless anger, the Jewish community was forced to pay compulsory "contributions" as well as taxes in cash and taxes in goods.

The acts of terror perpetrated by the Germans on the Jewish population have an important place in the diary. However, the stress is placed on the daily struggle for survival in the ghetto, events in its internal life, and on people—mainly public figures in Jewish life, their thoughts, feelings, and moods in the shadow of death. The actions and events recorded reflect the atmosphere of terror and depression of those days, and the diary also evaluates the events.

A valuable source on the intense social conflict that developed in the ghetto, the diary contrasts the servants of the conquerors—the profiteers living a life of luxury—and the starving masses. Czerniakow stresses the crying evil of a ghetto where bodies wasted by starvation lie near the restaurants and dance halls of those who live well.

Statistics and diagrams on the extent of starvation in the ghetto, and on epidemics and death, give us valuable insight into the German system of slow starvation. Because sources of income were cut off and German food supply to the Jews was poor, it was impossible to give everyone the minimum number of calories to support life. By the end of 1941, death from starvation was a common occurrence in the ghetto and the number of deaths per diem increased daily. In alms houses, Czerniakow wrote on November 19, 1941, mothers hid children for up to eight days after their deaths in order to get their food rations. The following day he wrote about "endless complaints that there isn't anything to bury the dead in. They are laid in the ground naked, without even a piece of paper in place of cloth." On February 20, 1942, at 11:32 A.M. Czerniakow copied the message he received from the Chief of the *Ordnungdienst* (Order Service, or Jewish police) "On Cannibalism in the Jewish Quarter." The next day Czerniakow reported to German officials on this, adding his opinion and what conditions led to this crime.

The diary confirms the fact that the *Judenrat* represented mainly the well-to-do, was closer to the upper classes, and more frequently backed these classes during the selection for the camps where the Jews were sent for forced labor and extermination.

Czerniakow's efforts to thwart the favoritism of the Jewish Council were not very successful. Discrimination was applied noticeably in the numerous indirect taxes, especially those on food coupons, medicaments and the like; the weight of these taxes fell mainly on the poorer people. The wealthy were almost entirely freed of direct taxation, for the Jewish Council took the inequitable stand that the direct taxes were to be levied only on income, whereas in the conditions prevailing in the ghetto they should have been based on levels of expenditure, that is, on the standards of living. The diary speaks of the injustice of the Jewish Council's budget being derived principally from indirect taxation.

The personal element—including quarrels between Jewish Council members—was recorded by Czerniakow. On May 26, 1940 Czerniakow wrote about attending a stormy meeting concerning a special levy on bread, a tax that severely affected the masses. The decision taken depressed him terribly. However, many were exempted from this tax. On January 6, 1942 Czerniakow wrote that he succeeded in freeing another 10,000 individuals from it. Altogether 150,000 people were exempted. Czerniakow called a meeting of the Jewish Council on May 16, 1941 to discuss the suggestion that 30,000 food coupons be collected from the wealthy and distributed among the poor.

On April 20 and May 21, 1942 Czerniakow commanded the ghetto police to carry out surprise searches in restaurants and to confiscate expensive foods such as chocolate, sardines, oils, and cakes. The cakes and cookies were distributed to children and the other items were given to orphanages and alms houses.

A public kitchen was opened on July 20, 1941 for children whose fathers had been sent to the labor camps. Czerniakow contributed to the success of "Children's Month" in the ghetto, which raised over a million zlotys. On January 31, 1942 Czerniakow told about his speech at the opening of an orphanage on 27 Ogrodowa Street. He stressed that he would continue to fight the wealthy, who refused to contribute to help the poor.

At the meeting of the Economic Council on February 1, 1942, members expressed dissatisfaction with the new line he wished to take by demanding contributions from the rich to meet the needs of the poor. Members of the Jewish Council firmly opposed Czerniakow's policy. The Germans, who well knew how to exploit conflicts within the ghetto to weaken Jewish unity, sided with this protest.

Ringelblum stresses this point in his essay on Itzhak Giterman, head of the Joint Distribution Committee in Poland. He says that Czerniakow adopted Giterman's idea of raising large amounts of money for aid. This project was headed by Giterman, with the participation of public figures such as Bloch, M. M. Cohn, and Dr. Ringelblum. Using compulsory measures, such as the placing of refugees in the homes of the wealthy and forced labor, this project brought in over a million zlotys. But they failed to achieve the main objective because "those around the Chairman [Czerniakow] did all in their power to thwart the plan to levy taxes on profiteers" (Ringelblum, *Writings,* vol. II, p. 135).

With great emotion, Czerniakow writes about hungry children, street children, beggars, naked and barefoot skeletons. We read his note of June 14, 1942: "I commanded that the children be brought to the garden from the detention room organized by the local *Ordnungsdienst* station. They are living skeletons, street beggars. Some of them came to see me at the community offices. These 8-year-old citizens conversed with me like adults. I'm ashamed to admit that it's been long since I cried so. . . . Cursed are those among us who can eat and drink and forget these children."

Czerniakow's concern for expanding a system of social self-help is made clear in the diary. He describes work carried on quietly in dormitories and public kitchens for thousands of children. Over

100,000 meals a day were often distributed, and on July 1, 1941 there were over 118,000.

Czerniakow's unremitting devotion to education is also reflected in his diary. The establishment of a network of educational institutions, schools, and professional courses in mechanics and chemistry were among his many accomplishments. Dozens of educational institutions, including elementary and high schools, worked in secret or semi-secret in the ghetto. Under cover of children's homes run by Centos, an orphans' aid society with 50,000 children in its various institutions, Jewish schools such as *Tarbut, Zisho, Shulkult, Yavneh, Horev,* and *Beth Yacov* held classes.

The "Nutrition Board" was the pseudonym of the Central Committee for Jewish Education, made up of school principals from all movements. In his lengthy essay on labor leader Szachne Sagan, Ringelblum credits Czerniakow with saving these movements and ensuring the survival of prewar educational systems. Thus, Borochow School at 68 Nowolipki Street flourished under the guise of a children's kitchen.

Over 50 vocational training courses were given. ORT gave agricultural courses and also crash courses in farming and gardening; 175 people completed the agriculture course. Disguised as courses for artisans, there were university-level studies in medicine, chemistry, technology, and education. Professional medical courses were disguised as lower level anti-epidemic training of hospital staff.

The Jewish Council's official report, prepared for the German authorities, stated that in the year between May 15, 1941 and May 15, 1942 100 courses were given in the ghetto to 4,300 students. In spite of tremendous difficulties, lack of textbooks, economic hardship, and uncertainty about the future, a fierce desire for knowledge imbued masses of young people in the ghetto.

When the Germans allowed Czerniakow to open primary schools and vocational courses, he spared neither labor nor financial resources to give the students everything possible. Czerniakow found this effort very rewarding. On August 15, 1941 he wrote: "I visited a number of refugee centers. In one of the centers, ZTOS (Zydowskie Towarzystwo Opicki Spotecznej—Jewish Organization for Public Care) I discovered a child's corpse. . . . Afterwards I visited the vocational school on Stawki Street. A breath of life after the depression of the *Punkten* [Centers]."

Czerniakow participated in science lessons, discussion groups, lectures, various meetings, and exhibitions. He played an active part in the intensive research carried out in the ghetto on starvation and typhus fever. Mention of this is made by Dr. Israel Milejkowski, who initiated this work on the basis of the rich clinical material that the ghetto hospitals afforded. The material collected in five months' time could not have been collected in a year under normal conditions. On July 6, 1942 Czerniakow wrote about a conference at Dr. Milejkowski's. Among others, Dr. Emil Apfelbaum, Dr. Jozef Stein, and Dr. Julian Fliederbaum read papers. At this meeting the results of the research on hunger were summed up.

Czerniakow also supported cultural life in the ghetto. He backed actors, musicians, and artists. With his help, a symphony orchestra was founded, and it gave a number of concerts. The diary mentioned nearly all the important cultural and educational events in the ghetto. They are listed below:

August 18, 1940—German authorities gave permission to start vocational training courses.

August 19, 1940—Appointment of committee to run vocational training courses.

August 20–21, 1940—In the course of three days vocational courses were started. A document forbidding confiscation of vocational school equipment.

August 22, 1940—Vocational school consultation, meanwhile organizing courses for 300 pupils.

September 25, 1940—A meeting about starting the school system. Czerniakow suggested that vocational schools be maintained by the community and maintenance of primary schools be in the hands of educational institutions. An organizing committee was elected.

May 24, 1941—A meeting devoted to vocational schools.

August 28, 1941—A list of schools for 4,300 children given to the *Kommissar.*

August 30, 1941—The opening of graphic arts exhibition in Sienna Street. Distribution of 50-zloty grants to a few dozen pupils.

September 1, 1941—Exhibition of pupils' work at the vocational school on Stawki Street. Distribution of 6-month grants (50 zlotys per month) and one-time grants of 50 zlotys.

September 5, 1941—Permission was received to open elementary schools and to hold committee meetings.

December 7, 1941—Opening of pharmacy courses.

December 21, 1941—Ceremony in honor of the community's educational network.

January 20, 1942—Czerniakow visits four types of primary schools and decides that where idealists teach, the education is good.

January 22, 1942—Czerniakow discusses with the supply authority fat and sugar rations for 2,700 pupils.

February 11, 1942—Czerniakow visited the Council's Institute of Chemistry and Bacteriology and offered them 5,000 zlotys to buy equipment.

February 16, 1942—Preparations made to open teacher-training pedagogic courses.

February 26, 1942—First meeting of Board of Governors of the about-to-be-established vocational education secondary school. The principal, Buchweitz, was given the task of drawing up a curriculum, together with his colleagues.

March 17, 1942—The technical school was opened.

May 5, 1942—Jewish Children's Day *(Lag B'Omer)*. A show presented by the pupils of the Council's schools.

May 24, 1942—A concert given by the Jewish Police band, conducted by Kataszek. Jewish works were presented. Played very nicely.

May 31, 1942—Meeting of lectures in higher education.

June 20, 1942—A reception given by the JSS for the teacher's seminar students.

July 5, 1942—Jewish police band concert in the garden. Review parade of 600 primary school pupils.

July 6, 1942—A conference giving the results of scientific research on hunger. Papers presented.

July 10, 1942—Opening of an in-service teacher training course.

July 12, 1942—Opening of prison workshop to commemorate the first year of Jewish prisons.

Czerniakow gives us new information and insight into the ghetto's religious life. On January 20, 1940, the Germans, under the pretense of preventing epidemics, ordered the closure of all synagogues, yeshivas and mikvas. Public prayer was forbidden even in small minyans, and those who disobeyed risked imprisonment. In spite of this, 600 minyans gathered in secret. But after the discovery of an illegal minyan in Grzybowska Street, the Jewish Council published a warning saying that Jews who arranged or participated in public prayer would be punished according to the government decree. Thanks to the efforts of Czerniakow, permission was granted at the end of April 1941 to open three synagogues. On April 27, 1941 Czerniakow appointed a committee to raise funds for renovation of the Great Synagogue on Tlomackie Street. On that same day Czerniakow proclaimed throughout the ghetto that from henceforth Saturday was to be the day of rest, and Sunday a regular workday. When a delegation of rabbis headed by Rabbi Michelson came to thank Czerniakow for the Sabbath proclamation, he suggested that they choose a Chief Rabbi and begin work on rebuilding the synagogues. On Shavuot (June 1, 1941), Czerniakow prayed in the Great Synagogue and was given the honor of removing the Torah from the ark.

Czerniakow saw a degree of apathy toward religion in the fact that the Jews could not maintain the three synagogues. He discussed this in his diary on January 29, 1942. The Moriah Synagogue committee came to Czerniakow with an appeal to aid religious ministrants and funds for rebuilding. Czerniakow mentioned in surprise that funds for repairing the roof of one of the synagogues came from non-Jewish sources.

In any case, the Jews didn't have long to enjoy the reopened synagogues. On March 3, 1942 Czerniakow received a letter from German Kommissar Auerswald saying that the Great Synagogue and adjoining houses had to be evacuated and closed by the twentieth of the month. In spite of all, the assembly of the religious committee opened on March 9, 1942, chaired by Rabbi Frydman; Czerniakow spoke of the need for religious spirit and was answered by Rabbi Kanal and Rabbi Frydman. Only a month before the big expulsion, permission was received from German authorities to open Yeshivas.

The diary describes the main lines along which the ghetto economy ran and gives most valuable details concerning the day-to-day struggle for existence. Czerniakow wrote briefly about the ghetto factories. We know from sources in Ringelblum archives, "Oneg Shabat," that a network of factories was established on a shoestring. These factories produced all sorts of objects but their many innovations, necessitated by extremely difficult conditions, are lost to us. Czerniakow praises the ingenuity of the ghetto Jews on February 25, 1942. As proof of the vitality of the Jewish population, Czerniakow cites the wonders worked in the production of raw materials and substitutes.

Not only did the Jews build various large-scale production facilities, but they found means of smuggling the goods to "Aryan" consumers. The Jewish manufacturers and artisans knew how to overcome with ingenuity many of the obstacles and repressions imposed by the Germans. The imprisonment of the Jews behind the walls of the ghetto had been intended to prevent any commerce between Jews and the outside world. Jewish manufacturers and businessmen managed to find some raw materials within the ghetto; still other materials were procured outside and smuggled in. The links between the "Aryan" world and the ghetto were so multiform that whenever some new raw material appeared in the "Aryan" section of Warsaw, it also showed up in the ghetto. After the raw materials were processed, the goods were smuggled out of the ghetto and sold to non-Jewish wholesalers. The money or goods bought were smuggled back into the ghetto. At one point the manufacture of brushes, metal, leatherware, textiles, underwear, and haberdashery reached tremendous proportions. For example, the monthly income of private carpentry shops in the first half of 1941 was 5 million zlotys; brush manufacture earned approximately 3 million zlotys. From the middle of 1941 on, 2,000 families made their living in the brush industry. This activity created employment opportunities in the thread and lathe industry. During the peak of activity, September and October 1941, the ghetto turned out 25,000 brushes a day.

The output of the carpentry shops and brush factories did not go through the *Transferstelle* (the German office that was the sole legal channel for imports and exports of the ghetto), for that institution's prices were controlled. Instead, the calculations were based on the open market prices. The *Transferstelle*, whose activities were mainly noticeable in its hindering of bringing food into the ghetto, concerned itself only with the products of workshops in German hands, mainly tailoring, shoemaking, and the fur trade. The official production of the ghetto industry, through the *Transferstelle*, came to over

1.7 million zlotys in November 1941. But the official figure represents only a small part of output, because most merchandise was exported from the ghetto illegally.

Private carpentry and brush firms in the ghetto produced goods for the German army from the end of 1940, usually through Polish contractors. Army trucks would come into the ghetto without being stopped at the entry checkposts. These trucks brought raw materials and picked up the finished products. Part of this production reached the open market. With the outbreak of the German-Soviet War, the flourishing business with the army came to an end. The German army moved far to the east and ghetto manufacturers began to furnish hospitals, offices, and other institutions. Upholstery and tinsmithing were also successful in the ghetto. For a long while, 1,000 heating pipes a day were sent out of the ghetto for the army.

Wherever there was demand, ghetto manufacturers tried to fill the gap. Thus, when in the second half of 1941 there was a shortage of beds for hospitals, ghetto plumbers undertook to fill the need and used old gas pipes because of a shortage of materials. The ghetto produced gloves for the army in the winter of 1941. They used rabbit fur from Kraków, tanned secretly in the ghetto.

It must be remembered that many Jews supported themselves by selling off their possessions when their livelihood was cut off with the establishment of the ghetto. At first they sold clothing and furniture, then underwear and linens, then finally pots and pans. For every three Jews who sold their belongings in order to eat, there was a fourth who earned his living as a dealer. Furniture, clothing, shoes and even jewelry were bartered for bread. According to a poll conducted by Ringelblum's archive, 20 million zlotys' worth of clothing and furniture was traded in the ghetto monthly.

Czerniakow tells us that the legal imports to the ghetto in November 1941 reached 2 million zlotys, while illegal imports reached 80 million. This means that the alert Jewish masses were in large measure able to frustrate the conqueror's intentions, acting secretly and in indirect ways to do everything possible to deceive the tyrants and outwit them. In December 1941, official exports totaled 2 million zlotys—in June, 12 million. As Czerniakow points out, these figures represent only a small part of total export, because most of the trade was smuggled out. The relation between official and real supplies paralleled the relation between official and real trade. The tremendous shortage of supplies in the ghetto was covered in part by illegal imports. If Warsaw's Jews had had to live on the official bread ration, they all would have died of starvation in the first year.

Czerniakow tells stories of smugglers and underground trade, and he especially praises the bravery of children who brought food into the ghetto. The German plan, to starve the Jews to death quickly, was foiled.

Everything possible was done to try to avert German orders and restrictions. A technique was developed to smuggle over walls, through gates, cellars, through all the hidden places the conqueror could not control. Professional smugglers worked in cooperation with bribed German, Polish, and Jewish police. Many of the impoverished adults sneaked out the gates in order to smuggle in food. Children did so, too, children who could squeeze through every crack in the ghetto walls. Thousands, Jews and non-Jews, were occupied with smuggling.

On October 14, 1941 Czerniakow writes that smugglers killed Yankel Katz, a Jewish policeman. On January 19, 1942 Czerniakow notes that 443 males (of whom 121 are boys) and 213 minors, both boys and girls were in prison for having crossed the border of the ghetto in order to get food for their families. In his diary entry for February 26, 1942 we read, "I waited for Auerswald in the Housing Office on Nowolipie Street at 12:30. As he was getting out of the car, a package thrown over the wall flew over his head." An entry dated April 9, 1942, says that near the *Wache* a truck belonging to smugglers had been stopped. For a long time it had been getting into the ghetto under cover of a sign that stated that it belonged to the gas company.

Of utmost importance in Czerniakow's writings are the terse and carefully considered entries about the instances of heroic resistance in the face of pursuit and torture. He notes the vitality and dynamism shown by the Jews of Warsaw, their tenacious resolve to hold on to life in spite of everything.

On July 8, 1941 Czerniakow states that in proportion to the enormity of the tragedy facing them, the Jews were calm and balanced. There is no doubt that Czerniakow was referring to the moral self-discipline of the deprived and starving masses and the sense of responsibility that motivated them. Thus, in spite of all harassment, acts of cruelty, threats, and cynical sadism, not one irresponsible act is recorded that could have seriously affected the entire

Jewish population. However, Czerniakow writes about two instances where Jews beat up *Volksdeutsche* [Ethnic Germans], on January 26, 1940 and May 28, 1940. After the first instance the Jews were given one day to pay a fine of 100,000 zlotys. If they did not pay the following day, the Germans threatened to shoot 100 men. After the second instance, 43 men between the ages of 18 and 50 were arrested. On October 30, 1940 Czerniakow was called to the Gestapo when Rabbi Najhaus' illegal synagogue was discovered in Grzybowska Street. On September 3, 1941 Czerniakow wrote that Auerswald was complaining that thousands of Jews flee the ghetto monthly, and so he had decided to cut the southern portion of the ghetto off from Sienna to Chlodna streets. "The walls are to be erected along the middle and will run the length of the street . . . smuggling of people and possessions is to stop," Czerniakow wrote.

With the intensification of German measures to destroy the ghetto and its inhabitants, Jewish resistance grew. "To stand and outlive the enemy" was the motto. The ghetto population fought heroically in a desperate battle for life. Systematic disobedience of the conqueror's laws, many of which a Jew had to break in order to survive, was fired by a spirit of passive resistance. Of course, the disorder frequently evident among the Germans made it possible to disobey many laws.

A good example of ghetto sabotage of German laws was the reaction to the order to hand in all fur garments. Most of those who complied did so out of fear of informers. On December 30, 1941 Czerniakow mentioned a persistent rumor, confirmed by other sources, that many people preferred to sell their furs to Poles, or give them away, hide, or destroy them, rather than obey the German order.

In his diary entry of April 21, 1942, Czerniakow confirms that the Gestapo threatened even greater reprisals than the mass murder of April 17 and and 18, 1942, if the underground periodicals continued to appear.

Two carefully worded hints about the Jewish underground appear in the diary. "B. claims that the organizations have been discovered in the ghetto," Czerniakow wrote on April 22, 1942. "B" was K. G. Brandt, the Gestapo expert on Jewish affairs. Actually, there was a big change in Jewish political organizations after the "Night of Blood" (April 17 and 18, 1942). Many leaders of the underground were killed, as well as publishers and distributors of illegal periodicals, and so political activity retreated even deeper into the underground. Until that time, all the parties acted semi-legally and "underground publications multiplied to such an extent that the bulletin of a certain group [the Bund] appeared twice a week." Under cover of a publicity campaign against disease, parties and organizations held meetings. At one of these meetings, Ringelblum mentioned in his notes, "A speaker addressed a crowd of 150. The subject was active resistance. I attended a party meeting of 500 youths. Heated arguments came close to curses." The Night of Blood weakened the parties, but they recovered quickly and became more hidden and secretive.

Czerniakow again refers to the underground on April 29, when he quotes K. G. Brandt, "again there is disquiet in the ghetto." There is no doubt that Brandt is expressing his dissatisfaction with the continual signs of rebellion in the ghetto.

In one of his last entries, that of July 22, 1942, Czerniakow records that a piece of glass was thrown at a passing German police car. "We were warned that if this happened again all hostages would be shot." Czerniakow is referring to the members of the Jewish Council and to the adminstrators of its supply board headed by Abraham Gepner. They were arrested on July 21, 1942, one day before the great deportation to Treblinka.

The diary gives us numerous details on the relations between Poles and Jews as seen by Czerniakow in his daily contacts with Jewish and non-Jewish public figures. During the siege of Warsaw, Czerniakow notes in his diary (September 15, 1939), no Jewish representative was invited to Civil Guard Central Command *(Straz Obywatelska)*, in spite of the fact that over 1,000 Jews volunteered in the Jewish quarter on the first day of enlistment. All Czerniakow's attempts to secure a post in Central Command were in vain. A. Hartglass writes, "He was rejected and after the defeat of Warsaw they said that he, as head of the *Judenrat,* was a German appointee." On a note of defeat Czerniakow writes on October 14, 1939 that when he was in the SS headquarters the commander of the Civil Guard, Regulski, took his Civil Guard armband and certificate without any explanation. He intended to complain to Mayor Starzynski.

From his first days as head of the Jewish Council, Czerniakow constantly stresses the organic link between the ghetto and the rest of the city. Julian Kulski, the appointed mayor of Warsaw and successor to Starzynski, confirms this approach. He said, although his words must be taken with a grain of salt, "It is as if Czerniakow recognized the city's inability to contribute toward its Jewish population and so never made impossible demands. When he made a request it was possible to meet it and so relations between the municipality and the *Judenrat* were very good, thanks to Czerniakow."

In order to drive a wedge between the municipality and the Jewish population, the Germans tried to involve the municipality in a vicious attempt to limit the living space of the Jews and create crowding in the ghetto. Thanks to his connections in the municipality, Czerniakow managed to get better terms, especially since the German plan involved moving thousands of Polish families to make room for Jews.

Though he is often circumspect in his remarks, Czerniakow does not overlook the sympathetic attitude of many Poles to German persecution of Jews. Thus, he notes on October 18, 1940, before the establishment of the ghetto, "Bargaining for certain streets." This refers to quarrels between Poles and Jews, each wanting more streets for their own quarter. The Poles were insistent and streets such as Swietojerska, which previously had been entirely Jewish, were not included in the ghetto.

Czerniakow mentions on December 2, 1940 that Jewish shops on the "Aryan" side of Warsaw were confiscated by the police. On November 16, 1940, 1,700 shops and 2,260 businesses were taken over, or as the officials put it "secured." All the Jewish stalls in the market on Mirowska Street were taken over and all the goods were stolen by Poles.

The Germans knew that by giving to the Poles part of what had been plundered from the Jews, the Nazis gained ardent supporters. And yet the bulk of the plunder remained with the German. There is no doubt that Polish satisfaction with the fate of Jews under the Nazis stemmed from economic considerations. Poles, neighbors of Jews, acquaintances, perhaps even friends, who were given Jewish possessions, shops and factories, turned into bitter enemies of the Jews during the German occupation.

Czerniakow writes about pogroms on Jewish streets at the end of March 1940, May 31, 1940, August 19, 1940, and October 26, 1940. During the riots, hooligans armed with sticks and light weapons fell upon passersby, beating them cruelly with no regard to age or sex. They broke shop windows and looted while the Polish police looked on complacently. The labor intelligentsia and unions condemned the rioters, but nothing was done to correct the impression that the Polish population was firmly behind the anti-Semitic Poles collaborating with the Germans.

The Germans spared no effort in deepening hatred toward the Jews. The main task of the Polish-language German press was to spread anti-Semitic poison among the Poles. The Polish underground papers incited the people against the Jews as well. It is no wonder, then, that Polish ruffians threw stones over the ghetto walls. Czerniakow mentions this a number of times. He writes on July 9, 1942: "In the afternoon Polish hoodlums throw stones over the walls into Chlodna Street. Ever since we removed the bricks and stones from the middle of Chlodna Street, they don't have much ammunition left. I often ask myself if Poland is Mickiewiez and Slowacki [two Polish poets] or the street gangs. The truth lies in the middle."

From the diary we learn of the German mechanism of destruction that operated with malevolent cunning against the Jews and of the multiplication of authorities, all of which regarded themselves empowered to treat the Jewish Council at their whim, to demand from them whatever they wanted, and to impose on it whatever duties and restrictions they desired.

Czerniakow tells of his constant attempts to have anti-Jewish decrees revoked or at least modified to lessen Jewish suffering. He pleaded with every government agency he could reach and faithfully recorded his discussions in brief. In addition to his work for the whole ghetto, he often tried to help individuals arrested for attempting to leave the ghetto, failure to wear the special armband, and other similar crimes.

In his contacts with the authorities, Czerniakow conducted himself as a representative of the Jews who would surrender nothing of his dignity and honor. His bearing and modest way of life, his power of organization and work, his courage and his firmness gained him the respect of some of the Nazis. In his feeling of responsibility, his devotion and persistence, which knew no bounds, Czerniakow was outstanding. For example, when the Gestapo fined the ghetto on November 24, 1939, the Jewish Council had to hand over 17 hostages; 6 rabbis, 6 public figures and 5 members of the Jewish Council. When Czerniakow offered himself as the solitary hostage, the demand was withdrawn.

He contacted leaders of other large Jewish communities to formulate a unified Jewish stand.

Frequently Czerniakow spoke sharply to German authorities. Thus on March 27, 1940, as a member of a delegation to the government of the *Generalgouvernement* in Kraków, he said bluntly that the armbands Jews had to wear were an indignity which encouraged crime. He gave details of the pogrom just perpetrated in Warsaw, the like of which had not been seen since the terrors of 1880.

In the memos and reports Czerniakow had to submit to the authorities, he often included harsh criticism of the policy toward the Jews. On August 10, 1940 Czerniakow wrote, "In the last weekly report, I mentioned the impression the new restriction banning Jews from parks had made." Durrfeld sent him a letter chiding him for daring to criticize the orders of SA-*Oberführer* Leist: "Let me point out that if this happens again, severe measures will be taken."

In a meeting on October 23, 1941 with Professor Kudicke, commissioner for the fight against typhus; Dr. Lambrecht, the district doctor of Warsaw; *Kommissar* Auerswald; Dr. Koman; Professor Hirszfeld; Dr. Milejkowski; and Dr. Ganc, Czerniakow repudiated the simplistic conclusion of the assembly that typhus is caused by body lice. In Czerniakow's opinion, typhus stems in the first instance from crowded living conditions and starvation rations. He protested that "Warsaw is a cursed city where Jews receive thirteen kopecks' worth of food."

In a December 2, 1941 conversation with the German *Kommissar* and his assistant Rodeck, Czerniakow claimed that the Jews should not be made to pay for the ghetto walls, that it should more correctly be the liability of those who were being "protected" from epidemic.

Auerswald, the *Kommissar,* furious that the strong and healthy were not being sent to the labor camps, threatened punishment if the Jewish Council would not do its job of supplying them. Czerniakow answered on May 23, 1941 that "Degenerates are destroying the community like a malignant cancer." Actually these factors brought the ghetto to the brink of chaos and all Czerniakow's efforts to restore order were futile. The Germans were glad of the disorder and did everything possible to encourage it.

In reply to Auerswald's complaints that the Jews were always coming up with unrealistic plans, Czerniakow asked him to look out the window at the street built according to "unrealistic" Jewish ideas (entry June 30, 1942).

Czerniakow also communicated to the Gestapo the difficult conditions in the ghetto, stressing the physical and spiritual torture. On May 19, 1941, for example, he reported that in the first half of May over 1,700 people died of starvation. That report included pictures of starving children in communal shelters *(Punkten)*.

It is no wonder, then, that on November 4, 1940 the SS stormed the Jewish Council, broke into Czerniakow's study, and arrested him. Meisinger, head of the security police, warned him before he was released that he did not speak properly of the SS. Early in April 1941, Czerniakow was arrested again, this time in connection with a special fund set up by the Jewish Council. Because the fifth notebook is missing, we do not know Czerniakow's reactions to his imprisonment. It is known that while in prison he was tortured and degraded. In spite of this, Czerniakow did not modify his behavior.

In his contacts with the Jewish masses, Czerniakow always spoke to them with dignity. He always made it clear that he was not a blind instrument of the Germans, nor one who carried out his duties trembling under the watchful eye of the barbarous conqueror.

Czerniakow severely criticized Mordecai Rumkowski, head of the Łódź Jewish Council. Czerniakow disagreed with Rumkowski's justification of the spiritual and physical ghetto walls. In Czerniakow's opinion, Rumkowski, whom he called, "that arrogant foolish man," harmed the people by trying to convince the authorities that things were fine in the ghetto.

Czerniakow poured out his wrath on Jews who served the Germans, the informers, extortionists, and underworld figures who degraded and corrupted the ghetto. Czerniakow often criticized Gancwajch, head of Trzynastka, a Gestapo agency working under the cover of the Office for Fighting Speculation in the Jewish Quarter of Warsaw. Czerniakow described Gancwajch in an entry on February 25, 1942 as "a revolting, abhorrent figure" and had no contact with his office.

Czerniakow knew that money was extorted from workers in the labor battalion and that clerks in the Housing Office took bribes. He went so far as to take the labor battalion clerks to court, but Czerniakow realized that the Jewish Council was forced to seek the help of the underworld in order to carry out the Germans' corrupt commands. He knew that the intolerable conditions in the ghetto encouraged degenerates.

In his negotiations with the Germans, Czerniakow never ceased bringing up new suggestions and plans, even though his efforts seldom produced results. Only rarely does the diary record positive achievements.

The following are some of the achievements he was proud of: arranging a loan of one million zlotys for the ghetto (entry of August 2, 1941); the prohibition of the confiscation of technical school equipment; a 15-day extension of the closing off of the ghetto (entry of October 21, 1940); permission to open vocational training courses; a quota of 36 tons of flour granted by Auerswald for the needy on June 25, 1942; the agreement of the Germans to set up the Jewish Police instead of *Lagerschutz* (the camp guards) in the three camps where Jews did forced labor, the Kampinos and Szymanow (entry of May 8, 1941).

In his own eyes, the zenith of Czerniakow's achievements as a negotiator was the release of 151 prisoners from Jewish jails on March 11, 1942 and 260 prisoners on April 10, 1942 in exchange for over 1,500 sheepskins prepared in Jewish Council workshops or bought on the free market. This event was celebrated in a public meeting of the Jewish Council with 24 members and 200 guests from all social strata. Czerniakow reported on "endeavors leading to the successful release of 500 prisoners," and gave an account of the expense involved. Gepner, Balaban, and Frydman lectured and Rabbi Kanal blessed the chairman.

These instances are exceptional, for though Czerniakow received many promises, rarely did his efforts bear fruit. Ludwig Fischer, the District Governor, in a discussion with Czerniakow on May 21, 1941, lied when he said that he had no intention of starving the Jews. Fischer also mentioned that the corpses lying in the street made a bad impression and should be removed as quickly as possible, adding that the Jews had better follow German orders or else. (Czerniakow did not record the actual threat, for reasons easily understood.)

Czerniakow knew how to exploit rivalries between government offices and yet the Germans always had the upper hand. For example, the Food Supply Office *(Ernährungsamt)* was opposed by the Population Transfer *(Umsiedlung)* Office. On December 4, 1940, Czerniakow wrote that Hörschelmann, a representative of the Food Supply Office, refused to follow the orders of the Population Transfer Office. On June 3, 1941 Czerniakow stressed that Bischof, in charge of *Transferstelle,* was ready to help the Jewish Council buy potatoes on the open market, but Palfinger, the head *Transferstelle* official, objected. One villian, Waldemar Schön, chief of the *Umsiedlung* division, Warsaw district, called Czerniakow to an urgent meeting on Yom Kippur, October 12, 1940 to tell him that it had been decided "in the name of humanity" to establish a ghetto.

Depressed, Czerniakow wrote in his diary on November 1, 1941, "As I see it, nothing comes of all my labor. My head begins to swim. . . . Not a positive step! The food rations were supposed to have risen. The mountain gave forth a mouse." This tone is evident in other entries: on January 23, 1940, "The community—the daily suffering . . . a wonder I'm not confused"; on August 9, 1940, "Torture all day." During the mass arrests of January 1940, Czerniakow, experiencing intensely all the ghetto's problems, tried to resign as head of the Jewish Council, but the Gestapo would not allow him to resign. Although they admitted he had a difficult job, he noted, "they don't advise me to do so."

Having no alternative, Czerniakow, a man with formidable self-control, adapted his policy to the prevailing conditions, in the hope that most of the Jews would hold out until release came. He castigated Jewish leaders who fled the inferno; he felt they were deserting their people in the hour of need. On February 12, 1940 he wrote, "I was offered a visa to Palestine but I refused it." He was proud that he remained at his post, one with the many, trying to do his utmost to ease the lot of his people.

In spite of disappointments, Czerniakow was continually active, aware, and responsive. Brokenhearted by personal suffering and the tragedy around him, he managed to turn inner pain and bitterness into motivation for public activity. He was not naive nor unaware of the horror, but his inner strength pushed him on to tireless labor. He hoped that in spite of all he would accomplish something and save what could be saved even though it might cost him his life. He never lost faith in the nation's vitality, in its will to live. It was this faith that gave him the hope that most Jews would survive.

So immersed was he in his labor that perhaps he did not pay sufficient attention to the rumors in the ghetto and to the serious portents concerning the ghetto's fate. Even some of the Germans hinted to him of what was to come. Auerswald hinted on July 8, 1941 that if the Jews did not volunteer for the labor camps the noose would tighten around their necks and the masses would slowly starve. At the end of October 1941, Czerniakow wrote about the worrisome rumors emanating from Kraków regarding the fate of the Jews. On January 31, 1942, Probst, an employee in Auerswald's office, told Czerniakow that hard times were coming for the Jews. This was a hint that a wave of destruction was approaching the borders of the *Generalgouvernement.*

Czerniakow recorded the echo of the *Aktion* in Lwów and Lublin. In February 1942 the rumors of "expulsions" from the Warsaw ghetto became more frequent; they peaked in the latter half of May. However, on May 15, 1942 Czerniakow wrote, "To work according to plan under these conditions is admirable. We do our daily work and weeping will not help us." Faithful to this line, Czerniakow inaugurated parks for schoolchildren at the end of June and the beginning of July 1942. When faced by bewildered questioners, Czerniakow compared himself to the captain of a sinking ship who requested the band to play to raise the morale of the passengers.

Surprisingly, even a few days before the "expulsion," Czerniakow doubted the reliability of the rumors of the great *Aktion* about to take place. The Germans to whom he turned for information denied there was any truth to the story. On the contrary, they gave him firm assurances that the expulsions would not apply to Warsaw. At that time, Czerniakow wrote a brief report on the economic condition of the ghetto and its industrial production, which he submitted to "the various authorities on which our fate depends." Only in work, he believed, lay salvation; he could not believe that the Germans would deprive themselves of the Jews' usefulness and destroy them because of some lunatic theory. Another naive assumption was that Auerswald and the staff of the *Transferstelle* were young men who wanted to avoid going to the front and who depended on the ghetto for their posts. "And there are others who point out impressive numbers, of tens of thousands, working in shops and supplying for the German Army," said Ringelblum.

Even three days before the expulsion that was to end in death, the day panic broke out in the ghetto, Czerniakow admitted that he did everything to give people encouragement in those stark moments. He was still deluding himself that there was some misunderstanding and that some possibility remained of averting the threatened evil.

In the final passage of his diary on *Tishe B'Av,* July 23, 1942 he wrote, "It is 3 o'clock. So far there are 4,000 ready to go. According to orders, there have to be four thousand [more] by 4 o'clock." [Czerniakow's handwriting makes possible a different reading: 9000 by 4 o'clock.] These orders opened his eyes to the meaning of the *Aktion* to be continued nonstop through the week, according to SS-1st Lieutenant Hermann Worthoff, one of the principal officers of the *Aktion* headquarters. It was this that decided Czerniakow to end his life at once. During the entire time he had served as head of the Jewish Council, Czerniakow had kept ready a potassium cyanide tablet which he intended to use, should he ever receive an order which went against his conscience. Before swallowing the tablet he wrote two notes, one to the Jewish Council executive and the other to his wife. In the first he said that Worthoff had visited him that day and told him that the expulsion order applied to children as well. They could not expect him to hand over helpless children for destruction. He had therefore decided to put an end to his life. He asked them not to see this as an act of cowardice. "I am powerless, my heart trembles in sorrow and compassion. I can no longer bear all this. My act will show everyone the right thing to do."

His notebook was found resting on the table before him when he died. The previous day, he had refused to sign the expulsion order, preferring to die himself rather than assist the enemy by sending others to death. Czerniakow had feared that the day would come when he would have no way out except suicide; he took his life when it became obvious that he had misled himself and others in calling on the public to remain tranquil during the terrible days before the *Aktion* began.

The poet Yitzhak Katznelson, author of the Vitel diary, correctly saw Czerniakow's death as "a sign of his desire to free himself of guilt feelings, to expiate a sin that weighed on his conscience."

It must be pointed out that Czerniakow's faithful and devoted service was highly appreciated in his lifetime. A Jewish crowd in Krochmalna Street for example, tried to take vengeance on a Jewish traitor responsible for Czerniakow's being arrested by the Gestapo. Czerniakow himself calmed the crowd and prevented bloodshed.

Chaim A. Kaplan, the author of a Warsaw Ghetto diary, wrote this of Czerniakow's bitter fate and tragic end: "Some people earn eternity in a single hour. Czerniakow earned eternity in one moment. His end justifies his beginning; he acted and labored for the people whose well-being and preservation he sought, even though not all done in his name deserves praise or commendation."

A Polish Catholic wrote, "I honor that death because he was asked to become a weapon for the destruction of his people. This was the only honorable way out. . . . He did much on behalf of the poorest of the poor and refugees, and in organization. The activities of the Ghetto's public institutions are to be credited to him . . . and you have to admit he was a brave man. He suffered beatings and insults but as long as he was able, he stood to his post. He is to be compared to the man [Stefan Starzynski] who in the historic days of September [1939] was the living spirit of the tortured capital."

Czerniakow's diary is a rich storehouse and fascinating source of information and detail, which fills out the background to the events of those days and gives us a greater understanding of them. By reason of its exactness and its faithful recording of facts, it enables us to test the reliability of other sources and is of great help in our understanding of problems and occurrences in the ghetto. It is an invaluable record of significant details in the history of the ghetto, providing us with the most important documentation on the history of Polish Jewry's Holocaust and Resistance since the discovery of Ringelblum's archives.

# Introduction

## Raul Hilberg and Stanislaw Staron

Who was Adam Czerniakow? In the literature of the Holocaust, the name is found in an index or a footnote, one of many names. Czerniakow killed himself in the summer of 1942, a lethal period of Jewish history, just midway in the war. He was little known in prewar days and has been remembered vaguely since then. Yet in the years to come, he may well emerge in print as he has not risen in life, for he has left behind a document the contents of which are .unique. It is a register of sorts, a diary, the most important Jewish record of that time.

If we were to look back at Poland under the German occupation, we could see several million Jews incarcerated in closed-off sections of hundreds of cities and towns—the ghettos erected by the Nazi regime. Most of the ghettos were gone by the end of 1942, their occupants choked in gas chambers of camps nearby, but their relatively short existence in the interim period between prewar freedom and wartime annihilation marks the last moments of organized life in the Jewish communities. Adam Czerniakow presided over the largest of those captive city states, that handful of blocks filled with nearly a half-million people—the ghetto of Warsaw. While he occupied the post of Chairman of the Warsaw Jewish Council, he noted events as he saw them, day after day.

What sort of man was he? One is tempted to speak of him as overwhelmingly ordinary. Often enough, he has been recalled as a kind of non-villain and non-hero, non-exploiter and non-saint. Several of his contemporaries have even attributed to him all of the qualities of nonleadership. His appearance may have furthered that image. A photograph taken in the days of the ghetto shows Czerniakow as a somewhat portly man with forceful facial features underscored by a protuding chin. Bald and beardless, he stares from the picture, an image of bourgeois respectability, all saturnine and distant.

He was already 59 when the Germans arrived. A native of Warsaw, Czerniakow had pursued his higher engineering studies there and in Dresden, polishing languages and collecting diplomas. His subsequent career was respectable enough but short of spectacular. He taught in a vocational school, worked for the government, went into business himself (and lost), to end up as an official in a foreign trade clearance house. He was also an author of educational and technical publications and even a writer of unpublished verse. Most important, however, was his activity in the social and political domain. He devoted himself to the embattled Jewish artisans and at the same time pursued Jewish politics, persevering in attempts to gain office in the difficult atmosphere of an accentuated Polish nationalism and a diminishing Polish democracy.

Within the complex Polish political system, there were Jewish political parties which fielded candidates for Jewish community councils, the municipal councils, and the national legislature. The three main political groupings of Polish Jewry were the traditional Orthodox (Agudah), Labor (Bund), and Zionist (divided into religious, "general," and socialist factions). Each claimed electoral victories; the Agudah long dominated the Jewish councils, the Bund made significant gains in the municipal elections, and the Zionists were visible in parliamentary contests. Occasionally, there were splits and alliances. A slate could be formed with a non-Jewish party and it might also accommodate an organization, such as the Association of Jewish Merchants or the Association of Jewish Artisans. In 1928 some of the Zionists joined other ethnic groups in a national minorities bloc. Czerniakow, backed by the Jewish Artisans, ran for a seat in the Polish Senate on this ticket. He lost the election, but subsequently tried again.[1]

His idealism was restrained. Although he was not separated from

1. Aryeh Tartakower, "Adam Czerniakow—The Man and His Supreme Sacrifice," *Yad Vashem Studies* 7 (1967): 55-67. For description of Jewish politics in prewar Poland, see Celia S. Heller, *On the Edge of Destruction* (New York: Columbia University Press, 1977); Bernard K. Johnpoll, *The Politics of Futility* (Ithaca: Cornell University Press, 1967); and Harry M. Rabinowicz, *The Legacy of Polish Jewry* (New York: Thomas Yoseloff, 1965).

political movements, he was not identified with them either. Too nonobservant for religious orthodoxy, he was also too pragmatic to embrace socialism and too "assimilationist" to evolve into an ardent Zionist. Indeed, he is more often characterized for what he was not than for what he was.

Yet, he gained in experience and power. He was a participant in the local politics of Warsaw, serving on the city council. Later he was also a member and deputy chairman of the Warsaw Jewish community council. By that time, this body was no longer elected; it had been constituted by Polish authorities in 1937 and no longer included the most recently victorious Bundists in its membership. It still carried out traditional functions such as religious education, welfare disbursements, and the care of cemeteries, and it collected various fees and taxes from the Jewish population for these purposes.

Upon the outbreak of war, the council fell apart. Several members, including the chairman, Maurycy Mayzel, fled from the city. Czerniakow stayed. On September 6, he started his diary, writing down only a few words each day. By the 11th, Abraham Gepner, of the Jewish Merchants Association, formed a citizens' committee to deal with emergency problems. Czerniakow joined the group; he noted that it was recognized by the Polish mayor, Stefan Starzynski.

A few days later, while the city was still under German siege, a committee member accidentally met Czerniakow in the waiting room of the mayor's office. Czerniakow told his colleague on that occasion that he was attempting to obtain an official appointment as chairman of the Jewish community. On the following day, he showed his friend the letter signed by Colonel Starzynski. He had also printed up cards which indicated his new position. They were in German.[2]


## THE CHAIRMAN AND THE JEWISH COUNCIL

Poland was invaded on September 1; by the end of the month it was partitioned between Germany and the USSR. The western and central portions had become German; they were in turn divided into the "incorporated territories" and the *Generalgouvernement*.

2. Apolinary Hartglas, "How Did Czerniakow Become Head of the Warsaw Judenrat?" *Yad Vashem Bulletin* 15 (1964): 4–7. Starzynski was the Commissioner for Civil Affairs with the Warsaw Defense Command as of September 8, 1939.

The *Generalgouverneur* was Hans Frank; his area was composed of four districts: Kraków, Lublin, Radom, and Warsaw. About 1.5 million Jews were trapped in the *Generalgouvernement;* the Warsaw district alone contained nearly 600,000 of them, while the city of Warsaw had a Jewish population of 350,000, soon swelled by refugees to more than 400,000.

During the ensuing three years, from the arrival of the German army to the onset of mass deportations, the Jewish community of Warsaw was subjected to five phases of German rule. Each of these periods is marked by a distinct German purpose and in each a particular German agency may be seen as predominating and taking charge:

| Phase | Time | Principal German Agency in Charge |
|---|---|---|
| Takeover of Jewish Community | Early Fall 1939 | *Einsatzgruppe* IV—Beutel, later Weis and Meisinger (Security Police and Security Service) under Military Commander |
| Impositions and Exactions | Fall 1939–Fall 1940 | German city administration—Otto, later Dengel and Leist |
| Ghetto Formation | Winter and Early Spring 1940–1941 | German district administration/Division *Umsiedlung* (Resettlement)—Schön |
| Ghetto Maintenance | Spring 1941 to July 1942 | German district administration/*Kommissar* for Jewish district—Auerswald |
| Deportations | From July 1942 | SS Resettlement Staff—Höfle |

From one phase to the other, power was not always handed over with a view to total relinquishment of jurisdiction. There was a tendency to conserve functions and continue activities side by side with the operations of successor organs. The Security Police in particular retained its interest in all matters pertaining to intelligence, surveillance, fines, arrests, and the like. The army, though preferring distant observer status, was continuously concerned with Jewish labor, production, and, of course, overall tranquility. The German city administration was involved—even after the establishment of the ghetto—with taxes, public utilities, traffic, and the rather frequent boundary changes. Only the Resettlement Divison disappeared completely—its chief became head of the Warsaw District Interior Division.

Throughout all the administrative rearrangements and transformations in the German bureaucracy, Czerniakow remained at the helm of the Jewish community. He was at his post when *Einsatzgruppe* IV moved into Warsaw on October 1, 1939, and he was still in office when yet another Security Police detachment wrote out the deportation orders in July 1942.

PHASE I: THE TAKEOVER

Even as German armies were bombarding the city of Warsaw, the Chief of the German Security Police, Reinhard Heydrich, dispatched mobile units *(Einsatzgruppen* and *Einsatzkommandos)* composed of Gestapo, Criminal Police, and Security Service personnel into Poland. On September 19, 1939, he obtained, in agreement with the army's Quartermaster, General Wagner, wide-ranging power in Jewish affairs.[3] Two days later, in Berlin, he met with key security police officials and commanders of *Einsatzgruppen* to hammer out directives to the units in the field. The *Einsatzgruppen* were authorized and instructed to set up Jewish councils of elders, including influential persons and rabbis, in each community.[4] *Einsatzgruppe* IV entered the city of Warsaw on October 1 and established itself on 25 Szuch Avenue. On October 4, while Warsaw was still under military rule, a detachment under a lieutenant raided the Jewish Community headquarters on 26 Grzybowska Street. The Germans emptied a safe and wanted to know who the

3. Diary of Chief of the German General Staff Halder, Sept. 10 and 20, 1939, Nuremberg document NOKW-3140.
4. Conference minutes of Sept. 21, 1939, quoted in Staatsanwaltschaft beim Landgericht Berlin [Prosecution at the Berlin Court], 3 P (K) JS 198/61, "Schlussvermerk in der Strafsache gegen Beutel u. a. wegen Mordes" [Final Report in the Criminal Case against Beutel and Others for Murder], Jan. 29, 1971. Document in Zentrale Stelle der Landesjustizverwaltungen, Ludwigsburg. Heydrich order of Sept. 21, 1939 in Nuremberg document PS-3363.

chairman was. The janitor told them that it was Czerniakow and that he was expected shortly.[5]

When Czerniakow reached the Security Police, he was told to establish a council of 24 members. Already, the *Einsatzgruppe* had taken care of its primary mission. On October 6, the unit reported that a council of 24 "prominent" Jews was being named, that it would be responsible for a census, and that it would be expected to advance its own proposals for a concentration of the Jews in "ghettos." The *Einsatzgruppe,* for its part, was going to confer with military and civilian officials on the matter. In the meantime, it had "secured" the Jewish community "together with" its president and secretary, as well as the museum.[6]

Czerniakow and his associates from the citizens' committee now began to draft the list. In contrast to the situation a few weeks before, when everyone wanted to be on the committee, most candidates now expressed great reluctance to serve. In a matter of days, however, the Council was formed. It included all former councilmen still in the city and a number of new appointees. The next day, a witness noted, Czerniakow indicated to several of the functionaries a drawer in his table in which he had placed "a small bottle with 24 cyanide tablets, one for each of us, and he showed us where the key to the drawer could be found, should the need arise." [7]

The composition of the Council reflected at least minimally every social and political orientation in the Jewish community. All of the members were certainly prominent enough to qualify for their new roles. A third of them, including Lichtenbaum (an engineer) and Zabludowski, were holdover members of the prewar council. The others had attained visible success in public or publicized careers: one was a judge on a commercial court (Kobryner); two were attorneys (Zundelewicz and Rozensztat); one came from the trade unions (Kupczyker); one from the Bund or Jewish Socialist Party (Zygelbojm); one was a rabbi (Sztokhamer); one a physician (Milejkowski); two were from the banking community (Dr. Szoszkies, Cooperative Bank, and Sztolcman, Bank of Jewish Merchants); one represented merchants (Gepner); another (Jaszunski) was director of the Jewish social agency ORT; and so on.[8] Most of these men

5. Hartglas, "Czerniakow," pp. 6–7.
6. Text of report quoted in "Schlussvermerk gegen Beutel."
7. Hartglas, "Czerniakow," p. 7.

were familiar with communal politics and power, and despite the diversity of their various affiliations, they were in fact homogeneous enough to share many an unspoken perception or unmentioned assumption.

Differences emerged, however, in their personalities. In the constricting atmosphere of the next few years, each individual would acquire a distinct reputation, one as a cold, distant disciplinarian, the second as a suffering, sympathetic listener, the next as a self-assertive gesticulating debater, and yet a fourth as a rising star, influential and even indispensable, until some German bullet put an end to his success.[9]

## PHASE II: IMPOSITIONS AND EXACTIONS

The rule of the *Einsatzgruppe* was short-lived. A civil administration took over the governance of the city, as Security Police and Order Police stood by at its flanks, ever ready and eager to reach into Jewish affairs, but no longer in charge. "The community has been subordinated to Leist," a German city official informed Czerniakow on April 26, 1940. By then, the German city apparatus had already been dealing with the Council for some time, but the fact was underscored explicitly, if only to emphasize the effectiveness of the new regime.

Figure I shows the placement of the principal German functionaries, both at the district and city levels. We should note particularly the direct line of command running from the District Chief (Fischer) and his Plenipotentiary for the City (Leist) to the Chairman of the Jewish Council. Fischer, Leist, and also Schön of *Umsiedlung* were all high-ranking SA-men. The brownshirted SA [Sturmabteilungen] had been relatively powerless in Germany since 1934, but here some of its leaders were to acquire new functions and prestige. Leist, however, depended on experienced German municipal officials and they in turn made use of the acting Polish mayor (Kulski) as well as Polish auxiliaries in their own offices for the implementation of a variety of tasks.

8. Excerpts of memoirs by Jonas Turkow in Philip Friedman, *Martyrs and Fighters* (New York: Frederick Praeger, 1954), pp. 68–69. Excerpts of recollections by Shmuel Zygelbojm in Isaiah Trunk's *Judenrat* (New York: Macmillan, 1972), pp. 22–23.
9. The most illuminating description of the ghetto personalities is to be found in the unpublished manuscript by Stefan Ernest, "Trzeci front: o wojnie wielkieh Niemiec z Zydami Warszawy 1939–1943 [Third Front: the war of Greater Germany against the Jews of Warsaw, 1939-1943]," written in a bunker early in 1943. Private collection of Dr. Lucjan Dobroszycki, YIVO Institute.

**FIGURE I**

PRIMACY OF CITY ADMINISTRATION, 1939–1940:
THE RULE OF LEIST

District Chief (*Gouverneur*)

Fischer————————Chief of Staff:  Hummel

(Palais Brühl)

*Umsiedlung* (Resettlement):  Schön
    Deputy:  Mohns
Interior: (Gauweiler)  Acting: Klein
Population & Welfare:  Auerswald
    Health:  Lambrecht
Economy: (von Coelln, Gaudig)  Schlosser
    Trusteeship:  Ballreich
Labor: (Espe, Sohnrey)  Hoffman
Food & Agriculture: (Grams)  Naumann

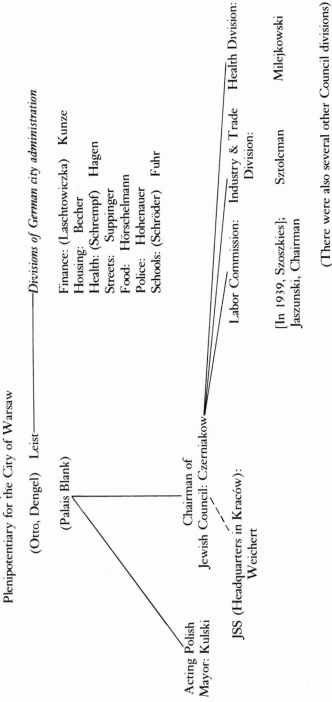

Plenipotentiary for the City of Warsaw

(Otto, Dengel) Leist —————— *Divisions of German city administration*

(Palais Blank)

Finance: (Laschtowiczka) Kunze
Housing: Becher
Health: (Schrempf) Hagen
Streets: Suppinger
Food: Hörschelmann
Police: Hohenauer
Schools: (Schröder) Fuhr

Chairman of
Jewish Council: Czerniakow

Acting Polish
Mayor: Kulski

JSS (Headquarters in Kraców):
Weichert

Labor Commission:   Industry & Trade   Health Division:
                     Division:

[In 1939, Szoszkies];   Sztolcman   Milejkowski
Jaszunski, Chairman

(There were also several other Council divisions)

The Jewish community was weakened at the outset. From prewar days, it had inherited an economic problem; the war brought damage and disruption; the German occupants added discriminatory measures. These consecutive developments had a pervasive effect on Warsaw Jewry; each contributed to its burdens and reduced its resources.

For many years, the occupational structure of the Warsaw Jews had been unbalanced. Their distribution in various economic sectors (in considerable measure traceable to exclusionist policies pursued by the Polish Republic) shows heavy Jewish participation in the following areas: independent professions (doctors and lawyers—but *not* teachers); skilled trades in which people were self-employed or working in small shops as tailors, furriers, and leatherworkers; piecework in the home; residential real estate ownership and operation (particularly in the Jewish sections); ownership of small stores or stalls selling food and sundries; auxiliary and marginal activities conducted mostly in the street (rag pickers, peddlers, porters, etc.). There was weak or sparse Jewish representation in management and in the work force of: wholesale trading; large-scale industrial enterprises; municipal government; and state enterprises (distilleries, etc.). It is likely that this stratification made Warsaw Jewry specially vulnerable to the great depression which had spread also to Poland's cities and which lingered in them for years.

With the beginning of war and occupation, there was a further disintegration of economic conditions, and before long the progressive impoverishment of the community was intensified by such German actions as looting, requisitions, fines, prohibitions on sales of Jewish property, and blocking of bank deposits. The decline in the number of Jewish industrial and commercial concerns was precipitous: before the war, there were 193 of them with a labor force of 20 or more; by the end of April, 1940, only 38 were still operating.[10] The German Trusteeship Office in Warsaw liquidated small Jewish enterprises and seized their inventory, selling the merchandise and banking the proceeds in three separate accounts credited to the office and labeled as receipts from the disposal of Jewish textiles, leather, and furs. The Trusteeship Office also

10. Statistical bulletin No. 1 of the Jewish Council, May 3, 1940, in Szymon Datner, "Dzialalnosc warszawskiej 'Gminy Wyznaniowej Zydowskiej' w dokumentach podziemnego archiwum getta Warszawskiego ('Ringelblum II')," *Biuletyn Zydowskiego Instytutu Historycznego*, No. 73 (January-March 1970), 107.

sequestered Jewish real estate and systematically collected the rent from tenants. The office paid the taxes and wages and undertook renovations. A small sum was allocated as an "advance" to "Aryan" co-owners of houses. A cash reserve was maintained and the remaining surplus was banked in yet another account.[11] The Jews of Warsaw were thus deprived of assets and income, both big and small. The result was a monetary loss from which there would be no recovery.

The two most visible manifestations of breakdown during the first winter were the large number of welfare-dependent families in the Jewish community, and a major group of more or less able-bodied Jewish unemployed.

Jewish welfare in Poland had been well established before the war, and the Jewish private agencies that existed then, mainly TOZ (for medical and communal purposes), Centos (for children), and ORT (for vocational training), continued to operate in the community and later in the ghetto. They are mentioned frequently in Czerniakow's diary and in his reports to the Germans. The one change in their operations, decreed on January 23, 1940, by *Stadt-präsident* Dengel,[12] was organizational: a central Jewish welfare body, the JSS *(Jüdische Soziale Selbsthilfe*—Jewish Social Self-Help) was established to coordinate all Jewish welfare in the *Gen-eralgouvernement,* and branches of the JSS in each city were super-imposed on the local offices of TOZ, Centos, and ORT. We leave out of account here the foreign welfare agencies, including the American Jewish Joint Distribution Committee and HIAS, and a coordinating committee of Poles, Ukrainians, and Jews, through which some funds were received from officially sponsored overseas sources such as the American Red Cross. The Jewish welfare effort became more and more dependent on the resources of the Jewish community itself and on the ability of Czerniakow and his colleagues to mobilize these means for children, refugees, or starving people generally. Often enough, Czerniakow—outraged by the sight of some island of luxury—would launch an exhausting fund drive, but his successes were insufficient, and insufficiency remained. .

A second conspicuous problem was Jewish unemployment. Fre-

11. See detailed report by Warsaw District Trusteeship Office for October, 1940; Nov. 8, 1940, Yad Vashem microfilm JM 814.
12. Dengel to Czerniakow, Jan. 23, 1940, Yad Vashem microfilm JM 1113.

quently, German agencies would impress Jewish men in the streets for rubble clearance and other heavy labor without compensation. This practice engaged the Council's urgent consideration and provided it with a test case for its basic philosophic stance.

Czerniakow notes in his diary that as early as mid-October 1939 the Jewish Council formed the idea of a labor battalion which would supply the Germans with workers in an orderly manner. The Germans accepted the proposal: supposedly they were going to give the laborers some money and food. By the end of 1939, central German offices in Kraców had visions of subjecting all of the *Generalgovernement* Jews to compulsory manual labor. In Warsaw, the municipal German overlord, Dr. Dengel, ordered the Council to register all Jews aged 13 through 59 in the city. The Council formed a labor commission, and after much bureaucratic labor, sent out 121,265 registration certificates.[13]

The daily quota of workers for the Warsaw Labor Battalion turned out to be 7,000–10,000. Virtually all of these laborers, however, were not being paid by their German employers. The Council instituted a surtax to fund the wages, but the amounts raised in this manner were grossly insufficient. The solution thereupon adopted by the Council was a provision to excuse most of the able-bodied conscripts for a fee of 60–100 zlotys monthly, with reductions for "socially active" persons and certain hardship cases.[14] At the same time, Czerniakow attempted to persuade the Germans to pay some wages to their Jewish workers. He records several conversations to this effect with one of the major German employers, Captain Schu of the army's Raw Materials Command. Schu at one point assured Czerniakow that he did not want slave labor, but in the bookkeeping of the German Army the labor of slaves it was.

The Council's outlays continued to rise. A financial statement for the first four months of 1940 reveals a precarious balance sheet.[15]

Clearly the Council could not meet its ongoing commitments. Czerniakow needed a major new tax, and on May 20, 1940, the Council held a "difficult meeting" in the course of which it ap-

13. See its report of February 18, 1940, JM 1113.
14. Czerniakow to Leist, May 21, 1940, JM 1113. Text in appendix of this volume, p. 386.
15. Jewish Council Statistical bulletin No. 3, June 2, 1940, containing financial report for January-April, 1940, in Datner, "Dzialalnosc," *Biuletyn*, No. 74 (April-June 1970), 103-105

*Revenue* (figures rounded to the nearest zloty)

| | |
|---|---|
| Taxes and exactions | |
|     Community levy | 206,010 zl. |
|     Surtax for labor battalion | 261,109 zl. |
|     Labor exemption payments | 388,366 zl. |
|     Labor registration fees | 203,859 zl. |
|     General registration fees | 11,785 zl. |
|     Hospital tax | 3,306 zl. |
| Special revenues | |
|     Receipts for social welfare | 114,737 zl. |
|     Other (including receipts | |
|        from hospital patients) | 75,094 zl. |
| Cemetery taxes | 639,015 zl. |
| Borrowing | |
|     From Emigration Fund | 363,770 zl. |
|     Loans from unstated | |
|        sources | 687,673 zl. |
|     Notes | 9,186 zl. |
|     Other borrowing (including | |
|        unpaid salaries) | 118,190 zl. |
|              Total | 3,082,101 zl. |

*Expenditures* (figures rounded to the nearest zloty)

| | |
|---|---|
| General (mainly salaries) | 272,860 zl. |
| Cemeteries | 102,066 zl. |
| Health and Social Welfare | 184,044 zl. |
| Hospitals | 961,616 zl. |
| Labor battalion | 816,129 zl. |
| Buildings | 22,549 zl. |
| Interest payments | 119,446 zl. |
| Payments to the authorities | |
|     (mainly reimbursements for | |
|     labor registration) | 238,035 zl. |
| Supplies | 54,592 zl. |
| Repayments (mainly to | |
|     Emigration Fund) | 285,681 zl. |
| Cost reserve on April 30, 1940 | 25,082 zl. |
|              Total | 3,082,101 zl. |

proved a levy on bread. With a "heavy heart" Czerniakow submitted the proposed revenue measure to the Germans. Leist gave his consent to the tax in June. The ordinance was implemented in that all Jews, with the exception of the poorest households, were required to pay one zloty a month for a bread ration card. Initially the money was collected by Kulski's city administration, and a credit of 300,000 zlotys in anticipation of receipts was awarded to the Council.[16] Czerniakow had his funds.

PHASE III: GHETTO FORMATION

As early as the fall of 1939, German Security Police and civil agencies in Poland were talking and corresponding about the ghettoization of the Jews, but as yet the concept was open-ended. No workable plan had been laid down for the timing or location of ghettos, and no principle spelled out their ultimate purpose. Over a period of a year, closed Jewish districts were being established all over the occupied territory by the hundreds. In each city, however, there were special problems.

Warsaw in particular was the scene of a long, drawn-out process of initiation, veto, agreements, and directives. These vacillations filtered into Czerniakow's diary. The summary below is an administrative history of the ghetto's formation—as reported in German sources [17] and as perceived by Czerniakow.

| GERMAN DOCUMENTS | THE DIARY |
|---|---|
| On November 7, 1939, Fischer emphasizes in a conversation with *Generalgouverneur* Frank that a "special ghetto" is to be erected. Frank agrees. | In November 4–5, 1939, a "zone" is considered by the military commander. The section in the old part of the city largely inhabited by Jews is thereupon designated a *Seuchensperrgebiet* [quarantine], off-limits to German soldiers. |

16. Czerniakow to Leist, enclosing draft of ordinance, June 10, 1940, and Leist to Czerniakow June 26, 1940, approving final version, JM 1113. Czerniakow to Leist, July 22, 1940, enclosing correspondence with Kulski's Food Office on credits, JM 1113.
17. In particular: report by Schön, Jan. 20, 1941, reproduced in large excerpt in Jüdisches Historisches Institut Warschau [Jewish Historical Institute in Warsaw], *Faschismus–Getto–*

## GERMAN DOCUMENTS

Schön reports that by February 1940, he was deputized by Fischer with the task of planning a ghetto. There is an abortive attempt to set up a Jewish district on the eastern bank of the Vistula River. It is rejected in a conference on March 8, 1940, on the ground that 80% of all artisans in Warsaw are Jews and that since they are "indispensable," one cannot very well "encircle" them. Moreover, a closed ghetto cannot easily be supplied with food. At that point it is also thought that all Jews might be dumped in the Lublin district, but that idea is rejected in April.

Division *Umsiedlung* (Resettlement) considers two ghettos, west (Kolo and Wola) and east (Grochow), in such a way as to minimize disturbances in the city's economy and traffic flow. This plan is dropped when word is received that Hitler wants to ship all of the European Jews to Madagascar "after the war."

Subdivision Health of the *Inland* (Interior) Division, pointing to increasing German troop

## THE DIARY

From the end of March to the middle of May 1940, Czerniakow is told that a wall must be built (around the quarantine). He presents arguments against this project and loses. Work is begun. On April 18, construction on a border street is suspended.

From the end of June to the middle of July 1940, Czerniakow wonders where the ghetto might be set up. By July 16, he makes note of a report that the ghetto idea was abandoned.

During the middle of August 1940, Czerniakow talks about expulsions of Jews from various

*Massenmord* (Berlin: Rütten and Loening, 1961), pp. 108-113, and Frank–Fischer discussion of Nov. 7, 1939, in Frank Diary, Nuremberg document PS-2233. See also oral report of *Generalgouvernement*'s Health Chief Dr. Walbaum to Frank, Sept. 6, 1940, urging ghettoization, especially in Warsaw, for "health-political" reasons. Frank Diary, PS-2233.

| GERMAN DOCUMENTS | THE DIARY |
|---|---|
| concentrations in the area, demands the formation of ghettos in the district. The nonmedical representatives of *Inland* acquiesce in the idea on August 20, but argue against sealing the ghettos "hermetically," lest they would not survive economically. From a number of documents, it appears that, nevertheless, German doctors, fearful of a typhus epidemic, want the Warsaw ghetto closed as tightly as possible. | sections of the city. There are references to questions about ghetto boundaries. He still has hopes for an "open" ghetto (compulsory residence with freedom of movement). By September 26, however, he writes "the ghetto" without any further doubt about its nature. |

Geographically, the ghetto was the original "quarantine," somewhat reduced in size. It consisted mainly of apartment houses with small rooms and very few open spaces. All Poles had to move out and all those classified as Jews by reason of parentage had to stay or move into the delimited zone. The exchange, according to Schön, involved approximately 113,000 Poles and 138,000 Jews. It proceeded over a period of six weeks in October and November, "without bloodshed," as the Germans noted, thanks to the employment of the Polish mayor on the one side and the Jewish Council on the other. Some 3,700 Jewish shops in "Aryan" Warsaw were sealed and an elaborate trusteeship system was instituted for the administration of Jewish-owned real estate on both sides of the wall.

The border of the ghetto was drawn with a view to maximum utilization of fire walls and minimum need for security measures. A bridge was to connect the northern and southern sections, which were separated by an "Aryan" street (Chlodna). Initially, there were 22 entry and exit points, which were used by 53,000 persons with crossing permits.[18] Dr. Lambrecht, who headed health services in the district, objected to the number of passes, pointing out that they defeated the whole purpose of the ghetto.[19] By January 1941,

18. Schön report of Jan. 20, 1941, and summary of interagency conference on ghetto, Dec. 2, 1940. JM 1113.
19. Conference of Dec. 2, 1940, JM 1113.

the gates were reduced to 15 and a First Lieutenant with a force of 87 German policemen (augmented by Polish and Jewish police) was assigned to guard the walls.[20] Schön's deputy Mohns also approached the new commander of the German Protective (street) Police in Warsaw, Lt. Col. Petsch, with a request to plant land mines in likely hiding places at the border.[21]

For the next few months, Leist and Schön contended for control of the Jewish Council. To solidify his position, Schön created a *Transferstelle* as an organization of public law with a board composed of representatives of several interested agencies, for the purpose of regulating all ghetto exports and imports. Soon Czerniakow was writing letters and reports to *Abteilung Umsiedlung/Transferstelle*, but copies went to Leist, who would make detailed notes in the margins and take positions on various issues. The transition regime was thus constituted somewhat as is diagramed in Figure II.

In the Jewish community, the sudden transformation from an integrated life to one of isolation was to have far-reaching effects. Jewish leadership was faced with a whole array of new concerns. The very multiplicity of these problems and requirements necessitated organization and structure. At the apex, the Council's deliberations became formalized. Its regular agenda were now being drafted by "commissions," which were initially composed only of Council members, but which were soon enlarged to include various "experts" from whose ranks had come a demand for a voice in policy formulation. In weekly reports to the Germans for December 1940, Czerniakow discusses a Trade and Industry Commission and lists commissions for the hospital, health, labor, social welfare, personnel, auditing, finance, economy, and grievances. The Industry and Trade Commission was assigned the pressing task of working out principles for the allocation of raw materials and distribution of food in the ghetto.[22]

Along with the expansion of the Council's functions, there was a buildup of its administrative apparatus. At the forefront of that development was the appearance of the Jewish Police, a housing office, and an elaborate health organization. These were the agen-

20. Schön report, Jan. 20, 1941.
21. Memorandum by Mohns, Jan. 14, 1941, JM 1113.
22. Weekly reports by Czerniakow for Dec. 13–19, 1940 and Dec. 20–26, 1940, JM 1113.

## FIGURE II

TRANSITION, 1940–1941: THE RULE OF SCHÖN

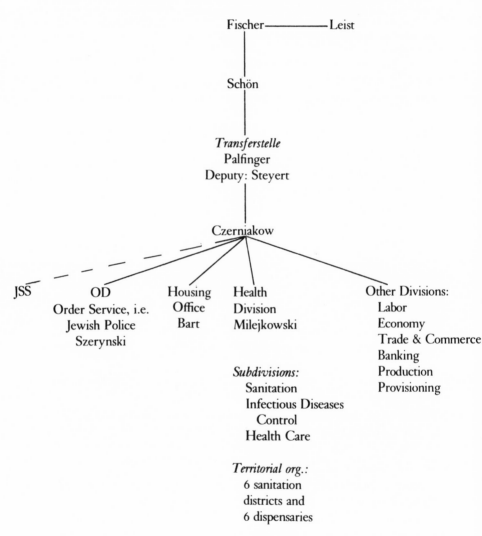

cies that were expected to cope with the most immediate impact of ghettoization.

The proliferation of administrative offices was accompanied by a rapid increase of staff. A full-fledged Jewish bureaucracy was born. Its growth began with the ghetto and continued for several months before leveling off. The Community employed 1,741 persons on July 1, 1940; [23] the number reported by Czerniakow's successor for early August 1942 showed an increase that was five-fold: [24]

| Divisions reporting directly to Council: | | 5,425 |
|---|---|---|
| Hospitals | 1,530 | |
| Health | 470 | |
| Labor | 312 | |
| Other (mostly police) | 3,113 | |

| Other task areas (administratively autonomous): | | 3,605 |
|---|---|---|
| JHK *(Jüdisches Hilfskomitee)* | 2,980 | |
| Provisioning Authority (originally Provisioning Division) | 502 | |
| Association of Jewish Artisans | 123 | |

| Total | | 9,030 |
|---|---|---|

Czerniakow was concerned with the professional competence of applicants for positions. On several occasions, important offices, particularly in the police, were filled with converts to Christianity who had been free in the Polish Republic to pursue careers not open to Jews. Such appointments caused widespread resentment in the community and on July 27, 1941, Czerniakow notes that a 4½-hour "fruitless" Council meeting was devoted mainly to this topic.

He was troubled that the police, and others as well, were not receiving pay. Not until March 1942 was a regular wage instituted for the *Ordnungsdienst* (Order Service—or Jewish Police). To be sure, the police were entitled to some important nonmonetary benefits, mainly, as we shall see, meals and larger bread rations. Czerniakow, incidentally, remained loyal to his controversial police. When in the Spring of 1942, the Order Service chief Szerynski was arrested by the Germans on suspicion of having smuggled some furs, Czerniakow repeatedly interceded for his freedom with the

23. Statistical Bulletin No. 8, September 4, 1940, in Datner, "Dzialalnosc," *Biuletyn,* No. 74 (April-June 1970), 122.
24. Lichtenbaum to Auerswald, Sept. 5, 1942, enclosing monthly report for August, Akten Auerswald [Auerswald files] (Polen 365e). Zentrale Stelle, Ludwigsburg.

Gestapo. The ordinary Jewish policeman was also in Czerniakow's thoughts, particularly if he was observed by the chairman in the act of a small kindness extended to a child. Of course, Czerniakow may have had a personal need for Order Service protection, not so much from any vengeful Jews as from those who would have accosted him at all hours with their problems.

Parenthetically, it may be pointed out that alongside the institution of Jewish officialdom, there were also other organizations in the ghetto. One of them was the network of house committees.

Czerniakow first mentions the committees on May 17, 1940, as having been formed to collect furniture for the Germans, but they remained to perform a variety of other functions, such as the distribution of relief funds and the informal education of children in the ghetto. There is no question of the fact that on occasion Czerniakow wanted to co-opt the house committees for unpleasant assignments or responsibilities, and that at other times he viewed them as an irritant. They in turn were not friendly towards the Council, with which they were in competition and which they criticized.

More sinister was the appearance, under reputed German Security Police auspices, of two tightly knit organizations, one styled "Control Office for Combating the Black Market and Profiteering in the Jewish District" and popularly known as "The Thirteen" for its address on 13 Leszno Street. The other—the "Ambulance Service"—like "The Thirteen," was suspected of having members who served as informants and agents of the Germans. Both forces wore caps and armbands like the Order Service, but with different colors: green for the 500-man "Thirteen," blue for the smaller Ambulance Service. Czerniakow was particularly affronted by The Thirteen and one of its co-directors, Abraham Gancwajch. By August 1941, he managed to have the "Control Office" dissolved—a major administrative victory.

The encirclement of the Jewish population in the ghetto produced an upheaval which reverberated through the entire city. The dislocations in the economy had their effects on both sides of the wall.[25] Artisans were unemployed in the ghetto and labor shortages

25. They are discussed by Hummel in his reports for Dec. 1940 and Feb. 1941 to the *Generalgouvernement* administration in Kraków, Jan. 25 and March 10, 1941, Yad Vashem microfilm JM 814 containing *Lageberichte* [Situation Reports] for 1940/41. Hummel, as Governeur Fischer's Chief of Staff, prepared the district's monthly reports.

were surfacing in the "Aryan" sector. Jewish rag pickers were cut off from Polish plants, and the plants from the pickers. The rag trade fell from a daily quantity of over 150,000 lbs. to barely over 30,000 lbs. Ghetto buildings without sewage connections were accumulating human waste; now German firms were vying for the business of carting it away. The precipitous decline of private income and savings in the ghetto entailed large arrears in the payment of taxes and rents. And so on.

The consequences for the Polish population were not all adverse. Many Polish tenants who obtained middle-class Jewish apartments outside the ghetto had a little more space. Polish retailers, without the presence of their Jewish competitors, were looking forward to much greater turnover. The black market was becoming more active, with prospects of good profits to Polish suppliers.

Conversely, the Jewish community was more enfeebled. We do not have Czerniakow's diary for much of this period (the entries for December 14, 1940, through April 22, 1941, are missing), but letters written by the chairman to his German supervisors during January have been found in German files, and from the tone of these communications we know something of the traumatic effects on Jewry of its incarceration.

In the first instance, Czerniakow requested permission to institute a variety of new taxes to finance welfare and other immediate needs.[26] The proposal was not going to cost the Germans anything and *Umsiedlung*'s Deputy Chief Mohns supported the Council chairman in sweeping language. "In the interest of the difficult administration of the Jewish District," he wrote, "the authority of the Jewish Council must be upheld and strengthened under all circumstances." [27] Leist, however, wrote in the margin of the Mohns letter: "New taxes may be raised only with auth. of finance supervisory agency." City Plenipotentiary Leist, having been overshadowed by *Umsiedlung* in ghetto affairs, was now a little more jealous of his prerogatives, and the difficult administration of the Jewish district was going to be somewhat more difficult still.

PHASE IV: GHETTO MAINTENANCE

By early spring 1941, the transition regime of Schön melted away. Division *Umsiedlung* was abolished—Schön placed in charge

26. Czerniakow to *Transferstelle*, Jan. 8, 1941, JM 1113. Text in appendix p. 388.
27. Mohns to Leist, Jan. 11, 1941, JM 1113.

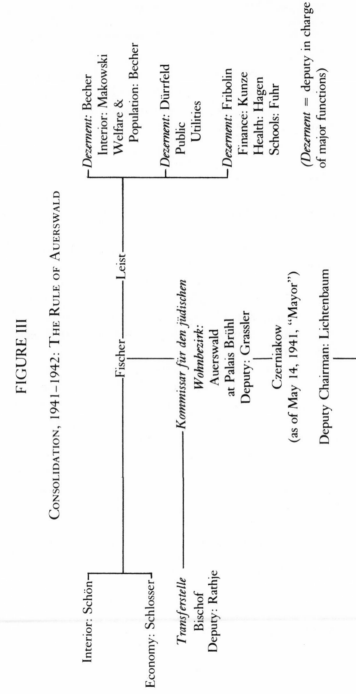

FIGURE III

CONSOLIDATION, 1941–1942: THE RULE OF AUERSWALD

Production
Division

transformed
into
Jüdische
Produktion GmbH
(a corporation)
Co-managers:
Orlean and Glicksman

Provisioning
Division

transformed
into
Provisioning
Authority

Board:
Sztolcman,
Gepner, Winter,
and Graf

Bank Division

transformed
into
Genossenschaftsbank
für den jüdischen
Wohnbezirk

Other Divisions:

Appeals & Grievances
Vital Statistics
Audit
Legal
Contributions
Economic
Cemeteries
Education
Archives

Other Agencies:

Order Service
(Jewish Police)
Housing Office
Personnel Office

Finance & Budget
Executive
Public Health
Hospitals
Labor
Social Welfare
Trade & Industry
Real Property
Postal

Independent
bodies:

Economic
Council,
Chairman:
Altberg

Jewish Welfare
Association,
Director:
Giterman

JSS
(Operational
arm: JHK—
Jüdisches
Hilfskomitee):
Wielikowski

of Interior, his deputy Mohns going with him. A new official now attempted to centralize and monopolize all control: The Ghetto *Kommissar.* Figure III depicts the main features of the new administration, which held sway over the ghetto for more than a year.

*Kommissar* Heinz Auerswald was a young lawyer who had previously served as section chief in Division *Interior* for Population and Welfare. Now he was the equivalent of a *Stadthauptmann* or city supervisor for the ghetto, even as Czerniakow was named "Mayor" to emphasize that the relationship of Auerswald to Czerniakow was parallel to that of Leist to Kulski.

Technically, the ghetto *Kommissar* had plenary power over the Council, its organization and activities. Auerswald claimed total enforcement authority *(Polizeihoheit)* in the ghetto, and to that end he disposed of three police organs: [28] The newly constituted Jewish Order Service *(Jüdischer Ordnungsdienst,* or ghetto police), ultimately about 2,000 men; a detachment of *Sonderdienst* personnel, i.e., ethnic German auxiliary police attached to local German civil authority (not as yet to the regular police); and, upon demand to Leist's Police Director, Polish police forces in the city. Of course, the Security Police and Protective Police were ever present in the wings. Neither had ever abandoned its claim to responsibility for insuring the peace of the ghetto, and Czerniakow in fact maintained continuous contact with representatives, albeit low-ranking ones, of both organizations. The structure of the police, under an SS and Police Leader, is reproduced in Figure IV.

In his diary, Czerniakow says a great deal about his meetings with Auerswald. At times, the *Kommissar* appeared to have been cold, official, and unyielding in conversation. Thus he admonished Czerniakow in connection with forced labor recruitment, saying that the ghetto could easily be surrounded with plentiful supplies of captured Russian barbed wire, and that the grip could be tightened until the entire population died out.[29] Occasionally, however, there are hints of Czerniakow at ease in Auerswald's office. For example, Czerniakow once allowed himself to say to Auerswald that the *Kommissar* as a recently married man could not completely understand what it meant to support a family.[30]

28. Summary of conference on public jurisdiction in ghetto, Nov. 8, 1941, JM 1112. Auerswald and Schön (Interior) were the ranking participants.
29. Czerniakow Diary, entry for July 18, 1941.
30. Entry for Nov. 1, 1941.

# FIGURE IV

## SS and Police in Warsaw District

*Gouverneur* Fischer
SS and Police Leader (Warsaw district)
SS-Maj. Gen. Paul Moder (to August 1941)
SS-Senior Col. Arpad Wigand (Aug. 1941-June 1942)
SS-Senior Col. Ferdinand von Sammern-Frankenegg (from June 1942)
Staff: SS-Major Max Jesuiter

Security Police
(Szuch Avenue)

*Kommandeur:*
SS-Lt. Col. Josef Meisinger
  (Nov. 1939-March 1941)
SS-Maj. Johannes Müller
  (April-Sept. 1941)
SS-Lt. Col. Dr. Ludwig Hahn
  (from Oct. 1941)
    Deputy: SS-Maj. Dr. Ernst Kah
    III Security Service, Chief: Kah
      B (Ethnic): SS-2d Lt. Kraatz
                  SS-Sgt.-Maj. Avril
      C (Culture)
        Chief: SS Capt. Bonifer
      D (Economic): SS-2d Lt. Dr. Stabenow
        Other personnel in III
        SS-1st Lt. Levetzow
        SS-2d Lt. Otto Fischer
    IV Gestapo, Chief: SS-Capt. Walter Stamm
      Deputy: SS-Capt. Höhmann
      A (Political):
        Chief: SS-Capt. Höhmann
              SS-1st Lt. Nicolaus
              SS-1st Lt. Boehm
      B (Sects):
        Chief: SS-Capt. Werner
              SS-1st Lt. Scheerer
              SS-2d Lt. Brandt
              SS-Sgt. Mende
    Other personnel in IV: SS-2d Lt. Müller

Order Police
*(Orpo)*

*Kommandeur,* in charge of Protective Police *(Schupo)* in cities and *Gendarmerie* (rural)

Order Police consisted of units and stationary personnel. Largest unit in Warsaw district was police regiment. Commander of regiment functioned (until some time in 1941) also as *Kommandeur* of *Schupo* and in lieu of a *Kommandeur* of *Orpo,* was responsible for all Order Police in district.

In succession:
    Lt. Col. Daume (1939-1940)
    Lt. Col. Petsch (early 1941)
    Lt. Col. Jarke (from second
      half of 1941)

The three battalions of this regiment were:
    6—from Sept. 1940: 301
    43—from Sept. 1940: 304
    8—from Oct. 1940: 307

The second battalion was directly involved in Jewish matters.

In 304th Bn.:
    ghetto guards  1st Lt. Welsch
    labor camps    Capt. Meissner

In the second half of 1941, 304th Bn. was replaced by 61th Bn.

No change of function was intended for the *Transferstelle,* which now as before was to concern itself with economic questions, but it was placed under the *Kommissar* and acquired new leadership. Its director, Max Bischof, was an experienced banker whose association with the Länderbank Wien (Vienna) dated from 1920 and who was most recently engaged in bank supervision in the *Generalgouvernement* administration. His association with Auerswald was contractual, and Bischof accepted the post in the *Transferstelle* only after some negotiations with Fischer about conditions of employment. In one conversation with the District Chief, Bischof wondered if the closed-off ghetto could ever become self-sufficient, and pointed to a German economic study which projected a need for an annual subsidy of 100 million zlotys.. Fischer, according to Bischof's summary, replied that first of all every effort would have to be made to solve this question and in this manner some "spade work" would be done "for the subsequent conclusive solution of the Jewish problem." If, despite every exertion, subsidies should become necessary later on, they would be granted.[31] They were not to be granted, and "self-sufficiency" was achieved by cold-bloodedly depriving the ghetto of essentials, month after month. However, during Bischof's tenure, there was an outburst of capitalist activity. At the end of 1941, he arranged for 76 million zlotys in unpaid taxes to be forgiven.[32] He created a climate for private enterprise, both Jewish and German. The administrative apparatus of the Council itself underwent structural transformations as several Council divisions acquired entrepreneurial independence. The Provisioning Division (imports) was turned into the Provisioning Authority, the Production Division, into a corporation *(Jüdische Produktionsgesellschaft),* the Trade Division became a firm (the *Lieferungsgesellschaft),* and after some time the Banking Division was constituted into a bank. Czerniakow writes about these changes with discernible reservations. For him the drawbacks were clearer than the advantages. He expressed vexation with some of the managers, resented their direct initiatives and approaches to the Germans, and was finally incensed by the suggestion of one of his own labor officials that the local German Labor Office approve applicants for positions in the Provisioning Authority.[33] In a word, he was losing control.

31. Bischof to Auerswald, May 12, 1941, enclosing summary of discussion with Fischer, April 30, 1941, JM 1112.
32. Bischof to Auerswald, report for November, 1941, JM 1112.
33. Entry for Feb. 15, 1942.

He might have consoled himself with the thought that Bischof was having his failures as well. The *Transferstelle* never acquired full mastery over ghetto trading either. Although the ghetto traded with the outside world as if in foreign commerce, Bischof's reports contain few statistics from which one could reconstruct a balance sheet of payments. We can only surmise that official imports and exports were only a part of the total volume of transactions. In short, the great bulk of trading was uncontrolled. The complexity of the situation may be summarized somewhat in Table I, which does not take account of exchanges of goods or money within the walls.

It is important to remember that Bischof in his reports and Czerniakow in his diary discuss mainly the official markets—the only portion of ghetto economic life that was fully visible to them. This is not to say that Bischof was an economic czar even in that sector of trade which passed through his *Transferstelle*. Thus, prices of ghetto exports were subject to approval of the District Price Control Office and, as late as December 1941, Bischof fought with that office for "sensible" (higher) prices, lest he never acquire control over contracts between ghetto suppliers and "Aryan" purchasers, which continually managed to short-circuit the regulatory mechanism, especially when border changes frustrated visual supervision.[34] Bischof also strove to consolidate small Jewish operators (e.g., manufacturers of brushes) and fuse subcontractors with prime manufacturers, with a view to reducing Jewish profits.[35] At the same time, he pushed for an expansion of German business activity inside the walls and invited the Commander of the Armament Inspectorate in Danzig, Admiral Strähler, to survey the labor resources of the ghetto for himself.[36]

By 1942, the list of the principal firms operating in the ghetto was as follows:

*German firms*
Walther C. Többens K.G. (clothing)
Schultz & Co., Danzig (mattresses, furs)
Waldemar Schmidt, Warsaw (straw shoes)
A. Ney, Berlin (straw shoes)
Metallwarenfabrik A.G., Bromberg (furniture)

34. Bischof's reports for Nov. 1941, and Dec. 1941, JM 1112.
35. Bischof's report for May 1942, JM 1112.
36. Bischof's report for Jan. 1942, JM 1112.

## TABLE I

### GHETTO TRADE: EXPORTS AND IMPORTS

| | Bischof in control | Bischof not in control | Mode of payment |
|---|---|---|---|
| **Exports from Ghetto** | | | |
| Scrap collection, etc. | To official market outside ghetto | | Into deposits in account of *Transferstelle* at Emissionsbank |
| Manufactured products (by "Aryan" and Jewish firms in ghetto) | To official market (i.e., "Aryan" firms, German Armed Forces, Nazi Party) | | |
| Manufactured products by firms | | To black market outside ghetto | Direct cash flows |
| **Imports of Goods and Services into Ghetto** | | | |
| Official allocation of food, coal, soap, raw materials, etc. (food subject to import tax) | To official market (Provisioning Authority and firms) in ghetto | | Payments by ghetto Council, Provisioning Authority, welfare organizations, and individuals through Council's Bank Division (later Genossenschaftsbank) cleared with Emissionsbank |
| Rents, Electricity, Gas, Taxes, etc. | | | |
| Smuggling | | To black market inside ghetto | Mostly direct payments by individuals using earnings, valuables, or cash |

Fa. Brauer, Danzig (leather products)
Astra Werke, Chemnitz (adding machines)

*Jewish firms licensed for district exports*
"Prohan" (electrical, mechanical, photographic)
"Galkos" (toys, cosmetics)
Lieferungsgesellschaft des jüdischen Gewerbes (distribution of finished products)
Jüdische Produktionsgesellschaft (uniforms)
Kohn & Heller (supplies for National Socialist Welfare)
D. Sternfeld
I.J. Margoses
"Gegeha"

In the course of a year, the increase in the zloty value of the exports was noticeable: some 400,000 in June 1941, 2 million in July, nearly 4.2 million in January 1942, to a peak of over 15 million (without Többens and Schultz) in July 1942, the month when the deportations began. The great bulk of this production was contributed by the Jewish firms.[37]

The economic upswing was registered also in employment statistics. Less than 34,000 Jews were "economically active" in September 1941—and that figure included the more than 9,000 people in the public sector.[38] By July 11, 1942, Czerniakow could list a total of more than 95,000, most of them in the workforce of the firms.

Standing alone, such data had a seductive effect; they implied productivity and viability. Economic enterprise could not, however, ensure survival. The volume of exports, even at its highest point, did not suffice to procure the essentials for a half-million people, and in the end it could not be used as ransom to buy their lives.

During Czerniakow's last year, profound impairments afflicted the Jewish community. Mounting stresses permeated ghetto life; there was crowding and illness, starvation and dying.

Population density was a direct result of ghettoization itself: the average occupancy per room was seven. Space was also a problem

37. The export statistics are gathered from Bischof's monthly reports. The number of Jewish and "Aryan" export firms was 41 when the deportations began. See enumeration in Bischof's report for August 1942.
38. See table in Emanuel Ringelblum, *Polish-Jewish Relations During the Second World War.* Edited by Josef Kermisz and Shmuel Krakowski (New York: Howard Fertig, 1976), footnote on pp. 71–72.

for institutions: the Jewish hospital (Czyste), lost on the other side, was re-established in multiple locations within the walls.

Again and again, the Germans pushed Jewish refugees by the tens of thousands from surrounding towns into the ghetto, simultaneously chopping off blocks and streets in the almost continuous process of boundary revision. The refugees, in particular, were vulnerable to disease and hunger—they lived in institutional buildings, bereft of possessions, waiting for their daily portion of soup.

The shrinkage of the ghetto's territory plagued Czerniakow constantly. In the late Summer and Fall of 1941, the ghetto was in fact threatened with the loss of its entire southern section. Dr. Hagen, chief physician in Leist's office, protested that the rising incidence of typhus among the Jews would bring about an unchecked epidemic and that the panic which already gripped the Jewish population in anticipation of the move would make an orderly transfer impossible. He characterized the plan as "insanity" *(Wahnsinn)*.[39] The outcome of this debate was the severance of more streets, in effect a widening of the "Aryan" corridor between the northern and southern ghetto sectors. In the meantime, of course, there was to be more wall building along the shifting 11-mile boundary. The construction project was entrusted to German contractors, but the Jews had to furnish stones and labor and the Jewish Council was responsible for the costs.[40]

The Germans had originally justified the establishment of ghettos because of reports that typhus was occurring in the Jewish population. In fact, such cases in 1940 were relatively isolated and, more significantly, the lice-born disease was seldom transmitted directly from person to person. It was the ghetto, and the consequent breakdown of hygiene, which provided ideal conditions for an epidemic. The number of cases began to increase in the Spring of 1941 and reached a peak of 3,434 reported cases in October of that year. The epidemic was being combatted with quarantining entire houses and subjecting the inhabitants to bathing. During the second half of 1941, Dr. Ludwik Hirszfeld, a scientist incarcerated in the ghetto, wrote a critical report of these procedures. Disinfection, he said, could encompass at most 2,000 individuals per day, and the bathing of clean persons was unproductive. He quoted the prewar

39. Hagen to Leist, Sept. 22, 1941, JM 1112.
40. Auerswald to Czerniakow, Oct. 22, 1941, JM 1112, and other documents in the microfilm. Principal contractor was Schmidt & Münstermann Tiefbaugesellschaft.

German scientist Martini to the effect that an infestation could be overwhelmed only when more lice were dying than were being born. To this end, nightclothes and underwear would have to be changed more frequently, and that was what the weakened victims could no longer do on their own.[41]

A large part of the Jewish population was suffering from gnawing hunger. In the German administration, the consignment of food-stuffs to the ghetto was a subject of debate from the very beginning. At a meeting of Warsaw district officials in late 1940, agriculture director Naumann wanted all deliveries cut off in December, in order that the Jews be forced to use up smuggled food. He also wanted the Jews to pay for any supplies with foreign currency which, he believed, had been hoarded in the ghetto. Dr. Lambrecht, of district health, opposed Naumann. An artificially induced starvation, he said, would breed more dangers of epidemics. Division *Umsiedlung* (at that time still responsible for the ghetto) sided with the health chief, but no one insisted on adequate provisions.[42]

Food was allocated on a 3-tier system, with a small number of German residents in Warsaw at the top of the scale, the Polish majority in the middle, and the Jews at the bottom.[43] When, in December 1940, the more than one million people in the city were required to share 15,000 quarts of milk daily, each German child received three-quarters of a quart. That month the German inhabitants also had exclusive access to apples and citrus fruits. Poles were permitted to buy other fruit at high prices, and they could obtain varying quantities of meat, poultry, and green vegetables. As for the ghetto, a typical shipment might be made up of rye, coarse-ground grain, some barley and bran, plus beets, carrots, and turnips. In its final form, the official ghetto diet was therefore going to consist mainly of a few slices of bread, a tiny amount of sugar, odds and ends as available, and—for some—a bowl of soup prepared primarily with cereals.

The food was purchased by Bischof on the basis of a rationing system authorized by the Food and Agriculture Division. The sheer quantities were kept low. In his reports, Bischof does not dwell on

41. Memorandum by Hirszfeld, undated, in *Faschismus–Getto–Massenmord,* pp. 147–49.
42. Inter-agency conference, Dec. 2, 1940, JM 1113. Mohns to Makowski, Jan. 2, 1941, JM 1113. Notation by Hörschelmann (Food Office), Jan. 9, 1941, JM 1113.
43. Hummel spells out details of policy toward Germans and Poles in his report for Dec. 1940, JM 814.

these imports; instead he speaks only vaguely of increases in potato shipments, a resumption of sugar allocations, or a substitution of "vegetables" for some other missing food. He is more specific about a direct grant, approved by the Labor Office for the benefit of some of the more important export firms that wished to maintain the efficiency of their workforce. These enterprises received a subsidy in the form of additional bread in exchange for which they were to offer their products at lower prices. Offsetting such a grant was another decision, noted by Czerniakow, to divert bread from the ghetto supply to the "Aryan" workers of the Münstermann firm which built the walls.

Czerniakow petitioned the Germans to mitigate their food embargo. He asked for permission to buy unrationed items in the free market of "Aryan" Warsaw. He was turned down. He then asked for larger allocations. Again his requests were in vain, and bitterly he noted his failure. The Germans, however, were fully aware of the precariousness of the situation. On October 1, 1941, *Gouverneur* Fischer, in the presence of Frank himself, requested additional food rations for the Warsaw Jews. Naumann, now acting food chief for the entire *Generalgouvernement*, pointed out that the supplements would involve 10,000 tons of wheat. Such amounts could not be made available, he said, although he could consider 50 grams of fat, 300 grams of sugar, and one egg. Meat shipments were impossible. Frank then said that any additional supplies for the Jewish population were out of the question.[44]

The staple reserved for the Jews thus essentially remained ghetto-baked bread. These loaves were subject to a threefold regulation: there was an apportionment taking account of different groups *within* the ghetto, the price of the bread was fixed, but the ration cards, as we have seen, were taxed.

A monthly report (reproduced as Table II) by Czerniakow to Auerswald, dated April 7, 1942, reveals the key that was used "pursuant to directives of the authorities" for the distribution of the bread to the Jewish population.[45]

44. Summary of *Generalgouvernement* and District officials' meeting, Oct. 15, 1941, Frank Diary, PS-2233.
45. Czerniakow's report for March 1942, Akten Auerswald (Polen 365e), Zentrale Stelle, Ludwigsburg.

## TABLE II: MONTHLY BREAD ALLOCATIONS

| Supplementary rations | Number of Individuals | Monthly Ration | Total (in lbs.) |
|---|---|---|---|
| Laborers in: | | | |
| armament plants | 5,000 | 8 lbs. 13 oz. | 44,100 |
| commercial enterprises | 500 | 5 lbs. 12 oz. | 2,867 |
| important export firms | 10,000 | 8 lbs. 13 oz. | 88,200 |
| Council employees | 6,000 | 8 lbs. 13 oz. | 52,900 |
| Order Service [Jewish Police] | 2,000 | 22 lbs. | 44,100 |
| Laborers in useful enterprises and persons usefully occupied | 10,000 | 8 lbs. 13 oz. | 88,700 |
| | | | 320,387 |
| *Basic rations* | 421,000 | 4 lbs. 6 oz. | 1,856,610 |
| *Welfare allocation* | | | 416,745 |
| | | | 2,593,742 |

The basic ration could be altered from month to month (it was lowered to 4 lbs. 6 oz. in January 1942, and raised to 5 lbs. in March). In the main, however, it was roughly equivalent to an American-sized loaf per person per week. The consumer paid the controlled price for the bread (by weight) and a tax for the card (per person). Czerniakow stressed in his entry of January 6, 1942 that 150,000 people were exempted from the tax.

The rationing system was designed to provide 33,500 of 421,000 ration card holders with additional food, somewhat in proportion to their "usefulness" or importance. Early on, Czerniakow himself had asked that a larger quota be given to Council personnel and the Order Service (Jewish Police). His calculations, however, were based on the expectation that these extras would be *added* to the ghetto supply; later, as he states in his diary on June 23, 1941, he learned that the Jewish Police were going to receive their supplements at the *expense* of the Jewish community.

The welfare allocation, which was supposed to approximate 15% of the total quantity, was doled out to refugee families or those who could not even afford the rationed bread.

There was a secondary food distribution through official channels in the form of low-cost (or free) midday meals. Czerniakow's report for January 1942, itemizes these lunches as follows: [46]

|  | *For the month* | *[Daily average]* |
|---|---|---|
| Children | 760,551 | [24,534] |
| Plants | 145,264 | [4,686] |
| Returned laborers and families | 23,040 | [743] |
| Council employees | 62,872 | [2,028] |
| Hospitals | 132,256 | [4,266] |
| JSS employees | 30,066 | [970] |
| Order Service [Jewish Police] | 32,385 | [1,045] |
| Refugees and indigents | 1,363,568 | [43,986] |
|  | 2,550,002 | [82,258] |

As one glance at the categories of this table will reveal, the soup kitchens—like the special allocations of bread—were available for two kinds of people: the privileged and the destitute.

The black market was even less egalitarian than the rationing system. Some of the smuggling was in the hands of organized rings; a great deal of it was also carried on by laborers (Poles and Jews) with passes. In January 1941, *Gouverneur* Fischer's Chief of Staff Hummel reported that Jews on daily outside work assignments were "dragging" in food and selling it at "phantasy" prices.[47] In fact, black market staples became more expensive as soon as the ghetto was formed; after a few months the cost of illegal bread, beans, sugar, potatoes, horsemeat, lard, etc., had increased severalfold. Czerniakow, who obtained his information about such shopping from experiences related to him by his own office staff, mentions steep bread prices by May 1941. The inflation, however, was not merely a product of profiteering; smugglers were always in jeopardy, they paid bribes, and they even devised insurance coverage against losses from confiscations and arrests. On the German side, incidentally, there was a good deal of correspondence

46. Report for January, (Polen 365e), Ludwigsburg.
47. Hummel report for Dec., 1940, JM 814.

about the disposal of confiscated food; that subject too was a matter of jurisdictional disputes.

Both Czerniakow and the Germans were ambivalent about the black market. Czerniakow wanted to render it unnecessary, but the Germans made it essential. German officials did not like the trade, which was by definition a subversion of their rule, but they could not bring themselves to increase rations. Consequently, they combatted the black market while recognizing its function. Finally, Jews and Germans alike understood the social implications of the illicit importations. In a remarkable statement, Auerswald himself observed that smuggled food could only benefit those Jews who had the means to pay for it.

One aspect of the illegal crossings troubled Czerniakow particularly. Children were venturing out repeatedly at the risk of their lives, sometimes for no more than a meal charitably provided by a sympathetic Polish family. Czerniakow writes about these children a great deal. They were for him an acid test of his whole institutional structure. He wanted them in the ghetto and spared no effort to take care of as many as he could.

Rationed bread and black market food were the mainstay of the ghetto; there was very little else. During 1941, a number of families could still look forward to parcels from relatives and friends in the smaller Polish towns or in neutral countries. By late summer, the Germans were systematically confiscating the larger packages if they contained leather, flour, or fats, and the smaller ones if two or more were addressed to the same recipient. Czerniakow notes these requisitions, 15,000 of them in September. With the spread of the war on land and sea, parcels were no longer arriving from the Soviet Union and the United States, and the total flow was greatly diminished.

The ghetto also maintained a small farm outside the walls. It was permitted to operate for a while. Attempts were made to grow vegetables in small spaces within the ghetto itself, but these attempts produced a minuscule supply for a few.

The impact of food deprivation was actually measured. The historian Isaiah Trunk cites a ghetto survey of consumption in December 1941 which revealed that Council employees averaged 1,665 calories, artisans 1,407, shopworkers 1,225, and the "general population" 1125.[48] Dr. Leonard Tushnet, who made a detailed

48. Trunk, *Judenrat*, pp. 356, 382.

study of medical aspects of ghetto life, believes that some adults, their movements reduced and blood circulation slowed, subsisted on 600–800 calories for months.[49] These were beggars and refugees, the beaten and collapsing elements of ghetto society. The Jewish community as a whole, socially stratified in a system of relative starvation, was gradually sliding downhill. Czerniakow made that point obliquely when he observed at the end of 1941 that the intelligentsia were dying now.

From January 1, 1941, to June 30, 1942, the Council recorded 69,355 deaths; one-seventh of the population had died in these months. The highest numbers were reached in the summer of 1941 (5,560 in August) but the rate did not drop much below 1% monthly thereafter.[50]

By November 11, 1941, Czerniakow attempted to obtain land from a Polish sports club whose soccer field was adjacent to the Jewish cemetery. There was no longer enough room for the dead.

Franz Blättler, a Swiss Red Cross ambulance driver with the German army stationed in Warsaw during the winter 1941–1942 decided to visit the Jewish cemetery at the edge of the ghetto. Because of his strange uniform, a guard let him pass. He saw "children's bodies, one day old to ca. three years of age, piled up like a heap of dolls." In the mortuary lay half-naked corpses of men, one shot, one with a swollen blue face who, he imagined, might have been hanged. Many bodies were bruised, they had been hurled during the night from the windows of upper stories. The two sexes were being buried separately in mass graves. For 700 zlotys, he was told, a family could buy an individual plot. Sometimes, however, the same grave might have been sold twice and two visiting families colliding at the site would discover to their consternation that each of the deceased had been given a companion.[51]

Phase V: The Deportations

In February 1942, Czerniakow watched a Jewish workman install stained-glass windows in the Council chambers. Did he reassure himself with that symbol of permanence? Was he surrendering to a mirage? The diary is evidence that Czerniakow was not

49. Leonard Tushnet, *The Uses of Adversity* (New York: Thomas Yoseloff, 1966), 62 ff.
50. See table of monthly figures in *Faschismus–Getto–Massenmord*, p. 138.
51. Franz Blättler, *Warschau 1942* (Zurich: F.G.M. & Co., undated, probably 1946), pp. 28-31.

altogether ignorant of happenings all over Europe, nor unaware of the closeness of a catastrophic German intervention.

Already in early October 1941, Bischof told him enigmatically that Warsaw was "merely a temporary haven for the Jews." The October 27 entry states: "Alarming rumors about the fate of the Jews in Warsaw next Spring." On January 17, 1942, he asked if Lithuanian guards were coming. Two days later he heard that Auerswald had been summoned to Berlin, and now he could not shake off the fearful suspicion that the Jews of Warsaw might be threatened by mass resettlement. Four days thereafter, Auerswald indicated to him that the trip was "private." We know from German documentation that on January 20, 1942, a high-level interministerial conference was held in Berlin on the "Final Solution of the Jewish Question." [52] The participants, who were discussing the fate of European Jewry, included two ranking representatives of the *Generalgouvernement* administration. Auerswald was not invited to the meeting itself, but he may have been with the *Generalgouvernement* delegation in the German capital.

More rumors reached Czerniakow on February 16. Disquieting news came on March 18 from Lwów (30,000 resettled) and from Mielec and Lublin. On April 1, he learned that 90% of the Lublin Jews were to leave their ghetto within the following few days.

His wife remarked on April 26 that it was important to die with dignity. When, on the 29th, one of Auerswald's assistants asked him for ten maps of the ghetto, Czerniakow feared "a decision in the offing" for Warsaw. Following a German demand for a list of working people on May 3, he conjectured that preparations were being made to deport the ghetto's unproductive elements.

All through the month of May, there were "disturbing," "alarming," and "persistent" rumors of deportation. "It appears," said Czerniakow on the 18th, "that they are not without foundation." On June 14, the *Gazeta Zydowska*, official newspaper of ghettos in the *Generalgouvernement*, had a report of changes in the "Jewish residential quarter" of Kraków. The article did not refer directly to deportations of women, children, or old people, but it spoke of a new "economic" character of Kraków's Jewish community and corresponding alterations in the composition of Kraków's Jewish Council. Czerniakow cut the report out of the paper and placed it into the diary.

52. Summary of conference of Jan. 20, 1942, Nuremberg document NG-2586.

On July 1, there were rumors to the effect that 70,000 Warsaw Jews were going to be deported. "The rumors," said Czerniakow, "are groundless (so far)."

Throughout that time, Czerniakow continued with his routines. He was trying to obtain more money from Fribolin, the *Dezernent* in charge of Finance, Health, and Education; to alter the rationing system in favor of the children; and to collect the garbage. He managed to raise some revenue and succeeded with an appeal for an extension of the curfew hour. The ghetto had a chess tournament, concerts, children's festivals. When, on July 8, Czerniakow was criticized for the music and the singing, he thought of a film he had once seen in which the captain of a sinking ship had ordered the band to play jazz. He identified with that captain.

By mid-July, the rumors became more specific. On the 16th, he heard that all but 120,000 Jews were going to be removed; two days later, he asked: all?

In his diary, Czerniakow does not ask himself where the deported Jews of Lwów, Lublin, or Kraków had been taken. It was not a question commonly verbalized by ghetto leaders. There was in fact no Jewish intelligence network, no systematic acquisition of information, no organized verification of rumors and reports. At that very moment, Nazi Germany was "solving" the "Jewish problem" in death camps created on Polish territory. Two of them were located in the nearby Lublin district; both were operating at full capacity, Bełżec as of March, Sobibór from the month of April. The news of gassings was penetrating the Warsaw ghetto by word of mouth, but the tormented possessors of that knowledge, some of them Jewish functionaries on the periphery of the Council, took no steps to initiate an alert. They feared the consequences of sporadic outbursts of resistance for the community at large and, like Czerniakow, they were clinging to residual hopes.[53]

Meanwhile, at the edge of the Warsaw district near the Bug River, a "labor" camp was being rushed to completion. Its name was Treblinka. The camp commander, Dr. Eberl (a euthanasia physician) wrote several letters to Auerswald, requesting nails for railway tracks, cables, measuring sticks, and sundry materials.[54] Apparently,

53. See entry of June 17, 1942, in Emanuel Ringelblum's diary, specifically mentioning gassings of Jews in Sobibór and discussing the implications of that information, in *Yad Vashem Studies* 7 (1968): 173–83, at 177–80.
54. See Eberl to Auerswald, June 26, 1942, *Faschismus-Getto-Massenmord*, p. 304.

construction was behind schedule. Czerniakow mentions the camp quite frequently; clearly, however, he did not understand its purpose. On January 17, 1942, Auerswald told Czerniakow that *Generalgouverneur* Frank had agreed to allow Jews held in Warsaw's Pawiak prison to be sent to Treblinka for work. On February 19, Czerniakow actually complained that German prosecutors had failed to produce the appropriate papers for the "release" of prisoners *to* Treblinka. A day later, the prisoners did leave. On March 10, he recorded the departure of five Jewish clerks to the camp, and in April some 160 young German Jews, recently arrived from the Reich, were sent there. All that time, Czerniakow did not know that Treblinka was going to be equipped with gas chambers.

Time was running out all along. On February 23, 1942, Bischof and his deputy Rathje were drafting terms for their continued employment with the *Transferstelle*. Their new contracts were open-ended; there was no stipulation for another year.[55] In July, the *Generalgouvernement* deportation and killing center expert, SS-Major Höfle (attached to the SS and Police Leader, Lublin), arrived in Warsaw. The deportations were at hand. In his report for July 1942, Bischof notes that inasmuch as jurisdiction over the "resettlement action" had been transferred to a special office outside the existing administrative structure, the *Transferstelle* (with Auerswald's agreement) had decided on principle to abstain from attempting to "influence" the process.[56]

Czerniakow tried not to accept the truth until the very last moment. As panic gripped the ghetto, he even asked a number of SS men whether he might deny the rumors. When the instructions for deportations were handed to him with provisions for the exemption of limited categories, he tried to widen the protected group. Although some of his requests were granted, he did not receive an assurance that the orphans would be safe. He continued to go to the office and still made entries in his diary. The last one was written on the afternoon of July 23. According to a number of accounts, Czerniakow went home for supper that evening, but was recalled by the SS. Back at Council headquarters at about 7 P.M., he received

55. Bischof's original contract ran to May 15, 1942 and provided for automatic extension thereafter, subject to three months' termination notice. The February 1942 amendment merely changed the May 15 date to May 31 and retained the termination clause. Rathje's terms were the same as Bischof's new ones. Document in JM 1112.
56. Bischof to Auerswald, report for July 1942, JM 1112.

new directives. Left alone in his office, he asked for a glass of water and shut the door. An employee heard the telephone ring. When it was not answered, the clerk stepped in and found the body of the chairman. Two farewell notes were on the desk. During the night, the Council met to select Czerniakow's successor. The position was given to Marek Lichtenbaum, Council deputy chairman and wall expert. Czerniakow was buried during a small, brief ceremony very early the next morning.

Almost a half-million Jews had lived in the Warsaw ghetto. By the time the war was over, 99 percent of them were dead.

## THE MAN AND THE DIARY

In the course of the German administration of Warsaw, several power centers had surfaced in the district, each leaving its mark on the Jews in turn, from the first appearance of an SS *Kommando* that established the Jewish Council, to the rule of Leist who burdened it with new problems, to the transition regime of Schön when the Jews were crowded into quarters behind walls, to the Auerswald *Kommissariat* that institutionalized starvation, to the re-emergence of the SS, which reached into the ghetto and deported its people. Throughout this time, Czerniakow stood at the helm of the Jewish community and took up the struggle for its existence. His was a world of recurring nightmarish problems, of crushing German demands and desperate Jewish needs. Even as the Germans widened their power and enlarged their aims, a surrounded Jewry was constantly reduced to searching for its remaining means.

The Jewish Council did not draft any manifestos or sets of assumptions. It did not have a plan of action. Nothing in Czerniakow's diary and correspondence is so conspicuous as the sheer frequency of his meetings and reports as such, the wide-ranging agenda with which he dealt, the diversity of subject areas which constantly claimed his attention. He worked a seven-day week, almost every week, year round.

The routine began about 8 o'clock in the office, often with the countless complaints of suffering Jews. He held meetings with his staff to map out the implementation of German directives or ad hoc orders, and to prepare proposals for internal changes, many of which had to be approved in advance by German officials. A considerable part of his time was spent in conferences with German functionaries. In the beginning, these meetings were frequently initiated by the Germans, who would summon him at a moment's notice to deal with specific problems or to issue threats and reprimands. Gradually, with the sealing of the ghetto, Czerniakow would report to his civilian supervisors on Tuesdays and (less regularly) on Thursdays and he would visit SS offices on Saturdays and (less regularly) on Wednesdays. Very seldom did Czerniakow confer with high-ranking individuals. The civilians with whom he maintained contacts were experts in Leist's office, later on also Auerswald, Bischof, and some of their assistants. In the military he would occasionally see Lt. Col. von Kamlah. They would discuss a variety of subjects, but the army, as von Kamlah once reminded Czerniakow, was no longer in charge. Within the SS, Czerniakow would speak mainly to lieutenants and sergeants. Once, when he tried to meet with SS-Lt. Col. Hahn, he was told brusquely that the *Kommandeur* was receiving no one but his own experts. Significantly, even the Gestapo chief under Hahn (Walter Stamm) is mentioned only once in the diary. Every once in a while, Czerniakow would also see Polish officials, but these contacts became infrequent after the ghetto was formed.

When a weekend was partially free, Czerniakow might use his pass to inspect the Jewish sanatorium and children's home in Otwock. During evenings he would read Polish novelists, or Shakespeare and Cervantes in Polish translation. He wrote sonnets and talked to his wife Niunia.

Czerniakow was a caretaker, not so much of a community, as of its countless afflictions, and his entire official life was much less a singular daily effort to save a people than a whole series of efforts to save people every day. Often there were salient issues to which Czerniakow and the Council gave priority and which were stressed in verbal and written appeals to the Germans. Such representations were made for segments of the Jewish population exposed to exceptional privation or special danger: forced laborers in 1940, homeless families in 1941, hostages in 1942. At other times, Czerniakow appealed for relief from the pressures of perennial problems: more money to pay community employees, more rations to feed the hungry population, more shelters for children.

The continuous process of intercession, so visible in the pages of the diary, is not an unknown phenomenon in Jewish diaspora history. It has a name, *shtadlanut,* and its essence is stated most succinctly by the holocaust historian Dr. Israel Gutman in his essay about Czerniakow: [57]

> *Shtadlanut* becomes necessary when Jewish rights are not safe-guarded by law, when Jews are unable to claim proper political representation and cannot engage in an active political struggle. *Shtadlanut* is based on negotiations between an individual, who is agile of tongue and quick to act and who knows how to behave with tyrants, and a ruler, who has the power to order matters at will and under whose patronage the Jews live. In return for the concession he requests, the *shtadlan* offers the ruler material benefits and unrestricted loyalty. Emancipation and civil equality eliminated the *shtadlan* from Jewish life, but the Nazis recreated him and made intercession the only possible form of contact between the Jews and the authorities.

Generally, Czerniakow assumed that almost every German agency could be approached in almost any problem area and that virtually every German official—however low his rank—would listen to a plea and perhaps pass it on to a superior.

So great was his expenditure of energy in these appeals that one might well ask: What were the results? Most of the time, he failed. There was never enough food, space, or security. Yet, on occasion, there are also successes: one or another prisoner is released, a loan is approved, the bothersome Thirteen are dissolved, and (by May 1942) 6,700 of the ghetto children are attending 19 public schools. Such small achievements, temporary stabilizations, and phantom victories were an important factor in fostering an illusion of progress and sustaining the official Jewish faith in the survivability of the ghetto.

Czerniakow's diary is a mosaic of many small facts. He recorded his experiences without analyzing their meaning. A chronicler of events rather than a historian, his writing is studded with details, prosaic rather than lyrical, and above all subdued. The shooting of 109 hostages is rendered into "tragedy in Wawer," the killing of

---

57. Israel Gutman, "Adam Czerniakow—The Man and his Diary," in Israel Gutman and Livia Rothkirchen, eds., *The Catastrophe of European Jewry* (Jerusalem: Yad Vashem, 1976), pp. 451-89, at p. 466.

more than a dozen people "more than 10 deaths last night." His descriptions of the Germans include no sketches of their personalities, nor does he say what he thinks of them. People like Brandt and Mende of the Gestapo, or Auerswald, the civilian *Kommissar,* with whom he had dealings several times a week, have their deeds and words duly and meticulously recorded, but usually without comment. When he provides a criticism, it would often take the form of a recapitulation of arguments he had made against precipitate or impossible orders. The arguments themselves were generally limited to reciting problems confronting the Council in carrying out German demands, but occasionally he allowed himself a larger statement such as that which he advanced when presented with bills for the wall. Since the epidemic, he said, was to be kept from those outside, the Jews should not have to pay for the medicine.

He wrote the diary in notebooks roughly 7″ X 4″, just thin and small enough to fit into a coat pocket. Most entries begin with the morning temperature. Then he would state where he went and to whom he spoke. He must not have bothered much to read what he had written, for there are repetitive accounts of the same event, sometimes a page or two apart. Quite possibly he carried around whatever notebook was the current one, vaguely prepared that it might be lifted from him by some German guard. In all, he filled nine of these notebooks, and the fifth one is missing. He does not, however, refer to the loss of that book. Fear of discovery may have inhibited him with regard to any elaborate description of the Germans—clearly he feels free to talk about any number of Jews. Yet we must also consider that he could have been keeping his diary with a view to writing a book later on. For such a purpose, he would not have had to record his profoundest reactions; he would always remember what they were. He would only have had to make sure of dates, names, and a myriad of daily happenings that he would never be able to recall. This is not to say that the short, fragmentary sentences in his notebooks contain only such facts. The diary reveals also the man—his beliefs, attitudes, and above all his style.

He had a sense of life and death in the ghetto as bizarre. A musical band is playing in front of a funeral parlor. A man called Rappaport laughs before he dies. The hospital grounds are toured in a hearse containing the body of a newborn baby, with one man in the driver's seat urging on the horses, and two other men on the horses.

He was a modest man, not given to sophistry or self-praise. In that respect he was the antithesis of Rumkowski, the Elder of the Lodz ghetto, for whom he expresses contempt. He expects no recognition and he has no proud image of himself as a chief executive. When the Germans give him the rank of mayor, he compares himself to the puppet "King of Croatia." After a particularly miserable day, he notes: "Filled with glory, I return home at nine in the evening." In an almost surrealist scene, a mental patient who imagined having black candles in his body accosts him during a visit to the Otwock asylum and Czerniakow escapes, explaining that he is not the chairman.

Nor did he take advantage of his position for material gain. As chairman, he draws no salary, even after Auerswald suggests that he do so. When the ghetto boundaries are changed, he foregoes the opportunity, offered to him by the Germans, to keep his old apartment. For his lunch, he eats ghetto soup. In one passage he remarks that he owns nothing except his furniture and clothes.

In September 1939, Czerniakow did take steps to secure his appointment as chairman. That single act was probably giving him much cause for subsequent thought. He even dreamt that Mayzel, the prewar leader of the community, had returned to reclaim his post. Czerniakow stayed on, convinced that he could not quit, and—in an allusion to Greek mythology—imagined the cloak he was wearing as poisoned. He persevered, almost with a feeling of propriety, expecting to endure troubles in small ways and large. Characteristically, when a colleague once asked him how he managed to remain calm, Czerniakow answered that he had been trained that way in his childhood under the specific circumstances of his parents' home. That is, he tells us, where he learned to suffer.

Some of his complaints were physical. Following a tradition in the Polish middle class at the time, he would diagnose his ailments, referring to "liver pain," "lumbago," and other maladies. He consumed headache powders galore. A good many of his annoyances, however, were administrative: the incompetence of Council members, staff, or house committees, the intrusion of the Gestapo informers, the constant jurisdictional conflict over agencies or functions. He is exasperated with corruption, wondering [58] (in the early

58. Entry for May 18, 1940.

days) if identification documents for staff would not have to be issued in different colors every month. And what, he asks, if such scum were to have its own state? Would not the currency have to be changed every month?

He had to cope with critics, detractors, and reformers. "He who is unhappy with his own house," he states, "becomes a social activist." He was plagued by petitioners and his ears were periodically assaulted by the din of wailing women at the door of his office.

Czerniakow was somewhat fastidious. Once he could not have his clothes pressed, another time he was repelled by a library book that had been handled a great deal, and on a third occasion he discovered to his dismay that a many-footed louse had invaded his apartment. Later on he made increasing references to unsanitary conditions in the streets, houses, and schools. He was bound and determined to clean them.

Only seldom does he mention a subject that was troubling him most deeply: his son, living in Lwów, and missing after the German assault on the USSR had begun. One day, Czerniakow notes that his little dog Kikus disappeared and then, no longer able to repress the pain, he asks: And where is my only son Jas? [59]

Czerniakow had his villains and heroes. Not deserving of much consideration were prosperous individuals who would not even donate money for charity. The Polish municipal finance official Ivanka tells us that Czerniakow once claimed to have jailed such a Jew. The culprit had reportedly spent 4,000 zlotys in a luxury establishment and when Czerniakow called upon him for a welfare contribution, the man offered 15 zlotys. "You will give not 15, but 25," the chairman told him, "and not in zlotys but in thousands of zlotys." Czerniakow thereupon ordered the man's detention until the family delivered 10,000 zlotys and a pledge for 15,000 more.[60]

Villainous are those who fled or deserted their posts, emigrating while there was still time, and they are hypocritical besides if they did so with the promise of seeking help abroad. Despicable is Gancwajch in whose saliva everything turns to filth. But there are also good men, like Dr. Ludwik Hirszfeld, whom Czerniakow respects not only for his ability but also his apparent coolness. He mentions with sympathy a poverty-stricken individual who wants

---

59. Entry for Feb. 13, 1942.
60. Aleksander Ivanka, *Wspomnienia skarbowca* [*Memoirs of a Treasurer*] *1927–1945* (Warsaw: Panstwowe Wydawnictwo Naukowe [State Scholarly Publishers], 1964), p. 536.

some money, not for food, but to pay the rent, lest he die in the street.

Czerniakow appreciated competence and understood dignity, but in the final reckoning he probably valued loyalty most of all. As he saw it, loyalty was not easy, for it demanded a kind of steadiness and tenacity that might even have to be physical. He gives two telling examples of such dedication.

On January 10, 1940, he relates the story of a woman singer in love with an actor. The man was badly injured in an air raid that blew out his insides. She pushed them back with her hands and brought him to a hospital where he died. When he was buried in a common grave, she dug him up and reinterred him in a private plot.

Almost two years later, on October 5, 1941, he relates another incident with some of the same imagery. That episode is especially significant because of the way in which it is introduced. He starts with an account of a meeting in which one of the Jewish leaders had contrasted those that were present with the "true mentors of the people." Who were the true mentors, countered Czerniakow, were they the men with passports who had left the community in the lurch?

In the very next paragraph, he goes on abruptly to write about a 15-year-old youth who, while substituting for his parcel-carrying father, was shot at during his rounds. Despite a stomach wound, intestines breaking out of the abdomen, and a damaged spinal cord, the youngster crawled to a house and rang the bell of an apartment, asking that the parcel be turned over to an Order Service man. Czerniakow says no more.

Throughout it all, he gives voice to an overwhelming sense of powerlessness and futility. He describes the situation of a newly formed relief committee as wonderful, but hopeless. He notes the experience of a child who was given a little desk. The child was elated with the present, but before the day was over, the toy was taken away from him.

The survival of the children was the ultimate test of his efforts in the ghetto. It has been reported that after Czerniakow made the last entry in his diary on July 23, 1942, he left a note to the effect that the SS wanted him to kill the children with his own hands.

# The
# Diary

# Notebook One

*September 6, 1939*—I could not sleep from midnight to 5 in the morning.

*September 7, 1939*—Burdened with backpacks all kinds of people set out for the unknown.[1]

*September 8, 1939*—Restless night.

*September 9, 1939,* Saturday—Shellfire.

*September 10, 1939*—I joined the Civil Guard. A rain of bombs. Went to the [Jewish] Community [office].

*September 11, 1939*—During the night the orphanage at Jagiellonska Street was smashed to smithereens. Radio appeal to the population to make lint bandages. Could there be a shortage even of those? Parenthetically this brings to mind the following passage from *Don Quixote* about a soldier: "They will place a tasseled doctor's cap made of lint upon his head, to dress some wound from a bullet passing through his temples or leaving him maimed in arm or leg."

Horsemeat—Emir Rzewuski's famous steed. After guard duty Jas [2] leads a blind man home under fire.

---

1. The Polish government was evacuating its offices from the capital and called upon able-bodied civilians to leave for the rear.
2. Jas was Czerniakow's only son.

*September 11, 1939* [3]—[Jewish] leaders frightened to death. I was working in the Community at 26 Grzybowska Street. At number 27 an explosion, three dead. The wounded were treated in our offices. *Chalutzim* [4] were hired to work for the Jewish [citizens] committee now being formed. A meeting at Gepner's [5] for this purpose.

*September 12, 1939*—A meeting of the committee: Gepner, Hartglas, Czerniakow, Lichtenbaum,[6] Koerner, Hartglas [sic], Prof. Weiss. The committee is now duly constituted.

In the evening a telephone message that the military authorities are requisitioning the M. Bersohn Museum, the Technical High School, and the [offices of the] rabbinate. I will intervene tomorrow. Bombardment light today.

*September 13, 1939*—The museum will have a guard. The Community organization is functioning again. The Jewish Citizens Committee of the capital city of Warsaw received legal recognition and was established in the Community building.

*September 14, 1939*—At the Jewish cemetery, 130 bodies burned by incendiary bombs on Sept. 13. First at the Community then at the meeting of the Citizens Committee. Zahan [7] will probably take charge of enterprises whose owners fled. At last a horde of refugee squatters left our apartment. The idea of making an appeal to world Jewry for assistance. The Citizens Committee voted in favor of it.

*September 15, 1939*—Heavy artillery fire mainly in the area where I live. Blazing fires lit up the city. The Citizens Committee was recognized by the city president [mayor], Starzynski,[8] who also

3. There were two entries under this date.
4. *Chalutzim* were young Zionists preparing for agricultural settlement in Palestine.
5. Abraham Gepner (1872–1943), a Jewish businessman, was chairman of the Association of Jewish Merchants in Poland.
6. Marek Lichtenbaum, an engineer, and member of the Jewish Community Council before the war, was Czerniakow's deputy in the *Judenrat* (Jewish Council), involved with wall-building in the ghetto. In July 1942, he took Czerniakow's place. Killed by Germans, April 1943.
7. Zahan *(Instytut Rozrachunkowy Zagranicznego Handlu)*, the Polish foreign trade clearing-house where Czerniakow was employed. When Czerniakow talks about going to the "office" in subsequent entries, he means Zahan.
8. Stefan Starzynski was the Polish mayor of Warsaw until the fall of the city; arrested by the Germans in October.

named the members of the executive committee: Gepner, Koerner, Szerezewski,[9] Czerniakow, Lichtenbaum. To date no Jews have been assigned to the headquarters of the Civil Guard.

*September 16, 1939*—During lunch at "A la Fourchette," shell fragments tore into the building. After taking brief shelter in the underground movie theater under construction, an hour's trek home to cover the distance between Zlota and Wspolna Streets. Bombardment in the afternoon and all night long.

*September 17, 1939*—Sunday—Early morning concentration of gunfire on the railroad station and vicinity. In the afternoon very heavy artillery fire. The Royal Castle and the Church of St. John damaged.

*September 18, 1939*—A meeting of the Citizens Committee. Formation of sections.
Presidium—press and propaganda
Weiss and Miss Kahan—information
Milejkowski [10]—health and medical assistance
               —financial commission
               —list of Jewish organizations
We are organizing a 100-bed hospital under the aegis of the Community at 35 Zielna Street. We will provide first aid and drugs. From 11 to 2 at night on guard duty at the gate of the apartment house.

*September 19, 1939*—Inspecting the [Zahan] office at Sienkiewicz Street, hit by a shell which failed to explode the day before and still lies on the floor with its fuse alongside. In the morning a meeting of the Citizens Committee. As usual [am] scrounging for groceries.

*September 20, 1939*—All night terrifying bombardment. Shells exploded over the house. They hit the Soviet Embassy at Poznanska Street nearby. I stood guard at the gate of the building until 5 in the morning. Forty bombers struck today.

9. Stanislaw Szereszewski, an engineer and a Council member, who was associated with the Warsaw JSS (Jewish Self-Help). He was killed by the Germans in April 1943.
10. Dr. Israel Milejkowski was to be in charge of the ghetto's health services.

*September 21, 1939*—Morning at the office. Arranged for the translation of a proclamation to the Jews. Visited Colonel Eile [11] on rights and duties of Community administrators. A relatively quiet day. What will the night be like? In the morning a bomb hit police station XI where Jas and I are registered. A difficult night; our school [12] was hit.

*September 22, 1939*—In the morning a meeting of the executive of the Citizens Committee. Letter to Starzynski concerning [Jewish] participation in [city-wide] Citizens Committee. In the afternoon two air raids on Warsaw. Mrs. Malwina Goldsobel came to stay with us.

Today, the Day of Atonement—atonement indeed. Cannonade through the night. Jas on duty from 4 until 8 in the morning.

*September 23, 1939*—For quite a while a shortage of bread. There is no meat. They started selling horsemeat, praising its taste in the newspapers, even as stock for soup. Mayor Starzynski named me Chairman of the Jewish Community in Warsaw. A historic role in a besieged city. I will try to live up to it.—All night the city was bombed, perhaps more heavily than before. Damage to buildings and loss of life very extensive. Sparks from the gutted railroad station were falling on our school. The office (at 4 Sienkiewicz Street) was hit for a second time by shrapnel which landed on the fifth floor, demolishing two rooms. We are moving to the fourth floor.

*September 24, 1939*—Gunfire all night. There is no gas, water, electricity, or bread. Horrifying day. Our apartment building was hit by four incendiary bombs and a shell. Jas was extinguishing them with sand. Later bombs from planes. Then fires on all sides. All windowpanes are out. In the evening the family moved to Wilcza Street. I am spending the night at Wspolna Street.

*September 25, 1939*—The family returned from Wilcza Street together with the landlord. All night in the shelter. Warsaw under continuous terrifying bombardment.

11. Col. Henryk Eile, a Jew, held a position in the municipality.
12. "Our school" was an elementary school under Mrs. Czerniakow's direction.

*September 26, 1939*—There is no news. Still no water. Bread utterly unobtainable. Night—heavy fire. In the morning, hysterics at home. Night—the shelter. Truskier's son-in-law, daughter, and granddaughter buried in debris.

*September 27, 1939*—A night of intense gunfire. Large numbers of dead and wounded. In the middle of the day an easing-off. People gather around in the streets in an optimistic mood. Something has happened. Many rumors. Starzynski issued a proclamation about water, etc. Gunfire stopped in the afternoon. We are sleeping at home. A quiet night.

*September 28, 1939* [13]—In the morning planes with a cross of as yet unknown origin. In my office salaries are paid out. In the streets people are carving out chunks of flesh from dead horses. Guard duty at the gate of the building 2–5 at night. Salaries paid in the office.

*September 29, 1939*—In the morning looting of a warehouse at Barbara Street. A nightmarish sight. Looting of the warehouse and robbing of the looters. I have offered myself as a hostage to the Germans.[14]

I inspected the Community offices. Saw Bryl. Saw Mrs. Mayzel [15]—her house in ruins, she was left with one shirt on her back. The head of the burial section crushed to death under rubble. I was burying corpses in the little square near Wegierkiewicz [café]. On my way home saw a woman refugee pulling possessions piled on a wooden horse. J. [Jas]—a stretcher—the deceased fled from the stretcher.

*September 30, 1939*—Morning at the Community. I called a meeting for Sunday. They did not accept me as a hostage. At 1 P.M. a meeting of the Jewish Citizens Committee. Poland is to be reduced to 15 million ethnics [16] including 2 million Jews.

13. Warsaw fell that day to the Germans.
14. Twelve prominent Warsaw hostages were provided for in the surrender agreement. Only Gepner and S. Zygelbojm were Jewish hostages.
15. Mrs. Maurycy Mayzel, wife of prewar Jewish Community chairman, who fled.
16. The fifteen million "ethnics" were in a part of Polish territory later called the *Generalgouvernement*. Not included in this region were western areas incorporated into Germany and eastern areas occupied by the USSR. Poland's prewar population was 33 million, including 3.3 million Jews.

*October 1, 1939*—Allocation of functions in the Community. *Sind Sie ein Jid?* [Are you a Jew?] [17] Starzynski requested me to issue a proclamation in the name of the Community calling upon the Jewish population to maintain order during [food] distributions.

*October 2, 1939*—Visiting with Mayor Starzynski.
(1)   Proclamation to the Jewish population
(2)   Armbands for functionaries of the Community
(3)   Food allocation
Dead horses were buried in the courtyard of the Community at 26/28 Grzybowska Street. A meeting of the Jewish Citizens Committee. Proclamation sent to the printers. Meeting of the Community Council. Search for food. Bought onions at 0.80 zlotys per pound.

*October 3, 1939*—At the office. Meeting at the Community. Searched for food. Civil Guard apropos expulsions. Proofs of the proclamation seized in the street. The messenger taken to forced labor. Kajut received the proclamation. The Community was paid for a burial with the blood-stained banknotes removed by a relative from the victim's pocket. Bersohn Museum is fine. We will open the Community schools. Complaints.

*October 4, 1939*—At the office. My wife standing in line [for food]. Father of Chairman Wencel [18] paid us a visit looking for his son. I assigned him to a 3-room apartment of Mrs. Nowerow. In front of the Community building the son of Prof. Dickstein informed me that his father was dead and asked me to give him a funeral. Unfortunately, before I could enter the building, I was stopped [by the police] and for the time being can do nothing. I was driven to Szuch Avenue [location of Security Police] and was ordered to co-opt 24 men for the Community Council and to assume its leadership. I prepared a statistical questionnaire.

*October 5, 1939*—It was impossible to cross Jerozolimski Boulevard until 1 P.M. I sat waiting in a little garden near the water filtration plant. At 1 P.M. I started walking to Gepner's. I did not

17. The question *"Sind Sie ein Jid?"* (derogatory for *Jude*) was apparently asked by German soldiers of pedestrians.
18. Wencel: citizens guard.

Chairman Adam Czerniakow in his office at the Warsaw *Judenrat*.

Facsimile pages of Czerniakow's diary.

Entrance to the ghetto at Chlodna Street, showing part of the overpass.

Jewish police and Warsaw Polish police controlling entrance to the ghetto.

Ghetto street scene.

The masses of people on the streets give some indication of the number of Jews who were crowded into the shrinking confines of the ghetto.

To the hundreds of thousands of Warsaw Jews incarcerated in the ghetto were added Jews expelled from other Nazi-occupied areas.

Nalewki Street, 1942.

Typical street scenes.

The overpass
photographed from
Chlodna Street. The
street itself was in the
Aryan section.

The poster advertises a
ballet to be performed in
the ghetto.

In desperation, even rags
were offered as
merchandise.

A market stall in ruins.

find him at home as he is imprisoned as a hostage in City Hall. I am calling a meeting for 9 A.M. tomorrow on the subject of the 24.

*October 6, 1939*—The meeting on the 24. It was scheduled to be! [Instead] a meeting at Szuch Avenue.
Mr. Batz [19] Captain of Security Police
Executive (5–6)
*Ausweis* [identity card], stamp
*Kasse* [treasury]
*Schulen* [schools]
*Friedhof* [cemetery]
*Taufe* [baptism]
It did not take place; I waited from noon to 6 P.M. I was told to get in touch with Meisinger [20] at 10 A.M. tomorrow. Armed with *Ausweis*, I was walking home through a dark night. Banks display announcements about the status of accounts.

*October 7, 1939*—A meeting at Szuch Avenue.
*Lebenswichtige Betriebe in der Lebensmittel Branche* [critically important enterprises in food products].
*Leute—Aeltesten Rat* [men, Council of Elders]
*Statistik* [statistics]
*Bauern?* [peasants]
*Ordnung* [order]
*Name, Wohnung, Beruf* [name, address, occupation]
*Mittwoch—11 Uhr* [Wednesday—11 A.M.]
    *(zu Meisinger)* [to Meisinger]
*Beirat (Zustimmung meine)* [Advisory Council, my appoval]
Stopped at the corner of Poznanska and Zulinski Streets.

*October 8, 1939*—Morning from 8:30 to 12 at the SS. Waiting for the keys. Later a policeman accompanied me to unlock the Community hall. The remaining rooms were locked and sealed. Twenty-four chairs were placed in the hall and inventory was taken. There is no glass in the windows and a shell has made a hole in the ceiling.

19. Batz: probably Bernhard Baatz, SS-Captain, administration of the Gestapo section in *Einsatzgruppe* IV. The *Einsatzgruppen* were mobile units of Security Police (Gestapo, Criminal Police) and Security Service in newly invaded territories.
20. Josef Meisinger, *Regierungsrat* and *Kriminalrat,* then chief of Gestapo section in *Einsatzgruppe* IV. Later, full SS-Colonel and *Kommandeur* of *Sicherheitspolizei* (Security Police) and *Sicherheitsdienst* (Security Service). That office, abbreviated KdS, was stationary.

Inspected the trade school at Sliska Street. No damage. Several families are now squatting there.

*October 9, 1939*—One of the Council members is wounded. Another one good for nothing. It is necessary to replace them. A labor activist offered his services to the committee. I dispatched invitations to the 24 for noon tomorrow.

*October 10, 1939*—Morning in the office. Klin Dawid—Barkowa Street 2a apt. 17.
[*Jewish*] *Handwerker Verband* [craftsmen's union]
member of the secretariat.
A meeting of the *Aeltesten Rat* [Council of Elders]. Election of the 24 and proposals. Mr. Starczewski of the municipality visited the Community and requested the cemetery taxes for the German authorities. Kaminer [21] drove to the cemetery and issued instructions. Late at night I was summoned to the municipality. Troubles all night.

*October 11, 1939*—There was no meeting at the SS.

*October 12, 1939*—In the office. Meeting with the SS.[22]
   (1)   List
   (2)   Statistical questionnaire
   (3)   Finances
   (4)   Labor contingents
   (5)   Gutszechter, Kahan, Rogozinski
   (6)   Schools, welfare, rabbinate, contributions, cemetery, bookkeeping—personnel
   (7)   Museum

*October 12, 1939* [23]—Clearing rubble at Jasna Street. In the office. The SS—
   (1)   *Aeltesten Rat* [Council of Elders]
   (2)   *Stat. Formuler* [statistical forms]
   (3)   *Schulabt., Fuersorge, Rabinat, Steuerabt., Buchhaltung,*

---

21. Meshulam Kaminer, Agudah, member of Jewish Council and first chairman of its Labor Commission, in charge of cemeteries.
22. First entry for October 12 crossed out by Czerniakow.
23. In second entry under that date, points 1–3 crossed out.

*Friedhof, Museum* [school department, welfare, rabbinate, tax department, bookkeeping, cemetery, museum]
(4)  *Arbeit* [labor]

Dr. Rosinski's grave—maid. Cemetery problems—visit with Starzynski. Restrictions on foreign currency. I found nobody at the SS. Summoned for tomorrow about *Rat* [The Council of Elders].

*October 13, 1939—*
(1)  The SS—*Liste der Mitglieder des Aera, Ausweise für die Mitglieder* [membership list of Council, identity cards for members]
(2)  *Stat. Formular—Evidenzbureau* [statistical forms—registry]
(3)  *Gemeinde* [community]
       *Kanzlei* [chancellery]
       *Fuersorge* [welfare]
       *Rabinat* [rabbinate]
       *Steuer Abt.* [tax dept.]
       *Buchhaltung* [bookkeeping]
       *Schulabt. (Fachschulen)* [school dept. (trade schools)]
       *Friedhof* [cemetery]
       *Statistik* [statistics]
(4)  *Arbeiterbrigaden* [labor columns]
(5)  *Veroeffentlichung der Kompetenz des Schulrats* [publication of School Council's jurisdiction]

Went to the SS—they informed me about prospective visit to the Community. Ba[a]tz showed up in the Community with a colleague. He announced the opening of some departments. In the meantime, everything was sealed again. Bonifer [24] 45.[25]

*October 14, 1939—*

| | |
|---|---|
| *Friedhof* | —*Zimmer* 4 [cemetery—4 rooms] |
| *Steuer* | —*Zimmer* 6 [taxes —6 rooms] |
| *Kasse* | —*Zimmer* 1 [treasury—1 room] |
| *Cabinet* | —*Zimmer* 1 [cabinet—1 room] |
| *Fuersorge* | —*Zimmer* 5 [welfare—5 rooms] |
| *Konferenzsal* [sic] | —*Zimmer* 1 [conference room—1 room] |

24. SS-Captain (later SS-Major) Adolf Bonifer, in the administration of the Security Service, *Einsatzgruppe* IV, later chief, Kds/III C [III = Security Service].
25. Number 45: Probably a room number.

| *Buchhaltung* | *—Zimmer* 2 [bookkeeping—2 rooms] |
| *Wirtschaftsabt.* | *—Zimmer* 2 [economy dept.—2 rooms] |
| *SS-Cabinet* | *—Zimmer* 1 [cabinet—1 room] |
| *Rechtsanwalt* | *—Zimmer* 3 [legal counsel—3 rooms] |

26

They will arrive 10–10:30 [to] *entsiegeln* [unseal the rooms].
   *Ausweise* [identification] (privileges)
     *Aera* [council]
     *Angestellte* [employees]
     *Armbinden* [armbands]
     *Lebensläufe* [vitae]
   *Kasse* [treasury]
     *Steuer—Beitragspflicht—Vorschlag (in welcher Hoehe?) Fuer die Zwischenzeit eine Anleiheaufnahme bis die Steuer eingehen.* [treasury—taxes—compulsory dues (proposed amount?) In the interim a loan until taxes can be collected.]
   *Statistik für jeden Stadtbezirk* [statistics for every city district]
   *Arbeiterbrigaden* [labor columns]
   *Aufruf* [conscription]—Project for Monday.
Son [?]—statistics.
*Organisations Plan mit Personen* [organization chart with names]
Schoeffler 8–9—*Lederhandschuh* [leather gloves]
   (1) *Parteien—Organisation:* [political parties—organization]
     (1) *Ganz Polen* [All of Poland]
     (2) *Warschau* [Warsaw]
     (3) *Institute* [institutions]
       (1) *Wirtschaft* [economy]
       (2) *Kulturleben* [cultural life]
         *Theater* [theater]
         *Wissenschaft* [intellectual life]
         *Volkstum* [Jewish studies]
       (3) *Gesundheitswesen* [health]
       (4) *Kunstinstitut* [Institute of Fine Arts]
       (5) *Literatur* [literature]
       (6) *Agentur* [news service]
       (7) *Presse* [press]
   (2) *Jued. Kulturgemeinde—fuehrende Leute—wo sie sind?*

[Jewish cultural community—leading personalities—where are they?]

(3) *Der wirtsch. Aufbau der Gemeinde* [economic reconstruction of community]

    (1) *Vermoegen wie verwaltet* [property—how administered]

    (2) *Budget* [Budget]

(4) Mayzel

(5) *Organisationsplan der Jued. Gemeinde* (Warschau) [Organization chart of Jewish community (of Warsaw)]

(6) *Kommunismus—Judentum* [Communism—Jewry]

(7) Classification—Zionism, Orthodoxy, etc.

(8) The 24—Who is who? (4 *Durchsch.*, room 45) [?]

(9) *Deutschland—Verhaeltnis*[Germany—relations]
    *Russland* [Russia]
    *Polen* [Poland]

(10) Foreign currencies (position on this matter)

(11) The problem of converts [baptized Jews].

(12) Hartglas [26]—*Montag 9 Uhr* [Monday 9 A.M.]

Ba[a]tz.

*Auswanderung der jued. bevoelk. nur mit vorher. genehmigung der deutschen Behoe[rde]n erfolgt* [Emigration of Jewish population may proceed only with prior permission of German authorities.]
*Arbeiterbrigaden—Montag* [labor columns—Monday]
*Ausweise* [identity cards] for personnel
*Baender* [armbands] for everybody
Museum—No.

In the corridor of the SS I encountered the commander of the Citizens Guard, Regulski (whom I have not previously met), with coterie who took away my Citizens Guard armband and identification card. I intend to bring this matter to the attention of Starzynski.

26. Apolinary Maksymilian Hartglas, Zionist leader, longtime member of Polish parliament, and for a short while in the Warsaw Jewish Council. At the beginning of 1940, he emigrated to Palestine.

*October 15, 1939*—At the Community in the morning at 10 briefing the personnel. From 12 to 2 P.M. a search by the SS. In the meantime a meeting of the *Aera* [Council]. Later Ba[a]tz addresses the 24. In the evening preparing materials for the SS meeting tomorrow. A building about to collapse at the corner of Merszalkowska and Wspolna Streets was dynamited. Fun and games in front of the Community offices—beards.[27]

*October 16, 1939*—Working from 5 A.M.—on census questionnaire and logistics of census taking. In the morning at the office. Community from 12 to 4 P.M. At 5 the Community submits to the German authorities the materials previously demanded. At 4 in the afternoon return of the keys to different department offices and to the safe. Removal of records from the safe. In the evening I received the *Ausweisy* [identification cards] for the members of the Council.

*October 17, 1939*—On my feet since 6. Summoned to the Civil Guard. Explained my functions to them. 12:20 at the SS. Ordered to appear at 6 P.M. At 6 P.M told to come October 18, '39 at 10 A.M. Discussing work with staff at the Statistical Office. I was visited by the *Tausendkünstler* [Conjurer] "Alfred Nossig." [28]

[There is no entry for *October 18, 1939*]

*October 19, 1939*—Office in the morning. From 12 at the Community. A meeting of the *Aera* [Council]. Getting the Labor Battalion ready for Saturday 7 A.M. After lunch conference with the Statistical Office.

*October 20, 1939*—Office in the morning; 11 A.M. at the community. Two visits from the SS about ritual slaughter. At 3 P.M. Ba[a]tz at the Community while I am looking for him at the SS. He threatened retaliation if I did not show up. At 5 P.M. discussed census statistics, finances, education, and the Labor Battalion at the SS. Plans for the Labor Battalion finalized. I am ordered to provide 500 men for the municipality at 7 in the morning. Proclamation about the census etc. will be issued by the SS.

27. Beards of orthodox Jews were cut off by the Germans in the streets.
28. Alfred Nossig, born 1864 in Lvov, lived in Berlin for many years, writer, communal worker, sculptor. Believed already to have been in German intelligence service in the First

*October 21, 1939*—At the Community at 7 in the morning. A crowd of 2,000 unemployed waiting for work. At 8:30 the SS arrived. Several dozen taken to the SS etc. Later 120. Representatives of the municipality failed to appear. Several dozen workers ordered for Sunday and so on. Tuesday again 500 for the SS. Supposedly they [the SS] will take care of meals and wages.

Office in the morning. From 12 until 2 a conference in the Statistical Office. Between 3 and 6 P.M., at the SS. Conference with Ba[a]tz. I point out that the lst is All Saints' Day and the 2nd All Souls' Day; hence the Jewish census should be postponed until the 3d. Ba[a]tz sends me to another official. A long and difficult conference—it is decided that the census will take place on [October] the 28th. He sends me to the Currency Control Office to make arrangements for the Community's census expenses. At his own request, at 6 P.M., I rode home with him, picked up a printer and drove to the printing shop at Twarda Street. The census forms were discussed and approved. I have to see to it that this German announcement is posted on the walls throughout the city. At night, I returned part of the way in the official car. At the corner of Jerozolimski Boulevard I was stopped by a patrol. My *Ausweis* [identity card] was not sufficient. Vomiting at home.

*October 22, 1939*—At the Community in the morning. Getting the census ready. Naming the 26 commissioners.

*October 23, 1939*—7:30 at the Community. The Council meets with the SS present. Census preparations.

*October 24, 1939*—Early in the morning 300-man contingent from the Community for work. Office, later the Community. Going to see SS at 3:30 P.M. B. [Baatz].

*October 25, 1939*—Office in the morning. Surrendering the radio set.[29] From 11 A.M. the Community. Influence peddlers—reassurances—complaints.

---

World War. In Warsaw, reported to Gestapo. Assassinated by Jewish underground, January 1943.
29. Poles and Jews had to turn in their radios.

*October 26, 1939*—Thursday, Office in the morning. The Aryan question.[30] From 12 the Community. After 1 an inspection tour of the census stations. After lunch complaints—assurances.

*October 27, 1939*—Friday. Office—12 the Community. Checking up on the census commissioners. Szoszkies.[31] Do I have a radio?

In the Community until 6 P.M. (census, etc.). Curfew 7 P.M. Proclamation of the *Generalgouvernement*. Death of Koenigstein [Imprisoned Warsaw industrialist]. Szoszkies' tactics.

*October 28, 1939*—Office, Community, SS. Submitted a memo on reopening of schools, on the authority of the Elder in Łódź, and on the payment of outstanding salaries. The census is going well—the forms in large majority of cases returned by the house superintendents. From all sides questions about the purpose of the census. Somebody brought a corpse to the Community and left it by the gate.

*October 29, 1939*—Morning—the Community. In the afternoon the SS.

*October 30, 1939*—Bonifer's demand.[32]

*October 31, 1939*—Bonifer. The number of the Jews 360,000. Requisition for 100 workers. Reward for those saving the house. The janitor and the watchman are letting apartments at Sliska Street [Jewish vocational school].

*November 1, 1939*—Ordered to provide 300 workers for Nov. 2, '39. Told that they will be paid. Memoranda. Ordered to submit a complete report on the census by the 12th. In addition to management we need 60 staff.

*November 2, 1939*—*Devisenstelle* [Currency Office] in the morning. As of now, no permission has been granted for unfreezing the money paid into the Discount Bank. I have no money to pay the

30. Czerniakow, as "non-Aryan," was subject to dismissal from Zahan.
31. Henryk Szoszkies, a member of the Jewish Council, emigrated at the end of 1939.
32. Bonifer demanded of Hartglas information about the Jewish community and particularly about emigration possibilities.

staff's salaries, the expenses of the census, the Labor Battalion, etc. We were burying the victims of typhus and dysentery. Yesterday I received a delegation from the orphanage which was just denied a municipal subsidy (500,000 [zlotys for] 500 orphans) under the pretext that the Community should assume complete financial responsibility for the institution.[33]

Council meeting—approval of work. In the afternoon a meeting at the Zahan.

*November 3, 1939*—In the morning, at 7:30, at Marszalkowska Street, while I was walking to work, Szoszkies reports that some of the workers deserted, while others go around begging. Yesterday they were treated at Fort Bem in an unfriendly manner. He is walking there just now to discuss it with those in charge. We reported yesterday at Szuch Avenue that up to 1 P.M. our labor contingent was not given any work to do. I have been ordered to report to Bonifer at 12. I did.

*November 4, 1939*—Office in the morning. Community. Difficulties with the payroll. A German currency control official expected to arrive at 9:30 did not show up. A soldier from the SS came in, ordering a meeting of the Council for 3 P.M. At 11:30 an SS soldier demanded in the name of the authorities a meeting of the Council of Elders together with their alternates.[34] Some of the councilors and their alternates failed to appear. A unit of the SS ordered completing the list. We enlisted people who happened to be around. We were informed about the zone of settlement. The alternates were removed from the hall.[35]

*November 5, 1939*—An audience with the commandant of the city, General Neuman[n]-Neurode. He indicated that a possible zone would be the subject of written notification. In the afternoon to Ba[a]tz. The zone reduced in size. Crowds under the windows of the Community headquarters. At home hundreds of people.

33. According to Acting Mayor Julian Kulski, German city administration forbade muncipal subsidies to Jewish institutions.
34. The entry refers to an unsuccessful attempt by the SS to set up a ghetto under its control. The move was vetoed by the Military Commander. See diary entry for November 5, 1939.
35. The "alternates" were taken as SS-hostages. They were the alternates of Council members and (because some of the alternates were not there) stand-ins—in all, 24.

*November 6, 1939*—Crowds. To Ba[a]tz in the morning. Czerniewski [36] from the municipality was there. He decided upon the list of streets. A briefing at the Community at 4 P.M. Informing the expellees.

*November 7, 1939*—In the morning at the Community. A crowd burst into my office. Reproaches because of the hostages. Three hags are creating a disturbance because Wspolna Street is excluded. In the afternoon, to Bischoff [37]—postponement of all work until Monday. Szoszkies!

*November 8, 1939—November 9, 1939*—In the office in the morning. The Community. An order relating to the hospital at Czyste, 5,000 zlotys for the timber for the roof, glass, window pane installers, roofers, 500 beds, blankets, pillows, sheets.

In the afternoon, to Bischoff—memo on the schools, social welfare, the Department of Contributions. Tomorrow the SS will send someone to unlock the department offices. I pleaded to be arrested together with the Council in exchange for the 24 hostages. They promised to release them all tomorrow morning.

*November 10, 1939*—Eight in the morning—the SS. Waiting until 1 P.M. Intervention with Bischoff resulting in the release of 24 hostages at Danilowiczowska Street.[38] Two officers drove with me to Danilowiczowska Street and ordered the release. At 5 P.M. they walked out free. Later to the bank to arrange for some money. Later on to the Community to the Departments of Contributions and Welfare. On Monday I am ordered to the SS in the matter of the expulsions. God alone knows what that day will bring! Kobryner [39] thrown out of his apartment. In the Community's courtyard expellees from Sierpc.[40] Council member Eng. Szereszewski arrested along with many others.

36. Marian Czerniewski, a Polish colonel in the municipal Housing Department.
37. Presumably SS-Major Helmut Bischoff, commander of *Einsatzkommando* 1 of *Einsatzgruppe* IV. The battalion-size *Gruppe* was divided into company-size *Kommandos*.
38. Danilowiczowska Street—location of detention facility used by both German and Polish police, and of other German police offices.
39. Commercial judge Edward Kobryner, member of the Council.
40. Sierpc, a town northwest of Warsaw in incorporated territory, from which Jews were expelled into the *Generalgouvernement*.

*November 11, 1939*—In the Community in the morning until 3 P.M. Wailing in front of the building—some Jews shot in a car on a bridge. At 3 P.M., the SS orders 300 workers.

*November 12, 1939*—In the morning at the Community. Expellees arriving from small towns. Conferences about the taking over of hospitals. Adalberg is dead.[41] At home loneliness and gloom.[42]

*November 13, 1939*—In the morning at the bank. Lastowitschka.[43] After lunch, the SS. Lastowitschka, again the SS. Tomorrow I am reporting to Ba[a]tz to be told about the resettlement. Next morning I have to be in the Community on the matter of workers at Danilowiczowska Street. I must reduce the wages of the workers from 4 zlotys to 3 zlotys. Until this day I managed to pay them 4 zlotys. We are still not permitted to open the schools.

*November 14, 1939*—At 7 A.M. at the Community. The Labor Battalion is being paid. Getting ready for a meeting with Ba[a]tz about resettlement etc. Went to the SS. The matter of deportation is no longer being entertained. More and more complications between the *Deutschvölkische* [Ethnic Germans] and the Jews—accusations that the Jews owe money and do not pay it back. I received summonses for Jews to present themselves at the SS. It is the Community's responsibility to deliver the summonses. Tomorrow I am ordered to appear at 8:30 at the SS for discussion with Ba[a]tz on getting the Community Organization going. They gave permission today to withdraw 30,000 zlotys from the Discount Bank. What would have happened if they did not abandon the plan for resettlement? The recriminations from the Jews would have been unbearable!

*November 15, 1939*—A cloudy morning. It is now 6:30. It is pouring. I must be at the SS at 8:30. This is November. On the 30th I will be 59 and going on 60. Once, long ago, I made a

41. Samuel Adalberg, a specialist in Polish folklore, committed suicide.
42. Czerniakow's son Jas had left for the Soviet-occupied zone.
43. "Lastowitschka" = Karl Laschtowiczka, of Austrian origin, associated with German-owned bank in Warsaw before the war. After occupation began, classified an ethnic German. In German city administration, chief of Finance Division, 1939–1940.

theoretical plan to divide my life into three parts: I. study and play; II. accomplishments; III. reconciled with God and at peace with myself. Fate would have it otherwise. Since 1905, I, who never exploited anyone and never lived at anyone's expense, have been paying for those who did just that. Anyway people like me are legion. I go to bed every day, according to police hours, at 9. As a result I wake up at 2 and sleep only intermittently until 6 in the morning. When I am awake I read *Don Quixote*. How much we need you, errant knight, today!

My head is bursting from all the complaints. In Annopol all the [unemployed and homeless] Jews were thrown out of the public shelters. I now have to cope with four small towns, the hospitals, orphanages, Annopol, and on top of it all, the mentally ill. My head is spinning.

*November 16, 1939*—I begin my day at 7 with a funeral. The deceased, Likiert, struck by a heart aneurism, was a master craftsman at the vocational school. The question in point is a free funeral.

A meeting of the Council.

*November 17, 1939*—The SS is now agreeable to the establishment of the communal kitchens and baths. We must collect 30,000 zlotys for the Labor Battalion. In the evening I am called to the SS. An exaction of 300,000 by Monday.[44] Five hostages from the Council in jeopardy: drawing lots. On my desk a model of a Jewish gravestone. The Council meeting set for 10 A.M. tomorrow.

*November 18, 1939*—At 8 in the morning at the SS about the exaction in the course of which I report difficulties. They gave me a deadline for Monday, Nov. 21, 1939.

Ghetto postponed for a few months. The Community ordered to place at its borders signs stating *Achtung Seuchengefahr Eintritt verboten* [Danger: Epidemics—Entry Prohibited]. The taking over of the hospital, the orphanages, and the old people's home postponed until December 31, 1939. Ordered to get in touch with Dr. Schrempf [45] about [the] transfer of the hospital.

---

44. The 300,000 zlotys were needed to ransom 53 men arrested at 9 Nalewki Street in reprisal for the fatal shooting of a Polish policeman and the wounding of another. The shots had been fired at that address on November 13 by a Jew with a criminal record. He escaped.
45. *Medizinalrat* Dr. Schrempf was a German physician in charge of Warsaw city health. He was considered virulently anti-Jewish and anti-Polish.

Went to Laschtowitschka in the matter of the exaction to obtain a list of the frozen Jewish accounts. Received a fragmentary tabulation of only the unblocked accounts.

*November 19, 1939*—From the early morning a meeting of the Council. All day long the collection of money for the exaction. In the afternoon, a meeting with Red Cross delegate Junod. He promised some assistance for the Jews, drugs and food. In the evening the money collection continues. I managed to obtain about 260,000 zlotys in cash and withdrawals from new and old blocked accounts. Tomorrow more collecting. Then I must deliver the contribution to the SS. Baptisms! [46] Architecture.

*November 20, 1939*—The census of the Jews in Warsaw now completed. Eight in the morning—the Community—the exaction. At eleven I take 40,000 zlotys in cash and transfer deposits in the amount of 260,000 to the SS. Later at the Currency Control Office for a permit.

The "ghetto" will be marked with the sign *Achtung! Seuchengefahr. Eintritt verboten.* The military authorities will add signs placing the area off limits to the troops. Money collection in the Community continues. Ordered to take possession of the hospital etc. A landlady refuses to reward men who saved her building from a fire.

At 4 P.M. at the SS about the exaction. At 5 P.M. at the SS on the same errand. Then at the Currency Control Officer at Fret Street about cashing checks.

In the meantime I have neglected my office where I earn my living. What am I going to live on? God only knows, especially since I do not want to take a penny from the Community. Meanwhile, my job at the Community costs me money spent on transportation and tips—a droskha costs 4–5 zlotys each time. When I go to bed at 9 in the evening I read. At 2 A.M. I begin to fret. And so on until 5 or 6 in the morning when I get up. Shoes.

*November 21, 1939*—8:30 at the SS, planning to go to the Currency Control Office about unfreezing funds for the exaction. Waited fruitlessly until 11. Returned to the Community. Yester-

---

46. A reference to attempts by Jews to escape from application of anti-Jewish measures through conversion.

day, some Jews accompanied by guards demanded to be paid for some unspecified work. Those who happened to be in the office had to fork out 150 zlotys. A delegation of tenants from 9 Nalewki Street concerning the arrest of all the men there. In the evening I intervened with the Gestapo. I was told by a police officer to intervene with the Polish Police.

*November 22, 1939*—8:30 A.M. at the SS about unfreezing the funds for the exaction. Absences of Council members. Sterile newspapers. Roster of the Community staff. A revealing statistical finding about the number of Jewish craftsmen in Warsaw. Probably many craftsmen failed to obtain their licenses in the past, thus creating a misleading picture. The contractor Schreyer gets paid. Perpetual bickerings between housewives and their maids. *Shabbes goyim.*[47] How are we going to fund the new budget for the Community?

In the afternoon the SS. Mothers from 9 Nalewki Street. Infighting at the Community.

*November 23, 1939*—At the office in the morning; from 10 at the Community. Mothers' delegation (tears and screams). At 12 summoned to the SS. Waiting 2½ hours, later from 3 to 4:30. At 4:40 they rode with me to the Currency Control Office, but no one was there. On the street *Kommissar* [sic] Mende [48] informed me that the *Kommandeur* [Meisinger] will not accept any checks and wants cash by 6 P.M. Saturday. A most distressing scene.

*November 24, 1939*—At 7 A.M. the delegation of women from 9 Nalewki Street; at 8, a Council meeting. My proposal: lists of the tenants to be delivered to the landlords or apartment house administrators. Collection in the Community. It transpired in the evening that it may be possible to deliver 100,000 zlotys to the SS. Tomorrow we must pay the remainder. In the meantime at 12 o'clock I was ordered to appear at the SS at 3 with six rabbis, six leading members of the community, five councilors. I proceeded at once to

47. *Shabbes goyim* were non-Jewish persons employed by some religious Jews to perform essential tasks on Saturdays (turning on lights, etc.).
48. SS-Sergeant Gerhard Mende, then 28 years old, served in Warsaw Gestapo Jewish section. Gestapo and Criminal Police officers often had civilian rank of *Kriminalkommissar* and Czerniakow refers to a number of these officers as *Kommissar*. Mende, however, was only a *Kriminalassistent*.

Ba[a]tz and the whole idea was abandoned. I informed Brandt [49] of my willingness to offer myself as a hostage.

*November 25, 1939*—7 A.M.—the delegation from 9 Nalewki Street. At 8 in the Community. Visit to the bank. Deputized a bookkeeper to the Currency Control Office to unfreeze some of the deposits. By noon, 40,000 zlotys were collected. The machinations of the Currency Control Office. At 5:30 I took 102,000 zlotys to the SS. We need another 38,000. A very difficult moment, but in the end permission was granted to make the last payment on Monday. Intervening about those arrested at 9 Nalewki Street. Instructed to get in touch with Kluge or Bin at Danilowiczowska Street. We could not have used rabbis to solicit money for exactions, since the people stay away from the synagogues lest they be shanghaied for forced labor.

*November 26, 1939*—In the morning, mothers from 9 Nalewki Street behaving scandalously. Another ordeal with an employee of a funeral establishment (the past chairman's method—a crowd in the office).

*November 27, 1939*—In the morning intervening at the investigator's office about the Nalewki group. Ordered to come tomorrow at 9 A.M. Office. Then the Community.

*November 28, 1939*—Dr. Kluge informed me that the 53 residents of 9 Nalewki Street were shot. He refused to reveal the place of burial (9 in the morning). At 11 the relatives in the Community building. Some of the councilors advise postponing the notification of the families until tomorrow. I reject the suggestion. I summoned the waiting families into my office in the presence of one councilor (the others were only too happy to take advantage of my offer to leave). A scene very difficult to describe. The wretched people in confusion. Then bitter recriminations against me. I left the Community at 1:30. The poor creatures were clinging to the carriage. What could I have done for them?

At 3 I walked to the SS to arrange for the return of the bodies to the families. Unfortunately, I failed to find any official who could

49. SS-2d Lieut. Karl-Georg Brandt, Mende's immediate superior, whose office was Kds/IV-B-4 (IV = Gestapo). Throughout the diary, Czerniakow refers to the KdS as *Kommandeur*.

authorize it. I have to return tomorrow. At home a delegation of the victims. Tomorrow I am going to see Dr. Richter [50] in the matter of taking possession of the hospital at Czyste. Received a deputation from the hospital.

*November 29, 1939*—Richter in the morning. We were received by Schrempf. Because of conflicting instructions, ordered to proceed to Dr. Dengel *(Stadtpraesident)*, to which I replied that without permission from the SS I was not allowed to do so. At the Community, rumors about Nalewki Street.

*November 30, 1939*—In the morning the SS. I am 59 today. A meeting of the Council. Toward the end of the conference a newspaper *Nowy Kurier Warszawski* was brought in with an announcement on the Jewish armbands,[51] the marking of Jewish shops as well as the execution of the 53 from 9 Nalewki Street. The armbands are obligatory starting tomorrow. In the evening a summons from the SS for December 2, 1939, to see Fischer.[52]

50. Professor Richter was German army divisional physician.
51. According to a decree by *Generalgouverneur* [Governor-General] Frank, dated November 23, 1939, the Jews had to wear a white armband with a blue Jewish star.
52. SS-2d Lieut. Otto Fischer, who summoned Czerniakow, was stationed in the Security Service.

# Notebook Two

*December 1, 1939*—In the morning in the SS about the armbands. Couldn't sleep at night—took some headache powders. In the evening a summons to the SS (a different section) for tomorrow December 2, 1939. According to information just obtained in the Community, the families of the 53 have been looking for a scapegoat. Who could serve this purpose better than I? The cleaning lady tells me that one woman called me a murderer; others were spreading rumors that the exaction was paid too late; still others that I knew about the [death] sentence and kept this information secret. Typically, when I was all alone in my office and the wretched people were wailing in an adjoining room, one of my colleagues sent in a functionary "to defend me." He himself vanished into thin air.

At 8 o'clock in the morning they delivered the armbands with the crest of David. In this manner I received a new decoration albeit in different circumstances than at one time when I got the Commander's Cross from Hungary. I gave instructions for ordering a stamp to imprint this coat of arms.

Work at the Zahan impossible. In the first place there isn't any. Secondly I must resign from the management because of the Aryan paragraph. I have no idea where my livelihood will be coming from. I told Zarebski [1] that I am relinquishing the post.

I was received by Ba[a]tz. He refused to release the bodies. He ordered the preparation of the list of the Jews wishing to emigrate to

1. Zarebski was an official in Zahan.

the Ukraine. In his opinion, they will be permitted to take with them 5,000 zlotys each. I showed him the summonses to room 45 (Fischer). He took the note and ordered me to disregard it.

Nalewki Street. Again visited by the families and two new persons claiming to be family members. The Community until 2 P.M. In the evening working on Community matters at home.

Zar[ebski's] sister praises treatment of the Jews, since allegedly in [Soviet-occupied] Brest Litovsk they are mistreating the Poles. In the evening rumors that the armbands have been postponed for two weeks. N. had to put on an armband when she went out.[2] I cannot bring myself to do this yet.

*December 2, 1939*—In the morning at the Zahan. Yesterday I summoned to the Community offices new candidates to the Council. Szpinak, Zabludowski[3] [who owns a pharmaceutical enterprise], and Dr. Glücksberg [merchant] join the Council. Second typhus vaccination. Feverish during the night.

*December 3, 1939*—Sunday—In the morning I proceed through the city on foot with an armband. In view of the rumors about the postponement of the wearing of armbands such a demonstration is necessary. For this reason I even stopped for a while in a café. On the Community buildings I posted announcements about the requirement of wearing the armbands. I also distributed these posters to the 70 Community kitchens. Szpinak has been arrested; I am short one member of the Council. Attending to current business in the Community.

*December 4, 1939*—Monday—The Zahan in the morning. The matter of my dismissal. An inconclusive outcome, so typical with us. At noon a call from Mr. Piatkowski requesting the whole Council to appear at 10 A.M. tomorrow at Czyste in regard to the transfer of the hospital.[4] At 3 o'clock in the SS concerning P.

*December 5, 1939*—Nine o'clock the Community office; 10 o'clock the hospital. P[iatkowski] failed to appear. The appropriate

2. N = "Niunia," Mrs. Felicja Czerniakow, his wife.
3. Benjamin Zabludowski was to hold several positions: Council member, member of Labor Commission, Chairman of Personnel Commission, and Chairman of Fuel Allocation group at the Provisioning Authority. His prewar background was in real estate.
4. Stanislaw Pilatkowski was a municipal official. Czyste, a municipal hospital partly

documents were drawn up and forwarded to the SS. A rabbi who was seized for compulsory labor promised 50 workers from the Community, and indeed the Community will supply them (150 zlotys).

*December 6, 1939*—A decree concerning the resettlement of the Ukrainians, Byelorussians, etc. The Zahan in the morning. After lunch the SS. Gossip. Lists of Christian converts. An Aryan asking for a job. The armbands to be worn on the arm and not on the forearm. Work certificates for our messengers. In the afternoon, at the SS. Efforts to obtain the release of Gamarnikow. [5]

*December 7, 1939*—At the Zahan in the morning. The baths are profitable. A bath for the [Labor] Brigade. At the Community an incident with a worker. A theft of 1200 zlotys donated to the hospital at Czyste. Requesting Piatkowski to remit a new sum of money. A difficult, very difficult day. A landlord of an apartment house, Lotte, laments in the office how poor he is. Later he becomes abusive.

*December 8, 1939*—A holiday. Morning in the Zahan office. A Zahan board meeting about the removal of the Jews from the board and management. Sugarcoated Jesuit hypocrisy. Behind my back "a new member of the management" (Zarebski's inspiration?) Midech. Later in the Community offices. Practical training for the life of a saint. They demand that I supply bread for those expelled from Nasielsk and Serock. This cannot be done.

*December 9, 1939*—Morning in the SS. I present the case of the workman. Later on, ordered to give a job in the Community to Dr. Nossig. I was informed that in January we will receive from Berlin the directives on emigration. (Could this mean a reservation?) [6] Julek has been ruined. [My] wife does not cease crying. I was seized yesterday for compulsory work at Zielna Street. The young Jews, like geese in a coop, transported for labor in a truck. My papers

supported by Jewish fund drives, became the responsibility of the Jewish Council as of January 1, 1940.
5. Jakub Gamarnikow, attorney, was an alternate member of the Council.
6. For a while the Germans entertained a thought of establishing a large reservation for Jews in the Lublin area, and Czerniakow may already have heard something about such a plan, although the date is early.

helped and I was not impressed for work. One of the members of
the Council was summoned by the police for compulsory labor. He
had to provide a substitute right from the street for 8 zlotys.

I was ordered to open a new hospital with 500 beds. I was
summoned to the *Reichskommissar* (an official of Danilowiczowska
Street) in the matter of the hospital.

The SS intimated today that they are not our immediate superior
but merely an executive channel to carry out the decisions of several
other authorities. They were interceding about the hospital. The
final outcome was that the city would cover the December costs but
we must regard these outlays as a loan which we must repay. In the
Community treasury 20,000 zlotys. Tomorrow, workers' wages
alone amount to 40,000 zlotys. And what about the salaries for the
Community's personnel on the 15th? And what about the taking
over of the hospital, the orphanages?

*December 10, 1939*—In the coffers 5,000 zlotys. In the waiting
room of the *Reichskommissar* (his deputy), Kowalski's son works as
an office boy. In the morning the departure of Pawel. I paid a visit
to Lastowitschka. The Community is about to receive a loan of plus
or minus 250,000 zlotys from the blocked accounts in two banks. I
could not find Bartel [7] who was to take care of this business at the
Szereszewski and in Łódź Deposit Banks.

The Baroness—the palace—thankful for its condition—demands
replacements (wine, etc.). [?]

*December 11, 1939*—In the morning at 8:30 in the Łódź Deposit
Bank; I am waiting for Bartel. It is sad that there is no one who
could take my place on such an errand. How poorly the Jewish
community provides for its needy. I am toying with the idea of
going to Holland, if they let me, to arrange a charity drive "for the
Polish Jews in the *Generalgouvernement.*"

Dr. Nossig who was hired two days ago did not show up for work
yesterday. I paid him for a month in advance. It appears that he
won't be any solace to us. The Jewish pharmacies ceased to exist.[8]
We are not permitted to open the Jewish schools.

7. Rudolf Bartel was a German trustee of two Jewish banking institutions: the Szereszewski
Bank and the Łódź Deposit Bank.
8. Jews were forbidden to operate private pharmacies. Later on, in the ghetto, pharmacies
were reestablished under the control of the Council.

*December 12, 1939*—In the afternoon, a visit at home by the three officials from the *Devisenschutzkommando* [Currency Control Office] ordering the Community authorities to submit the addresses of the rich Jews for the purpose of requisitioning furniture, lamps, bedlinen, etc. In the evening a call to appear at the SS at 8 A.M.

*December 13, 1939*—In the morning at the SS, where a regulation was read to me to the effect that the Poles and the Jews who had been deported to the *Generalgouvernement* from the Reich would be shot, if they returned to their former domiciles. In the matter of the dead worker the Community must make a request that the body be returned to the family.

In the morning I was summoned to the office of the investigator *(Sittendelikt* [crime of moral turpitude]). It turned out that we must increase the number of posts with the sign *Achtung, Seuchengefahr* [Attention! Danger of epidemics]. Then in the *Devisenschutzkommando* about a loan for the Community. Rabbi Zylberstajn's defense counsel Frydman.[9] Today a Jew donated 10 zlotys to the Community. It turned out that a German health officer fined this Jew for filth and ordered him to pay the fine to the Community.

Talked with *Kommissar* [trustee] Bartel about the loan of 250,000. It appears that the blocked funds belong to the very poor, who are permitted to withdraw 20 zlotys, a month only (Szereszewski's bank).

An idea on [Jewish] collections instead of [German] searches and seizures. Apart from that, the hospital support in kind. A meeting of the Emigration Commission. Nossig refuses to work in a collegiate manner but would like to hold talks with each one separately. Gepner had a talk with Barcikowski about the compensation from Zahan. So far nothing but words on the part of [. . .].

An idea to start a Community paper *(Flugblatt)* [single sheet].

*December 14, 1939*—A joke about me, that whenever I go to the authorities I am seized for compulsory labor, became a reality a few days ago. Thanks to my papers [*Ausweis*], but not without difficulty, I was let go while the young Jews, packed tightly in the trucks and sticking out their heads like geese in a coop, looked on amazed.

9. Avigdor Frydman protested to an ethnic German guard the tormenting of the rabbi, and was himself tortured and killed.

Julek—the accessories [?]. The behavior of the porters. The behavior of the porters at Gesia Street.

The distrust on Nalewki Street (75,000) [sic]. Digging out corpses in a little garden at Kredytowa Street.

*December 15, 1939*—In the morning at the SS. An attempt to obtain the release of the furniture belonging to the carpenters' cooperative. A project of collecting supplies for the hospitals. The opening of another room. An attempt to reopen workshops for locksmiths, tailors, shirt and linen manufacturers. A query concerning photographs of the Community in the *Berliner Illustrierte Ztg.*[10]

Schrempf in the hospital in Czyste.

Rotstadt [11] and his three comrades. A demand to fix broken windows in the quarantine facility. The Emigration Commission.

*December 16, 17, 1939*—The Community. Three people escaped from the quarantine in Leszno, stealing blankets. On the street a madwoman molests the Jews, striking them and grabbing their hats. I am opening up a Department of Hospitals and I have engaged as department head Fliederbaum,[12] the former superintendent of the Czyste hospital.

*December 18, 1939*—Morning. On the street Jews escorted by soldiers are carrying the so-called *spanische Reiter* [barbed wire]. I proceeded to the Łódź Deposit Bank about the loan. Bartel tells me to communicate with Lastowitschka. Bischof[f] demands an authorization from the SS.

H[artglas] and K[oerner] [13] inform me that they received permits for Palestine. K[oerner], a holier-than-thou hypocrite, felt it necessary to add a comment. H[artglas] was silent throughout. As a result of my efforts Rotstadt and his comrades will be released on Wednesday.

*December 19, 1939*—Eight o'clock in the morning—Lastowitschka. He will arrange for the 250,000; in the *Devisenschutz-*

---

10. The photographs appeared under a heading proclaiming that arms had been found in the Jewish cemetery.
11. Dr. Albin Rotstadt headed the Physiotherapy Department of Czyste hospital.
12. Ignacy Fliederbaum, hospital administrator.
13. Mojzesz Koerner, Zionist leader, formerly in Polish parliament as senator.

*kommando* [Currency Control Office] payments into the banks; 123,000 from the BGK [Bank of National Economy].

At this point my trip to Holland is out of the question. It is not their decision, the SS says.

At 1 P.M., Council meeting to constitute commission. At 2:30 in the SS. They are not permitting prayers in a number of the synagogues. Not the SS, but various other authorities.

At 6 P.M. at Schrempf's about the hospitals. Quarantines have been imposed in the hospital for the doctors and other personnel.

A present of water poured down the neck.

In the evening at Schrempf's. Downstairs, a party in progress. Upstairs a problem of being welcomed. Discussed with Schrempf the matter of the hospital services, of the release from the quarantine of the doctors, etc. (in Czyste). Overcoats from a cloakroom.

*December 20, 1939*—In the morning I proceed to visit Lastowitschka. At the gate a soldier lectured me on the necessity of learning the language. L[aschtowitschka] sent a message through an office helper asking me to come next morning. At noon, the Community. Prayers in synagogues prohibited. Rumors about Praga [ghetto].[14]

*December 21, 1939*—Lastowitschka in the morning. The approval for 260,000 zlotys. Later with Bischof[f], Bartel. The collection of linen, etc., pretty good. A merchant seized on Polna Street to clean an apartment—bread with marmalade. At the Zahan prevarications on the subject of compensation.

Yesterday several German military personnel were present at the funeral of three of our workers killed unloading ammunition (a grenade had exploded). A complaint that the Community buried them by the fence.

The scoundrel Lebenfisz!

*December 22, 1939*—At the SS at eight in the morning about the release of Rotstadt, etc. Raschitsch [15] instructed me to communicate with Schrempf's assistant. I sent First [16] on this errand—promise of release. By evening no release.

14. Praga, on the east bank of the Vistula River in Warsaw, was considered as possible ghetto site.
15. "Raschitsch": presumably Herbert Raschik, in IV-B-4, office of the KdS.
16. Israel First, prewar administrator of Jewish Student House, about 30 years old when

*December 23, 1939*—At the Community in the morning. About Rotstadt, etc. A corpse at the gate carted in by a policeman. Wawrzecki invited me to Celestynow.

*December 24, 1939*—The Community offices closed on the 24th and 25th. A few officials left on duty. Also operating are the funeral section and the treasurer's office. I received 25,000 zlotys on account of the 250,000 zlotys; the cash is kept in the Community's safe, not without misgivings.

I decided to devote my time today for a visit to the hospital in Czyste, and the hospitals for the convalescents and those suspected of infectious disease at the corner of Zelazna and Leszno Streets.

What superb municipal schools. At a delousing facility in Czyste I had to take special precautions. The typhus suspects play dice. I tried to be as careful as possible. Others still need my health; I need it least of all. Korczak [17] joined me for lunch. The only ray of sunshine—a letter from J[as]. Our maid left for the whole night.

*December 25, 1939*—A holiday in the Community offices. I was there all morning until 1 P.M. At home a mistreated woman pleads for intercession. Unfortunately, there is nothing I can do. Wawrzecki was killed by masked bandits in Celestynow.

*December 26, 1939*— Wawrzecki's death, no sleep all night. Disturbing thoughts about the new *gzajrach* [18] in January (emigration) [19] and about the complaints of ill treatment which I have no power to remedy. At night I read a lot, constantly envying all the heroes of my novels because they lived in different times. I am about ready to go to the Community offices. Walking down the staircase I notice on the doors of the second-floor apartments that visiting cards, naturally "Aryan," now serve as amulets.[20]

A special charge for delivering coal [to wearers of] the armbands.

---

German occupation began. In charge of ghetto Economy Division, he supplied Germans with items they wanted. Killed by Jewish underground, November 1942.

17. Janusz Korczak (pseudonym for Dr. Henryk Goldschmidt), a well-known educator and author involved in the care of Jewish handicapped children. In the ghetto, he headed an orphanage on Krochmalna Street; in August 1942, he accompanied his orphans to Treblinka.

18. *Gzajra* (Yiddish from Hebrew *gezerah*), a term covering persecutions, pogroms, or harsh decrees for which no reasons are given.

19. "Emigration" refers to deportations into the *Generalgouvernement*.

20. Czerniakow lived in a mixed neighborhood and he comments on non-Jewish neighbors affixing their non-Jewish names on doors.

Deianira's coat.[21] Jugs of cherry brandy. A. Rotwand, Wasong (Christians of Jewish descent). It is reported to me in the evening that one of the workers from the Labor Battalion has been arrested (a section leader?). Later Mrs. Rotstadt about her husband. I will be going to the Gestapo in this matter tomorrow morning. Pawel was robbed.

*December 27, 1939*—In the morning at the Gestapo on the release of the prisoners from Czyste Street. Later at the Zahan (Mrs. Wawrzecki), eventually at the Community. I was visited by a certain Dr. Feldschuh [22] on the subject of emigration. I advised him to contact Jaszunski,[23] the chairman of the [Emigration] Commission. Ba[a]tz had been recalled to Berlin. In his place Bauer.

Kon's work of art.

*December 28, 1939*—At the Community in the morning. The hospital. On the street a madwoman (!) in a white hospital coat keeps on striking Jews. A tragedy in Wawer.[24]

*December 29, 1939*—At the Community in the morning. A meeting of the Hospital Commission. Intervening with the police with regard to the madwoman. Nossig's antics.

*December 30, 1939*—At nine, Wawrzecki's funeral. It is very cold—6°F. The death of Gamarnikow.

[Jews] mistreated, it is said, in Praga and Wola. A meeting on the budget of the hospital in Czyste: 150–200,000 zlotys monthly, apart from the cost of repairs and new investments, etc.

In the afternoon at home petitioners visit about funerals. Some woman found the remains of her father in the hospital of the Holy Spirit—calls it good fortune. Szereszewski in trouble.

21. Deianira: In Greek mythology, she was attacked by a centaur. Her husband, Hercules, shot him with a poisoned arrow. She was convinced by the dying centaur that if his blood were to saturate her husband's cloak, it would be a special charm of love. The poison spread to Hercules' body until, driven by pain, he killed himself.
22. Dr. Ruben Feldschuh, a Zionist, was concerned with emigration to Palestine. He survived and lived in Israel, where he changed his name to Ben-Shem.
23. Jozef Jaszunski, an engineer, directed ORT (Organization for Rehabilitation through Training) in prewar Poland; member of the Council, considered a socialist. In council's Labor Commission, directed registration. Later he was involved with vocational training and JSS; deported to Treblinka, January 1943, and killed there.
24. Following the killing of two German policemen in an inn, 107 men (ten or more of them Jews) were shot in reprisal at Wawer and Anin.

*December 31, 1939*—Worried about the Balaban Library.[25] Admonishing Nossig. In the Community several funerals: (1) a worker fell out of a window (?) in the Royal Castle, (2) Gamarnikow, (3) father of the Nalewki Street woman found in the rubble of the hospital of the Holy Spirit. She remarked that it was truly good fortune that she had recognized her father. A new definition of good fortune.

Thus, filled with glory I return home. Two strangers paid us a visit and informed us that our apartment will be requisitioned. As for New Year's we have indeed had enough.

*January 1, 1940*—In the morning at the Community. At 1 P.M. a reception at Koniawa's. Dresden reminiscences.[26] A delegation of the refugees from Kalisz.

*January 2, 1940*—In the morning at the Gestapo. It has transpired that the "requisitioner" of our apartment is a certain Alfred Paczkowski, 16a Pius Street, registered as "Szulc," 62 Wspolna Street. Apparently a driver delivering or distributing soups. The SS, to whom I complained about the requisitioning of my apartment, promised to intervene. At this point I am not too keen to punish the "requisitioners," but perhaps this should be done.

This morning I saw the "fine" Mr. K. Barcikowski from the Zahan on the street. He didn't stop. An altogether charming person. They came to the conclusion that even as a mere functionary I may "harm" the corporation. A typical Jesuit argument! The more so, since Lastowitschka, a German, clearly stated that there is no directive which would prohibit my employment.

*January 3, 1940*—In the morning at the PKO.[27] A rude clerk. A sign on the wall about "callousness to clients." A veritable pedant— three documents are not sufficient to identify me. Later the Community offices. Lack of funds. Schrempf threatens arrest if the disinfection chambers are not ready by the 7th instead of the 12th. At the PKO a sign that any attempt to withdraw funds would be futile!

25. Meir Balaban, historian of Polish Jewry, was in charge of Council's archives.
26. Czerniakow received his engineering training in Dresden.
27. PKO: a nationwide savings bank.

*January 4, 1940*—In the morning at the Community. Yesterday for a second time [our] workers were beaten up at the Praga cemetery [by a gang] while searching for diamonds [rings?]. Rinde *(Bote* [messenger]) came to the office black-eyed from Nalewki Street and Wasserman [28] arrived with a bloody nose that a street mob gave him at Teatralny Square, when he came to the rescue of a Jew tormented by the crowd.

I arranged for a subsidy for the orphanage at Wolska Street. I have just engaged some more intelligent help in the office. I also transferred a certain Mrs. Szperling from Accounting to the Labor Battalion. The functionaries around her act apprehensively for fear of her husband, a good-for-nothing whom I ordered thrown out of the Community office (he was continuously lurking in the corridors). I gave orders for the posting of an announcement proscribing the activities of the middlemen in funerals.

*January 5, 1940*—Reminiscing about my youth when I myself was looking for a position (Dickstein, Fleischer, handshaking). There are so many applications now. The bureaucrats and the speed of work (a lame turtle behind a funeral procession). Attempts to create a Jewish bureaucracy. *Wus iz mir anafkemine?* [What's the difference?] *Avos'* [perhaps]. Or, "we are in high spirits, except that things are getting worse." A Jew about a burnt synagogue—"this is a matter for God to worry about."

Today I was called to the *Stadtpraesident.*[29] I also went to 3 Danil[owiczowska Street] summoned by Kluge. He ordered me in Richter's name to close all the places of worship. synagogues, and ritual baths. To top it all I was hit by a snowball in a droshky by some boys for being *"Jude"* [Jew]. "A la Fourchette" has been requisitioned. At night I was reading a novel by Nalkowska. She does not seem to write for the public but rather for the critics.

*January 6, 1940*—In the morning to the Community. On my way two Polish men and one Polish woman warned me that people are being seized for work at the corner of Krolewska and Marszalkowska Streets. Many staff are absent for this reason. A female convert at my home asked me to check if she is listed on the

28. Pinchas Wasserman headed the Council's Registration Division.
29. *Stadtpräsident,* the city's German administrator: then Dr. Oskar Dengel.

Community rolls, since she does not want to wear the armband. Diamand at compulsory labor at the Polytechnic.

*January 7, 1940*—Community offices in the morning. Studying a report on emigration. Schrempf demands a new quarantine facility (100,000 zlotys).

Madame Wiktoria relates that her neighbor from the burnt house in Swietokrzyska Street told her that the tenants owed their lives to her prayers alone. The proof is in the fact that only a Jew, Pompianski, a musician, died in the fire with his mother and wife. Incidentally, the Pompianskis were unable to carry their bedridden mother from the fourth floor and succumbed to the fumes. Madame W. told her acquaintance that she was also Jewish. Yes, was the reply, but you were baptized ten years ago and that saves you.

*January 8, 1940*—At the SS at 8 A.M. on diverse matters. Later questioned in the Blank Palace [30] why the upper strata are not wearing the armbands. I pointed out the consequences of wearing the armbands on the streets. Later tried to see Lastowitschka, but did not find him. In the SS they told me that no one who left for Russia will be permitted to return.

*January 9, 1940*—I arranged for beds to be manufactured in the Community workshops. Later in the Community offices attending to current business. An offer from friends (Zablud[owski]).

In the morning Lastowitschka sent a message (through a clerk) to come to see him tomorrow. The JDC lent us 50,000 zlotys for hospitals.[31] A "Jew" from the USSR who was mistakenly listed as a Jew in the census. He claims that he is a Russian from the Baltic states. Eagerly he showed me his passport.

*January 10, 1940*—For the last few days we are in the grip of a maddening cold spell (in the morning -12, -13°F) and there is no coal. In the Community we sit in cold, unheated rooms.

In the morning with Lastowitschka. A more general conversation. Some misunderstandings have been cleared up and we will soon know what is permitted and what is not. Later in the Commu-

---

30. Blank Palace, seat of *Stadtpräsident.*
31. The JDC, American Joint Distribution Committee, disbursed Jewish charity funds abroad.

nity. On my way there I was stopped by a soldier demanding "50 zlotys for a ransom of a Jewish woman who was caught without an armband." In my office I found a note from a sergeant who came with a soldier demanding a ransom for ten Jews and Jewesses, caught without the armbands—100 zlotys each. I directed Councilor Rosenthal to intercede with the Gestapo. They will apparently take care of this matter. In the afternoon, I am having a hospital meeting at home. Tomorrow a conference with JDC about social welfare. Yesterday m[orning] Bart [32] was caught for compulsory labor. Working without an overcoat in freezing temperatures. Somehow he managed. In the evening a meeting at home about the hospital in Czyste. It seems they will give us a *Kommissar* in the hospital.

A lady singer occupies an apartment just below us. She was in love with a fellow actor. During an air raid a bomb tore out his guts. With her own hands she pushed them back. Then she drove him to the hospital where he died. He was buried in a common grave. She dug him up and reburied him in a private plot.

*January 12, 1940*—At the SS in the morning. Later in the Community—they demand 2,000 zlotys, 100 zlotys per person, for violations of the armband regulation, or else threaten arrest of Council Member Rosenthal.

*January 13, 1940*—In the morning to Blumenthal at the NVF [33]; he demands a Jewish Committee for Warsaw. Rosenthal took care of the 1,000-zloty ransom, since there were only ten without the armbands and to tell the truth they possessed the bands. At the Zahan they have finally terminated my employment after all these years (3 months' salary to be paid over one year instead of a full year's compensation). Later with a heavy heart I proceed to the Community offices. A meeting of the Coordinating Commission.[34] A decree about compulsory labor.[35]

---

32. Tadeusz Bart, a Council member, headed the Housing Commission. Deported to Treblinka, January 1943.
33. NVF: probably Czerniakow means NSV (*Nationalsozialistische Volkswohlfahrt*), a German welfare organization. Blumenthal was at that point head of Welfare Division in German city administration.
34. The coordinating Commission on Jewish welfare organizations: JDC, ORT, and others.
35. The *Generalgouvernement* decree of October 26, 1939, established the principle of forced labor for Jews aged 14–60. A second decree of December 12, 1939, signed by the Higher SS and Police Leader Krüger, spelled out its implementation.

*January 14, 1940*—In the morning at the Community. Called to the SS about an arrest of a certain Dr. Szalman, an official in the JDC. Apart from this attending to current business.

*January 15, 1940*—In the morning at the SS. The release of Dr. Szalman of the JDC. *Nachrichtenblatt* [Jewish Community newspaper] not permitted. Interceding about the robberies and assaults on the streets. Little, as yet, known about the implementation of the compulsory labor decree. Later in the Community offices.

*January 16, 1940*—As fate would have it, in the very apartment house where we live there resides also a notorious anti-Semite O., who is now appealing to the SS for an exemption from the armband requirement.[36]

At the Community in the morning. We just received a letter from Zurich about assistance in clothing and drugs *(Hilfsaktion fuer notleidende Juden in Polen, Zürich* [Appeal for needy Jews in Poland, Zurich]).

A letter dated January 15, 1940, from *"Generalgouvernement fuer die besetzten Polnischen Gebiete"* [General Government for the occupied Polish territories]. *Abteilung Volkswohlfahrt* [The Welfare Division], which (in response to a report that 7,000 refugees irrespective of their religion and nationality found shelter in the Jewish Relief Agency) forbids us to take care of the Aryans. During the night I recalled that even before the entry of the Germans a policeman conscripted me for labor. Not so long ago when I was leaving the Hungarian Legation after a reception in honor of [Premier] Gömbös who was then visiting Warsaw, a comrade of that policeman had offered to bring my automobile to the door, an automobile which I did not have.

*January 17, 1940*—Today, I must prepare a report on my "Jewish property." [37] Alas, I do not possess much [although] in these times this is a blessing.

*January 18, 1940*—The Community offices in the morning. Later summoned to the SS and detained from 12:30 to 6 P.M. as a hostage,

36. The anti-Semite O. must have had Jewish origins.
37. Dengel ordered registration of specified Jewish property exceeding 2,000 zlotys in value.

until 100 others were arrested. Some kind of conspiracy. Apparently a Jew participated in it.[38] Lohengrin.

*January 19, 1940*—The Community in the morning. Families of the arrested. A meeting of the Council. I issued instructions. During the night I read a novel, "The Pilgrims of the Forest"—Grey Owl—*Szara Sowa*. The forest, little wild animals—a veritable Eden. Lichtenbaum is told: *"Sie wollen unsere Sachen nicht Kaput machen"* [You don't want to ruin our thing].

*January 20, 1940*—Summoned to the SS with Rabbi Alter, who, it transpired, was not at home. His apartment was locked and sealed. His family has disappeared. I was told that he must appear within a week and that nothing will happen to him.—Searching for Mendel Rozenpud. But Mendel is a given name, not a surname. Then let's have another Mendel. There is a Mendel Rosenduft, an informant says. It turns out that Rosenduft had been dead for two years. In the meantime the informant has disappeared. Such was an anecdote that somebody told me.

Today announcements were plastered all over the city with Kot's photograph offering 2,000 zlotys for his capture.

Tomorrow the usual toil in the office. In response to my efforts I was permitted to petition for a release of the Czyste doctors from among the many arrested.

Because of the regulation that 500- and 100-zloty banknotes must be deposited much of the commerce is dying out.[39] In the Community I am unable to purchase coal for the hospitals, food, etc. Only the Credit Office [*Reichskreditkasse*] accepts deposits. Rumor has it that many have been sentenced for black market activities.

*January 21, 1940*—At the Community in the morning. A letter to the authorities about the arrested. Caught at the corner of the Krolewska and Marszalkowska Streets for compulsory labor. I persuaded them that it is pointless to obtain labor in this manner

---

38. The Jewish participant was Andrzej Kazimierz Kot, a convert to Christianity and a member of a Polish underground organization. He was wanted by the Germans (see diary entry of January 20, 1940).

39. There was fear that the notes would be confiscated. Later on, they were exchanged for new bills.

since the Community would supply the required workers. After my arrival in the office I dispatched 20 workers. A meeting of the Emigration Commission concerning Feldschuh, etc. A scene between a tinker and a Jewish woman. The lady shopkeeper who had just collected some supplies at the post office after paying the Customs duties, was robbed by some scoundrel. Torn woodcut depicting a monk.

*January 22, 1940*—I have noticed this morning that one of my pants buttons is missing.[40] Even the greatest of men may look ridiculous because of that. The families of the arrested, in the evening, called to the SS about my petition for the release of the doctors, etc. I was informed that 100 were shot. They intimated also that further executions will take place.

At home a hospital reception. I go to bed with a headache.

*January 23, 1940*—In the morning visiting (on instructions of the SS) with chairman of the Kraków Council [41] in his hotel. Later in the Community offices the daily anguish. A large number of arrests. Tomorrow I am ordered to go to the SS with a doctor, who works in the Hospital Services Department, and a rabbi.

We have announced that we are looking for 2,000 workers to clear the snow. I called on those who were delinquent in paying the labor exemption tax.[42] We cannot change the Community's cash into small denominations because they do not accept 500- and 100-zloty notes at all, or when they do, someone has to wait in a long line for hours. In the meantime I cannot pay the staff, the workers, and the suppliers. It's a miracle that my head is not spinning.

*January 24, 1940*—At the SS in the morning about the release of Dr. Wortman.[43] It has been arranged. I also accompanied Rabbi Alter to the SS. He got off safely. Later the office. We must pay 1,200 zlotys in the VII Police Precinct for the twelve people without armbands.

40. Pants in those days had buttons instead of zippers.
41. The chairman of the Kraków council (Marek Biberstein) was the Jewish representative on a central relief council, composed of Polish, Jewish, and Ukrainian members.
42. On labor exemption, see Czerniakow's letter of May 21, 1940, appendix.
43. Dr. Antoni Wortman, Council's Hospital Division.

Again they would not change our currency. Due to the indolence of my staff I must see Lastowitschka in this matter tomorrow. What miseries because we don't have competent Jewish bureaucrats!

*January 25, 1940*—In the morning more agony about the 500s and 100s. Lastowitschka would not see me. Later he promised to help. The Discount Bank might lend us a modest sum in small denominations. Later in the Community. Two policemen summoned me to *"Polizei Regiment Warschau"* [Police Regiment, Warsaw]. Throngs from the families of the arrested. There is nothing I can do for them.

*January 26, 1940*—Summoned to the police *(Oberstleutnant* [Lieutenant Colonel] Daume).[44] By tomorrow the Community must pay 100,000 zlotys for the beating up of a *"Volksdeutschin"* [Ethnic German Woman]. Otherwise 100 Jews will be shot. I appealed to the Gestapo for the annulment of the fine, then, for permission to pay it in installments, and finally for the release of the Community from the obligation of clearing the snow, which would let us save some money. Nothing came out of it. We must pay up and tomorrow morning at that. Under these circumstances I began a money collection in the Community. We must borrow 100,000 and then get it back from the taxpayers.

At the same time the police are pressing us to pay 6,100 zlotys for 61 Jewish men and women who were caught without the armbands.

In view of all these tribulations I asked the SS to be released from the chairmanship since I find it impossible to manage the Community under these abnormal conditions. In reply I was told that this would be inadvisable.

I was given a letter to the *Reichskreditkasse* on the exchange of the hundreds and five-hundreds for smaller denominations. Tomorrow another day of agony.

*January 27, 1940*—Today I am supposed to deliver the 100,000. Right now I am waiting for the cash to be brought to the Community. The task of bringing the cash here and then carrying it to the

---

44. Police Lt. Col. Daume, commander of Police Regiment (Order Police) in Warsaw district.

authorities poses a serious problem due to the danger lurking in the streets. Will I be given a receipt? I paid and received the following:

*Polizei Regiment Warsaw* 20. I. 1940
  *Bescheinigung*
*Von der Juedischen Kultusgemeinde Warschau (Aeltestenrat)* 100,000 zloty *(Hundert Tausend) als Geldbusse fuer einen Ueberfall auf eine Volksdeutsche NSV-Helferin empfangen zu haben. Bescheinigt*
      Daume
*Oberstleutnant d. Sch.*

[Police Regiment Warsaw] [January 20, 1940]
  [Receipt]
[Received from the Jewish Community Warsaw (Council of Elders) 100,000 zloty (Hundred Thousand) as fine for an assault on an Ethnic German auxiliary woman in the NSV (National Socialist Welfare). Certified]
      Daume
[Lieutenant Colonel of Order Police]

I was warned that if a similar incident occurred in the future the punishment would be more severe.

I was kept waiting three hours in the corridor. *Setzen Sie sich* [Sit down]. A German police officer of the VII Precinct arrived in the Community offices and asked payment for eight "armbanders," 100 zlotys each, or otherwise they will starve to death. The remaining 19 paid on their own and were released. I promised to make the necessary arrangements tomorrow. Jews were beaten up on Marszalkowska and Poznanska Streets during the day and in the evening.[45]

*January 28, 1940*—In the morning (I am now taking headache powders daily) off to the Community. At 2 P.M. a gang of teenage hooligans, which for the last several days was beating up the Jews, paraded in front of the Community offices breaking the windows in the houses on the other side of the street. An emissary of the Community, Engineer Friede, was beaten up by a second group at Elektoralna Street until he was bleeding. Tomorrow I will present the SS with a bloodied piece of paper.

From the municipality we have received a communication con-

45. Polish anti-Semitic groups participated in the violence. See diary entry of January 28, 1940.

cerning registration for compulsory labor. We are in the midst of preparing the registration centers, posters, and forms. Tomorrow I must go to the SS at 8 A.M. to obtain permission to post announcements on the walls. As usual we received this order at the very last moment, and must be ready with the posters "tomorrow." Only from us does the municipality demand this speed. The day after tomorrow is a German holiday [46] and everything will be closed.

*January 29, 1940*—The SS at 8 in the morning. After a few days the temperature fell again from [a morning temperature of] 21°F, to 15°F, and coal is as unobtainable as before. Jews are to receive smaller bread rations and no meat at all.

The SS—8 A.M. Concerning the affair of the Rabiner family, about which I lodged a complaint; it was decided that the woman should come forward and tell their side of the story. The text of the announcement about the registration for compulsory labor was approved. I called attention to the need for *Ausweisy* [identifications] for the new members of the Council. I also related the incidents of Jews being beaten up. I was instructed to submit a memo to the *Polizeiregiment IV* [Police Regiment IV], 23 Szuch Avenue. In the Community offices a German soldier with two Jews—one without the armband. He demanded [a] 200-zloty fine, or else the Jew—prison, etc. I refused. He proposed contributions of 10 zlotys each from members of the staff to help their brother.

I returned home at 3 P.M. I found that the apartment was searched by two men in uniform. They rummaged through all our belongings taking two bottles of oil, a leather briefcase, chocolate, tea, etc. I immediately registered a complaint with the SS. The cowardice of the tenants at #62. In the Community offices some staffers were beaten up, etc., in connection with the incident of the two Jews without armbands.

[There is no entry for *January 30, 1940*.]

*January 31, 1940*—At the Community in the morning. The censors approved our placards (registration for compulsory labor).

The *Reichskreditkasse* had exchanged 70,000 zlotys (100- and 500-zloty notes) for lower denominations. The remainder amount-

---

46. January 30 was the anniversary of Hitler's rise to power.

ing to 115,000 was kept as a deposit. In the evening, as usual, full of anxiety lest somebody break in again. I go to bed hoping that my sleep will not be disturbed. At home throngs of people inquiring about the registration. Tomorrow morning will visit the SS and the *Ordnungspolizei* [Order Police] about the goings on in the streets.

*February 1, 1940*—In the morning an *Ordnungspolizei* memo (Regiment IV—*Oberstleutnant* Daume) concerning the excesses against the Jews. Earlier at the Gestapo about the registration procedure for compulsory labor. Again hordes of people visiting my apartment to get some news. I was summoned to Krasinski Square about the armbands—penalties for not wearing them. I made a formal complaint about the policeman who was collecting a few zlotys from the Community staffers for two Jews without the armbands. Labor registration census forms are being sold on the street. Thus we have already a second industry (the first one—the armbands made of linen, cellulose, rubber, and artificial silk). Today I saw a policeman arresting, for not wearing an armband, the vendor of same.

*February 2, 1940*—9 A.M. at the Community. The building over-flows with crowds of people (registration, labor brigades, etc.), I walk home uncertain that my belongings will still be there. A new questionnaire has been issued for listing Jewish property (cloth-ing . . .).

*February 3, 1940*—9 A.M. the Community. About noon a police-man from Krasinski Square walks in with a rifle and promptly arrests me. At Kras. I "wait" until 1:30 P.M. It turns out that we must pay 6,600 zlotys for some *Entlausungsscheiny* [delousing cer-tificates], since some Jews have not reported for delousing. I was ordered to pay by 12 [o'clock] Monday, Feb. 5.

I finally arrive home at about midnight. One of my toes is frostbitten—the result of the Krasinski Square interlude. At night terrible pains.

*February 4, 1940*—In the morning at the Community. At 6:30 an instant convert to Christianity. Yesterday throngs of converts. I am filling out my registration form for compulsory labor.

I received a reply to my complaint, about the incident of Jews being beaten up (tormented) by a madwoman etc., from *Kommandeur der Ordnungspolizei fuer den Distrikt Warschau: "Ich teile mit, dass ich die mir erforderlich erscheinenden Anweisungen gegeben habe."* [Commander of Order Police, District Warsaw: "I am informing you that I have issued the instructions that appeared necessary to me."] (Feb. 2, 1940.)

A Jew wearing an armband is addressed by a stranger: General, Sir. But I am not a general. Yes you are, there is your star.

*February 5, 1940*—In the morning at the SS about the payment of the 6,600 zlotys to the *Ordnungspolizei*. Left empty-handed. There was a discussion about the possible subordination of the Community to the *Stadtpraesident* [Dengel]. It was pointed out to me that the memo about emigration is academic and devoid of realistic prospects. The Community was ordered to supply information about the departure of Council members. I sent the 6,600 zlotys to the police at Krasinski Square, but did not permit payment itself until the authorization from the SS would arrive. I received a letter from the City President [Dengel] to the effect that the disinfection of the Jewish houses must be paid for by the Community.

*February 6, 1940*—In the morning a messenger from the SS about adding further information to a letter about the destination of the departed Council members. Before 10 at the Brühl Palace.[47] I fail in my attempts to see Dr. Ilg [48] (a matter of subordinating the Community to the *Stadtpraesident*). I sent him a memorandum. Tomorrow I will try again.

During my absence in the morning, somebody visited the apartment again for requisitioning. Mania's mattresses—a fine of 150 zlotys. My frostbitten toes (wounds). In the Community offices (almost never heated) I am never left in peace. I go to sleep full of anxiety about being awakened in the middle of the night.

*February 7, 1940*—At the Zahan in the morning—a refusal to make a settlement. Later in the Community. Our staff etc. now exceeds 800. Several staff members were beaten up in front of the quarantine at Zelazna Street. Teenagers are doing that. I took down

47. Brühl Palace was the seat of German district adminstration.
48. Dr. Alfons Ilg, chief of Division of Administration (including, at that time, welfare) in German city administration.

the name plate from my door. In a house on the opposite side of the street—requisitioning. Tadeusz a victim. Yesterday a truck was loaded with "virgins" from the Polonia [Hotel].

*February 8, 1940*—In the morning at the SS. They informed me that the madwoman in the streets will be restrained. I discussed the subject about registration for compulsory labor. The problem of the baptized Jews. I asked that a number of Jewish lawyers be authorized [to practice].[49]

Our staff now numbers 245 in the Community offices, 496 in the hospital at Czyste and 32 in the Quarantine hospitals, altogether [sic] 782.

Julek—a new disaster—A rubber coat.

*February 9, 1940*—In the morning at the Community. Jews have been forbidden to travel by train. Two men with an authorization demanded twenty Jews to transport some horses to Siedlce. The Community must pay for the arrangements and feed the men. We supplied the twenty. The intensity of typhus on the increase. A new quarantine looms large.

*February 10, 1940*—In the deep-freeze again—8°F. I walk to the Community offices at 9. As of yesterday 105,000 persons registered for compulsory labor. The authorities insist that converts be treated as Jews. By today 112,620 persons were registered. The registration offices will continue to be open at Elektoralna, Brzeska, Nowolipie streets. Today, a delegation of physicians' families reproached the Council for handing over [to the Germans] the names of 100 (!) doctors.[50]

I stopped at a modest luncheonette just in time to witness a requisitioning of tumblers and glasses.

I am invited to Dr. Ilg at the *Stadtpraesident*'s for 10 A.M. on Monday. In the afternoon I prepared materials for him with Dr. Weichert.[51] On the way to the office I tell the sled driver: "To the Community." He answers: "I drove the Chairman there yesterday." "What, me?" "No! It was Pinkiert." [52]

---

49. Special German authorization was required for the practice of law. Jewish lawyers had not been able to obtain these permits.
50. The hundred hostages seized January 18 included many professionals.
51. Dr. Michal Weichert, a prewar theater producer, resident of Krakow, headed Jewish Self-Help (JSS), first in Warsaw and then in the entire *Generalgouvernement*.
52. Mordche Pinkiert ran a funeral business.

*February 11, 1940*—In the morning at the Community. I was visited by an unknown *Dolmetscher* [interpreter] who was asking to provide assistance for a Jew to whom I am favorably disposed. I helped this man.

We have received a serum against snakebite from Belgium.

*February 12, 1940*—In the morning with Dr. Weichert at Dr. Ilg's in the *Stadtpräsident's* office. "We do not want any Jews around here." A disinfection chamber in the quarantine at Zelazna Street caught fire. I was offered a certificate to Palestine—I refused to have my name placed on the list.

*February 13, 1940*—At the SS in the morning.

*February 14, 1940*—The Community offices in the morning. On the street they are seizing people for work. Rumors about the ghetto and expulsions. A Jew is helped by a Christian.

*February 15, 1940*—The Community in the morning. *Obmann* [Chairman of the Jewish Council] from Sosnowiec.[53] At 3 P.M. to the SS—the matter of passports. A fruitless search for the Director. In the afternoon working on the organizational structure of the JSS. My head is bursting from complaints. Tomorrow I am getting up at 6; at 8 I will be signing passports or release certificates from the Community for them [prospective emigrants].

*February 16, 1940*—In the Community at 7 in the morning. A column of Community workers (thousands of them) with shovels along Marszalkowska Street. I visited a forge where we are producing shovels and handles. At 1 P.M. a meeting of the Health Commission. It was agreed to organize a soap collection, etc. The SS collects from emigrating Jews certain sums of money for the Community. Today the Community received through Mr. Berman, Chief of the Budget and Finance Department, 5,000 zlotys from ten emigrants. I am gathering reports from the several departments of the Community organization. Our efforts to secure the gift from Zurich are all in vain. J[as] kisses our photographs.

53. The chairman of the Council in Sosnowiec (eastern portion of Upper Silesia, outside the *Generalgouvernement*) was Moshe Merin. As of January 1940, headed central organization of Jewish Councils in Eastern Upper Silesia, including Sosnowiec.

*February 17, 1940*—One of the bank directors has repeatedly invited me to visit him. Unfortunately, I cannot find the time. The difference between the saint and me is that they have more time than I. A well-known economic "nationalist" allegedly has a salary from abroad of 180 zlotys a month (today a ton of coal costs 600–800 zlotys in Warsaw). For consolation he has the "import" and the "export" taken away from the Jews.

*February 18, 1940*—At the Community in the morning. A storm combined with bitter cold. The municipality informed us that the whole registration is useless because of new directives. I am calling a meeting of the Council on this matter for tomorrow. My lunch was interrupted several times by a lady in charge of an orphanage. I had to proceed at once to the SS on this errand. Not a moment of peace.

*February 18, 1940*—[Another entry] In the morning I am visited by Mrs. Maliniak. Referred to the SS. At 10:30 a meeting about the new registration. Wives of those arrested sent to me by their lawyer. At lunchtime a pounding on the door. It was Mende from the SS. He immediately drove me to East [Railroad] Station. There, after a considerable delay in the biting cold, I was informed by a *Bahnhofsoffizier* [railroad official] that we must deliver food for one lot of 150 and then another of 350 prisoners of war.[54] The first group is to remain in Warsaw, the other is proceeding to Lublin. He wanted me to find accommodations and take full responsibility for the 150, reporting to the 5th [Division of *Stadtpräsident*'s office]. I left the station to drive to the city. A soldier ran after me, grabbed me by my collar and led me to the guard post. My *"Ausweis"* [identity card] was studied by a German railroad man and I was barely let go.

I proceeded to the JDC on Jasna Street. Not a soul there. From there to Dr. Weichert; I did not find him. In the end to Bornstein.[55] He promised to send bread and tea today. Tomorrow the Red Cross will take over. I directed Lustberg to check on these arrangements tomorrow morning at 8 o'clock. Cowardice on Jagiellonska Street [location of a Jewish orphanage].

54. The prisoners of war were Jews.
55. Izak Borenstein, JDC secretary in Warsaw.

*February 19, 1940*—In the morning at the Community. Yesterday the JDC did deliver some bread, marmalade, sugar, and tea to the prisoners.

A letter from the *Stadtpraesident* arrives today to contact a Lieutenant Hesse at the *Entlausungsanstalt* [delousing facility] concerning the Jewish prisoners of war. I gave orders for Dr. Weichert, Rosenthal, and an aide to proceed to the institution. Not unnaturally, Rosenthal complained of "being very cold" and vanished. After lunch I received a letter from Dengel:

| | |
|---|---|
| *Durch einen militaerischen Transport sind 79 juedische Kriegsgefangene in Warschau angekommen. Dieselben werden Ihnen hiermit übergeben. Sie haben ueber sie Liste zu führen und sie im Rahmen der bestehenden Gesetze zum Arbeitseinsatz zu bringen. Ebenso haben sie bei meiner Abteilung V die Anmeldungen einzuliefern. Sie haften in jeder Richtung fuer die Entlassenen. Stadtpräs. Dengel.* | A military transport of 79 Jewish prisoners of war arrived in Warsaw. They are hereby being handed over to you. You must keep track of them, employ them under existing regulations in labor assignments. In the same manner my Division V is to receive the registrations. You are liable in every respect for the released men. City President Dengel. |

In the evening I was informed (by the official Goldfeil) [56] that 78 prisoners of war were brought to the Community offices and then allowed to go home. Tomorrow they are to report in the Community offices.

*February 20, 1940*—At the Community in the morning. Another message about 45 prisoners of war. I am dispatching some aides to the East Station. A directive from the *Stadtpraesident* to convert securities and paper into cash for the support of the hospitals.

At the Vistula [River] they took off the armband from a Jew who was working quite hard and put it on a Pole.

Supinger [57] anticipates the utilization of people aged 14 to 25 primarily to tear down war-damaged buildings, etc.

A certain Kirszblum, a louse, is leaving for Palestine and claims that he does not have the 600 zlotys payable to the Community as the emigration tax. Just before he leaves, after refusing to pay, he

56. Norbert Goldfeil, Labor Battalion, later Council's Labor Division.
57. Supinger = Suppinger, of the German city administration, in charge of Division of Streets and Sanitation.

declares "I will not forget this," to which I retort: "You louse, I will not forget, you louse, how you pretended to act as a leader and are now running away with others like you, leaving the masses in this horrid situation."

*February 21, 1940*—In the morning with Dr. Ilg at "*Stadtpraesident's.*" In the evening I was visited by some people from the TOZ [58] reporting that several score of prisoners in quarantine at Spokojna Street will be sent to the provinces. We were asked to consider them under the Warsaw municipality to avoid their transportation under escort to the countryside.

At Dr. Ilg's I presented the subject of the new "registration"—he knows nothing about this—so far as the persecution of the Jews is concerned he suggested writing a memo.

Delingowski [59] tells me to prepare the registration of 35,000 people (16–25 years old) for February 29, 1940. Interceding with Becher [60] fruitless—he refused to receive our delegation. In the evening preparing the organization plan of the JSS.

*February 22, 1940*—At the SS in the morning about the registration. Advised not to intervene with the higher authorities about the deadline. I was instructed that the payments from the emigrants must be paid into a special account of the Community without a right of using these funds by the Community except with SS permission.

In the matter of Mrs. Maliniak, I was told to report on the incident, which I did.

In the Community I was told that Sztolcman and Rozenstadt [61] were instructed in the municipality that the registration of the 35,000 must be completed (in type) without fail by February 29,

58. TOZ was a Jewish health care organization.
59. Jan Delingowski, a head of Registration Department in Warsaw municipality.
60. Max Becher, chief of Housing Division, German city administration. A reorganization in January 1941 resulted in the creation of an administrative level above that of division. An office on this upper level was called a *Dezernat*, its incumbent a *Dezernent*. Each *Dezernent* was in charge of two or more of the old divisions. (A division was now renamed *Hauptreferat*.) Becher seems to have become the *Dezernent* with responsibility for Personnel, Interior, Population and Welfare, and Food, while assuming personal direction of the *Hauptreferat* Population and Welfare.
61. Abraham Sztolcman and Boleslaw Rozensztat were Council members. Sztolcman headed Industry and Trade Division; he was killed by the Germans in April 1943. Rozensztat was a legal expert.

1940 and that everybody must appear in person. Ten doctors must be available to give medical examination. A visit by Drs. Kubicki, Sikorski [62] . . . at the Community.

Registration: "watching the eggs," "standing behind the counter," "cropping the boys."

*February 23, 1940*—In the morning at the Community. Preparations for the registration. Summoned to the SS I drove with two SS men to the quarantine facility at Zelazna Street. The prisoners of war are there. It is all about finding a permanent spot for these Jewish prisoners. I just signed 53 letters to Jewish doctors drafting them for a limited period of time to conduct medical examinations during the registration. I was visited by Dr. Stein [63] from the hospital in Czyste about various complaints.

*February 24, 1940*—At the Community in the morning. Proofreading the announcement about the registration. I issued 80 exit certificates. At 3:30 I left the office and headed home by droshky with Lichtenbaum. At Zielna Street, in front of the Radio Building, we were pulled out for compulsory labor. L[ichtenbaum] was struck with a whip. We barely extricated ourselves from this predicament. An appendix to my memo to the *Stadtpraesident* about street impressments.

In the morning we were ordered to free the prisoners of war detained in the quarantine at Zelazna Street. They delivered some new ones to us, about 47. A thaw, very slippery.

*February 25, 1940*—In the morning at the Community. 27°F. It is very slippery. Work. I walk home scared stiff. A visit from Kraków.

*February 26, 1940*—At 8 A.M. a conference with the JDC and the chairman of the Kraków Community about Bornstein's (JDC) visit to Kraków. Directives: The JDC [main office] in Warsaw and its branch in Kraków, etc.

---

62. Kubicki and Sikorski were Polish medical officials in Warsaw municipality.
63. Dr. Jozef Stein, a baptized Catholic of Jewish origin, was an anatomist, pathologist, and specialist in typhus fever; he was the director of Czyste hospital. He was killed with his family in Treblinka 1943.

The Community received a letter from the *Praesident* summoning us for 4 P.M. today on some very important business pertaining to crafts. Rozen [64] and Hazensprung [65] called to the SS about failure to deliver sufficient number of workers. Registration yesterday quite slow; it picks up today. I left the Community offices after 3 P.M. and reached my house without complications. During evenings on Grzybowska Street, etc., teenagers are beating up Jews and extorting ransom. Today's registration was less than successful.

*February 27, 1940*—In the morning at the Community. No trouble getting there. Grzybowska Street covered with ice. Walking between the ruins a real hazard.

They have arrested the superintendent of the cemetery in Praga with his assistant. The invitation to the *Stadtpraesident* was about the Jewish crafts. We were told to organize an association. The registration proceeds with great difficulty. I was jumped upon by some women complaining about the traffic in wage vouchers.[66]

I inspected the offices of the Labor Battalion. The *Selbstschutz* [67] issues 6 orders—for an architect, carpenters, piano-porters, and workers for reconstruction of a building. I sent Lichtenbaum and Zabludowski. A sister of a section leader, Grynberg, remonstrates about her brother who has not returned from Siedlce (horses transported by members of the Labor Battalion from Warsaw to Siedlce). I asked for the preparation of a large Community organization chart. The artist hastened to frame me (the *Obmann*) with laurel leaves. Wouldn't the "crown of thorns" be more appropriate?

*February 28, 1940*—In the morning at the Community. An inspection of the registration work by Director Delingowski. Rumors about a ghetto in Praga. At the Community, mothers and children of those arrested. Search for a chairman of the Craftsmen's Association. The candidacy of Wolfowicz. Today we supplied about 7,000 workers. Bornstein and Weichert to Kraków.

64. Hiel Rozen (Czerniakow sometimes spells his name "Rosen"), was a Council member, later member and chairman of Labor Commission. Also in Fuel Allocation group, Provisioning Authority. Reported shot and killed while trying to save two brothers during deportations, September 1942.
65. Hazensprung, Labor Battalion.
66. Wage vouchers, received by workers, were redeemed by the Jewish Community for money.
67. The *Selbstschutz* were ethnic German auxiliary police.

*February 29, 1940*—In the morning to Danilowiczowska Street to see Engineer Supinger about city public works. I submitted a proposal of a possible public works plan. S(upinger) announced that the Jews must make obeisance [to the Germans]. I replied that without a written order I cannot transmit this announcement to them. Later Lastowitschka (an automobile, labor, Zielna St., JSS) etc.

"Why don't you take two chairs?" Safely home after 3:30.

*March 1, 1940*—At 9 A.M. at the Community. Honorary Aryan Or [?]. Preoccupied with emigration daily. The registration to go on through the 28th: plus or minus 23,000 youths in the age group 16 to 25. A call to the SS about possible meetings (the hospital tax, crafts). At 3 P.M. safely home. The superintendent of the Praga cemetery has been released. I name a new superintendent.

*March 2, 1940*—The SS in the morning—emigration business. Later summoned by Klaus about the possibility of supplying the armbands; I told him that a whole new industry has sprung up. Thirty [German] dead report to St. Peter. They will not be admitted because only 20 were on the [casualty] lists.

Roundups in front of the Community building. Home safely. In the afternoon a conference about the hospital—joint purchases of food supplies with the JDC and the payment of salaries for December 1939.

*March 3, 1940*—In the morning—23°. There was another heavy snowfall. Again we are facing extraordinary expenses, since the Community must do the work of the Municipal Street-Cleaning Department.

Not so long ago I used to stop for coffee at Hirschfeld's. In view of the street impressments I now proceed directly to the Community offices. When, on rare occasions, I do drop in, the waiters of the café say that they were worrying that my absence was an indication of some new calamity.

In the Community building, a candy vendor lurks between the two glass doors. The janitor in the hallway, chatting, pretends not to see. The sloppiness in the Community offices is unbearable (the appearance of the documents, desks, the outgoing letters, etc.).

Today we had more workers reporting than needed. They did not want to go home.

*March 4, 1940*—In the morning (9 o'clock) I am waiting for Lastowitschka. Perhaps I should go to the Discount Bank and see Pres. Mikulecki [68] to save time. But then, they will seize me for work on the way. So I keep waiting. All in vain. I do pay Mikulecki a visit. He refuses to postpone the deadline for the loan of 100,000. On the other hand, he might be able to give us a new loan later. Weichert returned from Kraków. Has Mrs. Oderfeld become a convert?

In the afternoon, Rinde comes from Mende and requests me to give Halber [69] two rooms in a five-room apartment belonging to another Jew.

*March 6, 1940*—In the morning at the SS. A request for a loan out of the Emigration Fund. I will give Halber a loan, but not an apartment. Mende informs me that the Community is heading for bankruptcy.

In the morning Rozenthal, Kupczykier,[70] and Wolfowicz confer with Snopczynski.[71] The latter announced that the Jews will be allowed to form only workers' associations, not guilds. He dropped a hint about the ghetto—not for the workshops, but for the population. Czerniecki [72] from the Housing Department about requisitioning some furniture; wants the Community to do it for the City. Somebody paid us a visit from the Health Insurance Fund demanding payment of well over 200,000 zlotys. A new blow.[73]

*March 7, 1940*—Daily temperature—19°F. Heavy snow on the streets. The Health Insurance Office (Schayer) informed us that unless we pay 32,000 zlotys by noon today the "leadership" [Council] will answer for it. Right now I am waiting in Lastowitschka's

68. Dr. Wiktor Mikulecki, prewar president of Warsaw Discount Bank and trustee of the bank under the Germans.
69. Maurycy Halber, Labor Battalion official.
70. Leopold Kupczykier, prewar chocolate manufacturer, was a Council member and member of Labor Commission.
71. Antoni Snopczynski headed the Crafts Guild of Poland.
72. "Czerniecki" should be Marian Czerniewski; headed the Housing Department of the Warsaw municipality.
73. Jews were required to continue their contributions for health insurance, although they were no longer entitled to benefits.

outer office hoping that he will help. Alas, it is 10:30 and he has not arrived. Eating one's heart out—that is it. The Community originally owed 500,000 zlotys. This sum had been reduced in course of time by more than a half. Why didn't they pay, at least in installments? A commentary on how they ran their business. At 12:30, liens were attached to our cash in the Community offices. In the meantime, I sent attorney Goldfeil, on Lastowitschka's orders, to Schayer so that together with Jurek and Weryho he would approve an installment plan. [Goldfeil] returned at 3 p.m. We must pay 5,000 zlotys at once and submit our proposal of repayment in a week's time.

Received from the acting mayor of Warsaw [74] a letter dated March 6, 1940, naming me a member of the Municipal Relief Committee. Chairman: Sliwinski, Artur. Deputy Chairmen: Klarner, Czeslaw; Strzelecki, Jan, 40 Polna Street. Members: Landsberg, Emil; Starzewski, Jan; Machnicki, Janusz; Czerniakow, A.

*March 8, 1940*—In the morning at the Community. At 3 P.M. a meeting with Dr. Weichert in the office of the *Stadtpräsident;* I am accompanied by Lichtenbaum and Sztolcman. Weichert wanted information concerning shoe and textile dealers. Home safely.

*March 9, 1940*—In the morning at the Community offices. Preparing a charter for the new Crafts Association. The financial difficulties of the Community. Our debt of 100,000 zlotys. The value of the securities is on the decline. The Discount Bank, on Lastowitschka's orders, gives us 50,000 zlotys for the securities we sold. A thimbleful—tomorrow's payroll for the [Labor] Battalion alone is 40,000 zlotys for the week. On top of that the hospital which eats up enormous sums of money, the prisoners of war, etc. We must pay the cost of transporting the POW's to their places of domicile.

The return of the section leader Grynberg who at one time was in charge of delivering horses to Siedlce. Arrested as a result, he claims, of false accusation by one of the sponsors of the whole venture, he spent several weeks in jail. Now the informer himself apparently is doing time for embezzlement.

74. The acting (Polish) mayor of Warsaw was Julian Kulski.

*March 10, 1940*—In the morning 34°F. Heavy snow in the streets. Will I get to work undisturbed? A little coffee house on Grzybowska Street—off limits to the Jews. I work 7 days a week. Why has not God given us an 8th day of rest?

*March 11, 1940*—Starting at 10:30 A.M. inspecting some charitable institutions with Radziwill,[75] Count Ronikier,[76] Nicholson, and Taylor,[77] etc. In the afternoon, TOZ, the Jewish orphanage on Leszno Street and a shelter for the refugees on Dzielna Street.

At 5:10 tea at Radziwill's. An address by Professor Richter announcing another quarantine. During the day the Community was ordered to supply by the 15th of the month an extraordinary quantity of furniture, bedlinen, 15 grand pianos, boot removers, etc.

*March 12, 1940*—In the morning at the Community. At Okecie airport 30 workers from the Labor Battalion were arrested together with a section leader. I went to the office of the *Stadtpraesident* about the furniture. Nobody would see me. Summoned for 3:30 to the SS. They will not intervene in the matter of furniture requisition. Instead a stern complaint that today our workers refused to go to Okecie for fear of arrest. If this continues, 100 will be sentenced.

In a private apartment the appointed trustee demands three months' rent in three days. I was notified by the Community offices that some uniformed and civilian officials entered the Community Museum about 4 P.M. At Szeroka Street the workers employed in excavations found some weapons.

*March 13, 1940*—In the morning to the offices of the City President [78] about the requisition of furniture in Jewish homes.

At Danilowiczowska Street a toilet with an inscription.

Lastowitschka instructed me to go to Becker on the matter of the

---

75. Prince Janusz Radziwill was a prominent member of prewar Polish parliament and major landowner.
76. Count Adam Ronikier was chairman of a national relief council made up of Polish, Ukrainian, and Jewish components. Ronikier also headed the Polish contingent. The Jewish group was the JSS.
77. James Thomas Nicholson, American Red Cross Delegate to Germany for Poland, and Wayne Taylor, American Red Cross Delegate in Paris. Nicholson negotiated with Germans for distribution of relief in Poland on "basis of need and without regard to race, religion, or politics."
78. City President *(Stadtpräsident)* Dengel.

furniture and he himself went there. Becker told me to go to the Brühl Palace to see Dr. Gaudich. In his place I found Schlosser.[79] He in turn summoned Maurer. I explained to Maurer [80] that the Community cannot take care of the requisitioning. He called Czerniewski instructing the Community to form House Committees for the purpose of collecting the furnishings and ordering the city to make the deliveries to the Germans. First, who saw Czerniewski, returned reporting that it was Czerniewski who sold the idea of the Community taking over the requisitioning to Maurer. Tomorrow I am going to Lastowitschka again. I called together 80 people for tomorrow on this matter.

The families of the workers who went to Okecie are wailing in the Community. There are no children. An *Unteroffizier* [noncommissioned officer] from Okecie who visited the Community disappeared yesterday. Mende arrived and arrested Hazensprung. The *U(nter) O(ffizier)*, however, turned up on the street.

The museum was requisitioned yesterday.

*March 14, 1940*—In the morning at the JDC. Guzik and Neustadt have returned.[81] Later at the Community. The Okecie families are weeping. Kraków is going to invite us.[82] Mende at the Community: the offices of the Labor Battalion must be manned nine hours a day. Tomorrow at 6 A.M. a meeting at 6 Twarda Street of the Community Furniture Committee.

650 zlotys.

Schreyer—Hazensprung
   Dr. Milejkowski—5 Orla Street
   Lustberg—5 Wspolna Street
   Fiel—49 Ogrodowa Street, m 17
   Fuerst [First]—Okrag III b
   Kot. [?]—Czernichowska Street, m 7
Bornstein—35 Krolewska Street
Weichert—8a Dluga Street (warehouses—13 Leszno Street)

79. "Dr. Gaudich," should be Dr. Gaudig, temporarily director of Warsaw district Economy Division. On March 8, he was succeeded by Schlosser.
80. Maurer served in district administration.
81. Dawid Guzik and Lejb Neustadt, JDC directors, had just returned from Belgium.
82. The *Generalgouvernement* administration invited Czerniakow and other Council members for continuation of discussions on distribution of American relief supplies.

Dr. Ringelblum—18 Leszno Street
*Steuerbezahler Vermoegensanlage als Basis 50%* [Taxpayer assets as
   basis 50%]
*Keine alte Konten anerkannt* [No old accounts recognized]
Mende 109
Raschisch Tel. [ext.] 270
Lastowitschka 569–20 Ext. 120
Nossig—21 Krasinski Street, m 33

[Material from "Schreyer" through *"Keine alte Konten anerkannt"* is
crossed out in the notebook.]

# Notebook Three

*March 15, 1940*—5 A.M. at Twarda Street (inspections of the labor contingent on its way to work). M[ende] appeared with a retinue. The workers began to gather at 6:30. The latecomers were punished on the spot. [His] horse whip in need of repair.[1]

In the Community, familes about Okecie, weeping and shouting. Czerniewski arrived reporting that Becker got in touch with Maurer and they were threatening to hold the Community responsible for the requisitioning of furniture.

*March 16, 1940*—In the morning at the SS. Intervening in the matter of the thirty [workers] at Okecie (not hostages but *Untersuchungsgefangene* [detained suspects]). They must remain in jail until the completion of the investigation. Mende will be gone. Brandt is acting in his place.[2] He asked for the data on the typhus deaths in 1939 and 1940 (January and February).[3] On Monday a conference on the finances of the Community. I do not have a penny in the Community coffers, not even to meet the payroll.

At 10 a meeting of the Municipal Relief Committee. The Gestapo expressed sympathy with my fate which is worse than that of a street snow shoveler. When I come to the Community there

1. Czerniakow had been summoned by Mende to watch punishment of workers arriving late. Due to night curfew lasting until 5 A.M., promptness was difficult for men living far from Twarda Street. Mende himself participated in beatings, breaking his whip.
2. Brandt was actually Mende's superior.
3. The Jewish Council reported 944 typhus dead for December. 1,004 for January. Many of the victims were refugees.

will again be the wailing of the families from Okecie. This morning the SS made the inspection of the labor contingent. According to Mende there was some improvement; that is, fewer latecomers. At 1:30 P.M. the released Okecie prisoners arrived.

A meeting of the Municipal Relief Committee has taken place at City Hall. Yesterday I did not meet the payroll. Today there is not a penny in the safe. All this is the fault of the Discount Bank which sold our securities and pocketed 120,000 zlotys as repayment of our old debt.

*March 17, 1940*—In the morning—18°F, the cursed snow keeps falling. Again I will have to supply thousands of workers to clean the city. Tuesday is our deadline for delivering the furniture, etc. We have formed the House Committees to take care of the collection. Registration for compulsory labor has been completed.

I receive an invitation to Kraków for March 27, 1940.

*March 18, 1940*—In the morning at the SS. The matter of a loan for the Community from the Emigration Fund. A demand that the Jews guard the coal at Krasinski Street which is being pilfered. A demand that the Community ring the "ghetto" with wire, put in fenceposts, etc., and later guard it all. Halber has informed the Labor Commission about certain misdoings in the Labor Battalion, but he did not go into detail.

*March 19, 1940*—21°. In the morning at the Community. The first day of furniture delivery. The voluntary collection resulted in obtaining one upright piano and hundreds of pieces of all kinds of furniture, beds, etc. Nonetheless, we are far short of the quota. Our coffers are empty. The salaries remain unpaid. The hospital services (Sikorski and Stein) are eating up our resources.

I was notified that a certain captain from Okecie visited our Craft School, ordering the opening of all the rooms for inspection tomorrow at 8:30 A.M. He added that the facilities were not suitable for *his* purpose.

*March 20, 1940*—Permission was granted for the matzos for the Jews. A meeting about a report on the Labor Battalion for the SS. The drafting was postponed until tomorrow.

*March 21, 1940*—I am waiting at 9 A.M. for *Oberfuehrer* Leist, to whom I was sent by Lastowitschka. Somebody from the *Warschauer Ztg.* [German newspaper in Warsaw] was trying to get in touch with me several times about an interview. He is going to contact me today. A conference at 1 P.M. about the Kraków trip.

Received by Leist.[4] He issued orders for a transfer to the Community of an automobile without charge. I acquainted him with the incident of labor impressment at 25 Zielna Street. He promised to take care of that. I reported on the financial situation of the Community stressing the endless new demands upon us. I asked him to rescind the furniture requisition directive. He told me to cease our work on this. Summoned by Brandt for 2:30 to the SS. Richter makes a demand for new quarantine facilities for the POWs and refugees.

*March 22, 1940*—32°. Good Friday. In the morning to the Community. No money in the till. At the Zahan at 12. Leaving at 2:30. Safely home.

*March 23, 1940*—37°. Office work suspended because of the holiday. In the Community at 8:30. Our labor contingent on its way to work. No money for the staff's salaries. The SS refused permission for a loan of 100,000 zlotys from the Emigration Fund. The situation, as they say, without hope. How many such burdens it had been my lot to live with. At home, my wife in tears—a letter from J[as], all tenderness and love.

*March 24, 1940*—For the first time since the Germans entered the city I stay home. Preparing a memo for Kraków, where I was summoned together with Councilors Jaszunski, Milejkowski, Sztolcman as well as Dr. Weichert and Bornstein (JDC). The Community offices are closed anyway. In the afternoon, on the Jewish streets, beatings of the Jews and windowbreaking. A sort of a pogrom.[5]

*March 25, 1940*—In the morning in the Community at 9. A meeting on the subject of Kraków. In the coffers not a penny. I owe

4. Leist, Dengel's successor, was the newly appointed German Plenipotentiary for the city of Warsaw.
5. On March 24 and 25, Polish mobs engaged in Easter pogroms.

the Labor Battalion 90,000 zlotys, the hospital staff 25,000, the registration staff 50,000. Pogroms on the streets. At the corner of Zurawia Street beatings and window breakings. The hag that was beating the Jews is again roaming the streets.

*March 26, 1940*—In the morning preparations for the Kraków trip. More street beatings (at the vegetable market). I am forwarding a report to the proper authorities.

Left for Kraków at 4:43, arrived after midnight. During our journey a discussion with Weichert, Jaszunski, Milejkowski, Sztolcman, of the agenda for our meetings.

*March 27, 1940*—Kraków. Up at 6. I prepared my presentation.
1. Security
2. The Community—a paper
3. The economic situation, *Rechtslage* [Legal situation]—Sztolcman
4. *Arbeitsproblem* [labor problem]—Jaszunski
5. *Gesundheitszustand* [health conditions]—Milejkowski

In the afternoon, received by Dr. Arlt[6] and his colleague Heinrich.[7] I spoke on the topic of the security of life and property. I described one day in the life of the Community and concluded with an appeal for the security of life and property, pointing out that armbands degrade the Jews and mark them a target for criminals. I described the present pogroms in Warsaw, the like of which have not been heard of since 1880. Last, I reported on the financial condition of the Community.

Arlt questioned the beatings. Then, he observed that the soldiers would not be able to distinguish [Polish from Jewish] ladies of easy virtue without armbands. It was pointed out to him that the ladies in question would not wear armbands anyway. I suggested that some [Jews] are already exempted, that I myself was advised to petition the *Stadtpraesident* in my own behalf (for instance, if summoned in the middle of the night by the authorities I could not report), that there are also green armbands [sic] exempting [sic] Jews, all of which goes to show that the authorities themselves are cognizant of the danger. Jaszunski, Sztolcman, Milejkowski reported on the issue

6. Dr. Fritz Arlt, Chief of Population and Welfare in the Interior Main Division of the *Generalgouvernement* administration at Krakow.
7. Herbert Heinrich, an official in Arlt's office.

of the compulsory labor decree, restrictions, epidemics.[8] Arlt asked for some additional data on the Community's finances, public works, and births (abortions).

*March 28, 1940*—It is 8 in the morning. Engineer Reicher [9] (he came with Bornstein) informs us about a pogrom yesterday: Buchweitz [10] could not reach the Community offices at Grzybowska Street. In view of this we decided to see Arlt. In the meantime a caretaker, Mrs. Wojnarowska,[11] appears with news that there were more beatings and harassments: she has a letter for Lichtenbaum that Rozen and Rosenthal were injured on their way from the SS to the Community and that the Community offices are under siege. The Labor Battalion was only 1,500 strong. Arlt received us and made a call to Dr. Gauweiler,[12] who reported that the appropriate steps had already been taken. I read him the letter to Lichtenbaum. At our request he agreed to call Meisinger. (He did in fact get in touch with the SS [Higher SS and Police Leader] Krueger [13] and—I suppose—with Meisinger.) He told us to leave today for Warsaw and get in touch with Leist, Meisinger, and Gauweiler on arrival.

Between 12 and 1, there was a telephone message for us to see Arlt again. We were received by Heinrich and one after another reported what we have observed in Warsaw. These statements were being taken down. I again mentioned the matter of the beatings. With Arlt's approval we decided to leave Sztolcman in Kraków as our liaison man.

Arlt decided that, in accordance with a letter to that effect which will be sent to Warsaw (to the appropriate authorities and to us), we [sic] will clear with Dr. Siebert, Chief of the *Innere Verwaltung (Unterabteilung Bevoelkerungswesen)* *"Alleinige Befehlsgewalt Kreishauptmann,* or *Stadthauptmann* [Internal Administration (Subdivision Population) exclusive jurisdiction [14] of District Captain or City Captain], Concerning the *Judenrat, Arbeitseinsatz, Fuersorge, Finanzielle Moeglichkeiten der Gemeinde, Executiv—Gewalt lokale*

8. Jaszunski, using statistics, argued against exclusion of Jews from economic life of the country.
9. Reicher was a JDC functionary.
10. Rafael Buchweitz was principal of Jewish vocational school.
11. Mrs. Wojnarowski, not Jewish, could travel to Krakow without permit.
12. Dr. Otto Gauweiler was chief of the Interior Division, Warsaw district.
13. Friedrich Wilhelm Krüger, in charge of SS and Police in *Generalgouvernement.*
14. "Exclusive jurisdiction" of civil authorities refers to attempted elimination of police interference in Jewish affairs.

*Behoerde fuer die Finanzexecutive* [Labor utilization, welfare, financial resources of the Community, executive power—local authority for the financial executive].

Trustees to be made responsible [illegible word in parentheses] *Sperrconto einzelner Personen (bis zur Neuordnung des Bankwesen) (im Gange) alte Guthaben noch ohne Dezision* [For blocked accounts of single individuals (pending reorganization of the banking system) (in process). No decision as of yet on old accounts.]

An idea about the armbands. Leaving for Warsaw by sleeper at 10:20 P.M. According to Arlt's instructions, tomorrow I must see Leist, Gauweiler, Meisinger. I didn't sleep a wink.

*March 29, 1940*—Got up at 5 A.M. Arriving in Warsaw at 6:20. After the arrival I stopped at the SS. In the Community new instructions about the walling up of the ghetto, preparing a shelter for 3,000 persons expelled from the Reich, etc. I summoned the Council for 1 P.M. and reported on the meetings in Krakow. At 3 P.M. Milejkowski will put through a call to Sztolcman. Many arrests from the police roundups, etc.

*March 30, 1940*—From the very morning, rumors about the ghetto. I visited Lastowitschka: he suggested I better not see his chief today. Later with Leist, I submitted Richter's instructions about establishing the Jewish postal service, the shelter for the 3,000 expellees from the Reich, and our own letter about the virtual impossibility of building a wall (damaging the water installations, electric and telephone cables, etc.).

I reported on our Krakow visit. He instructed me that he himself is our immediate superior and that we should not take orders from anybody else. He gave me his visiting card with his telephone number. In the Discount Bank, Minister Mikulecki promised a loan of 160,000 zlotys (repayable in quarterly installments). Kulski, whom I also visited and who had just seen Leist, informed me that he was told to act as a liaison between us and Leist (contradiction). At Gepner's in the afternoon. I leave with him. Complaint from M[ayzel]'s wife that I do not give up half of my salary, a salary that I do not draw at all.

*April 1, 1940*—Getting ready for whatever I may be doing is an effort as if I were embarking on a long journey. In the morning with

Lastowitschka. He advised me to see Leist about the walls, etc. In the meantime, on orders of the *Ordnungspolizei* [German Order Police], at 7 A.M. we started digging the ditches in preparation for wall construction. The clocks were moved forward one hour last night. The temperature is 34°. For the last several days I have been riding around in a car. I visited Rozen yesterday. He suffered a broken arm and a fractured rib. Tomorrow he will be taken by an ambulance to a clinic.

Leist—problems.
(1) the walls
(2) the postal service
(3) shelter for the refugees
An interlude with Leist's adjutant.

*Krochmalna bis 38 abgesiegelt, ein Teil von der Rynkowa und Walicow. Ciepla bei der Kreuzung um Krochmalna muss geschlossen werden.* [Krochmalna Street sealed off to 38, one segment from Rynkowa and Walicow Streets. Ciepla at the intersection of Krochmalna must be closed off.]
1 – 38.
*3 Stellen zu machen (nicht Mauer mit Bretter—Holzpfaehle)* [3 sites to be erected (not wall with boards—wooden piles)]
*(2 Polizisten)* [(2 Policemen)]
*Lebensmittel gestattet* [Foodstuffs permitted]
*So hoch wie die Mauer* [As high as the wall]
*Durchfahrt—Krochm. 56* [Throughway—56 Krochmalna Street]
He orders the closing of Krochmalna Street from Rynkowa Street to Ciepla and Walicow Streets. We are to erect the fences and transport the food to inhabitants who must not leave their buildings. The walls must be built in several parts of the city. Tomorrow Lastowitschka will inform me who will pay for all this. They will also decide what to do about the postal service. Feldschuh and someone else discuss emigration with me. They ask for advice and [at the same time] offer advice *ehrenhalber* [gratuitiously] about emigration.


*April 2, 1940*—In the morning to Lastowitschka. I am kept waiting from 8 to 10. Trying to obtain permission to borrow 160,000 zlotys from the Discount Bank; the matter of financing the walling up of the "ghetto," postal service, etc. L[aschtowiczka] asked for a note on our various departments, as he is about to inspect them.

The Community was visited by some city engineers from the streetcar department about the potential damage to the network. I directed them to Kulski, whom we had already seen on this matter. Weichert and Bornstein are going to see Messing and later Dr. Gauweiler. The registration of the craftsmen is proceeding at snail's pace.

*April 3, 1940*—At 8 A.M. I proceed to Lastowitschka. Yesterday in the Community building. courtyard workers' hands reach toward the car imploring to be paid. In the treasury not a penny. Summoned to Hufsky [15] (tax office). Threatened with a fine of 500,000 zlotys if the Jews . . .

*April 4, 1940*—In the morning at Braun's (Leist's adjutant), "The walls are being ordered to defend the Jews against excesses." The bricks must be supplied and carried by the Jews themselves, several bricks to every person between the ages of 16 and 60. The idea of the ghetto.

Lastowitschka authorizes withdrawal of 60,000 zlotys from two Jewish banks. For the 100,000 zlotys [loan] he insists we must take a mortgage on some buildings but not in the Jewish section. I am told to see Schubert of the [Warsaw] District about the postal service.

In the Community offices squabbling about the whole problem of Krochmalna Street. It was sealed from Rynkowa Street to Ciepla Street. Eighteen thousand people are without bread, because nobody is allowed in or out.

They refuse to allocate the matzos or the flour. Perhaps they will, but only for "foreign currency." Weichert went to see Herzog. I was instructed to see him instead of Schubert tomorrow. A communication from Hufsky (*Steueramt* [Tax Office]) ordering the Community to pay 500,000 zlotys by the end of April for the recalcitrant taxpayers.

Rosenthal visited Gestapo about those arrested, so far without results.

15. *Finanzinspekteur* Hufsky, one of seven in the district, whose territory apparently included the ghetto. The *Finanzinspekteur* collected direct taxes.

*April 5, 1940*—32°. Heavy leaden clouds. I am to go to Herzog at the Brühl Palace. Is the ghetto already at hand?

The conference with Herzog is fruitless. In the Community offices somebody. has a letter to the [non-Jewish] public servants instructing them to move out of the "ghetto." The Housing Department is inquiring whether we know anything about that in the Community Council since they are already getting applications from prospective tenants. A meeting about leaving for Krakow (Sztolcman). Today, a man from Krochmalna Street died of hunger in the courtyard.

*April 6, 1940*—28°. I am going to Meisinger and Kamlah [16] about the "ghetto." Received by Brandt to whom I stated my objections concerning the walls. Then with Braun, Leist's adjutant—same thing. I brought up the subject of the matzos. He responded that it was a matter for the *Wirtschafts Abtg.* [Economy Division] in the [Warsaw] "district." I left a note and said that I will come [again] at 9 in the morning. Two visits to the *Kommandantur* to see Major Kamlah, but he was out. His office is opposite Richter's office; and it is Richter's proposal that I am to discuss with Kamlah. I will try to see him on Monday.

I also visited Lastowitschka. He approves the loan if we mortgage the Community building at Jagiellonska Street. We are to see Minister Mikulecki on this matter. He [Laschtowiczka] agreed to give us a letter to the effect that we are not permitted to disburse any funds without the *Stadtpraesident's* permission; thus we should not take such orders from other authorities. A lieutenant from the *Rohstoffstelle* [Raw Materials Office] appeared in the Community and paid in 4,000 zlotys for 3 days' work by our labor contingent. He also gave us 1,500 green armbands with appropriate *Ausweise* for the men—both laborers and functionaries—who are going to work for him.

*April 7, 1940*—Morning. The Community offices. 27°. A meeting about the matzos. In reply to the mayor [Kulski] the Council adopts a resolution that religion forbids consuming bread [at Pass-

16. Major (later Colonel) Ferdinand von Kamlah represented Military Commander of Warsaw military district in Jewish matters.

over] and is petitioning the mayor to ask the German authorities for an allocation of matzo flour.

*April 8, 1940*—28°. On my schedule the *Stadtpraesident* and Major Kamlah in the *Kommandantur* about Richter's proposal. In the morning with Braun. He takes me to task for going to the "district" about the walls. The matzos are outside their jurisdiction. Major Kamlah in the *Kommandantur* listened to my presentation on the walls and will intervene in this matter. Mayor Kulski suggests a different form for the matzos memorandum; he will try to accommodate us, although, in his opinion, the results are doubtful. I mentioned the walls. For two days, in order to clear things with the Technical Department, they were suspended. The digging goes on.

A meeting in the Community (matzos). I am implementing my idea of making the Jewish house administrators responsible for order in their buildings.

Richter *befuerwortet* [supports] a letter to the SS about Bielenki's [17] release.

Supinger: If we are short of 1,000 people for the ZOM [Sanitation Department], he will take women directly from the street.

*April 9, 1940*—28°. Summoned for 8:30 to the SS. I mentioned the matter of Bielenki. Brandt asks to be notified about the arrival of the matzos. I mention the walls, submitting documentation.

In the Community a soldier with a Jew, demanding that the latter be paid for his work. A message from *Leutn.* [Lt.] Franke, that I will be arrested if the work [i.e., wall construction] does not begin in 15 separate locations by tomorrow. Lichtenbaum gets construction started on several sites. For tomorrow, I am summoning the house administrators to tell them to clean up the mess in their buildings. A delegation from the hospital doctors including their chief—a matter of a hospital superintendent, etc.

The Germans entered Denmark and Norway.

*April 10, 1940*—37°. A difficult night, liver pains, blood running from my nose, etc. In the morning in the Community occupied with current business. [Sztolcman] returns from Krakow without accomplishing anything.

17. Dr. Owsiej Bielenki, a physician and lung specialist. He was killed in 1943.

Milejkowski, impressed for labor (his *Ausweis* was not sufficient), asked a soldier why he stood in the rain when there was no work to do, to which the soldier replied, "And why do you?" Ten Jews were passing on one brick at a time.

A vendor of candy has no *Zionsstern* [Star of David] on his tray. The work on the walls is in progress on more than a dozen locations.

*April 11, 1940*—34°. It is 7 in the morning. The families from 9 Nalewki Street [18] weeping in my apartment. They were given permission to collect the bodies of their kin. They are pleading for a separate plot in the cemetery. I go to the Community and then to the Praga cemetery. I find about a score of corpses there and the Funeral Department will bring in the 40 remaining. In the Community the families are bickering with Kaminer about the plot at the Praga cemetery. I directed Zabludowski to Praga and the matter was settled.

I received summonses from the Tax Office on my income taxes for 1930, 1931, 1932, 1933—in point of fact paid long ago. Nossig keeps on writing unnecessary letters to the authorities. I reprimanded him.

Jaszunski was impressed for work on his way from Rozen to a meeting. He was ordered to sing a German ditty about the biblical Moses. I forwarded a complaint to the SS.

*April 12, 1940*—37°. It rains. In the morning I proceed to the SKSS [City Social Services Committee]. On Wiejska Street, near the famous Diet [Polish Lower House], singing. I sit in front of a door with a notice, that there are no funds for any cash subsidies, signed by the deputy treasurer, the equally famous Professor Rybarski.[19] Guzik and Neustadt are to go abroad again to solicit contributions. Difficulties with the matzos. Tomorrow I am to visit Wanderof at the *Distriktschef's* on this matter. In the evening I was gorging myself with Adolf Raciazer's, *The 35 Years of Struggle with Foot Distress.*

18. Families of 9 Nalewki Street: cf. diary entry of November 28, 1939.
19. Roman Rybarski, National Democratic Party ("Poland for Poles"). Died in Auschwitz, 1942.

*April 13, 1940*—30°. Beautiful weather. At 8 o'clock with Lastowitschka, next at the Community, then seeing Wanderof (the matzos). Last[owitschka] about the walls. The Emigr[ation] Fund to remain with the SS. We are to pay for the walls. Wanderof demands payment in either silver or gold for the 250 tons of wheat flour. I gave up. Supinger intends to introduce compulsory labor by the Battalion for the city of Warsaw.

A visit by Bonifer and two associates. He demanded a report on the activities of the Community. The remainder of the museum requisitioned.

*April 14, 1940*—An unpleasant conference with Rozen. In the afternoon his letter with apologies.

*April 15, 1940*—37° The SS—the walls (intervention with SS in the *Ordnungspolizei*). Bielenki.

I request the keys to the museum. I reported that I will reorganize the Battalion in the course of a week.

It turned out at Supinger's that it was the Community's own staff that suggested making labor compulsory. I mentioned that I fired Hazensprung and will reorganize the Battalion. Summoned to *Rittmeister* [Captain] Sch.[20] He informs me that he will pay part of the workers' wages. I will send a delegation to him tomorrow. In the Community I named the lawyer Goldfeil as Battalion Chief and added Zabludowski to the labor commission. I named Graf as head of the textile merchants. I am also appointing him to the Council.

Zabludowski went to see Hufsky. He passed on to me the text of a proclamation, which I must post, on the payment of taxes. I have no money to pay salaries. I am borrowing 60,000 zlotys from the bank; we should have that money in two weeks. A new industry: a woman who, for money, will take the place of another person at a disinfection steambath. A nun working at the hospital of Knights of Malta.

*April 16, 1940*—43°. In the morning at the Community. We are on the brink of bankruptcy, owing the [Battalion] workers 120,000 zlotys, and our staff their salaries. The hospital is eating up our resources. We go on building the walls, all of our efforts to the

---

20. Captain Sch. = Schu, in charge of organization collecting scrap metal.

contrary notwithstanding. Tax inspector Hufsky orders the issuing of the proclamation calling on Jewish taxpayers to make their payments.

The Community was visited by Capt. Baltazar from the *Rohstoff* [Raw Materials] office who told us that the workers will receive better treatment. He was investigating the odor of gasoline in the mouth of one of the workers. His superior, *Rittmeister* Schu, will pay part of the workers' wages.

At 3 P.M., Brandt from the SS, with two assistants, arrived at the Community offices to have a look at the drugs we received from Switzerland. Prior to this visit there was Avril [21] from the SS inquiring about the excesses, etc., and demanding a report on the activities of the Community. After the inspection Brandt wanted us to make a detailed list of our drugs.

*April 17, 1940*—50°. In the morning at the JDC. Guzik and Neustadt are still without passports. Anyway, Troper [22] will be in Europe about May 1. *Leutn* [ant] Teicher appears in the Community about nonpayment of 80 workers. In the afternoon, Rinde: Mende orders us to pay 69 workers (mattresses, Krolewska Street). He [?] reappears, announcing that Brandt will inspect the matzos in the Community.

*April 18, 1940*—48°F. All night liver pains. I must leave the apartment at 8 o'clock, but people come to the apartment even earlier. At 9 Brandt and Mende in the Community. I requested permission to deliver holiday [Passover] food to the prison. Permission granted.

Called to the *Ordnungspolizei* for 9 o'clock tomorrow. The work on the walls has been stopped at Zoliborska Street, etc. H., a partner in "Helianis," was ordered to pay up his income taxes for 1930 and a few subsequent years. It turns out that all the abatements granted previously by the authorities are now rescinded.

*April 19, 1940*—50°F. Captain Rochlin (!). Summoned with Weichert in the matter of exemption from the armband provision. Later at the SS (the Emigration Fund: the Battalion will not be

21. Franz Avril, SS-Sergeant, KdS/III-B-4.
22. Morris C. Troper, Chairman of the European Executive Council of the JDC; headquarters in Paris.

under Mende). Delingowski from the municipality or Korzeniowski (?) will wield the baton over the workers.

Dienstman came to the Community making a scene about the nonpayment of the workers. A doorman at the *Ordnungspolizei:* where did I get the automobile from? Rozen arrived at the Community offices with a "machine." [23] Zundelewicz [24] asks for a leave of absence. The registration of metals will be the responsibility of the CZK.[25]

*April 20, 1940*—48°F. I drove to Lastowitschka for an 8 A.M. meeting. The offices closed due to H[itler's] birthday. Later in the Community offices. Lack of funds.

*April 21, 1940*—57°F. In the morning at the Community. We are besieged by the poor (special assistance for the holidays). The JDC will provide 5,000 zlotys for tomorrow. Today, 2,000 zlotys were paid out. After lunch at home, a scene with a delegation from the quarantines about their salaries.

*April 22, 1940*—50° F. At 7 in the morning Mrs. Dawidson screaming that I sent her husband to work.

A poster, my own appeal to the Jews about the taxes (to the censor!). In the morning—Laschtowitchka [sic]—the Budget. Tomorrow a conference with Arlt. Lascht. I submitted the budget.

At the Community in turn a functionary clamored for the payment of the workers. Schrempf in the Community on the matter of the death certificates. He prohibited burial in the common graves at Praga. A conversation with Mrs. Miler.[26]

At 8 o'clock a message from the community clerk on duty that pillaging is in progress in Bagno. I interceded at the police station at Poznanska Street. It transpired that during a requisition there the looters' designs were apparently foiled.

In the morning three janitors and one orderly were impressed for work.

23. The "machine" was probably a rickshaw.
24. Bernard Zundelewicz, lawyer, Jewish Small Merchants Association, Council member. Labor Battalion and Labor Commission. Also dealt with legal questions. Deported with his family to Treblinka, January 1943.
25. CZK, abbreviation for Central Association of Merchants.
26. Mrs. Miler, wife of Dr. Miler, director of Zofiowka mental hospital at Otwock. Czerniakow visited there occasionally.

*April 23, 1940*—37° F. The Community offices are closed today with the exception of the Battalion. I drive to the Community. I am wondering whether the workers will appear with their protectors today. Honor, it seems, begins with prosperity.

Balaban gave me his tract about the ritual murders. What have I, poor devil, done to him?

*April 24, 1940*—44°F. (6 A.M..). At 8:30 I will be at Laschtowitschka's. Lasch[towiczka] scheduled me for Friday morning. Today and tomorrow conferences with Arlt. The *Hauptversorgungsamt* Zoliborz [Main Provisioning Office] seized 40 persons in the Community. At home a library book terribly dirty. I cannot bring myself to read books soiled by constant touch. These are the dullest and most banal books.

*April 25, 1940*—54° (8 A.M.). A certain Lesselbaum turned up in the Community with a German functionary who proceeded to demand 10 zlotys a day for L[esselbaum]'s work. Mende, to whom I reported this, called him [the German] to the telephone supposedly to tell him that this was extortion. The functionary repeated this to me. I told him that indeed "*Druck*" [pressure] was applied. Later, M(ende) telephoned, instructing me that I should always report to him all the cases of this type of intervention. Mende ordered me to engage Rinde, until now his orderly, for the Battalion. For several days I have had pains in the proximity of my heart.

*April 26, 1940*—57° (6 A.M.). A headache—powder. Niunia has been ill for several days—cough.

For 8:30 to Laschtowitschka. L[astowiczka] informs me that (1) the Community has been subordinated to Leist, (2) there will be an official for population affairs [*Bevölkerungsrat*], (3) the Community will have a budget, (4) new tasks will be assigned to the Community when funds are available, (5) Krakow will regulate revenue sources, (6) changes in respect of Jewish self-help, so that the foreign Jews are not discouraged from contributing money (*pflegliche Behandlung der Fuersorge* [careful treatment of welfare]), (7) part of the costs of the Battalion will be reimbursed (they will pay part of the workers' wages). All the final decisions will be made by Kraków.

*April 27, 1940*—In the morning I go to the Community on foot. Caught for work by a soldier with a Jew on a truck at the corner of Zurawia Street. In the Community Dir[ector] Delingowski declared that the authorities will pay each worker 2 zlotys a day and the Community the same amount. This would cost us 500,000 zlotys per month not counting the staff salaries. I telephoned Lastowitschka. I will see Kulski on Monday on this matter.

*April 28, 1940*—47°F. Drizzly. A 20-year-old neighbor died of T.B. Tomorrow I am to see Kulski with a proposal for the financing of the Battalion. In the morning at the Community. Later the cemetery at Okopowa Street. The Orphanage of the Social Self-Help demands a construction = 64,000 zlotys—through the German authorities. In the cemetery not one tree, all uprooted. The tombstones shattered. A fence together with its oak posts pillaged. Nearby at Powazki [Christian Cemetery] the trees are intact.

*April 29, 1940*—39°F (6 A.M.). At 8 I go to Laschtowiczka, etc. Las[towiczka] informed me that what is involved is merely additional pay for 2,000 workers (Schu). Later with Kulski on the same matter as well as about the municipal buildings and the request that the Jews give up some of their apartments (a case of an arrest of a family which refused to do so). Later at the Community. At 12:30 in the [Jewish] Crafts Chamber. (Chairman Mach) [?].

*April 30, 1940*—37°F (6 A.M.). I am driven at 8 to the friendly Tax Office. In the Community two men were injured during the impressments. A conference about the refugees. Schrempf ordered a quarantine shelter at Spokojna Street. The Coordinating Commission is not carrying out its objectives.[27] Tomorrow the Commission will be discussing this problem. From the Discount Bank 100,000 zlotys, a tough job.

Again, the tenants from the various streets who were called upon to sign a statement that they will leave their apartment voluntarily. The [nationwide] Chamber of Craft[s] amended the sections in the charter of the Association of the Jewish Craftsmen—instead of guilds, the "groups of crafts." These changes were proposed by the

27. The Coordinating Commission was designed to effect cooperation between the Jewish Council and relief agency in regard to refugees and social welfare.

Chamber to the chief of the district. I bought a supply of *kogutek* [headache powders].

*May 1, 1940*—Six in the morning 39°. The Community. Today an official German holiday. In the Community current affairs. A visit by two Germans enjoining the Community to issue an order that all shopkeepers must subscribe to the *Verordnungsblatt* [*Legal Gazette*].

*May 2, 1940*—45°F (6 A.M.). I go to the Community. In the morning visit to the Praga cemetery, later in the Jagiellonska Street orphanage. I gave the children some chocolate. Zbytkower's [28] tombstone damaged. Trees cut.

*May 3, 1940*—8 A.M. 50°F. In the morning at the Community. As usual until 3:30.

May 4, 1940—54°F. In the morning with Lastowitschka. A postponement until Monday 9 A.M. Later the Community offices. At 9:30 on my way to Mayor Kulski about the opening of schools.[29]

*May 5, 1940*—50°. Cloudy skies. The streets are empty. A philatelist whom I have entertained in the past, asked about my collection, selected some stamps and offered to buy them. Mende sent me his orderly Rinde to take up his new job with the Community organization. Because of the irregularities in the Labor Battalion it will be necessary for me to keep returning to the Community offices after lunch to clear this mess. The old management has failed. I fired the man in charge. It is essential that they get a dictator. The sanitation committees are working well. It appears that we must wall up the ground floor windows of the houses on Chmielna Street.

*May 6, 1940*—6 A.M. 48°F. Driven to Laschtowiczka for 9 A.M. meeting. L. has not heard from Krakow, although two weeks ago

---

28. Szmul J. Zbytkower, a late 18th century merchant prince in Warsaw who, following unsuccessful Kosciuszko revolt, saved the lives of many Jews and Poles during Russian occupation.
29. Elementary schools for Jewish children, unlike those for Polish children, were still closed. They received permission to reopen in April 1941.

Arlt promised to write. The Community Authority is given enforcement power. There was a visit from Schrempf on the matter of Haendel [30] (it must be something relating to Krochmalna Street). He loudly urged the completion of the walls by the 20th. Haendel, he claims, caught a [Battalion] section leader redhanded at Krochmalna Street. A German functionary in charge suspended the culprit and replaced him. H[aendel ?] and Milejkowski are to report to Schrempf at 4 P.M. today. Yesterday our receipts were 40,000 zlotys, the Battalion [exemption taxes?] alone bringing in 21,000 zlotys. Today we are exchanging our money in the bank for the *"mlynarki."* [31] The lines in front of the Bank Polski are several blocks long.

The rabbis are protesting against the non-kosher hospital food. I called a meeting of the Hospital Commission. Today yet another one of the frequent meetings of the House Sanitation Committees. The Self-Help people are complaining about a stupid hag who, they say, wants a wall around the cemetery to protect her cow; we cannot solve that problem.

In the afternoon I read that they have opened movie theaters somewhere. For how long have we been deprived of the opportunity to see a movie or to listen to the radio? I have just completed reading Zbyszewski's *Niemcewicz—Front and Rear View.* Apart from the sloppy style and its bawdy vulgarities I found the book to be rich in truths and so free of whitewash. What a pity that this scrupulous writer lacks an objective and humane approach to the people of Poland and their many problems. His strength is criticism; he fails in constructive thinking.

I received a letter from the Esperanto Union inquiring whether I could transmit money to the Zamenhof family.[32] Jasz [unski] visited Bitek [?] at my behest on the matter of schools.

*May 7, 1940*—In the morning at the Community Mende directs five Jews to the Labor Battalion for one month as a punishment. Delingowski asked for additional information to be entered on the

30. Marian Hendel, or Marjan Hendel, liaison man between Jewish Council and German offices. Later with Jewish police. Survived and moved to Caracas, Venezuela, after the war.
31. *"Mlynarki,"* new zloty notes which became legal tender, named for Feliks Mlynarski, at first head of Bank Polski, then placed in charge of Emissionsbank.
32. Eliezer Ludwik Zamenhof (1859–1917) was the creator of the artificial language Esperanto. His son, Dr. Adam Zamenhof, together with members of his family, was arrested shortly after the German occupation of Warsaw.

5,000 cards of the compulsory labor register by May 13 (the income of each individual). Krochmalna Street is sealed. In the closed-off area 30 new cases of typhus. Apparently two landlords did not remove garbage for nine months.

*May 8, 1940*—55°F. Summoned at 6:30 to the SS. Six who forged the Battalion seal were just arrested. The five Jews from May 4, 1940, were supposed to have bribed the functionary who seized them for work at Dynasy.[33] They were given 15 lashes and one month of compulsory labor. Drozdowski [34] from Self-Help telephoned on behalf of Sliwinski. Staniszkis refuses to give up his fence at Okopowa Street. I told him without mincing words what I think about people like that. The Staniszkises will never reform.

Esperantists from Geneva are offering help to the Zamenhof family. I instructed Sztolcman to discuss this matter with Messing in the *Distriktchef's* office. The *chalutzim* from the Grochow farm brought me a gift from their first crops (rhubarb and asparagus).[35] I am going to visit them on Saturday. Some Poles are beginning to wear Jewish armbands [to avoid being impressed for labor in Germany]. Somebody started a rumor that we have made special representations to the Germans, lest, God forbid, our bands were taken away.

*May 9, 1940*—55°F. In the morning at the Community. The receipts are small today. I return after lunch in the matter of Schu and the Battalion. The streets are empty. Majfeld has been burned with cigarettes.[36] Project Schu. At least 2,000 workers: even if he pays 2 zlotys per worker per day the result would be as before, since I give him and the others 3,000 [workers] and now on top of it will have to pay on the dot. Where will I get the money? I will go to see him myself tomorrow.

*May 10, 1940*—55°F. In the morning at the Community. Yesterday a Jewish mother with a [German] functionary terrorized the cashier; 4 cartridges, one fired in the direction of a building on the

33. Dynasy: location of SS garages.
34. Henryk Drozdowski, Artur Sliwinski, and Witold Staniszkis, Polish officials in citywide relief committee. Sliwinski was a former Prime Minister; Staniszkis, a National Democrat, was a known anti-Semite.
35. There was a Jewish training farm at Grochow (suburban Warsaw).
36. Majfeld, Small Merchants Association, was apparently mistreated.

other side of the street. The cashier gave him a certain amount of money. I instructed Halber to report this to the SS. We handed over to the prosecutor some functionaries of the Battalion for embezzlement. I received today the *Skizze des Sperrgebietes War-schau* [Sketch of closed-off area of Warsaw]. A ghetto in spite of everything. Some furrier threw out Typograf [37] from his apartment. He was told to move to the fourth floor.

At dawn today the German armed forces entered Holland and Belgium.

In the afternoon, with *Rittmeister* Schu. He informed me that he does not want *Sklaventum* [slave labor]. He will take 1,300 paid workers. With regard to back pay from the beginning of May, he instructed me to see Unger.

*May 11, 1940*—59°F. In the morning at the Community. At 6 in the morning some airmen showed up with workers (money, wages). Later, similar scenes. The Gestapo summoned to their headquarters three soldiers (with rifles) together with some of their [Jewish] comrades.

I made an inspection of the farm at Grochów. The young people are busy at work. A squatter refuses to leave one of their dwellings. The local scum are pilfering. The rhubarb is being stolen by a good-for-nothing in a student's cap. The visitors are telling *chalutzim* about the Rotszylds.[38] Not so long ago I had a visit from a lawyer B. He listened patiently to my negative opinion of those Jews who run away, or are about to run [i.e., emigrate], about the Jewish activists, like Koerner, who moreover promised hypocritically that they will send us assistance from abroad (money). He kept on nodding his head in genial approval and in the end declared that he himself wanted to emigrate, mainly to render us assistance. These utterances are made by a decrepit old man with a serious heart condition.

*May 12, 1940*—48°F. In the morning at the Community offices. The JDC is without funds; they are sending imploring wires to the United States for money. They have also asked the Community authority to do the same. The reduced receipts in the Community. Considerable difficulties with the workers because there is no

37. Dr. Typograf was a Physician.
38. "Rotszyld": Polish spelling of Rothschild.

money for them. Today and tomorrow, Christian holidays—the Community offices are open as usual.

Korczak is recounting that on his way home in the evening he sings: "To a very old uncle once said the maiden." Waiting on line for groats in a little shop he cajoles the female owner saying. "You do remind me of my elder granddaughter." The lady gets red in the face, quickly prepares the package and wraps it carefully in paper. On another occasion he asks a streetcar driver to stop. "If I were a young girl I would hug you for slowing down, since I want to jump off at the corner." "You don't have to kiss me, sir," the driver snapped and proceeded to break as Korczak wished.

*May 13, 1940*—41°F. I receive the second list of the baptized. Very meager receipts—some section leaders [39] are rebellious. One of the converts told me that his baptism is only temporary; that is, just like a comfortable seat in a streetcar.

A message from the lice-ridden Jozef. *Ot sumy* etc. . . .[40] "God hath so ordained that you will suffer all your life."

*May 14, 1940*—In the morning 37°F. At the Community. At 11, some armed men appeared and compelled our staff to pay them 1,700 zlotys. At 12, Major Kaczor turned up with two policemen about requisitioning some machines from the Craft Vocational School. I informed him that most of them belong to the JDC. They requisitioned three lathes, one borer, and one grinder.

The workers threaten the staff for their pay. It is my impression that Hazensprung and Halber have a hand in this, and later they circulate stories about the irregularities [in the Battalion]. Zundelewicz and Rozen have been a total failure—such small and incompetent men. I was summoned to Mende for tomorrow. Moreover, I am to see Lastowitschka at the same time.

*May 15, 1940*—In the morning at the SS. Ordered to pay the 150 workers on Szuch Avenue. Mende makes an assertion, on the basis of his graph tables of the Community structure, that the Jews are capable of being self-sufficient and could live off their own resources, if it were not for the fact that we just do not care to cash in 300,000 zlotys worth of our assets that might be needed for the

39. A reference to the section leaders of Labor Battalion.
40. The Russian proverb in full: "Don't forsake your beggar's sack and gaol."

*Umsiedlung* [resettlement] after the peace treaty is signed. Halber [41] should be co-opted into the Council. I pointed out that the Council members serve without pay, and he as a staff member should continue to receive a salary.

Lastowitschka, for whose appointment I was 30 minutes late, could not see me and informed me that he will telephone me about our next meeting.

According to the afternoon paper Holland surrendered. Leodjum [Liege?] fell. [Queen] Wilhelmina is reported to have fled to England.

*May 16, 1940*—41°F. In the Community offices a line of people on the matter of those recently arrested on the streets. A tragic state of affairs with the workers. No money to pay staff salaries. A cantankerous hag in town spreads rumors that I receive a salary from the Community. The 77-year-old Baroness Rostocki called up to work in the Battalion; on the other hand, so has a one-and-a-half year old child. In the *Warschauer Ztg.* [German Warsaw newspaper] a communiqué that the *Festung* [fortress] "Holland" surrendered. In the Community offices Avril and colleague with questions about the Jewish climate of opinion. Mende telephoned that Hazensprung should have his salary reduced to 250 zlotys.

In the City Hall a dark-haired dandy in a light-colored overcoat makes an allegation that the receipts for the Battalion are 150,000 zlotys and expenses 80 or 100,000. A certain historian [42] keeps on bringing his books for me to read. What have I, poor fellow, done to him to be so burdened now? A financial report from the Battalion indicates that we owe the Battalion 400,000.

*May 17, 1940*—45°F. In the morning Laschtowiczka: *Judenrat* [Jewish Council]—self-government with the powers of enforcement. The municipality is to have Jewish functionaries for that purpose. He instructed me to prepare an enforcement statute. He requests to be informed of the military units which come to the Community with creditors. He declares that the *Treuhaender* [trustees] of the [Jewish] real estate and business enterprises should pay receipts to the Community. The workers for the city and the

41. Halber probably was a Jewish agent for the Gestapo. See also March 4, 1940, May 19, 1940, and June 5 diary entries.
42. The historian is probably Balaban.

*Rohstoff* [Raw Material Staff] should be paid. The *Treuhaender* [trustees] should pay 3 zlotys per day.

Today, the Community receipts better. The registration of the documents (1 zl. per person) has already brought over 30,000 zlotys. The Battalion, on the other hand, has not been bringing anything for almost two weeks.

I was summoned by Schrempf about some boards missing from the fence on Krochmalna Street. He had to call *me* on this matter (from 3 to 6 P.M.). Supinger made a decision on the latest changes in the walls. In the Leszno Street quarantine—I have just found out—there must be lice, since they have just had a case of typhus.

Two powders for a headache—beautiful weather but changeable. News from Jas—he is on his way.[43]

*May 18, 1940*—In the morning at the Community. Later at the SS. In the Community, a report of racketeering in the Battalion. A Jew who contributed 100 zlotys for the Battalion for the month of May was asked to pay an additional 400 zlotys. He had a visit in his shop from our section leader and a soldier. A clerk is under strong suspicion and the whole matter is under investigation. Apparently, identification papers will have to be issued every month in different colors. What would happen if such scum had its own state? Would it not be necessary, for instance, to change the currency every month?

*May 19, 1940*—54°F. It rains. In the morning at the Coordinating Commission. During the night—a migraine headache. In the Community word that Goldfeil and Halber were summoned yesterday to Szopen Street. The former 20 lashes, the latter 10 lashes.[44] Our own worker executed this punishment. Tomorrow I will lodge a complaint. In the Battalion shameful doings—cases of extorting money from people (Lekachmacher paid 100 for May, they demand from him another 400 zl.).

*May 20, 1940*—55°F. The weather is improving. I proceed to the SS about Goldfeil. For my breakfast today I had "caviar." It is apparently frog spawn colored black. One little can 3 zlotys. I drank

43. Czerniakow's son Jas did not come back.
44. Apparently the reason for the beatings was the failure of the Labor Battalion officials to supply the requisite number of workers.

some artificial tea: a pint of this liquid 3.60 zlotys. At the SS I submitted the complaint about Goldfeil, etc. In addition, again the matter of the 300,000 from the Emigration Fund.

I presented Mayor Kulski with a memorandum about food rations for the Jewish population. Two rooms of furniture for Kulski.

In the yard behind the Community building some horses covered with lime have just been dug up. They look like immense herring, about to be fried.

*May 21, 1940*—50°F. Cloudy. My head is throbbing. A reprimand from Okecie that instead of 1,800 workers only 400 reported. In the *Warschauer Ztg.* a note about drainage and land reclamation work in the Warsaw district—another demand for unpaid Jewish manpower.

Delingowski appeared in the Community offices about the archives and informed us that Kulski will visit us on the same matter tomorrow.

Schu promised to give us by 4 o'clock an advance for the workers. In the meantime a *Dienstmann* [low-level German functionary] arrived with a section leader. I had to give him the money. Today, Schrempf inspected our refugee shelters. He received our report on combating epidemics today.

*May 22, 1940*—59°F. In the morning with Laschtowiczka. A draft of a tax statute (ration cards for bread). Expulsions from Krakow. The optimists, the pessimists, and the Sophists.[45]

Schu will at last pay the workers. No money for salaries. The debts: 160,000 zlotys apart from the Labor Battalion. A project for organizing a meeting of the four [Jewish] Communities.[46]

*May 23, 1940*—61°F. Tomorrow we expect the arrival of the Americans [47] who will visit the hospital at Czyste. At 8:30 I will be at the SS. They demand for the Berlin authorities information about regularizing Jewish life throughout the G.G. [General Government]. A news item from Kraków that 15,000 will be allowed to

45. Optimists, pessimists, Sophists—play on words: the Hebrew word for "end" is *soph.*
46. The four communities: probably the largest Jewish communities in the *Generalgouvernement*—Warsaw, Kraków, Lublin, Radom.
47. Americans were relief officials.

remain, the rest of the Jews expelled and resettled, at the rate of 5,000 per week.

*May 24, 1940*—63°F. I am headed for the Community to be there at eight. At 8:30 a visit from Mayor Kulski, accompanied by Delingowski, on the matter of the archives [record office?].

I signed the necessary papers at the notary public for a loan of 100,000 zlotys at the Discount Bank.

At last Schu is paying 2 zlotys per worker. One of our workers was watering flowers during the pouring rain. An old hag who had been raped appeared today, coiffured, with her lips painted, etc. Rejuvenated at least 20 years. Somebody told someone else to come to a pastry shop to collect some cakes that were supposed to have been paid for and forgot to order them. Pre-war worries in the context of today's more serious worries.

*May 25, 1940*—66°F. In the morning to see Berenson [48] (500). Later at the Community. Alas, Laschtowiczka is transferred to Kraków. Schrempf is furious about our report on combating epidemics. I am to be summoned on this matter to Leist. A touching letter from *"silaczka"* [49] of Zawichost. I am calling a meeting of the Council tomorrow on the tax statute.

In the *Voelkischer Beobachter* [principal Nazi newspaper in Germany], May 24, 1940, an interesting article: *"Franzoesische Kolonialtruppen demolieren belgische Wohnungseinrichtungen"* [French colonial troops demolish Belgian apartments].

*May 26, 1940*—66°F. Counselor Tempel [50] was arrested yesterday. His family in my apartment in the morning. According to the German communiqué Boulogne has been taken, Calais is surrounded.

Everything is terribly expensive. Only cigarettes and streetcar tickets are cheap. Somebody said that it would pay to buy 1,000

48. Leon Berenson, prominent defense attorney, proposed that fifty (not 500) Jewish community leaders volunteer for camp labor. He spoke after Council officials said that it was the duty of Jews to present themselves for labor in order to avoid greater German restrictions. The incident is reported by Emanuel Ringelblum in his diary.
49. *"Silaczka"* (strong woman), an allusion to a novel by Zeromski.
50. Tempel, an attorney, had returned to Warsaw from Soviet-occupied territory.

streetcar season tickets. In 1916 a black marketeer bought a freightcar of appendixes [?].

This is J[as]'s birthday without J[as]. A thunderstorm. A very difficult meeting of the Council on the issue of the bread tax. The "disgusting" [*parszywy*] ordinance voted on. With a heavy heart I am taking it to the authorities tomorrow. Lastowitschka is leaving.

*May 27, 1940—55°F.* Cloudy. I am being driven to Laschtowiczka for a meeting at 8 o'clock. I find it impossible to have my suit pressed.

At L[aschtowiczka]'s reviewing the tax ordinance. I suggested that I should periodically report to him in Kraków to discuss the financial matters of the Community. He will clear this suggestion with his authorities.

Summoned to the criminal police to notify Jewish fences and people hiding bandits that they will be treated the same as criminals.

Brandt appeared in the Community accompanied by an aide, demanding information about the Community, the JDC, the JSS. The 300,000 zlotys, plus or minus, from the Emigration Fund may not be touched. Later Avril arrived from the SS with a colleague to unlock the Museum. The keys did not fit and they announced that they will return tomorrow at 9, move the remaining Museum collections to one room, lock it, and release the rest of the space. They asked whether people are gossiping that the curfew will start at 6 P.M. I inquired if this were true and they responded that it is not. They told us that Calais was captured the other day.

At last I received the 100,000-zloty loan from the bank. The Commission divided up 40,000 zlotys.

*May 28, 1940—55°F.* Cloudy, 8 o'clock—Laschtowiczka. He could not get in touch with Leist because of the arrival of some dignitary in Warsaw. I handed in the ordinance. What the future will bring I do not know.

In the Community offices a delegation—all men 18 to 50 years old residing at Numbers 7 and 10 Gesia Street were arrested. The Gestapo was scheduled to open some rooms in the Museum building but did not. Summoned to the SS about Gesia Street. The residents must pay 4,000 zlotys through the Community Authority for beating up a *Volksdeutscher* [Ethnic German] and his wife. Forty-three Jews were arrested. The guilty ones will be punished, the others are to be released after a while.

I am reading Proust's *Within a Budding Grove*. He says: "According to the Japanese, victory belongs to an antagonist who knows how to suffer one quarter of an hour longer."

*May 29, 1940—55°F.* I took 4,000 zlotys with me to the Gestapo, the fine from the residents of Numbers 7 and 10 Gesia Street for the bruised *Volksdeutscher* [Ethnic German].

In connection with the increasing number of converts—here is a letter received today:

To: Mr. Goldfeil, The Labor Battalion of the Community
From: Aleksander Mietelnikow, 32 Zeromski St. (Bielany)

I have learned from several communications marked P/70, ordering me to report to the Labor Battalion, that I am considered a Christian convert. How else could it be explained that I am the only Jew in this suburb who receives these communications. This being so, I wish to state that I have never been baptized. I left the Jewish Community in 1933 to be a person without any religion. I did not leave the Jewish Community to embrace some better or worse faith—I only did it because I do not accept any religious beliefs. To list me as a baptized Jew—a category which I myself look down upon, identifying me with that group—is a grievous moral wrong. I am respectfully asking you, Sir, to correct this unintended injustice by removing my name from the "file" of the converts and placing it on the appropriate register. Warsaw, May 29, 1940, Aleksander Miet[elnikow].

*May 30, 1940—55°F.* In the morning with Makowski [51] in the matter of the passports for the directors of the JDC. Leist refused. They planned to travel to Budapest to meet with the JDC head, Troper.

A section leader whom I refused to see threatened to complain to the authorities. I had to react accordingly. The receipts are a little better today. In the *Warschauer Ztg.* an interview with *der Chef der*

51. Hans Makowski, Chief of Interior Division in German city administration, to whom Czerniakow sent the Council's weekly reports.

*Kanzlei des Führers* [Chief of the Chancellery of the Führer], *Reichsleiter* Bouhler, of the 30th of May. He states that the armbands, the ghetto, and the ban on Jewish travel by rail are all appropriate.

I just read, in the obituary columns, that a certain Bohatiuk, a director in the *Auswanderungsbureau* [Emigration Bureau], had passed away. Not so long ago this Ukrainian fellow with a physique like Hercules paid me a visit to establish a liaison with the Community, since he was about to organize emigration of the Jews from Poland. He showed me certification from the Gdansk [Jewish] Community. And now, one of the first, he emigrated himself.

*May 31, 1940*—59°F. Cloudy—a headache. In the Community. The JDC is without any funds. The receipts in the Community today fairly good; yesterday—a record 31,000 zlotys, and without any artificial injections at that. "Zofiowka" [52] threatened to discharge their mentally ill patients because of the lack of funds.

At 2 P.M. reports of incidents [53] against Jews at Chmielna Street and in the vicinity of the Community offices. A state of emergency has been put into effect. At 3 P.M. the situation apparently quieted down.

Niunia was taken ill in the afternoon; I called a doctor—injections. Tomorrow is her birthday.

The Compensation Association [the Zahan] is still Jewish [54] even though the Jews surrendered their stock and resigned from management and the board. It appears that it takes a Jew to make an Aryan firm.

Haendel heard that no one will be allowed to leave the "ghetto" or come into it from other districts. Biberstein is expected from Krakow tomorrow. I must organize with him a Chamber of Luminaries.[55]

*June 1, 1940*—55°F. Niunia's birthday. She is up after yesterday's illness. What is Jas thinking about us today? At 8:30 I report to the

---

52. Zofiowka was a Jewish hospital for the mentally ill in the town of Otwock outside Warsaw.
53. The incidents occurred after a Pole was killed on Franciszkanska Street.
54. The Zahan: under German definition, an enterprise was Jewish so long as any board member was Jewish or if in fact Jewish "influence" was predominant. Theoretically, the Zahan should have been "Aryan" by now.
55. Chamber of Luminaries: possibly a group of four major Jewish Councils.

Gestapo with Zabludowski and Goldfeil (the Labor Battalion). Jozef's condition very poor.

I read about the "Brześć Affair" [56] last night. We too were capable of such things.

In the Gestapo we presented the situation in the Labor Battalion. They informed us that they are conducting an independent investigation of the racket with the stamps used to authorize work exemptions. Okecie threatens reprisals if we do not supply the required number of workers.

The Szopen [Chopin] monument is no longer.

*June 2, 1940*—45°F. My thoughts are with Jas. Proust writes in *Within a Budding Grove* about a daughter's devotion for her father: she loves him "since ever." Rozen visited Okecie. All quiet. Halber schemes.

Better receipts in the Community. I discussed with Biberstein our potential cooperation in the sector of "social welfare." Payments for the Battalion considerable.

*June 3, 1940*—55°F. A headache at night. In the morning at the Community. The JSS admonished. A certain Geller has been calling on the authorities in the name of the *Judenrat.*

*June 4, 1940*—59°F. In the morning at the Community. At 10 A.M. at Brühl Palace to see Herzog (202). (1) In the streets, registration of children for elementary schools, on June the 4th a conference, at Danilowiczowska Street, between Schmidt [Education official] and the Polish elementary school authorities, (2) *Denkschrift* [memorandum], (3) *Eisenbahnbenutzung* [use of railways], (4) Statute.

Herzog claims that he spoke in favor of Jewish schools. In the meantime, during the meeting at Danilowiczowska Street it was stated that the opening of schools in the *Seuchensperrgebiet* [Quarantine] is in the hands of the doctor in charge of public health, probably Schrempf.

Today at 7:30 the walls were to be inspected for acceptance. A postponement until Friday.

In the Community offices a briefing of the administrators and

56. "Brześć Affair" refers to the illegal detention and brutal treatment of opposition deputies in Brzesc by prewar Pilsudski regime.

owners of the buildings. As usual, I addressed them, pleading for the contribution of free lunches by the more prosperous residents, cleanliness in the buildings, resolution of problems of work, etc. This was a very profitable day for our treasury as the result of a certain funeral [cemetery tax of] 18,000 zlotys. (Photographing the Councilors.)

I asked Herzog why the Community had to pay for the cost of the walls. He demanded more information: our memorandum to Kraków and the weekly reports.

*June 5, 1940—59°F.* Halber, the viper, has been stirring up the Battalion workers and their employers against the Council. He absents himself for days gadding about and conniving. I must cut off this hydra's head. A bad day, reduced receipts. At Sliska Street a quarantine again because of typhus. At the hospital they expect a delegate from Hoover [57] in the afternoon.

*June 6, 1940—55°F.* Summoned to the Gestapo. An order to [our] quarantine facilities for 500 lice (700 were supplied). Three hundred zlotys were paid for this.

In the morning Dr. Kuhn, a university lecturer from Tübingen. A discourse with Professor Balaban on archival and biblical topics. He examined the Archives. The Museum was unlocked—the collection and showcases are gone.

*June 7, 1940—68°F.* In the morning at the Community. Mende and Dr. Kuhn opened the Gdansk chest. Only some insignificant documents. Mende inspected the Labor Battalion; in the process he called Halber and reprimanded him. Poor receipts. In the afternoon a meeting about the charter of the JSS.[58] A committee is to work on the draft. Our tax ordinance was approved.

An inspection of the walls by Schrempf and Supinger. We were given a bird to be stuffed. A number of workers have been called to Szopen Street, apparently as a result of somebody's indiscretion.

It has been oppressively hot today. I have not eaten from morning until 8 P.M. I have not eaten for lack of time.

57. Former U.S. President Hoover was concerned with relief efforts in occupied Poland.
58. The charter for JSS refers to an American requirement for a coordinating committee including Polish, Ukrainian, and Jewish components. The JSS was the Jewish agency. It was required to have a presidium of seven, four of them from Warsaw.

The Italians are demanding Corsica from the French through [the good offices of] the USA.

*June 8, 1940*—52°F. Cool. In the morning at the Community. A certain Lesselbaum, who stays with the *Postbauleitung* [Postal Construction Office], appeared and inquired why he has been dismissed. He added that he was working for the Community at the behest of the authorities. A little while later there was a call from "Chef Ehrwulf" of the *Postbauleitung* that he [Lesselbaum] must be given a job and a salary. He gave us a Monday morning deadline. Lesselbaum is responsible for sending his associates to the residences of the "rich" Jews to extort contributions for the Battalion. This gang collaborates with Halber.

During a visit of the Administrator Sikorski from the hospital in Czyste, today, on Saturday [the Sabbath], his companion, Dr. Stein, wanted to light a cigarette and I pointed out that [today] smoking was forbidden. At the same time I assured Sikorski that this rule did not apply to him. I also told him on this occasion that the late attorney Korwin Krukowski, whose clients were mainly Jews and peasants, used to say on entering his office: "Praised be Jesus Christ," always adding "The Israelite gentlemen may remain seated." On his way out, Sikorski saw Dr. Milejkowski [a Jew] with a lit cigarette in the corridor, and shouted, "Smoking is forbidden here."

*June 9, 1940*—59°F. Cloudy. In the morning at the Community. A conference with a Battalion section leader. In the cemetery the keepers dealt effectively with the scum (Babice). I presented a plan for a bank loan to the JDC.

*June 10, 1940*—59°F. At the Gestapo with problems involving the Labor Battalion. They are, it appears, investigating the counterfeiting of Battalion stamps. The arrested culprits are excusing themselves saying that after all they have only cheated the Community. Functionaries who were fired from the hospital denounced the management for providing hiding places from compulsory labor for members of the intelligentsia. I am to report at 10 A.M. tomorrow to Leist. Our receipts very meager today. This is more than anyone can bear.

Italy entered the war.

*June 11, 1940*—54°F. Received by Leist who was accompanied by Kunze, [59] etc. I reviewed the matter of the JSS, the return of the Emigration Fund, compulsory labor, Jewish registration in the Community very poor. Rap [Raab?] appeared with a city engineer. We discussed the ZOM [City Sanitation Department].

*June 12, 1940*—58°F. In the Community. Today is Shavuot [Pentacost]. Poor receipts. Wachsmacher, the Karaite. In the afternoon, a meeting of the JSS (statute and candidates for the presidium). I forced through a resolution providing that possible amendments to the statute be submitted to a Committee of Three. As for nominations—Gepner and myself. We started receiving telegrams in the Community.

*June 13, 1940*—A holiday in the Community. I arrived at 9 A.M. At 2 P.M. the *Feldgendarmerie* [Military Police] appeared, ordering us to bring in a woman named Sadowska, who works in the Labor Battalion. She had left work and they apparently looked for her in her apartment. The receipts are nil. I am sending letters to 200 taxpayers to solicit a sum of money, however small, without which it will be impossible to carry on.

*June 14, 1940*—63°F. We are having beautiful weather of late. The Germans 12 miles from Paris yesterday. (In the afternoon) it was reported that Paris is taken.

I went to the JDC for money without success. Later in the Commercial Bank—there are prospects for 50,000 or perhaps even 100,000. In the Community Halber and others beat up a recalcitrant worker. An investigation is in progress.

*June 15, 1940*—64°F. Yesterday Halber et al. whipped a Jew who was ordered to work. Today I sent for H[alber] and suspended him. Prior to that Zabl[udowski] made inquiries at the authorities about their attitude toward him. They summoned H[alber]; later he reported to the Community offices. The receipts are good. A conference at the Community on the seven [representatives] to the JSS in Krakow and the guidelines for the statute. At 6 P.M. a

59. Friedrich Kunze succeeded Laschtowiczka as chief of Finance Division of German city administration.

meeting at Tlomackie Street on the JSS. The delegation to Kra-kow—Weichert and Jaszunski—a number of proposals for the JSS.

*June 16, 1940*—64°F. At the Community. A meeting of citizens with means about financial help for the Community. A vulgar letter from Halber to Zabludowski. The last 15,000 zlotys from the borrowed 50,000 expended. A message that the Commercial Bank will lend us 100,000 zlotys for future expenses. The 417 Jewish residents of Gesia Street [60] arrested for a beating of Januszewski were released.

*June 17, 1940*—68°F. In the morning [a meeting] in the matter of social welfare near Tlomackie Street. Later Kulski: (1) the tax ordinance, (2) the Jews will be expelled from city-owned buildings, (3) food rations apart from bread the same for everybody during the next month.

A meeting at the Community about the loan from various citizens. The receipts meager: 7,000 zlotys. Rap [Raab?] complains that instead of 500 workers due at the *Tiefbauamt* [Underground Construction Office] only 62 appeared. Haendel delivered the stuffed bird. Yesterday rumors that all of France is about to collapse. Paris has been in German hands for several days now. The German standard over the Eiffel Tower. The same in Versailles.

The High Command, June 17, 1940: "The premier of the newly formed French government, Marshal Pétain, proclaimed in a radio address to the French people that France has been forced to lay down her arms. He also referred to the steps just taken to notify the German Government of this decision and to learn the German terms for an armistice. Chancellor Hitler will meet with the Royal Italian Premier Benito Mussolini to discuss the position to be taken by the two states." (Special issue of *Nowy Kurier Warszawski*, Monday, June 1, 1940, 8:30 P.M.)

*June 18, 1940*—63°F. At the Community "Whom do you con-sider to be the most impressive among English politicians?" "Why, Winston Churchill, of course. Here is a man with a quick wit, exceptional intelligence, wisdom and imagination, talent and ambi-tion, a magnificent orator, and a gifted writer. To be sure, Winston

60. Gesia Street: see diary entries for May 28 and 29.

Churchill always backs the wrong horse. Enough to mention the Dardanelles, the Denikin affair and all the money it cost, his opposition to the ruling Conservative Party on the eve of the general elections and the government of national unity. He is always backing a lost cause." "Lord Reading: I consider him one of the greatest Englishmen. What a pity that he does not hold an official position in government now, and I daresay that much would improve in international relations if he were in charge of the Foreign Office." (An excerpt from Rom. Landau's *Paderewski*).

In the Community at 11 o'clock two German policemen with a certain Popiolek, a section leader at the University, demanding money for the workers. Raab threatens that a concentration camp for 20,000 Jews will be established if the Jewish labor contingents continue to fall short of requirements. At 12 a meeting with some citizens about aiding the Community treasury. The receipts today are about 17,000 zlotys, as usual not enough. Jaszunski and Weichert left for Kraków. Lastowitschka regrettably, after a brief visit to Warsaw, returned to Kraków. An unknown Pole stopped one of my associates at Danilowiczowska Street and on the pretext that my friend's armband was hidden by his coat, searched him and escorted him to one of the University buildings. A bargaining session followed: 20 zlotys, 100 zlotys, 200 zlotys. In the end he glanced at his quarry's wristwatch (worth 15 zlotys before the war) and asked how valuable it was—300 zlotys—"Gimme the watch," and he let my friend go.

*June 19, 1940*—59°F at 6 in the morning, at 7 already 63°F. During the night I read S. Wojciechowski's [61] diary, *My Reminiscences*. A dull, mediocre individual, C+.

In the Community two airmen with a section leader claiming that we owe him 400 zlotys. When I remarked that he should not resort to intercession he replied that he belonged to the Maccabees, but. . . . Then, in view of the strike of the workers and the threat of revolt by [their] women in the courtyard of the Community building, I proceeded to Kunze. He promised to talk to Meisinger tomorrow about the 300,000 zlotys. We had a telephone call from adjutant Braun who indicated that there will be consequences (a camp?) unless we mend our ways. I went to see him and since he

61. Stanislaw Wojciechowski, a former president of Poland.

was gone I told his secretary about my visit to Kunze. It appears that they will use the Polish police to procure the labor contingents. The receipts today are very meager. For several days we have been calling in Jews to conferences in which we are asking them to lend money to the Community. The typical outcome of these meetings is talk. I will have to impose a compulsory contribution.

*June 20, 1940*—At 6 A.M. 68°F in the shade. What a scorcher it is going to be! Health insurance payment—7,000 zlotys—is due today. And there is nothing in the coffers. As usual, we need 30,000 zlotys in addition.

In the morning the Community was visited by a German with a worker for whom he was demanding wages. The worker became incensed at my suggestion that perhaps he had been stirred up to come here. A section leader, who was present during this exchange, remarked that there was indeed considerable agitation against the Community.

Later, Mrs. Tempel, all tears, screams, and recriminations, said that I failed to do anything to help her husband and that he was sent away at 6 A.M. today. To calm her down I drove with her to the Gestapo and did my best to intervene. They knew nothing about the incident, but will investigate it. I returned to the Community offices to find the summonses to the *Finanz-Inspektion Warschau-Land* [Financial Inspection/Warsaw District] there. We drove with Zabludowski. Smetkala, who received us, made a scene about our doing nothing with the recalcitrant taxpayers.

Back in the Community offices the workers are milling around in anger; a segment of the Battalion went on strike. In the afternoon, at 5 P.M., I addressed a group of the section leaders. In the corridors the clamoring of the rebellious workers.

The representatives of the *Norddeutscher Lloyd* [German Shipping Corp.] arrived to discuss the registration procedure of the future emigrants.

On my return home a crack in the sofa. For the second time its leg collapsed.

*June 21, 1940*—At 6 in the morning, 66°F in the shade. Last night I was reading by turns the magnificent opus of Fabre, *Souvenirs entomologiques,* and the lackluster reminiscences of Wojciechowski. The latter [offers the] comment that among the Jews only the "child prodigy" Perl could be trusted. Unlike Perl, Mendelson would curiously keep on changing his convictions.[62]

The Commercial Bank was unable as yet to finalize the arrangements for the loan. It appears that they will be able to do so sometime next week. Guzik could not help either. I borrowed 8,000 zlotys from the [Jewish] Craftsmen's Association. All day long, workers with their armed protectors. A delegation from the hospital and the doctors, nurses, etc.—a stormy session with them.

I went to Kunze in the afternoon but he would not see me. Mrs. Zulkowski came out and said that I will receive a reply to my letters next week. To my query about the 300,000-zloty loan, she told me that our request had been turned down. More misery. I sat down while waiting in the hallway [of the police precinct] at Danilowiczowska Street. A civilian official who was passing by ordered me to stand up. Policemen and orderlies on the scene pointed out to me I should have told him who I was.

Balaban and Weisbert (the Judaic Library) summoned to Szuch Avenue in the matter of the Jewish books. Dr. Kuhn was also searching for Jewish books. Replete with glory I returned home at 4:30. Oppressively hot. From morning until dinner I only had a glass of tea.

The interventionists are probably being sent here by Halber and Co.

*June 22, 1940*—68°F at 6 A.M. in the shade in spite of rain. In the afternoon 79°F. Unbearable heat. In the Community offices there have been eight interventionists in the matter of the Battalion. Weichert and Jaszunski have just returned [from Kraków]. We must get the JSS going as soon as possible. Tens of thousands of Jews will be expelled from the Jewish quarter in Kraków. Four members of the presidium of the JSS must be elected from Warsaw (two from Kraków). I submitted a petition to the SS for the release of the 256 arrested in January (Jan. 18–25, 1940).

The *"Waffenstillstand* [Armistice] Germany-France" ([pending conclusion of] terms [with] Italy).

*June 23, 1940*—Morning, in the Community. Financial problems. The four nominations from Warsaw for the seven-member JSS

62. Feliks Perl and Stanislaw Mendelson were leaders in the Polish Socialist Party and theoreticians of socialism.

[council] in Kraków: Zabludowski, Weichert, Lawyer Wielikowski,[63] Jaszunski. The levy. Receipts average. A Jewish worker
came allegedly on behalf of M[ende]; a look at his identity papers
revealed that he was using an alias and a false address.

*June 24, 1940*—At 6 A.M. it is a scorching 70°F. Summoned for 9
in the morning by Leist, I was received by Braun, who informed me
that within three to four weeks they will have ready the *Selbstver-
waltung* [Self-Government] of the Jews. When I broached the
matter of the 100,000-zloty loan from the Commercial Bank he
responded that they would rather release 300,000 zlotys from the
Emigration Fund. I promptly hastened with a letter from the
Community Authority to Kulski. I am to report to Braun at 8
tomorrow morning. I discussed the matter of taxing real property
and industrial licenses. Leist mentioned in passing that he had read
the letter about the mistreatment of the Jews at work and that he
will take appropriate steps. With Braun I raised the problem of
collecting the taxes, and the dues from patients in the hospitals, etc.
  Balaban was ordered to requisition, with the assistance of a
Community functionary and two workers from the Labor Battalion,
our Judaica collections.
  Haendel went to see Fischer (the stuffed bird). Engineer Rinder-
mann (a German) forwarded a complaint to Schrempf about the
behavior of a sanitary detachment at Krochmalna Street. They
broke the front doors of cupboards and back walls, beating women
(wounds) who refused to bribe them, stealing silver spoons.

*June 25, 1940*—At 6 in the morning, 72°F in the shade. Cloudy
skies. Reported for an appointment with Braun, Leist's adjutant, at 8
o'clock, but he was not there. As a matter of fact nobody is working
today there because of the signing [7:15 P.M.] of the Franco-Italian
armistice agreement at the conclusion of which the Franco-German
agreement will be in force. The hostilities ended at 1:35 A.M. The
sentry instructed me before I entered the Blank Palace to take off
my hat *frühzeitig* [in advance].
  The usual worry in the Community. On top of everything the

63. Dr. Gustaw Wielikowski, author of a work on application of Kant's philosophy to
criminal law, published in Germany when he was a young man. In charge of JHK (Jewish
Relief Committee) in Warsaw. The JHK was operating arm of JSS. Wielikowski was named
to council, May 1941.

expellees from Kraków. Nine persons were placed in shelters. A crowded meeting with the house superintendents, etc. The matter of the bread ration cards has been discussed with the city administration. (Rozenstadt, Bart, Iwanko,[64] Jablonski, etc.). I have received a communication from Leist that the SS will not permit the use of the Emigration Fund for the purpose of paying the workers' wages. The letter was dated June 21, but yesterday, June 24, Braun instructed me to settle this matter with Kulski.

*June 26, 1940*—At 6 A.M. 70°F. Somewhat cloudy. Meager receipts in the Community. Schrempf was supposed to visit us. Fajnsztajn's endeavors at Krochmalna Street (Engineer Rinder-[mann])—our own Jewish sanitary detachment under German supervision. I could not get to see Braun. Mende demands that we take in two [more Battalion] section leaders and that we pay wages regularly. He will use these workers at Szuch Avenue.

*June 27, 1940*—63°F in the morning. It rained during the night. I had a telephone message from the Community that our offices have been surrounded by the police. On my arrival I found in the courtyard a dozen or so police from the *Ordnungspolizei* with a lieutenant and several sergeants. They are demanding money for the workers. My parley with them was interrupted by Brandt et al. who arrived for other business. I proceeded to attend to them and in the meantime the *O[rdnungs] P[olizei]* departed, leaving instructions for the money to be delivered to the O.P. in the Student Dormitory. Fifteen hundred zlotys were thereupon delivered there.

I went to Leist and when Braun telephoned Major Mayfeld [65] (?) in the O.P., the latter disclaimed any knowledge whatsoever of the incident. Then he [Braun] made another call, this time to the SS about the 300,000 zlotys, and ordered me to see Kunze. Kunze passed me on to an aide with whom I reviewed a number of different topics. In the meantime two Germans appeared from the Ursus [66] works remonstrating that they do not want "children" but adult workers and are prepared to pay 1 zloty per worker per day. It turns out that it was Berger (a section leader) who coaxed the

64. "Iwanko" - Aleksander Ivanka, Chief of Finance Department, Warsaw municipality. Czerniakow misspelled the name.
65. Mayfeld, probably Major Richard Maiwald, Police Regiment.
66. Ursus: a truck and tractor plant.

O[*rdnungs*] P[*olizei*] to seize the Community offices. Guzik, the Warsaw director of the JDC, was arrested yesterday.

*June 28, 1940*—In the morning 59°F. Cloudy skies. The community. The levy yields pennies. Incessant interventions. The prospects for the 300,000 poor. New junior official Heilmann.[67] Delegations again, with protectors.

In the morning intervening at the Gestapo about those arrested in January. I made a request for granting the prisoners a correspondence privilege that would not involve disclosure of the location of the camp. They want to fire all the Jewish apartment house administrators. The buildings are to be placed under the supervision of the KKO.[68]

*June 29, 1940*—After a storm at night, 63°F at 6 A.M. Yesterday more serious rumors about the ghetto. I must check them today. The financial condition of the Community—as if there were not enough to worry about. In the morning, at Danilowiczowska Street, Kunze sent me to H[eilmann]. I told his secretary Zulkowski about our predicament, asking her to pass this information to Kunze. A moment later she stepped out of the office and told me that 100 to 200,000 zlotys would be released today. In the middle of my meeting with Heilmann we were both summoned to Leist. Braun, who received us, announced that the sum of 300,000 had been released. I was told to submit to Kunze my plan for the payment of the back wages to the workers. At the same time he instructed me that the Jews must pay respect to the German military and civil service uniforms of all ranks by removing their hats. The Jewish women must bow their heads. I also touched upon some matters pertaining to the rabbinate and the schools. He sent me to Counselor Schmidt.

A vehicle was dispatched from Okecie to round up unwilling workers. Among the 150 that were caught today were some who possessed papers proving that they had paid their contributions to the Community.

Ganc[?] was summoned to the SS to explain why he is not wearing his armband. They also summoned his wife for Monday in the same matter.

67. Heilmann (Czerniakow also writes Heilman): see entry for July 4, 1940.
68. KKO: Municipal Savings Bank.

Jewish-owned buildings are to be taken over by the KKO. The rental income from these apartment houses is reputed to be 4 million zlotys a month. I am endeavoring to prevent the firing of the Jewish superintendents. All the Jewish employees at Gepner's were given notice. The municipality received a letter on the ghetto and is busy compiling data.[69]

*June 30, 1940*—At 6 o'clock in the morning it is 68°F in the shade. A clear sky. It is Sunday but, as usual, I proceed to the Community. I visited the cemeteries at Okopowa Street and in Praga. Zbytkower's tombstone has been badly damaged. A new grave of a mother and her seven children killed during the bombardment. The graves of the 53.[70]

The plan for the payment of the back wages for the Labor Battalion has now been prepared. Our indebtedness for July 1, 1940, amounts to 482,011 zl. including the workers' wages of 282,563 zl. The loan from the Emigration Fund account is 300,000 zl. We may even be able to extricate ourselves from this predicament provided, of course, that our minds are not overwhelmed by new ghetto schemes. I am afraid that unfortunately we will not be able to work in peace.

*July 1, 1940*—At night I tossed about in bed—the ghetto. In the morning 66°F. At Danilowiczowska Street I submitted to Heilmann my plan for the disbursement of the 300,000 zl., and I waited for quite a while to obtain an authorizing letter for the money, but did not get it. In the corridor I met Weichert, who immediately started to explain that I had been treating him unjustly in that I suspected him of disloyalty. He informed me that he was leaving for Kraków the next day and that his immediate assignment will involve touring the several communities with Heinrich for the purpose of organizing assistance committees. He is to meet with me before his departure. He himself is not counting on becoming chairman or even deputy-chairman. On the other hand, he asserts that Jaszunski lacks the proper qualifications for the job. Sztolcman was in Kraków and reported to Arlt on the expulsion of the Jews from Jewish enterprises.

69. According to J. Kulski, Acting Polish mayor under the Germans, the letter was sent by Leist to obtain data with a view to determining the boundaries of the ghetto.
70. A reference to the 53 victims of Nalewki Street.

The first victims of the obeisance decree reported in the Community; all of them were beaten up. The receipts today (July 1) somewhat improved. The hospital tax now makes it possible for us to pay the salaries. A plague of petitioners. One fellow pleads for a job (a legacy of Szoszkies) but it is easy to accommodate him since he wants to do manual labor. Lotte [71] sheds tears. The arrogant rich talk back, each and every one of them, trying to take advantage of my good will. Hordes of pleaders and the laziness of a university lecturer (the library).

I went to Mende to plead for Ganz[?]. He ordered me to obtain *Die Judenstadt von Lublin* [*The Jewish Quarter of Lublin*] by Balaban as he had not received it. In the meantime Balaban notified me that in addition to the copy he submitted, he owns more copies. Mende declared that the war would be over in a month and that we would all leave for Madagascar.[72] In this way the Zionist dream is to come true.

I ordered posters in the Community announcing the obeisance rule for all Jewish men and women.

*July 2, 1940*—At 6 A.M. it is 61°F. The temperature reached 68°F at 8 o'clock. I had a dream that I handed over my responsibilities to Mayzel. What a beautiful illusion. I went to see Avril. The tax office is demanding 10,000 zlotys from the Community for the 1934 taxes. I received a letter from Danilowiczowska Street about the 300,000. Mikulecki's red tape. We keep on receiving complaints from the Jews who have been beaten for not making obeisance. A conference with the Labor Battalion on the subject of the 300,000. In a meeting with Weichert before his departure to Krakow. I am insisting on Jaszunski for the chairmanship. Weichert himself will support Gepner and—in case Arlt will not agree— J[aszunski]. He keeps on assuring me of his loyalty.

*July 3, 1940*—6 A.M.—64°F., 8 o'clock 70°F. Dr. Typograf, Rubinstein, etc. have been arrested and tomorrow I will intervene on their behalf with the SS. The ghetto in many localities. The

71. Lotte was the owner of an apartment house, first mentioned December 7, 1939.
72. A reference to a recurrent German idea of transporting Polish and German Jews to Madagascar. The plan surfaced again, after the collapse of France, at the end of June. Madagascar Island was to be ceded to Germany as soon as England quit the war.
73. Eventually, Weichert became Chairman of the JSS; Jaszunski, Deputy Chairman.

receipts in our treasury somewhat improved. Today I received from the Bank the first 30,000 zlotys as a loan for the Coordinating Committee.

*July 4, 1940*—68°F. I presented a petition (a letter from the Jewish Council) to the SS for the release of doctors Typograf and Rubinstein, who have been employed in the Community clinics. I again referred to the matter of granting those arrested in January the privilege of correspondence without disclosure of their whereabouts. I tried city hall; unfortunately Kulski was arrested yesterday. I had a visit from Heilmann. This is a Pole who has been seconded by the municipality to Kunze where he oversees the section dealing with the finances of the Community. Today's receipts have been considerable. I withdrew the second 30,000 zlotys from the Discount Bank. The JDC sent me a letter about Guzik whom they consider indispensable in their organization. I am to plead with the authorities for his release on his own recognizance.

*July 5, 1940*—In the morning 68°F. Kraków is denying rumors about the ghetto. In Mińsk Mazowiecki [74] the ghetto is at hand—efforts to establish one in Kraków. Average receipts in the treasury.

*July 6, 1940*—6 A.M. 59°F—8 A.M. 64°F. Dizziness. At 10 in the morning in the *Arbeitsamt* [Labor Office] summoned on Battalion business. They received the files of the Jews registered for compulsory labor from Kraków. They claim that the Jews will take the place of the Germans and the Poles who have been drafted for work. *Regierungsdirektor* Hoffmann [75] comes from Dresden. His assistant's name is Kraft. He asked for some data on the [occupational] structure of the Jewish population, etc. A number of building administrators have come to the Community grumbling that Jewish-owned houses will be taken over and they will lose their jobs.

*July 7, 1940*—In the morning 63°F, later 70°F. Poor receipts. The authorities refused our request to release 123,000 zl. (from the Retirement Fund) in the BGK [Bank of National Economy], ordering payment of the pensions from unspecific sources instead.

74. A town in the Warsaw district.
75. Kurt Hoffmann, director of the Labor Division, Warsaw district administration. He was a ranking civil servant.

A delegation of building administrators. I am going [to intervene] in this matter, Guzik's, [76] etc. It is rumored that Kühn [77] will be taking over from Kulski.

The hospital is threatening a hunger strike, in spite of the fact that daily we pay 2–3,000 zlotys in salaries there. Those arrested on May 8 were released yesterday.

The English used force to capture [sic] part of the French navy (Oran).

I wanted to rest for a few hours yesterday or today at Otwock. For the last eleven months I have not had one day of rest, and nothing has changed today.

*July 8, 1940*—64°F (6 o'clock), 70°F (8). I go to see Güth in the morning (the criminal section of the *Devisenschutzkommando* [Currency Control Command]) about the affaire Guzik. He instructed me to return on Thursday, since by that time his assistant Zimmerman, who is in charge of the investigation, would be back.

In the Community a commotion due to the demands of the hospital (they are again threatening a hunger strike), orphanages at Wolska Street, etc. The crafts (their association) can't be bothered to supply the needed craftsmen; tailors, for instance, sit back looking on while the Community struggles, having to pay 70 tailors [a competitive wage of] 10 zlotys each day.

At 1 P.M. in the KKO on the matter of the Jewish-owned buildings. The municipal courts are in the process of sending letters about the registration of buildings. The individual owners are beginning to receive court orders to hand over their houses to the *Treuhänder* [trustees]. Many print shops, mainly Jewish ones, were closed today; the keys to the premises had to be surrendered. I receive a delegation and issue instructions for the drafting of a memo. The receipts for the Battalion are on the wane but the turnout is decidedly better.

Some time ago, according to the German newspapers, long before the defeat of France by Germany, Ironside [British General] was reputed to have remarked that German generals were too young. If he had indeed made this nonsensical statement he should

76. Guzik, of the JDC, was arrested for having accepted loans in US dollars from Polish Jews for relief purposes, with an understanding that the lenders would be repaid after the war.
77. Alfons Kühn, former Polish Minister of Transportation, was director of Warsaw Electric Department during the occupation.

be reminded that on June 14, 1800 (the Battle of Marengo) Napoleon Bonaparte was 31, Desaix 32, the young Kellermann 30, Marmont 26, Lannes 31, while Melas (the Austrian?) was 70. In the Battle of Austerlitz, Napoleon was 36, Bessières 37, Berthier 52, Bernadotte 42, Davout 35, Soult 36, Lannes 36, Murat 38, Mortier 37, Kutuzow was then 60.

At home in the afternoon, agony. I have to suffer in a stuffy little room which looks like a prison cell, while the rest of the apartment is used by my wife for receiving Community clients. Besides, all these Jewish complaints. They do not want to make payments to the Community, yet they keep demanding that I intervene on their behalf, be it in trivial private matters or in serious predicaments. And when my efforts fail, or result in delay, they blame me without end as if the outcome had depended on me. Often there are scenes. Gepner asked me today how I managed to retain self-control and remain calm. This is the product of my difficult childhood and the conditions of my parents' home. That is where I learned to suffer.

*July 9, 1940*—In the morning 73°F. Not a cloud in sight. Again we are heading for a scorcher over 86°F. My schedule for today still undetermined. In the morning at the SS on the matter of Typograf and the January people.[78] Later, the ghetto, etc. In the afternoon, guests—clients of the Community. The only distraction is provided by a woman who butchers the piano. The old hag weighs 240 lbs. She would choose of course *"La prière d'une vièrge"* [Prayer of a Virgin] by Bogdarzewska.

I can no longer write to J[as].

*July 10, 1940*—In the morning at the Community 70°F. It is cloudy, hot and sultry. I submitted the draft of the budget to Heilmann. Avril arrives with an aide and demands the budget draft and the labor charts. I saw Kulski in the matter of the Jewish-owned buildings. It turns out that in a number of buildings the trustees were already named.[79] The official debt collector by the name of Zaremba came to the janitor of an apartment building at Miodowa Street stating that the tenants must pay the rent to him and not to

78. In January, there were arrests in connection with the Kot affair. See diary entry for January 20.
79. Kulski asserted after the war that trustees were named by the Germans without the municipality's participation.

the owner and that the owner will receive 250 zlotys a month. In a block of ten houses, a rich lawyer, Antoni Jurkowski, has been named as trustee. The *Treuhandstelle* [Trusteeship Office] ordered the economic section of the municipal court to compile information on apartment houses. In turn this task was given to the public collector. The court is to name the trustee administrators from among the lawyers, judges, and other court officials. An item of news from Kraków that the administration of the dwellings will [eventually] be transferred to the Jewish Communities.

The receipts have been smaller, but not the expenditures.

*July 11, 1940*—In the morning 68°F. I went to intervene about Guzik. They permitted a meeting with the representatives of the JDC on current business in Güth's office.

In the Community a conference about exemptions for the poor from payment of the bread taxes. Very poor receipts today. Ten representatives have been dispatched to the recalcitrant citizens in the city about the payment of their contributions. A letter has arrived from the *Generalgouvernement (Abt[eilung] Treuhandstelle* [Trusteeship Division]) to the effect that the Community-owned building at 26 Grzybowska Street is being taken over by someone (signature unclear). It prohibits the collection of rent, announcing that after an investigation the landlord would be notified how much he will receive. The remainder must be paid into a *Sperrkonto* [blocked account]. Similar letters were received by a number of other landlords. I will see Leist about this tomorrow.

*July 12, 1940*—Although I had an appointment with Leist for 8 A.M., I found nobody there. I submitted a statement on the real property and on printing, lithography, and stereotype shops. A copy of the statement on real estate was sent to the SS.

I again broached the matter of the detention of Typograf, Rubinstein, Orzech,[80] etc., but so far no results. A talk with Guzik (Bornstein) was held today in the *Devisenschutzkommando.*

The Radom Community was reported to have taken over the administration of the Jewish-owned buildings there. At the Warsaw Community, a Polish attorney showed up as trustee.

A Jew, asked in prison why he was not wearing an armband,

---

80. M. Orzech, the leader of the Bund (Jewish Socialist Organization).

replied that—according to the regulations—one does not have to wear one at home and since he felt at home in prison he did not have to wear the armband.

It is a real sizzler today. In the afternoon, cloudy skies; then it rains at 73°F. Tomorrow I intend to leave Warsaw to go to Otwock for the first time in eleven months for a half-day.

*July 13, 1940*—Saturday—cloudy skies, 70°F, later 63°F. I am to leave at noon for Otwock for a rest until tomorrow morning.

It didn't work, I am biding my time at home.

*July 14, 1940*—55°F. It rains. In the Community a meeting about exemptions from the bread tax.

*July 15, 1940*—57°F. It has been raining all night and through the morning. A long line of people in front of the Community offices waiting to obtain exemptions from the bread tax. The taking over of the buildings postponed until Wednesday. On the same day I am to see Leist. Weichert. In the afternoon, a parley to prevail upon W[eichert] to behave. It ended with Weichert feeling affronted and walking out of the hall.

*July 16, 1940*——It drizzles, 61° F. At 8:30 off to the *Devisenschutzkommando* on the subject of Guzik. Unfortunately they refused to release him and I am to report again on this matter next week.

In front of the Community offices long lines of those asking exemptions from the bread tax. Forty thousand were given the exemption so far. At 1 P.M. we had to close the offices. Until yesterday, receipts for the 50,000 bread ration cards 100,000 zlotys, which is very little. Today there has been more activity. The deadline will be extended two days. It is rumored that there will be no ghetto in Minsk Mazowiecki. It seems that a meeting was held yesterday in Warsaw to reach a decision on the subject of the ghetto. The verdict—no ghetto.

The matter of the buildings postponed until August 15. A rumor that some of the Jewish houses would be administered by the KKO, some by the judges, and the remainder by another entity. Tomorrow I am going to see Leist about the houses, also the printing and lithographic shops, etc. Today two officers from the *Arbeitsamt*

[Labor Office] reviewed the question of compulsory labor and inspected our premises.

*July 17, 1940*—63°F. On my arrival at Leist's the meeting was postponed until Monday 10 A.M. Summoned to the SS to be told in response to my letter that out of the 260 arrested, January 16–25 of the current year, the fate of 113 has been checked. Of those, 37 are still alive.

*July 18, 1940*—In the morning 63°F. In the Community the families of those arrested in January storm my office. I agreed to receive a delegation of four people—I promised to have the details for them by Tuesday.

A meeting with Weichert and the rest of the delegation to Kraków. The bread ration cards brought 420,000 zlotys through yesterday. The distribution of the cards will continue through tomorrow.

*July 19, 1940*—63°F. Cloudy. [List of home addresses of Council officials]

1. Cajtlin Tauba — Sienna Street, 69
2. First Izrael — Okrag Street, 3-b/7
3. Fliderbaum Ignacy — Ceglana Street, 17
4. Goldfeil Norbert — Chmielna Street, 49/19
5. Horensztejn Szmul — Sienna Street, 44
6. Hazensprung Jozef — Grzybowska Street, 30
7. Halber Maurycy — Mila Street, 45/13
8. Lustberg Mieczyslaw — Wspolna Street, 5
9. Malamud Efroim — Rev. Mackiewicz Street, 3 m. 6
10. Milner Salomea — Ogrodowa Street, 5
11. Popower Izrael — Lubecki Street, 3/6
12. Seidman Hilel — Grzybowska Street, 22
13. Syrkis Dacha — Sosnowa Street, 8
14. Wasserman Pinkus — Zelazna Street, 101
15. Wortman Antoni Pawel — Leszno Street, 36

Hazensprung, Grzybowska Street 30/19

# *Notebook Four*

*July 20, 1940*—Today, at 7 in the morning, I gave myself a 24-hour holiday after all these months—I am leaving for Otwock. We are having beautiful weather; at 5 A.M. it is 61°F.

An inspection of the Brijus TB sanitarium and later of Zofiowka. I notice in Zofiowka the woman troublemaker who cost us 100,000 zlotys, adult lunatics and children. One child in a straitjacket to prevent self-injury, the face covered with flies. Another one is scratching wounds on his head. A female singer in bed executes some operatic arias: she used to perform in Italy. Other women by the piano were playing and singing; I joined them. Somebody built himself a tombstone in a cemetery with his name carved on it. It is to this address that he would direct his creditors.

*July 21, 1940*—After my return from Otwock I must notify the families of the arrested. Tomorrow is my appointment with Leist on the buildings.

All things considered, *man darf das Kreuz tragen aber nicht schleppen* [one may carry the cross, but not drag it].

*July 22, 1940*—Leist, who is said to be busy in conference with the *Treuhandaussenstelle* [Trusteeship Branch Office], will receive me tomorrow at 9. Ohlenbusch,[1] of the *Propaganda Abteilung* [Propaganda Division], ordered us to submit suitable materials for

1. *Oberregierungsrat* Wilhelm Ohlenbusch, director of the Propaganda Division in the Warsaw district, later director of Main Division Propaganda, *Generalgouvernement*.

the *Gazeta Żydowska* [*Jewish Gazette*] [2] to a certain Langier. Later on, Langier himself appeared with a prospectus of the gazette.

In our January tabulation Azriel Bojko is listed under A, and also under B. Here he is entered among the living, there among the dead. In light of this we have asked for another cross-check. A woman does not believe that her husband is dead because a for- tuneteller told her that he is alive. In the *Warschauer Zeitung*, No. 171, there was a report on university lecturer Dr. Seraphim's [3] peroration on the subject of the Jews. He writes [from the German]:

> Constructive solution required. One must thereby keep in mind the essential realization that, by itself, a restriction of Jewry is not sufficient. Rather, the limitation of Jewish influence and the isolation of Jewry must be replaced by a constructive solution through which these measures will be effectively supplemented.

*July 23, 1940*—63°F. Rain. I go to see Leist at 9 but am received by Braun. The matter of the Jewish-owned buildings must be referred to Kraków. Roughly speaking, the final outcome may approach our own suggestions. Franczke is being called to account. The lithographers and printers will not be hurt by an eight-day shutdown. Again there is a possibility of a loan of 300,000.

In the Community a delegation of the January women. The first issue of the *Jewish Gazette* came out today. I do not know why I just recalled, from childhood, a school of thieves at Ptasia Street.

*July 24, 1940*—79°F. The expulsion of all the Jews from Krakow has been decided.[4] Bersohn and Bauman [Children's Hospital], "Brijus," "Zofiowka" at the Community without means of support.

*July 25, 1940*—In the morning 61°F. A headache at night. The Community offices are besieged by a multitude eager to obtain bread ration cards. Today we have been distributing cards free of charge. Tomorrow and the day after tomorrow the deadlines for

2. *Gazeta Zydowska*, Polish-language newspaper for the Jewish population in the *Generalgouvernement*, published under German control. Publication stopped in July 1942.
3. Peter-Heinz Seraphim published a heavy volume on East European Jewry in 1939. Later on he was an *Oberkriegsverwaltungsrat* with the German Army in the Ukraine.
4. The Kraków expulsion order, providing for voluntary and involuntary phases, was published August 6.

this purpose. It appears that there may be a favorable resolution of the building issue.

*July 26, 1940—59°F.* Today, it seems that the issue of the buildings will be decided. I was told to await a reply. Throughout the city, there are more and more removals of house fixtures. I submitted a memorandum about the prohibition on the sale of books. Ujazdowski Park was placed out of bounds for the Jews.

*July 27, 1940—57°F.* A cool day. Business as usual.

*July 28, 1940—57°F.* Beautiful weather. At work. Lichtenbaum Jr. and Haendel are going to a party with caviar, smoked salmon, and brandy. A decree that the Jews are not allowed in Ujazdowski Park, as well as in a number of streets that have been posted to that effect. *Hexenschuss* [lumbago] in my shoulder.

*July 29, 1940—50°F.* I delivered our budget draft to Heilman, requesting a loan of 300,000. He is expecting a decision from Leist today about the buildings. I have been visited at home by a group of converts who are asking us not to send any more letters to their home addresses requesting contributions to the Community, etc. (they feel ashamed in the presence of their Aryan wives). A professional dancing school [5] in "Melody Palace": the only school apart from the nurses' school in the hospital. *Hexenschuss.*

*July 30, 1940—53°F.* At the Community in the morning. At 1:30 a very large meeting (at least 600 persons) of the building superintendents. We had barely recited our speeches, when Inspector Paemeler [6] from the *Arbeitsamt* [Labor Office] came and addressed the meeting, complaining that there were not enough workers reporting for the labor contingents and threatening that he would resort to sanctions if this state of affairs continued.

5. The dancing school was run by a Mrs. Regina Judt. Ringelblum states in his diary that she had been the mistress of a German officer when the German army occupied Warsaw during the First World War and that she exploited that relationship with the help of German military officers in the course of the Nazi occupation. According to Ringelblum, Germans (SS?) shot her on May 29, 1942. Czerniakow himself refers to her repeatedly in entries from 1940 to 1942.
6. "Paemeler" should be Peemöller, director of Jewish labor in the Labor Office, Warsaw.

At the SS I was informed that Dr. Zamenhof, his brothers-in-law, and Minc are dead.

I received a communication from Leist that an investigation has disproved complaints about mistreatment of the workers. In the future any false accusations will be punished.

*July 31, 1940*—54°F. A letter from Major Kamlah about a certain Judt.[7] The arrest of Mandelbaum, his wife, and two orderlies as a result of the house search at M's. Kraków will not expel all the Jews. Roma and her furniture.

*August 1, 1940*—55°F. We are petitioning for the movie theaters. We are extending the deadline for the registration of shop signs.[8] A discussion with Dr. Fraenkel in the Blank Palace on jurisdiction of the Community Chairman. We are asking for permission to have concerts in order to provide jobs for the musicians. The receipts for the Battalion, as well as the turnout for work, poor. My car was stopped at 4 P.M. at Krolewska Street and the chauffeur had to proceed on foot to get the travel authorization documents. For several days, fall weather. Tomorrow I will try to obtain information about the buildings.

*August 2, 1940*—54°F. Asked to the *Treuhandaussenstelle* [Trusteeship Branch Office] for Wednesday morning on the matter of the buildings. Ujazdowski Avenue closed to Jews. The Jewish residents there cannot go about their business. Endeavors to open it up as far as Pius Street. Out of 641,000 zlotys, our revenue from the bread tax, only 30,000 zlotys remain unspent.

The administrator of the Community building at Sliska Street demanded rent from the refugees. A session with the financial office at Danilowiczowska Street. The real estate taxes will be imposed for the benefit of the Community. Business enterprises will, it appears, pay a surtax of 50% as well.

On the steps of the Community Authority building, refugees from Kraków.

*August 3, 1940*—57°F. Cool. At 7:30 I go to work. The matter

7. Possibly Mrs. Judt, of the dancing school.
8. Store signs were taxed by the Community.

of buildings remains unclear. Tempel's situation not encouraging. The *Arbeitsamt* [Labor Office] will deal with the recalcitrant workers. According to some sources the Jews will be expelled from all the streets crossing Ujazdowski Avenue *(Lindenallee)*. In the provinces, directives for the handing over to various Polish men and women the shops with their inventories for a few zlotys.

*August 4, 1940*—64°F. In the morning at the Community. A meeting was scheduled to deal with the problem of the Kraków refugees. A lessening of tension has been reported and the conference was postponed until Tuesday. At 1:30 I left for Otwock for a few hours. At the "Brijus" sanitarium I met for the first time in my life a female veterinarian, Miss Neufeld. A lunatic who fled from Zofiowka was run over by a train and the police have brought in the corpse. By 8 o'clock I am back in Warsaw; a half-hour by car.

*August 5, 1940*—65°F. In the morning at the Community. A part of the shore area [adjoining the Vistula] is to be de-Jewed (Wiejska, Ksiazeca, Rozbrat Streets, etc.). In the afternoon a meeting on the ZSS.[9] (A memorandum to the authorities about the Community sharing in receipts from city taxes on streetcars, gas, electricity, and residence.) [10]

*August 6, 1940*—61°F. Leist refused to see me today in the matter of the buildings but instructed me to come the day after tomorrow. The *Treuhandaussenstelle* telephoned ordering me to appear tomorrow at 11:30. I went to the *Finanzabteilung* [Finance Division] about a loan for 300,000 zlotys. I also visited Kulski to inform him that I will take the necessary steps with the authorities for sharing in the charges for gas, electricity, etc. For tomorrow, I am summoned in the matter of Guzik. We did not receive the January list from the SS. It is supposed to be ready tomorrow.

*August 7, 1940*—61°F. Danilowiczowska Street. The 300,000 not settled. I called Gepner and Szereszewski for a discussion on reconstituting and reorganizing the JSS in Warsaw. Visit at 3 P.M. to Dr. Droessel.[11] He instructed me that claims to the *Treuhaender*

9. ZSS = JSS *(Jüdische Soziale Selbsthilfe)*
10. See subsequent letter by Czerniakow, dated January 8, 1941, in appendix.
11. Drössel: a trusteeship official.

[trustees] should be submitted to him directly together with a justification for each of the requested sums. Just before I was leaving, a Kazimierz Mahler, the *Treuhaender* for Braun and Rowinski, came to see Droessel. He accused me of not exempting his workers from service in the Labor Battalion or from [exemption] payments. I declared roundly that he should feel free to lodge a complaint in the *Arbeitsamt* [Labor Office].

In the afternoon a meeting in the Community about the orphanage at Wolska Street. I gave a speech and so did my wife.

Droessel refused to talk to me about buildings, sending me to Ballreich.[12]

*August 8, 1940*—61°F. Leist and Braun passed me on to Kulski today. Hoffmann from the *Arbeitsamt* [Labor Office] notified us that starting August 15 the authorities will pay the workers. On the other hand, a contingent of the Jews will be moved to a labor camp. This is what he learned in Kraków. In the afternoon a conference with JSS about the refugees from Kraków.

Schrempf agreed to the conversion of the quarantine shelter at Zlota Street into a staging center for the refugees. The same type of center will be organized in our school at Podchorazych Street. Today 333 persons were sent to Sliska Street, a few dozen to Jagiellonska Street. A settlement project on the Otwock line is being studied. I received a letter from Messing to the effect that the ZSS is to be considered part of the *Judenrat*.[13] He wants an organization chart.

*August 9, 1940*—59°F. Heilman, whom I visit in the morning, has no information whatever. His superior, [illegible], will not see me since he does not know whether Jewish affairs will come under his jurisdiction. I hastened to see Kulski. He was asked whether the 300,000 zlotys was paid into the Bank. A decree just published permits the Jews who live in the southern part of the city to exchange apartments for lodgings behind the walls. The refugees may only be accommodated in the ghetto. It is planned to expel the Jews from the shore areas [along the Vistula River]—Nowy Swiat,

---

12. Dr. Hans Ballreich, chief of Subdivision Trusteeship in the Economy Division of the Warsaw district.
13. Subordination of the ZSS (JSS) branch in Warsaw to the Jewish Council: A jurisdictional victory for Czerniakow.

Gornoslaska, Maczna, etc., streets. In the Community offices angry confrontations with the January families. They demand information about the fate of those arrested.

The *Arbeitsamt* [Labor Office] orders 600 workers for Wednesday and 600 for Friday to be transported to a labor camp. They must be fitted out by the Community. Several days ago the man in charge of the quarantine at Leszno Street discovered a radio in a cellar and made a report to the SS. I am summoned to the SS for 8 A.M. tomorrow about this.

A whole day of agony. On top of everything, the *Hexenschuss* [lumbago] in my neck and a headache.

*August 10, 1940*—57°F. Off to the Gestapo on the January matter, etc. Rozen and Zabludowski were supposed to inquire in the *Arbeitsamt* about living conditions in the camp and obtain a postponement of the project. In the Gestapo I was shown the January list. Rosenthal is to pick up a copy of it on Monday at 8:30 A.M. The *Arbeitsamt* continues to demand categorically the 600 workers for Wednesday and 600 for Friday. I am giving instructions for the collection of clothing.

In my last weekly report I described the impression made on Jews by the prohibition of the use of parks, etc. Today a reply arrived, dated August 9:

[Translated from the German]

On page 9, paragraph 11 of your activity report for July 26–August 1, 1940, you allow yourself to criticize the orders of SA Brigadier General Leist. May I call to your attention that any repetition of such conduct will be answered with severest measures. Dürrfeld.[14]

*August 11, 1940*—64°F. (5:30 A.M.) During the night I have been reading a book by Malicki, *Marshal Pilsudski and the Diet.* I was again reminded of the depravity of Mr. Staniszkis in connection with the commemorative plaque for Narutowicz.[15]

Several hundred persons volunteered for the labor camp. I or-

14. Ernst Dürrfeld, held rank of mayor. German city administration, Warsaw. As of January 1941, *Dezernent*, in charge of public utilities. Reported killed, August 1944.
15. Gabriel Narutowicz, president of Poland, assassinated by an artist on the ground that he was elected with the votes of the Jews and other minorities.

dered a collection of clothing and equipment for the workers. Too many people reported for work today. I inspected the cemetery at Okopowa Street. A conference with the ZSS about the organizations which have been dissolved by a plenary ordinance. Tomorrow I am to see Messing and Supinger. A reflection while at the cemetery: Will they leave us in peace here? My grandmother's tombstone was repaired. Instead of trees—acacias and weeds.

[From the German]

## ORDER

Subject: Jewish District

Based on # 10 of the Decree for the Administration of Polish Communities of November 18, 1939, the following order is issued for the city limits of Warsaw:

1. Jews moving into the city limits of Warsaw may take up residence only in that portion of the city which will be bounded by the surrounding wall.
2. Jews living in the Warsaw city district may change apartments only by moving into an area inside the surrounding wall.
3. Persons of non-Jewish ancestry may not establish residence inside the above mentioned closed off areas.
4. Owners and administrators of houses as well as those charged with registrations must observe this order when concluding new leases or executing registrations.
5. Violators of this order may be punished by fine or imprisonment. They may also be banned from the Warsaw city district. Compulsory police measures for the direct implementation of the conditions envisaged in this order will follow.

Warsaw, August 7, 1940

The Plenipotentiary of the District Chief
of the City of Warsaw

signed Leist

SA-Brigadier General

*August 12, 1940*—61°F. In the morning at Bo[l]lenbach's [16] and Kunze's about assistance to the JSS in Warsaw. Later with Heilmann about the JSS and the Council, the 300,000 zlotys, etc. The matter of the 4% [property taxes] on the buildings—a reservation by the *Finanzinspekteur* [Inspector of Finance], Warsaw II.

I learned that more than a dozen streets will be closed to the Jews.[17] Luckily [only] about 1,800 Jews live there. At 2 a mass meeting at the Community. Paemeler [Peemöller] arrived and spoke about the labor camp, adding that his own son and daughter were at such a camp. There are about 500 volunteers. They will be leaving on Wednesday. I received the list of the Januarians. Now I must tell their families. One hundred fifty-eight persons are dead out of 260. Tomorrow is *Tishe B'Av*.[18]

*August 13, 1940*—64°F. Cloudy skies. Permission has been granted to borrow the 300,000. The departure of the 600 workers has been postponed until Friday. Some of those called up by the *Arbeitsamt* have not reported. The same is true of some of the volunteers. The workers are to be sent to a staging area from where they might even be dispersed. At 3 P.M. there was a visit by Supinger. I raised the subjects of the buildings, vocational courses, movie theaters, parks, etc. He replied that they are looking for a park for the Jews. Krasinski Garden is not to be considered. They will permit some vocational courses. As for the buildings, they are under the *Treuhandstelle* [Trusteeship Office].

*August 14, 1940*—57°F. At 7:30 a visit from two women inquiring about their husbands who were, it appears, sent away. We have not yet received permission for the mailing of such information to the families. A visit in the Community by Heilman who reviewed the revisions to the tax ordinance. Out of the 300,000 I will have to allocate 100,000 for the JSS. The collection for the workers is already bringing results. A scene with Mrs. Rozanski. In the

16. "Bolenbach" = Heinrich Bollenbach, in the Interior Division of German city administration.
17. Twenty-seven streets were placed on prohibited list on August 14. Cf. August 19.
18. *Tishe B'Av*: The ninth day of the month of Av in the Hebrew calendar, a day of commemoration of the two occasions in antiquity when the Jewish temple in Jerusalem was destroyed.

afternoon a conference on the subject of the JHK.[19] Filled with glory I return home at 9 in the evening.

*August 15, 1940*—54°F. Leist did not give me the power to represent the Community in the courts. A refusal of our request to place Kraków refugees in the Community's home in Jarosław. Granted permission to obtain a 300,000-zloty loan for the Community and the JSS. A functionary showed up and beat up Goldfeil and Aronson for the nonpayment of wages. At 4 P.M. to the Gestapo to discuss Typograf and Rubinstein as well as the January list. Rosenthal, who accompanied me, was taken to task by M[ende] for admonishing [him].

*August 16, 1940*—59°F. To the Community. In the city, requisitioning of house fixtures on the basis of the *Generalgouvernement* decree signed by Dr. Hartmann. Today we received permission to notify the families of the January victims about the fate of their nearest relatives. Twenty orderlies,[20] in twos, to those whose relatives are dead. Those whose relatives are alive were also informed. All of this by word of mouth.

Today at 9 P.M. I am watching with Paemeler and our own Councilor Zabludowski the departure of the first contingent to the labor camp. It is not known whether they might be dispersed from the *Verteilungsstelle* [staging area]. We gave them cigarettes, shirts, boots, etc. Alas, there was not much to give!

*August 17, 1940*—At 7 in the morning I depart for Otwock to "Brijus." At 9 the wife of a certain Dr. Rubinstein came pleading with me to intervene again on behalf of her husband. At "Zofiowka" they informed me about the death of one of their patients, an old Jew, "the King of England." Another who "has black candles inside his body" tried to accost me but I managed to get away from him, claiming that I was not the Chairman.

19. JHK = *Jüdisches Hilfskomitee* (Jewish Relief Committee).
20. During the summer, the Council had about 100 orderlies, used mainly to escort labor columns. The orderlies were forerunners of the Order Service (Jewish ghetto police). See entry for September 20, 1940.

*August 18, 1940*—In the morning return to the Community. Yesterday and today our offices beseiged by 80% of the families [21] who have just been notified, demanding further information; among others Mrs. Zamenhof and Mrs. Minc. The authorities granted us permission to conduct some vocational courses. In the city Jews are being thrown out from their homes at Koszykowa and Marszalkowska Streets. They must leave their belongings behind. The transport which left on August 16 was composed of 57 [workers] from the town of Mińsk Mazowiecki, 23 from Mińsk county, 24 from Grójec and Warka, 27 from Piaseczno, 35 from Skierniewice, and 435 from Warsaw. One worker who tried to escape from the collection point at Kaweczynska Street was apprehended, and handed over by the *Arbeitsamt* to the SS. Fourteen workers escaped from the Piaseczno group. Those from the provinces were examined by the Battalion doctors who issued many exemptions. In the group of 435 from Warsaw, 360 were volunteers. Their equipment appallingly poor.

A complaint by Miss Knaster ("A la Fourchette"). In Bacelona [?] a Mrs. Block (née Datyner) died in a hospital. Zabludowski was not permitted to leave.

*August 19, 1940*—59°F. Cloudy skies. Shooting pains in my bones. In the Community a report that the German quarter in Warsaw has been enlarged. This area is bordered by the left side of Marszalkowska Street (starting at Krolewska Street) and the Vistula River. About 20,000 Jews are living in this area. In addition, Jews are being expelled [in] another area.

Wasserman, a Community official, was beaten up in the streetcar in Praga. Some rabbis dashed in today fear-stricken by a rumored "pogrom." Then Mrs. Rubinstein rushed in imploring me again to intervene with the SS. I went to the SS at 3 P.M. and was told that they would call the *Ordnungspolizei* [Order Police] to send some patrols to Praga. They also informed me that Rubinstein was alive but would not be released at this time.

In view of the tendency toward reducing the area of the ghetto, small as it is, we asked the German authorities for clarification.

[From the German]
Interpretation of the Order of the Plenipotentiary of the District

---

21. Families were relatives of dead hostages.

Chief for the City of Warsaw of August 7, 1940, with regard to the Jewish District

1. The designation "portion of the city which will be bounded by the surrounding wall" (closed-off area) noted in the above-mentioned order is to be understood as the city segment of Warsaw bordered by the following streets:
   Marszalkowska Street
   Chmielna Street
   Srebrna Street
   Towarowa Street
   Okopowa Street
   Mlocinska Street
   Blonska Street
   Dzika Street
   Stawki Street
   Zoliborska Street
   Bonifraterska Street
   Konwiktorska Street
   Zakroczymska Street
   Wojtowska Street
   Rybaki Street
   Brzozowa Street
   Celna Street
   Stare Miasto [Market Square]
   Swietojanska Street
   Zamkowy Square
   Senatorska Street
   Miodowa Street
   Krasinski Square
   Swietojerska Street
   Nalewki Street
   Nowolipki Street
   Przejazd Street
   Dluga Street
   Hipoteczna Street
   Teatralny Square
   Senatorska Street
   Bankowy Square
   Saski Garden

as well as the planned street which is to traverse Saski Garden from Bankowy Square to Marszalkowska Street.

2. All buildings, abutting the closed-off area from inside the boundary on the enumerated streets and intersections, belong to this area.

3. All buildings located within the area described in Paragraph 1 and all those referred to in Paragraph 2 may be occupied by newly arrived Jews who are to be registered there accordingly.

Warsaw, August 1940.


The father of the singer Mrs. Szereszewski collapsed and died at Koszykowa Street while they were vacating their apartment.

Kaminer has no greater worry than to bring in a consignment of crab apples from the provinces for the holidays. I named the vocational education commission to organize some courses.


*August 20, 1940*—57°F. Cloudy, drizzling. A report from Teatralny Square [Polish municipality] about the new district—there is less of a rush. Intervention concerning furniture and other movables in the houses outside this district. Plans of the (enlarged) Jewish district were approved and signed. Only Jews will be allowed to live in the odd-numbered houses on Marszalkowska Street up to the main railroad station. A document prohibiting the requisitioning of the machinery in the vocational school. One thousand Jews every week for the labor camps.


*August 21, 1940*—48°F. The Community. A postcard from a worker in Lublin to his parents, full of despair. A telephone call from the Lublin Council that the workers who arrived from Warsaw have nothing to eat. I promised to send 3,000 zlotys for food in three days. The *Arbeitsamt* has been informed and that is going to do no good. I am dispatching Zabludowski to Lublin.

We have taken the map of the Jewish district to City Hall. Registrations in accordance with the new rules will start on Monday. I paid a visit to Stawki Street. In the course of three days we have started our vocational courses.


*August 22, 1940*—57°F. In the morning at the Community a collection for the workers in the labor camp—one lady offered a brassière. One "Abramek" arrived with . . . a soldier. Abramek, who was thrown out of the Battalion, brought a letter from the *Hauptmann* [Captain] that he is indispensable. I refused and sent Signer [22] with an explanation. Zabludowski has left for Lublin on the matter of the camp. In the afternoon a telegram from Lublin, from an inspector *(Arbeitsamt?)* demanding the delivery of cups, blankets, etc., for the 500 workers. A meeting about vocational education. For the time being we are organizing courses for 300 students. It appears that some janitors, domestic servants, etc., in houses at the very edge of the walled-up district have petitioned the authorities for the expulsion of the Jews from those buildings. In the Chamber of Industry and Commerce one Glinicki proposed that the authorities be requested to eliminate the Jews from the street-vending trade.

*August 23, 1940*—48°F. Two representatives (Inspector Holzheimer) of the labor camp appeared in the Community offices reporting that our workers are in Józefow near Lublin, that they have a place to sleep and a canteen. He wanted from us, in accordance with his telegram, supplies for 500 workers. He remarked that we should not have given any money to the Lublin *Judenrat* as they clamor for money from wherever they can get it. He informed us that the workers are paid 1.50, 2, 2.50 depending on their productivity—land reclamation work. He invited several members of the Council to see the camp. There will be a conference with Paemeler at 3 P.M. on equipping the workers. We are successful in supplying 700 people for a transport today.

*August 24, 1940*—50°F. In the morning at the Community. At noon to Grochów [23]—shown a new stable. They have two horses and a borrowed cow. Bo[l]lenbach visited them several times and fell in love with his work. He tells them that he would give up everything and move in with them. He also promised that he would provide them with some cows by ordering . . . me to supply them. I then expressed my thanks to the hosts for this opportunity of making a journey from Egypt to Palestine. We were given sandwiches and borscht with potatoes.

A fellow in the process of requisitioning furniture from my

22. Signer, Jewish Council labor official.
23. Grochów: location of *Hechalutz* (young Zionists) farm.

friends remarked that he was sorry there was no encyclopedia *(Meyers Lexikon)*. I just received as gift from the Community an antique chair with an inscription *nec temere ne timide* [neither rashly nor timorously]. A Jew waiting in line, pressed by a streetcar conductor for the *Entlausungsschein* [Delousing Certificate], asked the conductor what business it was of his. Came the reply: it is my business because I make a zloty this way. Professor Centnerszwer [24] came to Grochów on foot. He cannot afford the streetcar fare.

*August 25, 1940*—48°F. In the morning at the Community. Someone asked me, what was my chairmanship all about? I replied that it made me lose my paunch.

Zabludowski is back. Our workers are in a camp at Bełżec [25] a long way from Lublin. The camp is not under the control of the *Arbeitsamt.* Whether they are paid is not known. We are sending four doctors there with instruments and drugs. According to Zabludowski, when our men return from work, they may not be in the worst of moods.

*August 26, 1940*—52°F. A message that 20,000 Jews from Warsaw will be sent to the camps. I had a conference with the Labor Battalion Commission and issued orders for this commission to continue permanently. Signer learned from the *Arbeitsamt* that recalcitrants will be handed over to the SS. Our effort to assemble 700 persons for tomorrow is not going well. Tomorrow morning we will dispatch orderlies to their homes.

*August 27, 1940*—59°F. In the morning at the Community. Not too many workers for the camp. At the start of the day about 300, and 700 are needed. Summonses are being sent to home addresses. We find it impossible to persuade any doctors to go. In the end we had 519 persons, including 470 from Warsaw. More than ten were taken off the street. One individual reported to take the place of his brother—both were taken. We must supply the remaining 180

24. Mieczyslaw Centnerszwer (1874–1944) was a professor of physical chemistry, Warsaw University.
25. The Bełżec labor camp in the Lublin district should not be confused with the Belzec death camp established in that area in March 1942. The labor camp, a large one, was set up for the construction of a defense line facing the USSR. The project was directed by the SS and police.

workers by Friday. Naftek bought back his bedroom furniture and a grand piano sold a long time ago.

*August 28, 1940*—Morning at the Community. The expulsion of the Jews from their homes goes on; they are losing all their belongings. Today Mosin was moved out, Glazer must hand over even his cologne and soap. In the afternoon a conference about organizing the JHK. A telephone call from Tomaszow Lub[elski] about Bełżec. Difficulties with provisioning, etc.

*August 29, 1940*—In the morning at the Bruehl Palace—three teller windows for (1) *Reichsdeutsche* [German citizens], *Volksdeutsche* [Ethnic Germans], (2) Poles, (3) Jews. I was waiting for Schubert [26] in the matter of the railroad passes for the Community.[27] All in vain because of an important conference.

Rumors about the ghetto on the outskirts of Warsaw, surrounded with barbed wire. Word from the Bełżec camp: poor food, etc. I arranged for two conferences, one with the participation of Neustadt. I authorized the *Obmann* [Chairman] from Zamość to engage doctors at our expense for Bełżec. Tomorrow I will try to obtain a loan for the camp.

It seems that Rumkowski [28] in Lódź issued his own currency "Chaimki." He has been nicknamed "Chaim the Terrible."

*August 30, 1940*—50°F. In the morning at *Zollfahnd[ungs]stelle* [Customs Investigation Office]. Guzik will not be released. Later in the SS on the matter of some craftsmen and complaints against me. In the afternoon with Paemeler, who read the *Erlass* [decree] from Kraków concerning workers in labor camps. I countered with a letter from one of our workers and furnished him with a copy.

A child Z. was given a little desk to cheer him up. He liked it and was quite elated but before the day was over his toy was taken from him.

*August 31, 1940*—52°F. It rains. *Hexenschuss* [lumbago]. A discussion with Heilmann on the topic of the finances of the Commu-

---

26. Schubert: German official, probably in Interior Division of the Warsaw district.
27. As of January 20, 1941, Jews could no longer use the rails without special permission.
28. Chaim Rumkowski was chairman of the Jewish Council in Lódź.

nity and the JSS. He claims that the [proposed] 4% real property tax and the tax from business licenses are not legal. Instead he suggests an [income] tax to apply to 20,000 people. I retorted that the law does not provide for the expense of the Community, either. An income tax would reduce revenues. We agreed that I would prepare an analytical evaluation of the issue.

A telephone call from the SS that some tourists will visit the Synagogue. I held a meeting on the subject of the camps. A money collection for the camps is in progress. Yesterday's contributions were 30,000 zlotys; today's also 30,000. Rapaport, the biologist—laughing in the face of death.

*September 1, 1940*—46°F. Morning to the Community. A story was being told about one Rapaport who burst into laughter just before he died.

In the Community the weeping of mothers. I gave instructions for the collection to begin tomorrow. About 70 persons will solicit assistance in the city. I will donate 500 blankets and 500 shirts from the quarantine shelters. I will purchase bowls, cups, and spoons. The guidelines: (1) married men to be exempted; (2) rabbis, the intelligentsia; those employed in their occupations with workshop licenses, work certificates, and health insurance cards; *chalutzim* in Grochow; (3) ransoms [exemption tax contributors]; (4) a commission to process applications for deferment; (5) a commission to regulate ransom procedure.

Today Saski Square was renamed.[29] Aryans are either vertical or horizontal.[30] The horizontal ones were carried to their baptism while the vertical ones are walking by themselves.

*September 2, 1940*—46°F. Morning at the Community. Later in Brühl Palace where Schubert (in the presence of Lustberg and one Wundheiler)[31] suggested that the Community itself issue the railroad passes. On the same occasion a discussion of the labor camp, Jewish-owned buildings, their administrators, the Labor Battalion, the Community finances, JSS. Schubert announced that he would invite me and the JSS (Weichert) for a conference with Kunze. I

29. Saski Square was renamed Adolf Hitler Square. It was barred to Jews.
30. "Vertical Aryans," adult converts to Christianity, actually "non-Aryan" by German definition, inasmuch as they were Jews by descent.
31. Dr. Aleksander Wundheiler was to head the Trade and Industry Division in the ghetto.

received a pass for Fuerstenberg [32] and Faust [33] who are going to Tomaszów and perhaps to Bełżec with Zabludowski. I am sending some blankets, shirts, bowls, cups, and spoons, etc. The news from the camps is dismal. In the afternoon I was summoned to report at the governor's house at 13 Szopen Street at 10. A house superintendent declared that the Jews will be expelled from Barbara Street.

*September 3, 1940*—54°F. Morning at the Community offices. At Kaweczynska Street there were hardly any workers. Paemeler deferred the transport of 1,000 workers until Friday. I went to Szopen Street and saw ... the *Oberscharfuehrer* [Sergeant] (*Schlosshauptmann* [captain of the castle]). He wants to fire Signer. I set his mind at ease. He also demanded 14 workers that would be paid, plus 200 workers, 50 women, and 35 skilled laborers to work for him without any cost to his office. In addition he came up with some other demands.

I went to Bo[l]lenbach. He will approve the lottery but wants more information. I submitted the bylaws of the JHK. Stopped at Heilmann's to deliver our legal brief on the subject of the 4% [property] tax. I went on to K. in the matter of the Jewish residential area. It appears that the project of the Jewish quarter has been abandoned. On the other hand, the ghetto issue is receiving serious consideration (Pelcowizna, Praga, perhaps existing *Sperrgebiet* [area prohibited to German soldiers]). A visit from Pressdorf who called for a report on the immigrants from Kraków, our collection, etc.

Zabludowski, Faust, and Fuerstenberg left for Lublin with the gifts for the workers, including 10,000 zlotys for the camp. Lambrecht [34] made a demand for 20 doctors for the camps.

*September 4, 1940*—48°F. In the morning at the Community. A commotion from droshky drivers whose concessions have been withdrawn. I submitted a request in this matter recently—they are impatient. In response to yesterday's Gestapo call a letter was submitted on the camps, etc.

---

32. Jurek Fürstenberg, son of a Jewish manufacturer, became an officer in the Jewish ghetto police (Order Service). Assassinated by Jewish underground in 1943.
33. Faust, ORT (Organization for Rehabilitation and Training) official, from Lódź.
34. Dr. Lambrecht (occasionally misspelled "Lamprecht") was chief, Subdivision Health, in the Interior Division of the German district administration, Warsaw.

The workers released from Jozefow told us their story. We are sending a delegation to Jozefow with money and equipment.

Because of conflicting attitudes between the *Arbeitsamt* and another authority, the problem of providing workers has become more complicated. Detainees now take the place of the workers.

*September 5, 1940*—61°F. In the morning at the Gestapo in regard to the workers from the Battalion and those arrested yesterday at Unia Square. According to M[ende] they have not been arrested but merely impressed for labor. They have been confined at Zielna Street since there is no other place to hold them. The whole business will take about two months. I told B[ollenbach] that the families of the craftsmen working for the SS will be looked after by Public Assistance (JSS).

Rumkowski of Lódź visited me at the Community in the company of an SS man and the chief of the *Ernaehrungsamt* [Food Office]. He boasted that in Lódź he has an assortment of ministries and a budget of MK [*Reichsmark*] 1,500,000. Asked why our letters do not reach him, he answered that this matter would be settled soon.

In Otwock, yesterday, nobody reported for the labor camp. Several persons shot.

*September 6, 1940*—48°F. At 8 o'clock I went to see Paemeler and his superior Boerner on the subject of conditions in the labor camps. Today we are required to supply 1,000 workers. Only a few have in fact reported. We were told by the authorities that unless we have numerous volunteers on Tuesday severe sanctions would be imposed. I reviewed the matter of Public Assistance and the wage rates for craftsmen working at Szuch Avenue. Just then a delegation arrived with the news that 25 had been arrested and the rest dismissed from work. The 25 will be working during the day. Our cart is being pulled by two horses; we are trying to obtain a truck for Józefów for tommorrow.

*September 7, 1940*—54°F. In the morning at the SS on the matter of the 25 craftsmen. They promised to take care of this problem. In the meantime they will continue to work in Pawiak [prison] where the equipment has been transferred. An item in the papers: [King] Carol [of Roumania] has abdicated and was escorted to the Swiss border by Marshall Antonescu. Luck is necessary for whatever one wants to do. Why is there no Iron Guard [35] in the Community to escort me to Switzerland?

Some officer telephoned from Bruehl Palace complaining that Jewish workers stole some of his money and demanding restitution by the Community. We paid. Yesterday 650 workers (including 250 from Warsaw) left for a camp. In the middle of the night the Polish police was pulling the recalcitrants out of their homes.

According to Leist's announcement the Jews are forbidden to cross Adolf Hitler Square. The curfew [for Poles] was changed from 10 to 9 P.M. (It has always been 9 for the Jews.)

A visit by a man in uniform demanding 300 zlotys for workers. Aronson beaten up. He was asking for me. Akselrad had his beds and linens taken away along with everything else.

*September 8, 1940*—54°F. A meeting of representatives of the Communities [in the Warsaw District], the JDC [American Joint Distribution Committee], and the JSS on assistance to [labor] camps, followed by a meeting at the Community (hundreds of people) on the camps.[36]

*September 9, 1940*—59°F. Rain and thunder. Because of the good possibility that the ghetto may be located in part of Grochów or in an area around Wola, I am preparing a memorandum. Wola [itself] has 32,335 inhabitants in 9,821 rooms, Koło (XIX Police Precinct) 13,523 in 4,000 rooms. [For the combined room capacity] 400,000 Jews = 30 persons per room. Grochów has 39,000 inhabitants and 17,000 rooms. Here 400,000 would result in 25 per room.

In the *Gazeta Zydowska* [*Jewish Gazette*] an attack on the Community Authority (bread ration cards, etc.).[37] The vengeance of a certain Langier. Three hundred and ten persons reported for transport to Hrubieszow camp. I sent Goldfeil to their assembly

---

35. The Iron Guard was a right-wing paramilitary formation in Roumania.

36. At the meeting, Zabludowski announced that there would be no German wages for camp labor, but that the Germans would supply the laborers with food, clothing, shelter, and medical services. According to a German army report on the Bełżec labor camp, September 23, 1940, meals consisted of bread, coffee, potatoes, and occasional morsels of meat (no fats, fruits, vegetables). There was widespread dysentery. Clothing was not issued; the workers were human figures in rags. Work was scheduled for seven days a week and there was no opportunity to wash. The men slept crowded on the hard floor. For medical care, they were dependent on Jewish doctors and "sanitation" men.

37. The article in the *Gazeta Zydowska*, September 10, 1940, charged the Council with failure to meet Jewish needs and specifically with taxing bread for the first time in Jewish history.

point with bread, etc. The receipts from the bread cards today only 700 zlotys instead of 70,000 zlotys. The city is admonishing us. Only one doctor has volunteered for the camp, and it appears that unfortunately he came from a public clinic.

*September 10, 1940*—57°F. Before 9 to Supinger. A note on the subject of housing conditions and size of population in Grochów and Wola. A visit from Potsdorf.[38] The *Gazeta Zydowska*. In the afternoon at the SS on the address register of the Jewish residents. Thereafter a meeting about vocational education and labor camps.

*September 12, 1940*—48°F. It rains. In the morning at the *Arbeitsamt* about the conditions in the camps. I am to go to Kraków *(Regierungsdirektor* [Government Director] Hoffmann and Boerner?). He warned that in case we fail to meet the labor camp quotas, people will be dealt with by the *Sondergericht* [Special Court].

At the Community. A telephone call from Lublin that they gave Fuerstenberg 6,000 zlotys for the camp. Fuerstenberg himself reports that he is spending 1,500 zlotys a day. He has visited the camps with the exception of Cieszanów—where there is no food—the conditions everywhere unsanitary.

Zukier returned from Józefów. Conditions in this camp are bad. He brought with him five sick workers (one typhus case). In every camp they desperately demand pants, used boots, shirts, and drugs. In the afternoon I am visited at home by the police with Zibkow. Questions about the *Obmann* [Chairman] of Pruszków Czernecki and his alleged cache of forbidden goods.

*September 13, 1940*—48°F. Rinde was stopped on the street and had to exchange overcoats with one of those apprehended. At Zlota Street Jews are being expelled from their homes. At Sienkiewicz Street, the poverty-stricken tailor Lasocki was thrown out from his tiny apartment. He had previously given his sewing machine for safekeeping to a carpenter Bednarski. B[ednarski] now claims that the machine was stolen during the night! Lasocki was in tears. Our camp contingent will not leave today. There are only 200 people.

Langier lodged a complaint with the *Abt[eilung]* *Volksaufklärung*

38. Potsdorf: possibly Pressdorf. See entries for November 18, 21, 1940, and December 4, 1940.

*u. Propaganda* [Division for Public Enlightenment and Propaganda] that we are not giving him the current materials for the *Gazeta Zydowska*. I received written instructions to submit such information to him regularly.

It appears that Fischer, Handke, Schubert, Supinger, and Lambrecht left for Łódź.[39] Could it have anything to do with the recent visit of Rumkowski to Warsaw?

*September 14, 1940*—48°F. In the morning at the Community. As of yesterday, the bread cards yielded 230,000 zlotys in all. Today is the last day. A talk with Ohlenbusch about one Langier of *Gazeta Zydowska* who preferred charges against me. Biberstein has been arrested. The project of the ghetto outside Warsaw has been abandoned. In its place the *Sperrgebiet.* A letter from the labor camp: I am all right and it serves me right.

*September 15, 1940*—48°F. Feverish at night. A delegation from the *Gazeta Zydowska* at the Community with apologies. I showed Langier the door. I lay down the law that in the future he should contact the statistical section and no one else.

In the garden Roma declaims: "Come to me Pericles, your pants are torn."

*September 16, 1940*—48°F. The installation of the JHK at Messing's in the presence of a delegate from city hall. Car taken away. Must buy a new one. The Falenty [estate] is to be liquidated. We have supplied a hundred blankets. I sent delegates to Biała Podlaska and Józefów. I remarked to Messing that because of a scarcity of means, *"die Lage JHK ist glänzend aber hoffnungslos"* [the situation at JHK is splendid but hopeless]. A lady in the Education Office summoned me through a secretary to appear after the first of the month. Kunze informed me that Kraków did not settle anything.

Korczak tells me he is spreading rumors about himself that he is a thief. He believes that this way he might be appointed to the management of a certain orphanage. He happened to ask Wedel [40] to sell him 120 lbs of grain. When Wedel indicated that sales to Jews were forbidden, Korczak replies that there was a way out: Let us have it as a gift.

39. The Łódź ghetto at this point had already been in existence for several months.
40. Wedel: a chocolate maker.

*September 17, 1940*—45°F. In the morning at the Community. At Kaweczynska Street 318 workers. At 3 p.m. Supinger inspected our schools at Grzybowska Street and in Stawki Street. During the visit in our offices Mende appeared with two Jews, etc. Jews were forging receipts for assistance to labor camps. Tomorrow I am to report at 8:30 in the morning to [Szuch] Avenue in this matter. Sup[inger] about the planned ghetto. The acceptance of applications to the camp has been halted.

*September 18, 1940*—57°F. In the morning at the SS in the matter of the two scoundrels. They were collecting money for the camps and the "police." I demonstrated that it is within my authority to organize collections. I was instructed to submit written reports on the meetings in the Community Authority.

There has been a deluge of reports about confiscations of homes and furniture. Today Dr. B. was thrown out in a matter of minutes. A clarification that the Jews in the *Sperrgebiet* are not to be expelled and that I must report every case to the contrary.

I received a delegation from several school organizations demanding schools with different languages of instruction. I paid 6,000 zlotys for the car; this was the amount Becher asked, in the name of the authorities, for the municipality.

*September 19, 1940*—57°F. In the morning with Heilmann. No news from Kraków except that it may be possible for us to sell the securities owned by Jewish institutions for the benefit of the JSS.

In the afternoon with Paemeler. Because of the poor showing in meeting the camp quotas the *Arbeitsamt* took the position that the recalcitrants must be handed over to the *Sondergericht* [Special Court]. I read the excerpts from Fuerstenberg's report. *(Nota bene* F[uerstenberg] claims that the Jews themselves are to a considerable extent responsible for the conditions in the camps.) Jewish camp councils trade in parcels which arrive for the workers. They have pushed the price of bread for these parcels to 6, 7, and 12 zlotys per kilogram. The provincial *Judenraty* [Jewish Councils] are compounding the chaos. Today I am dispatching an inspector to the camp in Cieszanow.

A woman official from the Community was caught today on the street. After it was ascertained that she was Jewish they let her go. The *Arbeitsamt* decided to post the proclamation about compulsory labor. Dr. D [illegible] asked Sztolcman whether rumors which have been circulated about me are true. I am supposed to have committed suicide after being asked to sign some 15, 16, 18 point document. The Truskier [41] family has been thrown out of its home.

*September 20, 1940*—In the morning at the Community I was notified to see Leist. During the conference L[eist] introduced me to some senior District officials. He declared that the workers from the Battalion must not pass through the Avenue and Square on the way to their assignments.[42] Later the officials suggested the creation of a unit of orderlies 3,000 strong. L[eist] retorted that the entire Polish [city] police has 3,000; thus 1,000 would be enough for us. He added that we were going to receive *Selbstaendige Autonomie* [independent autonomy (sic)]. The official then asked why we were continuing to use our Grzybowska Street headquarters, and whether we would not find Elektoralna or, possibly, Leszno Street more convenient. All of which would seem to suggest the open ghetto within the borders of the *Sperrgebiet.*

In the afternoon I was summoned to Dr. Klein,[43] Schubert, etc. in the Brühl Palace. There was a general review of Jewish affairs. To my remark that the Jews should be allowed to work in peace, he replies that all this is related to the question of the ghetto. I presented verbally a detailed account of the situation and submitted a written list of grievances relating to different restrictions. They telephoned the Deputy Governor asking him to receive me in their presence. He replied that at this point he would only receive them. I am to be invited to the Brühl Palace for Monday, Tuesday. Leist also announced a conference next week and said that he would give me certain instructions at that time. He will sign the ordinance regulating the Order Service [Jewish Police].

The transport for the camp has not left today because of insufficient numbers. Among the Jews extraordinary rumors are circulating about me, now that I have been arrested, then that I committed suicide.

It was announced that in the apartment building at 58 Wspolna

---

41. Adolf Truskier, a Jew, former Senator of the Polish Republic.
42. Prohibited route for Batallion workers: probably Jerozolimski Avenue and Adolf Hitler Square.
43. Dr. Hans Klein, Interior Division, Warsaw district. Acting director of the division, January–March 1941.

Street the Jewish tenants are forbidden to remove any of their belongings.[44]

*September 21, 1940*—57°F. In the morning at the Community. At 11 with Supinger on the subject of the ghetto. On Monday there will be a conference in the district about the ghetto. In the meantime, as a result of applications from [non-Jews] affected, he wants to reduce the *Sperrgebiet* by excluding Swietojanska and Swietojerska Streets. Moreoever, the boundary will run from Zielna and not from Marszalkowska Street. An apartment house at Wspolna Street was notified that the Jews will be forbidden to remove their belongings. One of the tenants, Czernecki, was thrown out without being allowed to take any of his possessions.

*September 22, 1940*—In the morning at the Community. I am preparing a report for tomorrow on our general situation. It looks like tomorrow there will be a struggle. In the meantime I do not know where we shall live in a few days. Will they take everything from us? And all we own is our furniture and clothes.

They stopped my car at Jerozolimski Avenue. What abuse was heaped on me! *"Jüdische Schweine"* [Jewish swine]; *"Wie lange werdet Ihr herumspazieren"* [How long will you be promenading around?]; *"So etwas"* [Look at this!]; and so forth.

*September 23, 1940*—50°F. 10 in the morning, the Community; 11 o'clock with Schubert in Palais Brühl. I delivered my memorandum on the conditions in the Jewish community. A prolonged parley: ghetto, etc. I think that there is not going to be any closed ghetto. Painful news from the camps. Schubert requests that Fuerstenberg tell him personally about camp conditions.

In the afternoon I have been preparing materials for a visit with the *Schulrat*.

*September 24, 1940*—57°F. In the morning at the Community. At 11 with the *Schulrat* at Danilowiczowska Street. He informed me that our schools cannot be private and must all be subordinated to the Community Authority. The language of instruction is at this point to be left to our discretion; 7 grades. We must organize a School Commission.

44. Czerniakow's apartment was located on Wspolna Street, outside the walls.

A soldier appeared with a worker from the Lublin camp insisting that the Community promised to pay the camp workers. A stormy exchange.

I was summoned to the Gestapo in regard to my alleged complaining about the money exactions obtained from the Community. I had to make an official deposition about the 100,000 zlotys paid at one time to the *Ordnungspolizei* [German Order Police] for the beating of a nurse from the NVW [45] by a demented Jewish woman. I also made a declaration to the effect that during 1940 the SS has not obtained any contribution whatsoever and that *"eigenmächtig"* [on his own authority] no SS official ever demanded any contribution.

Two Jews came to me with a letter marked *"Dringend"* [urgent] and *"Geheim"* [secret] in which some unknown official urges me to give them a job, or else he himself will have to *"eingreifen"* [intervene].

*September 25, 1940*—66°F. In the morning at the Community. Ghetto and more ghetto!

The *Sperrgebiet* has been reduced on the chart by the exclusion of Chmielna and Marszalkowska Streets and the Stare Miasto, etc. On the other hand the Jewish cemetery and the Jewish hospital which have been outside the boundary have been included. In Otwock the Polish authorities are to take over Brijus. Zofiowka is threatened, etc.

Fuerstenberg and Rozen gave a report on the conditions in the camps. In the afternoon I called a meeting about starting our school system. I made a suggestion that the Community should be responsible for the vocational schools, and that elementary schools should come under the educational associations or private initiative. The organizing commission was elected with the permanent one in mind.

*September 26, 1940*—48°F. In the morning at the Community. The ghetto!

A ghetto in Otwock.[46] A threat to our hospital in Czyste. In the afternoon a meeting about elementary schools, then about the vocational school.

45. NVW = NSV, German welfare organization.
46. Otwock ghetto (for local Jews in Otwock) was formed in January 1941.

*September 27, 1940*—43°F. In the morning at the Community. News about the ghetto. The area considerably reduced. Tlomackie with the Synagogue, the hospital in Czyste, are to be excluded from the ghetto. The wedge Zelazna Brama Square, together with the Mirowski Market, Elektoralna, Zimna, Rynkowa, Zabia, and Prze-chodnia Streets will likewise be excluded. I bought a chest to pack my books. Brijus and Zofiowka have been saved for the time being, although they are forbidden to register new patients. All of these are surprises for the [Jewish] New Year.

*September 28, 1940*—50°F. It rains. I am intervening today about the ghetto. The moment I arrived at the Community at 8 A.M. I was surrounded by a group of women, mothers of the workers in the camps. Weeping and shouting. Recriminations why I am not obtaining their releases.

I visited Schubert about Community finances and the ghetto. The ghetto—it seems to me—is in the offing. He asked me why the Jews are not leaving the southern part of the city. Leaving for which street? I retorted. He announced that he and Dr. Auerswald (Welfare) will inspect the camps.[47]

From another source the news that the boundaries of the ghetto are not yet definitively settled. Chmielna and Marszalkowska Streets are still in doubt (the wedge from Saski Garden to Mirowski Market: the latter should, one would think, be included in the *Sperrgebiet)*. Tlomackie and the Synagogue are also problematic.

Jablonski of the municipality questioned payment to us of half of the receipts from the bread cards. I telephoned Kulski who was angry because Jewish tardiness in obtaining the cards made their processing more difficult. It seems they are drafting a memo to the authorities on this subject.

*September 29, 1940*—In the morning 54°F. The Community. Ghetto. I ordered a survey of Zlota Street. It turned out that—contrary to false data that one tenth are Jews—Jews number 50%. Tomorrow a day of struggle.

47. First mention of Dr. Heinz Auerswald (a lawyer), then chief of Subdivision Population and Welfare in the Interior Division of the Warsaw district. Became ghetto *Kommissar* May 15, 1941. Inducted into the German army, January 1943. After the war, lived in West Germany. Auerswald was born in 1908; he was one of the young men in the Warsaw district administration. West German prosecutors investigated him in the mid-1960s, but he was not placed on trial. Now deceased.

Korczak suggests that entreaties placed on the graves of *Tzadikim* [holy men] be taxed for the benefit of the poor.

*September 30, 1940*—In the morning 45°F. Preparing a defense for ghetto (Zlota, the wedge Mirowski Market, the Old City, etc.).

I visited Kulski. I recovered the controversial 200,000 zlotys from the bread cards and reassured him on the matter of our future cooperation in the distribution of the ration cards.

Yesterday Orzechowski [48] et al. visited the hospital in Czyste. An impression that the hospital will be taken away from us. In Otwock Mayor Gadomski summoned the *Judenrat* [Jewish Council] to announce that the ghetto will be instituted there. The highest authority in Warsaw knows nothing about it.

The ghetto in Warsaw is to be instituted during the period October 15–November 15.

*October 1, 1940*—43°F. In the morning at the Gestapo but Mueller [49] was not there. Again at 12 I described the situation of the workers in the camps, the financial position of the Community, the circumstances of the Jewish population (expulsions from homes and requisitions of belongings), the problem of the Jewish-owned dwellings (administrators imposed by the authorities), of the hospital in Czyste which is to be taken away from us, of the ghetto. The last point a strong question mark.

There is a saying about me, *"Gott leistet Czerniakow"* [God has accomplished Czerniakow].[50]

*October 2, 1940*—48°F. In the morning at the Community. A report from the city that an apartment building at Zelazna Brama Square #8 is being emptied. The delineation of the ghetto boundaries completed yesterday. Karolkowa Street was added to the previous plan.

News from Kraków that upon R.'s intervention [sic] the response was that there would be no ghetto.[51] The SS is ordering me to appear tomorrow morning in this matter. I am to be summoned to

48. Dr. Konrad Orzechowski, head of Hospitals Department, municipality.
49. Probably an SS-2d Lieut., Erich (?) Müller, in the office of the KdS-IV.
50. *Gott leistet Czerniakow:* play on words—"leistet" refers to Leist, German Plenipotentiary for city of Warsaw.
51. R. = Count Ronikier?

Danilowiczowska Street for instructions on the ghetto. Schubert is calling that some dignitaries will tour the Community Authority, the hospital, Wolska Street,[52] etc.

I telephoned Braun that the Community will not be operating with the exception of the few clerks on duty. He told me to convey this information to Kulski. The word "ghetto" was used a few days ago in Ohlenbusch's announcement about the *Gazeta Zydowska*.

*October 3, 1940*—In the morning in the Community Authority. The Jewish New Year! Schubert drove in at 3 P.M. A half-hour later he was followed by *Staatssekretär* [State Secretary] Bühler [53] accompanied by Schoen,[54] Schubert, etc. After some explanatory remarks by me in the Community Authority they visited the vocational school, the orphanage at Wolska Street, the quarantine. Later on they drove around the cemetery and the whole *Sperrgebiet*. On the basis of Schoen's questions about the capacity of the delousing facility and whether I have 1,000 men in my "militia," I surmised that they are planning an open ghetto.[55] (Everybody leaving the ghetto would have to show a delousing certificate.) Even the itinerary of this cavalcade led by Schoen seemed to point to this. They made a special detour to the court building at Leszno Street (this is where the hospital in Czyste will be transferred to).

At 9 in the morning I went to the SS. A strange reception by Scherer.[56] He gave me the impression that he was sick. I submitted a letter to F.[57]

*October 4, 1940*—In the morning at the Community. 57°F. The second day of Rosh Hashana. There may be some easing up in the ghetto project. The news is that the Jews would receive free of charge Polish workshops and stores.

*October 5, 1940*—In the morning there are demonstrations in front of the Community building by mothers of the workers in the camps.

---

52. Wolska Street = site of Jewish orphanage.
53. *Staatssekretär* Dr. Josef Bühler was the deputy of *Generalgouverneur* Frank.
54. Waldemar Schön was chief of Division *Umsiedlung* (resettlement) Warsaw district. Subsequently, he took over Interior Division.
55. "Open ghetto"—Czerniakow means compulsory residence in a city area with relative freedom of daytime movement outside the boundaries.
56. SS-1st Lieutentant Rudolf Scheerer (misspelled Scherer by Czerniakow), in charge of Jewish affairs in Warsaw Gestapo (KdS-IV-B).
57. F. = District Chief Fischer?

Our Order Service [Jewish Police] stopped my car at the corner of
Grzybowska Street with this news and I had to go back by way of
Ciepla Street. I was irked by an incident in which Rozen, while
quarreling with Kupczykier, smashed an ashtray and had to have his
hand bandaged. Again we hear about the ghetto.

*October 6, 1940*—In the morning at the Community. Today I was
to be received by F[ischer]. So far nothing came of it. There was
supposed to have been a loudspeaker announcement to the effect
that the Jews outside the walled area were to be allowed on the
streets from 8 A.M. till 7 P.M. Within the walls until 9 P.M. For the
Poles the curfew hour would be 11.

*October 7, 1940*—In the morning at the Community. Lessening of
tension in the ghetto. I am to be summoned to F[ischer]. I received
a letter from *Schulrat* on the subject of elementary schools.

*October 8, 1940*—45°F. In the morning at the Community. I am
still in my formal clothes [Fischer]. The expenses of the Community Authority amount to 50,000 zlotys a day. The camps alone cost
20,000 zlotys a day. Today we dispatched to the camps two trucks
loaded with goods worth 120,000 zlotys.

One of the Council members told me today that I am a "legend."
Many years ago a merchant-industrialist—in the main, a usurer—
visited me in a cellar where I started a workshop producing berets.
Seeing me in that cellar he told me I was a "hero." This sounded as
if it came straight from Plutarch!

*October 9, 1940*—41°F. In the morning at the Community.
F[ischer] has left. He is supposed to receive me in four days.[58]

A proclamation by Leist about giving the right of way to soldiers
on sidewalks and about curfew hours from 5–9 in the ghetto and
from 8 to 7 outside the walls.

*October 10, 1940*—50°F. In the morning at the Community
Authority. The number of suicides among the Jews has been greatly
increasing during the last months. Not so long ago Freider and his
wife took poison. Yesterday it was Ludwik Bergson's [59] and his

58. Czerniakow waited in vain; *Gouverneur* Fischer did not receive him. The decision to
establish the ghetto was conveyed to Czerniakow by Schön. See entry of October 12.
59. Bergson, son of a former chairman of the Community.

wife's turn. The 83-year-old Ludwik Krakowski died in prison.

The plan of the ghetto is still being worked out. It seems they are trying to balance the removal of 104,000 Poles from inside with the transfer of 110,000 Jews from outside the walls. In the afternoon a conference on schools. A Jewish woman, Regina Judt, received a license for a night club.

*October 11, 1940*—In the morning at the Community. Eleven o'clock with Insp[ector] Szczerba. There have been rumors that, because of a fear of epidemics, Jewish schools will remain closed.

*October 12, 1940*—Cloudy. 54°F. Today is the Day of Atonement. Only a clerk on duty in the Community. I wanted to leave for the office rather late today, since my arrival in the Community building on the Day of Atonement would amount to a demonstration of atheism. And here was a letter summoning me to Makowski at Danilowiczowska Street for 10 A.M. A matter of 1,000 "workers."

At 10:30 a conference at Makowski's: Schoen, Braun, Drost, etc. Also, Czerniewski and an official from the municipality. At first an exclusively German conference, then with Czerniewski and his comrade, and finally I was invited. It was thereupon proclaimed (Schoen) that in the name of humanity and at the behest of the Governor, the Governor General, and in conformity with higher authority, a ghetto is to be established. I was given a map of the German quarter [sic] and separately a map of the ghetto. It turns out that the ghetto border streets have been allocated to the Poles.

I was ordered to form a Jewish militia of 1,000 men. Until October 31 the resettlement will be voluntary, after that compulsory. All furniture must remain where it is. When I raised objections with respect to the financial problem, I was told that the militia could be [unpaid] volunteers and again that there were enough material resources within the ghetto itself.

At this very moment (3 P.M.) municipal workers were busy with blow torches, cutting some iron railings around the gardens at Barbara Street.

*October 13, 1940*—48°F. I arranged for a meeting of the Council for 9 in the morning today. Three commissions were elected: (1) one to deal with the economic problems of the future ghetto, (2) the

Housing Commission, and (3) the Verification Commission to check on the credentials of the Order Service [Jewish Police]. Crowds are blocking access to the Community offices. Consequently, receipts today are minimal.

I decided to move our Housing Office to 4 Tlomackie Street.

*October 14, 1940*—58°F. Fischer's proclamation about the ghetto has just now been published. The boundaries do not correspond with the plan that was handed to me. In the morning a delegation from the Community went to see Hanika [60] who informed them that Kercelak and the court buildings on Leszno Street are to be excluded and that Swietojerska Street is still under discussion.

In the afternoon I called a meeting about the directives for tomorrow. I am going to Danilowiczowska Street.

Legions of Jews from Praga are trekking to Warsaw, their pushcarts filled with pitiful junk.

In city hall we were informed that housing offices will be opened in the Jewish zone to register Christian homes for exchange, and similarly outside the walls for the registration of the Jewish homes.

*October 15, 1940*—39°F. A letter from Stein about the transfer of the hospital. At 8:30 with Hanika. After checking with Schoen he informed me that the proclamation in the *Nowy Kurier Warszawski* is incorrect. The plan I received earlier is authoritative.

At 9 with Kunze. A confusion about a 100,000-zloty loan (from the Community's own funds): we have borrowed, we have not borrowed. In the end, I am to see Leist about it. It is possible that the new walls will be financed by city hall. A new loan could be discussed but it must be secured with a mortgage on Community-owned buildings. At 10 with Schrempf (he has been in contact with Schoen in this matter), who told me that the hospital in Czyste must be transferred. Involved in this swap will be part of the court buildings, the Protestant Hospital, etc. The hospital doctors themselves are to be the last to move (into the ghetto). I named eight representatives to the city offices to register the Christian homes in the ghetto for exchange with the Jewish homes outside.

Kupczykier has just returned from his tour of the camps. In one of these camps the "commandant" ordered the [visiting] members

---

60. Hanika, building inspector at Warsaw district administration.

of the *Judenrat* [Jewish Council] to stand in the middle. Around them he positioned the workers who proceeded to sing a vulgar song about the *Judenrat* and myself.

A little old woman appeared in our apartment to take it over at the behest of one Commissar Buht(?).

*October 16, 1940*—39°F. Goldfeil has now come back from the camps. A story about Dorohusk. Beaten and humiliated, he had to flee the pursuing workers three times. They would not accept our offerings—and demanded to return home. They were to receive 2–2.5 zlotys.

*October 17, 1940*—39°F. Leist's proclamation of the ghetto is published.

*October 18, 1940*—34°F. In the morning at the Community. I am looking for an apartment. Today our own and city officials from the housing exchange offices are touring the ghetto. Bargaining for specific streets. The problem of the corner houses (Aryan shops), of the numerical ratio of the Jews to the Poles. I abhor this haggling—anyway, I did not take part in it. And in the city all is frantic activity. The coolies are much in evidence, transporting in their carts the meager belongings of the poor from Praga.[61] On top of it all, janitors and all kinds of scoundrels extort from the poor wretches their last pennies.

There is a story about me that I go outside of the Community to find what goes on inside.

A letter from Zabludowski requesting an intervention with the authorities. He was visited at 6 P.M. by some emissaries of Major Ditman [?] from Bruehl Palace who wanted to requisition furniture, etc. His identity papers were of no avail.

*October 19, 1940*—34°F. Korczak has inquired if I secured a place to live. He added that if I didn't, he could give me the name of an official in the Community who, for a bribe, will give me an apartment. In the afternoon there was supposed to have been a loudspeaker announcement that the area of the ghetto was reduced by a belt from Zelazna and Wolnosc Streets (24,000 Jews out of a

---

61. Coolies and rickshaws took the place of cars and even droshkies in occupied Warsaw.

population of 62,000 are involved). The ghetto would be divided. Who would not be perturbed?

Late morning, a German official from Lilpop, Rau and Loewenstein [machine factory], invoking Makowski's authority, instructed us to supply 250 apartments for their workers by Monday, 9 A.M.; to make things worse, he wants apartments not in Praga.[62] Or else the Jewish occupants would be "thrown out."

*October 20, 1940*—37°F. In the morning at the Community. The question of the boundaries in utter confusion. Rumor has it that Wronia Street and not Zelazna Street will be the boundary, that Sienna Street is threatened. People seem to be rushing about as if they were demented. I will go to Leist tomorrow with a formal request for an authoritative delineation of the boundaries of the ghetto. Weichert left for Kraków.

*October 21, 1940*—30°F. In the morning at Leist's (Braun). I submitted to him our letter on the subject of the changes in the size of the ghetto. He knew nothing about this and when I showed him the appropriate issue of the *Warschauer Zeitung* he telephoned the district. It turned out these were the Governor's own orders and I was instructed to notify the Jewish population to that effect. I retorted that the prestige of the authorities was involved and that I would prefer that the authorities themselves made the announcement. In the end the only concession I obtained was the extension of the deadline for housing exchanges to November 15. When I broached the question of our 100,000 zlotys he replied that he was too busy to consider that matter.

*October 22, 1940*—32°F. In the morning at the Community. Instructions from Kraków that the parties concerned should themselves come to an understanding on the question of the ghetto boundary adjustments. The JSS has submitted a memorandum to Messing. In our coffers only a few thousand zlotys.

They found me an apartment. The deadline for housing exchanges has been extended until the end of the month [November].

For the second time they want to requisition some vises from our school at Stawki Street.

62. Apparently, Germans wanted some of the good Jewish apartments outside the ghetto. The Jewish occupants were therefore unable to arrange exchanges with Poles who held similarly good accommodations inside the ghetto.

*October 23, 1940*—34°F. Ceglana Street has been taken again. Haberbusch is touring the city (Mylna Street, etc.) and apparently he is being greeted with flowers.[63] Machnicki told the JSS that some prominent Poles were supporting the creation of the ghetto. My new apartment in doubt.

*October 24, 1940*—32°F. At the SS—the ghetto. They do not oppose [me]. Later, Director Makowski, who knows nothing about changes. Thereafter, to Kunze. I discussed the Community's finances with Heilmann. Kunze does not want to approach Leist.

*October 25, 1940*—37°F. Cloudy skies. Called from my office for 10 A.M. to Schoen. Mohns[64] in the presence of Makowski responded to my contentions: (1) there would be no further boundary adjustments, (2) there will be no extensions, unless I submit proof by Monday, Oct. 28, that the rate of Jewish resettlement had been fast indeed. I gave him a note about Zelazna and Ceglana Streets. Later with Schubert—talking about the rope around my neck.

In the afternoon, at the Office of the Plenipotentiary (Hanika)—winning back part of Zelazna, Skorzana, etc., streets. The orphanage at Wolska Street paraded 20 children who were to be sent to unheated quarters.

*October 26, 1940*—32°F. A mob was beating Jews today. The woman janitor asks if it is true that the Jews will have money made of wood. Rumors that a priest in Leszno Street [is distributing] leaflets appealing to the Poles to hold on to their apartments in the street. We are issuing questionnaires to find out the extent of resettlement.

*October 27, 1940*—In the morning I presented to Mohns the data on the resettlement: 5,400 apartments had been exchanged and 3,200 are in process, which amounts to 8,600 out of the total of 11,567 Aryan housing units in the ghetto. The remaining 3,000 consist of 2,500 (caretakers, factory personnel) which are not exchangeable, and 500 which are. The spaces already vacated have been occupied by 58,000 Jews and the 3,200 plus 500 housing units

---

63. Haberbusch, co-owner of a brewery, was being cheered by Polish inhabitants who believed that their streets had been excluded from the ghetto due to his intervention. The streets were part of a mixed Polish-Jewish neighborhood.
64. Otto Mohns, deputy of Schön, *Umsiedlung*.

will be filled with 22,000 Jews, all told, about 80,000. There remain 55,000 *Jews without a roof over their heads.* On .the basis of these figures Mohns went to Schoen and the Governor, who extended the deadline to November 15. Later on I reviewed the financial condition of the Community for Dr. Klein, Dr. Auerswald, and Schubert. I am requesting a 100,000-zloty loan from our own funds, a bank loan, the approval of two [tax] ordinances (real property and business enterprises, etc.) Mohns instructed me to set up an office for issuing passes to streets outside the ghetto.

Yesterday I engaged Lt. Col. Szerynski [65] as head of the Order Service.

*October 28, 1940*—Jas [Czerniakow crossed out the name of his son and made no other entry.]

*October 29, 1940*—25°F. Our treasury has been sealed by fiscal officers. It is rumored that Föhl and Kundt [66] will be coming to Warsaw from Kraków.

*October 30, 1940*—28°F. In the morning at the Community. We were told (Supinger) not to build walls except where construction is already in progress. I was summoned to the Gestapo and sternly informed that I, the whole Council, those who got together for prayer, and the organizers of these prayers will be held accountable [for disregarding regulations]. According to Mende, there exists an illegal house of worship [67] at 11 Grzybowska Street, apt. 79—Rabbi Najhaus. I was also asked about the ownership of the car parked at 36 Stawki Street. A representative of the Fiscal Office garnisheed our typewriters and calculators.

*October 31, 1940*—34°F. Inspection of the walls by officials of the Plenipotentiary [Leist]. An order—continue the building with the exception of the western side of the ghetto. Mohns promised to

---

65. Jozef Szerynski (original name: Szynkman), baptized a Christian in his youth. Before the war, Lt. Col. of Polish police and commander of Lublin area. In ghetto, chief of Order Service [Jewish Police] until his arrest by Germans on May 1, 1942. Released late July to take charge of the Order Service for the deportations. Subsequently wounded in jaw in the course of an attempt on his life by Jewish underground. Recuperated, once again led Order Service during deportations of January 18–21, 1943. Committed suicide on January 23, 1943.
66. *Unterstaatssekretär* Ernst Kundt, director of Main Division Interior, *Generalgouvernement* administration at Kraków. Subsequently *Gouverneur* of Radom district.
67. The synagogues were closed as of January 1940, ostensibly to curb epidemics.

announce today an extension of the deadline to November 15 (the loudspeakers were carrying the broadcast in the afternoon). Leist was interviewed yesterday and among other things talked about the Jewish question in Warsaw.

*November 1, 1940*—32°F. Drizzling. A holiday (also in the offices). No funds at the Community.

A proclamation by Leist. For 5 zlotys, the Jews must obtain special streetcar identification cards with photographs (from the Warsaw Transport Authority at 2 Mlynarska Street). Only the holders of such cards are permitted to buy streetcar tickets (in the Jewish streetcars). Without these cards a quadruple price for the tickets.

*November 2, 1940*—In the morning 32°F. At 2:30 46°F. All is quiet at the Community. Quiet, that is apart from the never-ending crying of mothers of the workers in the camps begging for help.

*November 3, 1940*—39°F. We drafted a memorandum to allow the Jews to stay in Praga, etc. Malicious people are referring to the ghetto as "the Garden City Czerniaków." [68] In front of the Community building and in the courtyard throngs of the mothers of the camp workers. On the opposite side of my window somebody has set up a coffin-making shop in a ruined building. This is all I can see from my windows.

A 27-year-old section leader in the Battalion committed suicide by taking poison, the reason being the resettlement and a beating that he received at a bridge while returning from work.

*November 4, 1940*—43°F. It is drizzling. The usual work at the Community until 3:30. At 3:30 I heard battering at the front door and the sound of windows being broken. A soldier with an officer were at the point of breaking in. They entered the building and, led by one Sachsenhaus,[69] proceeded to beat Popower,[70] First, etc.; then they went to the Battalion offices and beat up Signer, Zylberman (?). I called the Gestapo and was instructed to get one of the

68. Czerniaków was a section of "Aryan" Warsaw on the west bank of the Vistula River, not contiguous with the ghetto.
69. Sachsenhaus, was a Jewish agent for the Gestapo.
70. Izrael Popower directed Division of Finance and Budget, a position he held before the war. Survived and lived in postwar Warsaw as Karol Ignacy Popowski.

armed men to the telephone. I called on a soldier who happened to be nearby but he refused in an irritated tone, ordering me to follow him. When I appeared in the Battalion office, the officer in charge set upon me, hitting me on the head until I fell. At this point the soldiers started kicking me with their boots. When I tried to stand up they jumped on me and threw me down the stairs. Half a flight down they beat me again. In the end I was dragged to a truck but was soon ordered to move into another one. I was [then] transported with Signer, Zylberstajn, and Popower in turn to Szuch Avenue, to Pawiak [prison], the University, back to Szuch Avenue, and again to Pawiak, where we were all incarcerated. I was put into an underground cell with 5 fellow prisoners. The cell measures three paces in width and 6 paces in length. One of the prisoners occupies a bed, the rest sleep on the floor on very thin straw mattresses. To make things worse, one of the prisoners arrested for beating some *Volkdeutscher* [Ethnic German] (Sosnkowski), in a drunken state, has diarrhea and keeps on relieving himself all through the night next to my mattress. He insists that it was the water which he drank in prison that caused this misfortune. It is clear that he is not used to water. *(Wasser dient auch zum Trinken* [Water may be used also for drinking]—a sign in a Dresden Sanitation and Hygiene Exhibition).

*November 5, 1940*—After a sleepless night at 6 A.M.: Get up and clean the cell! Then coffee was distributed (every man a big bowl), *nota bene,* salted, and one-quarter of bread. Next a shower and delousing. Still wet I had to dress since some Gestapo men who have just arrived were waiting for me and my comrades. In the Gestapo, depositions were taken from us. Waiting for Meisinger's interrogation I was kept in an underground cell fixed like the inside of a streetcar. At 4:30 I was received by Meisinger. We are accused of making improper remarks about the SS, etc. (Sachsenhaus). In the end he released us all. At 6 P.M., after preparing a formal complaint about the beatings I returned home. They had brought my hat and overcoat for me to the Gestapo. In the evening I was examined by 3 doctors and a paramedic. They patched me up with bandages on my head, both legs, and one arm. I can hardly walk. Tomorrow I will go to the Community [as usual].

*November 6, 1940*—In the morning at the Community. Scherer, Mende, showed up with an interpreter. It turned out that somebody had beaten up Mrs. Sachsenhaus and had threatened her with revenge by [residents of] Krochmalna Street. I issued an appeal to the Battalion and used my influence with respect to local citizens to calm tempers at Krochmalna Street. At home a garden of flowers. I am informed that yesterday, on account of me, the value of the dollar fell [in the black market].

*November 7, 1940*—In the morning at the Community. Flowers keep arriving from all over. The sellers of greens in the market hall sent a delegation with more flowers.

I went to see Schubert and Kunze. Schubert's idea—the requisitioning of hidden merchandise partly for the benefit of the Community. He promised that within 2 days he would review our finances. Kunze asks for a written statement about financing the walls by the inhabitants and more about the postponement of repayment of 100,000 zlotys from the bread ration card receipts.

*November 8, 1940*—Leaden skies. 39°F. It rains. Summonses for tomorrow to Mende. Major Hohenauer [71] called me for a conference on the Order Service. I went to see him with Szerynski. On Monday I am to submit the draft ordinance.

*November 9, 1940*—It is dark at 8:30 in the morning. Called to the Gestapo with Signer. Also Brafman, Lesselbaum [72] and Mozdzenski (?). I was informed that they have been arrested. I returned to the Community. I made arrangements for my belongings to be moved.

*November 10, 1940*—All day at the Community. At home, packing. A meeting on the Jewish Police, resettlement. Tomorrow I am to report to Danilowiczowska Street in the matter of the police, etc.

Minimal receipts. Everybody is preoccupied with moving, I myself no less than the others.

*November 11, 1940*—A summons to Leist for 4 P.M. The call for me and several other members of the Council was made by one of Schoen's aides (Steyert). After we have presented ourselves at the

71. Major Hohenauer was in charge of Division for Police Affairs, German city administration.
72. re: Lesselbaum, see diary entry for June 8, 1940.

Blank Palace it transpired that Leist knew nothing about the summons. We thus proceeded to Danilowiczowska Street where I alone was received by Schoen in company of Mohns, Makowski, Steyert, etc. Starting with a few epithets about the Jews he informed me that any extension of the November 15 deadline is out of the question and that he had reported to the *Kommandeur* [73] on the lack of cooperation of the Jews. Starting on the 16th serious sanctions will be imposed on the recalcitrants. He asked some questions about the police.

*November 12, 1940*—In the morning with Kulski. He is writing to the authorities pleading for extension of the November 15 deadline by two weeks so that the voluntary exchange agreements are not at once replaced by compulsion, and the population may be resettled peacefully and on the basis of referrals. We have sent today a written communication to the *Umsiedlungsamt* [Resettlement Office] on the following: (1) a few weeks [postponement] of November 15 deadline; (2) the market hall; (3) the hospital, orphanages, etc.; (4) the militia.

At 3:30 I went with Szerynski to Major Hohenauer: the militia ordinance, problems, etc. He will summon us after studying it.

*November 13, 1940*—Called to Schrempf in the morning. He told me that this was my second call and that the third one will mean my imprisonment. What is involved here is our tabular report to the authorities on the *Judenrat*'s struggle with epidemic diseases.

Later in the Bruehl Palace. Those present were: Dr. Klein, Auerswald, Kreppel,[74] Schubert. They asked me what had happened to me. Klein observed that there are scoundrels like Sachsenhaus among the Jews. This I countered by asking if he remembers his physics and mentioned Newton's third law.[75] Later the topic of restoring to health the finances of the Community. He is against the real estate and commercial taxes but will very shortly inform me how we may obtain revenue from the sale of the ghetto's reserves. I tried to convince him that we should rather use taxation under law. We have sent to Steyert a copy of our plan to requisition for November 14 and 15 some Jewish horsecarts to transport the

73. *Kommandeur*: probably the KdS (Security Police).
74. Dr. Kreppel was director of legal office of the Interior Division, Warsaw district administration.
75. Newton's third law stated: to every action there is an equal and opposite reaction.

meager belongings of the Praga poor. He will inspect the militiamen on the 15th of this month.

*November 14, 1940*—With Kulski at 8:30 A.M. He is going to Leist at 10 about the ghetto. At 12 a message that Leist wants another memorandum on matters covered by the one just sent to him. I went to see Schubert about the Community's finances and in connection with my recent experience also talked to him about making things easier for me.

Steyert ordered me through Haendel and Szerynski to post an announcement about passes for leaving the ghetto and to organize their distribution.

*November 15, 1940*—At 8 in the Community. I had issued instructions for the Jewish owners of horsecarts and pushcarts to report this morning to move the Jews from Praga. As of this time (8 o'clock) hardly anyone has appeared. Haendel has just arrived from the District with a statement that out-of-ghetto passes are to be issued not by us but by the *Passstelle* [Check Point] (Fabisch-Okon) 76 and only to those who work in industry. Hearing this I went to the District myself. As it happened, I managed to extend the scope of the passes. Moreover, we shall be issuing them and the *Umsiedlungsamt* [Resettlement Office] will stamp them. I was ordered to have 10 of our militiamen posted at each of the street exits from the ghetto by 7 A.M. tomorrow.

After they arrived in the Community, Haendel and Lichtenbaum were called to the District. They are to block with barbed wire a number of streets which have not been walled up. -

At 4 in the morning First arrived telling me, on Steyert's orders, to dress and come down to the street in 5 minutes. Steyert has just been in the Community where he asked janitor Adler to take him to Haendel, First, and myself. He was driven to Malamud 77 and then to First. When we discovered that there was no car downstairs waiting for us we went on to the Community.

*November 16, 1940*—We were swamped all through the day with functionaries from units employing workers requesting passes

76. The *Umsiedlung* division (under Schön) set up a *Transferstelle* (Exchange Office) under Palfinger, whose deputy was Steyert. The *Transferstelle* regulated exports and imports from the ghetto. The *Transferstelle* official in charge of passes was Fabisch,
77. Malamud was Community treasurer.

which the Community is to issue for Steyert's approval stamp. At one point Steyert himself appeared with several aides and demanded energetically that the Community staff work all night preparing the passes for his approval by Sunday noon, that is tomorrow. He also demanded to be given two Torahs, some German books about the Jews, newspapers published by the Polish Jews in German, a prayer book, etc. Late in the evening I went home to go to bed fully clothed just in case I have to get up again in the middle of the night.

*November 17, 1940*—Sunday. At the boundaries of the ghetto the *Ordnungspolizei* [German Order Police]. Throngs of Jews pass by with bared heads.[78] At 12 Haendel, First, and Lewkowicz went to Steyert. He refused to approve the bulk of the passes. Lewkowicz mistreated. Steyert issued instructions for another emergency night operation in the Community: An official on telephone duty with the addresses of the members of the Council and my own.

Malamud limps. Jews can be seen doing calisthenics[79] in the streets and washing their hands in the gutters. Bo[l]lenbach made a telephone inquiry as to whether those working at Grochow have now been released: they had been arrested. He was informed that they were freed.

Schubert paid us a visit. For the last two days the doctors cannot get to the hospital.

*November 18, 1940*—In the morning at the Community. I myself had some difficulty in obtaining a pass. They have issued some additional passes today. I was called to the SD for 12:30.[80] I reported on the conditions in the ghetto; incidents at Zelazna Street (a shot at a cyclist, etc.). I was told that they would intervene.

Mende showed me a Polish anonymous letter according to which I, together with Czerwinski,[81] was taking bribes for apartments. Brandt added that there are scoundrels and informers among the Jews. When I broached the question of parcels to Signer,[82] Mende showed me a letter commenting that worrying about others is not worth the trouble. I asked Brandt about Tempel; apparently he is still alive.

78. Jews were required to take off their hats when passing German guards.
79. Knee bends, etc., were punishments imposed by the Germans.
80. SD = *Sicherheitsdienst* (SS Security Service).
81. Henryk Czerwinski, Community official; before the war a newspaper reporter dealing with courts. Cf. May 9, 1942.
82. Signer was under arrest.

Pressdorf arrived at 2 P.M. demanding charts of the ghetto and some statistical information.

*November 19, 1940*—The body of a stoker who hanged himself three days ago is still in the boiler room at Jagiellonska Street. He cannot be buried since the workers in the funeral home cannot obtain the passes. To make things more difficult they have forbidden burials at the Praga cemetery.

Our militiamen were given their dose of calisthenics this morning. They came back terribly filthy, covered with mud. The executive secretary of the Vocational School Board was doing his exercises with two bricks in his hands. It appears that the hospital at Czyste will be taken away from us.

Some of the passes were signed this morning. At 4 P.M. there will be more signing. I am to report tomorrow at 10 A.M. in the *Umsiedlungsamt.*

*November 20, 1940*—In the morning at the Community. At 10 in the morning in the *Umsiedlungsamt.* Schoen, Mohns, Fabisch (from Danilowiczowska Street), Steyert. Schoen went on to state (1) with regard to the post office 41 Zamenhof Street: by January 15, 1941, a Jewish post office will be established; (2) we must organize the *Stueckgut Warenlade Verladungsstelle* [Piece Goods Warehouse and Shipping Center], also for food produce, near the main railroad station; (3) they will set up the *Transferstelle* [Exchange Office] close to the ghetto. We are to provide furniture for 20 offices. We will pay a monthly charge of 10,000 zlotys. The deadline is December 1, 1940. By November 28, 1940, we are to submit a list of the articles and food that we need. Foreign currency (dollars) and finished goods will serve as payment. The *Transferstelle* will be in charge of contracts for craftsmen and workers. The *Tr[ansfer-stelle]* is to protect the interests of the German and Polish creditors against their Jewish debtors and vice-versa. The *Tr[ansferstelle]* will be in charge of the *Arbeitereinsatz* [labor allocation] together with representatives of the *Arbeitsamt* [Labor Office]. We were instructed to set up delousing facilities *(Backsteinoefen* [brick ovens] 100 per hour). The passes which we heretofore prepared and which the German authorities stamped are no longer to be issued by us, and the office staff (72 people) is to be dismissed. Fabisch will be issuing these passes and they will be limited to the workers employed by the SS and the Army.

The Praga cemetery is to be closed. The cemetery at Okopowa Street will be enlarged by the Skra soccer field.[83]

*November 21, 1940*—In the morning, wives of those arrested in connection with Sachsenhaus. In response to Pressdorf's demand 5 charts of the ghetto were prepared with several institutions (the Council, etc.) marked on them; in addition a report on the resettlement. I visited Brandt in the matter of Signer and comrades. They have not yet been sent away but a camp is in store for them. It turns out that it was Brandt, as duty officer that evening, who ordered my arrest.

Today they have excluded the fish market hall from the ghetto. Grzybowski Square is threatened as well. Jewish shopkeepers who own shops outside the ghetto now prefer to have Aryan partners.

At 3 p.m. Dr. Droessel appeared in the matter of the wholesale establishments, drugstores, and pharmacies. The question of the real property will be discussed at a meeting. The streets seem to be more quiet today.

*November 22, 1940*—In the morning at the Community. Later with Heilmann on the subject of new taxes. Then, with Schubert and Auerswald about real property. Sanitary napkins. On the matter of the buildings they suggested that I should see Schlosser's *Wirtschaftsabteilung* [Economy Division].

Today we had adjustments again in the various sectors of the ghetto. We are to erect a wooden overpass at Chlodna Street.

*November 23, 1940*—In the morning at the Community. A visit from Schubert on the subject of Warman [84] who is alleged to have behaved in an insulting manner. The episode involved a pass for the Jewish wife of a German.

*November 24, 1940*—In the morning at the Community. Since Nov. 11, 1940, we have been living in an apartment at 11 Elektoralna Street. Preparing the transit warehouse. Schoen's instructions: (1) for 7:30 November 27, 1940, 50 craftsmen, who are to fix the offices of the *Transferstelle* (23 Krolewska Street) in 24 hours; (2) 20 rooms to be equipped with office furniture, hanging and standing lamps, curtains, 2 rooms must have luxury furnishings. A

83. Skra, a sports club, had a soccer field adjacent to the Jewish cemetery.
84. Zygmunt Warman, secretary of the Council.

table for 30 people. Office supplies, etc., 6 new Continental type-writers, a telephone exchange; (3) we must pay to the Bank 26,000 zlotys including 6,000 zlotys for an Opel-Olympia; [85] (4) the biographical resumes with three photographs each for all the Warsaw rabbis.

*November 25, 1940*—In the morning at the Community. The last day of issuing passes by the Jewish Council. Summoned for 4 P.M. to the *Umsiedlungsamt*. I have been given the following information:

(1) The Council is under the authority of the *Transferstelle;* our dealings with other authorities will be through the U[*msiedlungs*] A[*mt*].

(2) The charge: the *Transferstelle* 20,000 zlotys

(3) We must set up the *Markstelle* [border post] in the vicinity of the Gdansk Station. A special siding to be arranged with the railroad authorities.

(4) Prepare an inventory of all the food produce, coal, and other raw materials in the ghetto. On the basis of this we must submit the list of our requirements on November 28.
Weekly requirements *(Versorgungsperiode* [supply period]).

(5) Furnish information about the number of bakeries and/or—less desirable—the number of loaves to be brought in.

(6) On December 15 the Jewish buildings in the ghetto will come under the administration of the *Judenrat*. Ten percent of the rent will go to the *Judenrat*. If this proves insufficient, a special tax may be imposed on the houses.

*November 26, 1940*—In the morning at the Community. Haendel went to see Steyert but received no instructions. The Aryan employees of the Community Authority have not yet received their passes. I am making arrangements through Kulski. The municipality has informed us that they have ordered to transfer as of December 1 the bread ration cards to the Community Authority, and that in the future they will not have anything to do with this.

85. The Opel-Olympia, a small car, was acquired for Czerniakow.

*November 27, 1940*—In the morning at the Community. Haendel went to see Steyert. Jewish travelers will be marched in a column through the city to the railroad station. I and the pact [sic].

Tomorrow we are to provide 50 craftsmen to fix the offices of the *Transferstelle*. Our efforts to obtain passes for our staff have been in vain. Pressdorf paid us a visit, asking about various current matters. A letter from the *Totenkopfreiterstandarte* [SS Death Head Cavalry Regiment] with a list of Jews to be recruited into the militia.

*November 28, 1940*—In the morning at the Community. With Mohns about the bread ration cards, which the municipality will no longer be distributing after December 1, 1940, the garbage in the buildings, and the coal and potatoes which are not being delivered from outside the ghetto.

I received a letter from the *Umsiedlungsamt* on the Community taking over buildings.

*November 29, 1940*—In the morning at the Community. At Ciepla Street it was pointed out to me that I could get out of the car and go about my business on foot altogether. Glücksberg was dragged out of the droshky and ordered to do calisthenics.

I went to see Mohns. The bread ration cards were extended through December and the garbage will be removed. I handed in a memorandum listing our food requirements, etc. I was informed that I will be communicating directly with Schoen or Mohns. I have been invited to a meeting of the *Transfer[stelle]* on Monday at 4 P.M. I had a tooth extracted today and a bridge taken out. Tomorrow morning I must go to the SS and to Dr. Ballreich on the matter of the buildings.

*November 30, 1940*—In the morning at the Community. On my arrival there I was greeted by a detachment of the Order Service who were lining the corridor and saying *"Czesc"* [Hail] as I passed. Later in the big conference room Gepner delivered an oration and then there were more speeches from the staff delegates. A profusion of flowers. I became 60 today.

*December 1, 1940*—In the morning at the Community. A conference about food supplies. Sachsenhaus made a demand through his wife that she be given some profitable position or else Sztolcman would meet with the same misfortune that I did.

Major Tunka telephoned yesterday from the Palais Brühl asking, and very politely at that, that we should take care of one Mrs. Strauchler (her husband is in Russia). She appeared today and declared that the major has told her that he would arrest all of us if she is not given a position. Hearing this I instructed Lustberg, right in front of her, to check with the major. At this point she proceeded to plead that we refrain from telephoning and in the end she told Lustberg that she lied to us. I gave instructions because of her poverty (a child) that she be paid 100 zlotys a month.

*December 2, 1940*—In the morning at the Community. At 4 P.M. with Mohns. If we find a building on the periphery of the ghetto, even outside the walls, we could locate our hospital [86] there. Then M[ohns] added that the Aryan-owned houses would also be placed under *Treuhand* [Trusteeship] and that in the future the Jewish houses will be exchanged for the Aryan ones. The question of the [Jewish] shops on the Aryan side.[87]

*December 3, 1940*—In the morning at the Gestapo. I was asked about the *Transfer[stelle]*. I tried to intercede with Scherer about Signer. He told me to remind him about it 10 days later.

At 1 P.M. 2 Gestapo men appeared in regard to Malamud and his wife, First, Adler, Haendel, Wojcik. They will be sent for tomorrow, because they have no passes. Gancwajch and Sternfeld [88] paid us a visit. I asked them not to use the name of the *Judenrat* in their announcements.

*December 4, 1940*—In the morning at the Community. At 10 o'clock we had a letter from *Umsiedlung* [Resettlement Office] on the 1,000 Jews expelled from Piaseczno. Shortly afterwards came the trucks. Later came the people on foot (12 miles) carrying their bundled possessions. We placed part of this crowd in the quarantine facilities, the other part simply dispersed. A visit from Pressdorf, then came Scherer and Brandt on the subject of Piaseczno.

---

86. The hospital in Czyste.
87. Czerniakow's reference is to shops outside the ghetto. According to a report by Schön, 1,170 Jewish grocery shops and 2,600 Jewish shops dealing with other commodities were sealed as of November 16, 1940.
88. Abraham Gancwajch and D. Sternfeld, two officials of the German-sponsored Control Office to Combat the Black Market and Profiteering, located at 13 Leszno Street and popularly known as "The Thirteen."

Hoerschelman[n] *(Emaehrungsamt* [Food Office]) refuses to honor a letter from *Umsiedlung.* Thus it is forbidden to import into the ghetto anything except flour for December. But not for the bakers, only for the Council, and the bakers have no passes.

At 4 P.M. I went to see Major Kamlah (the Praga cemetery, making obeisance to the Germans, etc.). He informed me that a regulation will be issued no longer requiring obeisance.

*December 5, 1940*—In the morning at the Community. Later with Mohns to whom I explained the discrepancy between regulations about the bread ration cards and actual practices. He promised to take care of this.

Haendel has just returned from Steyert who announced that he [Haendel] and Lichtenbaum are to wear the *Judenrat* armbands, etc. . . .

*December 6, 1940*—In the morning at the Community. At 11 with Fleming [89] in the Bank of National Economy. He lectured me on the principles of housing administration. He emphasized the fact that he made some inquiries about me—*"Sie sind ein ziemlich anstaendiger Mensch"* [You are a fairly decent man]. "But you are surrounded by crooks." I protested vigorously. He told me that out of the 57 Jewish *Beauftragte* [plenipotentiaries] over the buildings, he himself will appoint 20–30. I explained that out of a sense of responsibility I would like to avoid having people I do not know as subordinates.

*December 7, 1940*—In the morning at the Community. Haendel and Lichtenbaum went to the SS. A strange view and from 25 Chlodna Street [?]. It appears that Mohns will be away on leave. The SS will act in his place. I was instructed to post announcements about failure to wear armbands, black market, etc.

Taking one's shirts to the laundry presents a problem now.

*December 8, 1940*—A morning appointment with a dentist, then until 6 P.M. at the Community. Shortage of funds, problems, a meeting.

89. Fleming = Flemming, German official in Trusteeship Administration of Sequestered Real Estate in Warsaw. "Trustees" were installed on both sides of the wall. Inside the ghetto, the administration consisted of an upper level made up of 57 "plenipotentiaries" *(Beauftragte)* and a lower level of 450 house administrators *(Hausverwalter),* all Jews. A *Hausverwalter* administered several buildings.

*December 9, 1940*—In the morning at the SS about the Community Authority telephones. Later at *Umsiedlung*. I was received by Palawer who told me that he is my superior. Later at the Community.

*December 10, 1940*—In the morning at the Community. It is still warm. At twelve at the *Transfer[stelle]*. They have demanded payment of 15,000 zlotys tomorrow, and 200,000 zlotys in the next few days. We are receiving a loan from the [building] administrators. Tomorrow, I will submit the list of building plenipotentiaries to be named.

*December 11, 1940*—In the morning at the Community. Kaczka speaks like a Delphic oracle. I submitted to Fleming a list of the *Beauftragte* [plenipotentiaries] and administrators, assistants, and caretakers; he refuses to approve them. He upped, from 3% to 4%, the share of the net [rent] income which will go to us. He commented on my remark about the type of persons for assistant positions. Since the beginning of the month the receipts in the Community are nil. We manage to survive on private loans. The Jews do not pay direct taxes. My furniture today.

*December 12, 1940*—At the Community. The *Transfer[stelle]*. A longer talk with Steyert and Palfinger.

*December 13, 1940*—At the Community. In the morning Fleming called from the Bank of National Economy that a list of the owners of real property had been compiled. A letter from the *Transfer[stelle]* ordering us to dismiss 30 Aryan employees forthwith.

[Notebook Five has never been recovered.]

# Notebook Six

"Julius Caesar," Act I, Scene I

Flavius:  Hence! Home, you idle creatures,
                get you home.
             Is this a holiday? Know you not,
             Being mechanical, you ought not walk
             Upon a laboring day without the sign
             Of your profession? Speak, what trade art thou?

*April 23, 1941*—In the morning at the Community. Later at the Gestapo I presented to Mende the project of Zweibaum's [1] lectures, etc. for official approval. Today a ritual of circumcision was carried out under the aegis of Dr. Milejkowski for a physician and others of the Gestapo. Later the displaying of an adult.

*April 24, 1941*—In the morning at the Community. Berenson's funeral at 3 P.M. It is rumored that he referred to me in latter times as a "saint."

*April 25, 1941*—In the morning at the Community. Mende informed me that Palfinger is not pleased with me and the Council. He wants 30 million zlotys for the goods going to the Jewish

---

1. Julian Zweibaum, specialist in histology and embryology, Warsaw University. Gave covert medical instruction in ghetto.

Quarter. He is to summon me and the other members of the Council for a conference.

Dr. Nossig came pleading for financial assistance. In addition he kept babbling about my recent experiences.

*April 26, 1941*—In the morning at the Community. Later with Mende on the matter of the *Lagerschutz* [camp guards] and yesterday's lawlessness on Leszno Street.[2] With Brandt about the latest incidents. Later with Kratz[3] on the subject of the epidemic. I reported to K.[4] but he told me to come on Monday. The news from the labor camps is very sad. Very little food and much abuse. Yesterday the *Lagerschutz* took 3 Order Servicemen for the camp: two of them were excused, one had to go.

*April 27, 1941*—In the morning at the Community. I visited the workshops and the warehouse at Prosta Street, then 13 Tlomackie Street.[5] Later I inspected the interior of the synagogue. The altar had fallen in. The capitals and parts of the architraves badly damaged. One column bared (of ornaments). The roof is pierced with holes. I issued instructions for the setting up of a committee to collect funds for the renovation and the opening of the synagogue. I received a parcel—some sausage, flour, sugar, buckwheat groats, and candy. A meager little parcel, but dear.

At 7 P.M. an extra newspaper edition: *"Athen von deutschen Truppen genommen"* ["Athens captured by German troops"]. I have finished reading again a novel by Weyssenhoff, *The Dolega Affair.* How quaint is his "hero" Dolega.

*April 28, 1941*—In the morning at the Community. I delivered to Brandt a memorandum about the treatment of our workers in the camps (9 have already died). I told him a story of a young worker who has returned from Łąka minus the boots and clothing given to him by the Community! On our way to report with Szerynski to Ka[h] we were intercepted in a corridor by Bonifer[6] who then led

2. Camp guards, mostly Ukrainians, robbed Jewish shops on Leszno Street.
3. Kratz = Otto Kraatz, SS-2d Lieut. in Security Service, Warsaw. Kds/III-B.
4. K. was probably SS-Major Dr. Ernst Kah, deputy of KdS and chief, Security Service section (III). Kah, an agricultural economist, first arrived in Warsaw in September 1939 and served there until the end of 1943. Died in the 1960s.
5. 13 Tlomackie Street, prewar location of organization of Jewish writers and newspapermen.
6. SS-Capt. Adolf Bonifer, chief, KdS/III-C.

us to his own office. He proceeded to ask me whether I am familiar with the Control Office for Combating the Black Market and Profiteering and whether I maintain contact with it. I replied that they have reported to me, but in the absence of an order from the authorities, I did not establish lines of communication with them. He then asked me about the purpose of Merin's visit to Warsaw. Yesterday the placards with my proclamation about [keeping] Saturdays [as the sabbath] were posted. [See Diary entry of May 3, 1941] In spite of the rain large crowds gathering in front of the posters to read it.

*April 29, 1941*—The Community. Distressing news from the camps. Haendel and Fuerstenberg have just returned from Garwolin, where they went with Hentschke to release the Order Serviceman Pasenstein (?), who had been impressed for the camp the other day. A teenage volunteer who was in Garwolin arrived at the Community. His boots and clothing etc. had been taken away from him.

*April 30, 1941*—In the morning at the Community. Mende and some "tourists" from the *Wehrmacht* [German Armed Forces]. I briefed them about the Community. Later Zabludowski joined them to lead a guided tour. I paid a visit to Mohns but he was absent. The authorities have a holiday tomorrow (May 1).

Apparently there has been an announcement about the ghetto administrative structure and its relationship to the authorities in yesterday's *Verordnungsblatt* [Legal Gazette]. It seems that no newspaper will be allowed in the ghetto except the *Gazeta Zydowska*.

*May 1, 1941*—In the morning at the Community. A meeting of the Executive Committee of the Citizens Commission on the subject of the camps. Checking the jurisdiction of the Executive Committee with Rozen. A report from Haendel and Fuerstenberg on the conference with Zuchowski from Garwolin. Taking depositions on the conditions in the camps. Zabludowski feted by two tourists.

Our photographers and barbers are asking for permission to stay open on Saturdays.
[Translated from the German]

*Kommissar* for the Jewish District in Warsaw
Creation of a *Transferstelle*

Warsaw, May 1

The Governor General has empowered the District Chief in Warsaw by decree to set requirements and take measures for the maintenance of order in the Jewish District of Warsaw. For the performance of his task, the *Kommissar* for the Jewish District in Warsaw makes use of the *Transferstelle* Warsaw and the Chairman of the Jewish Council in Warsaw. The *Kommissar* is subordinated to the District Chief. A section for general administrative matters and another for economic questions will be established in his [the *Kommissar's*] office.

The *Transferstelle* as an institution of public law, regulates the economic relations between the Jewish District and the outer world in accordance with its bylaws which are issued by the District Chief. In this connection, the ordinance also contains provisions for the organization and budget of the *Transferstelle*. The District Chief in Warsaw is furthermore empowered to invest the Chairman of the Jewish Council of Warsaw with the responsibilities and powers of a mayor. The Chairman is subordinated to the *Kommissar* who supervises him. He prepares his own budget for the administration of the Jewish District in Warsaw.

*May 2, 1941*—In the morning at the Community. Nossig told me about a Jewish mother who abandoned two children on the street, disclaiming to the crowd that they were hers, although, they kept on crying: "Mummy!" A charity collection box with a few pennies was stolen from a telephone booth. At 8 A.M. a film crew arrived from the *Aussendienst* [field service] to take pictures of the Community workshops. In the afternoon I am going with Zabludowski to the theater.

*May 3, 1941*—In the morning with Szerynski in the S.P. [German Security Police]. Mende reviewed the subjects of meetings about which he must be notified beforehand. He accepted our reports about the treatment of the camp workers by the *Lagerschutz.*

I was received with Szerynski by Kra[a]tz who demanded data on births and child mortality. Mohns declared in the Brühl Palace that either he himself or Dr. Auerswald would become the Jewish *Kommissar.* Nossig sent me a message through an intermediary that I could not be received because of "lack of time." In the end they told me to report next week. I have a feeling that they will dismiss me.

Today was the first day of general Sabbath rest.

*May 4, 1941*—In the morning at the Community. The movie camera crews are with us again. They brought five corpses from camp. Zofiowka sent us 10 children. A confrontation between Haendel and Fuerstenberg. The rabbis arrived led by Michelson to thank me for Saturday. I appealed to them to set up a Rabbinate and advised them to elect a chief rabbi and to start the rebuilding of the synagogues.

*May 5, 1941*—In the morning at the Community. Later in the *Arbeitsamt* with Rozen and Altberg [7] submitting a declaration about the conditions in labor camps (it is rumored that 100 people have died). Rozen gave a detailed account of what is happening in the camps and submitted his reports. Then I drove to the Gestapo and gave Mende one of these depositions. I then described the conditions in the camps. I announced that the next day I would bring a Battalion memorandum on the camps. Later the conversation moved to the topic of the goings on in the *Transfer[stelle]*

We were visited at the Community by Dr. Gater and Meder [8] about work (economic production) in the ghetto, etc. They went on to suggest that the ghetto merchants establish direct contact with the merchants on the other side and that a cooperative be established in the ghetto. The *Judenrat* is going to be the sole self-governing authority [9] with the *Obmann* [Chairman] as a mayor.

---

7. Lucjan Altberg, a corporate lawyer before the war, may have been in the Council. Chairman of the Economic Council. Also served on Labor Commission. During summer deportations in 1942, he crossed the wall and disappeared.
8. Gater and Meder, Main Division Economy, *Generalgouvernement.*
9. The reference is not to real autonomy, but to exclusive jurisdiction of the Council vis-á-vis other Jewish bodies claiming administrative power. Czerniakow was going to be named "Mayor." See entry for May 19, 1941.

At 8:30 P.M. I had a visit from Rozen and Goldfeil. They gave me materials on the camps. According to their list 91 people died in 10 camps. They tell me that tonight a transport of 280 is scheduled to leave; the men are said to be very agitated. The employees in the Battalion are in a state bordering on hysteria. God only knows what will happen tonight and what tomorrow will bring. The news from the *Arbeitsamt* is tragic. Allegedly the higher officials do not give credence to our reports and claim that the *Arbeitsamt* is deliberately being misled. The difficult conditions in the camps are compounded by bad weather: it has been raining most of the time. Today it snowed. One can imagine working in water.[10] I received a letter from Steyert canceling his previous order about reporting all the cases of requisitions to him.

*May 6, 1941*—In the morning at the Community. Later I took to the Gestapo a memorandum about the camps (91 cases of death). Hagen,[11] as well as some German filmmakers who happened to be in the vicinity, came to see the corpses in the quarantine. Last night 280 candidates reported for the camp. Of these 180 went in spite of the fact that they have seen the victims.

Summoned by Palfinger who informed me that he will do everything to improve the food supply. Later he asked what Dr. Gater and Meder from Kraków were doing in the ghetto.

The governor [of the Warsaw District] is awaiting a special report on the camps from Meissner [12] who is inspecting them now.

Mende has asked who has been communicating with the *Trans-fer[stelle]*. In our treasury in the morning, 29 pennies.

*May 7, 1941*—In the morning at the Community. A meeting took place in the *Arbeitsamt* at Hoffmann's. Captain Meissner, the chief of the *Lagerschutz* [camp guard], contended that the causes of the misfortunes in the camps were: weather, the underfeeding of recruits, lack of seasoning and hard work, and partly the *Lagerschutz* is also responsible. He agreed to take two members of the Council

10. Working in water: river regulation and land reclamation projects employed tens of thousands of Jews, many of them working knee-deep in water in the Warsaw district as well as neighboring districts.
11. Dr. Wilhelm Hagen succeeded Dr. Schrempf as health chief, German City administration, Warsaw.
12. Captain Meissner, German Police Battalion 304, was in charge of camp guards.

with him to the camps. Zabludowski and Dr. Wielikowski will be leaving tomorrow at 6 A.M. on a three-day camp tour.

Gancwajch reports that the public is concerned as to whether the present chairman of the Council will be named the mayor. Not so long ago his wife's name figured on the posters of some dancing school as its "honorable" patroness.

One of the many jokes: they tell that some Jewish fellow gave his daughter, as a dowry, a hole in the wall, which is in use twenty-four hours a day.[13]

*May 8, 1941*—In the morning at the Community. I went to see Kamlah (I could not have gone to the theater, it is not fitting in view of what is going on in the camps). During our conversation I told him about the camps.

At 4 P.M. with Mohns. He announced that the ghetto is to receive a budget of 24,000,000 zlotys. We must establish a cooperative savings bank (It will not issue bank notes.) Emission [*Emissionsbank*] will have a branch in the ghetto. All requisitions are forbidden. If they occur they must be reported to him. At my request he agreed to replace the *Lagerschutz* with our own militia in the Kampinos camps (Szymanow, etc.). *(Nota bene,* yesterday our militia was introduced in Dąbrowica.) The *Lagerschutz* has departed and the workers rejoice.

Mohns informs me that we will have 10% of the rent income, etc. The governor is allegedly giving up his revenue from the Jewish buildings for the benefit of the Community. The *Amtschef* [Governor's Chief of Staff] will intervene with the *Wehrmacht* [Armed Forces] about the requisitions. We are to receive our own newspaper. He contended that soon he will put an end to the visits by our officials to the *Transfer*[*stelle*].

It looks like Dr. Auerswald will be named as *Kommissar* for Jewish Affairs and Mohns as District Chief [Governor].

Several days ago Gancwajch organized a gathering (a tea party) and kept his guests through the night.[14] Among those invited were Korczak (!!), naturally Stanislaw Rozenberg,[15] Glocer, etc. One of

13. The joke refers to a hole in an apartment wall facing "Aryan" Warsaw. The hole in the border wall was used for smuggling.
14. Gancwajch's guests stayed overnight because of the curfew.
15. Rozenberg, owner of printing plant before the war.

those present came to offer excuses for going there. Gancwajch kept on bitching about the Community Authority, lying shamelessly that he will get the workshop going and indeed "cultural life."

[Translated from the German]

Appointment by State Secretary

SA-Colonel Waldemar Schön was relieved of his post as *Kommissar* for the Jewish District of the City of Warsaw by the State Secretary of the Government and appointed by him, effective March 15, 1941, to be acting director of Interior Division in the Office of the Chief of the Warsaw District.

I went to see Auerswald, who contended that he was going to speak as a private person. Did we have enough members in the cooperatives? In the Brühl courtyard somebody in a car yelled to me "Off with your hat!" I took no notice. Horrible happenings in the hospitals and the refugee camps. Bread now costs 12 zlotys [per kilogram loaf] and watery milk 4–4.5 zlotys per liter. Children starving to death.

*May 9, 1941*—In the morning wet snow. A Jew came with Danke [?] from the *Totenkopfreiterstandarte* [SS Death Head Cavalry] who emphatically demanded a Jewish barber for the police. The Jew in turn, asked for a position as building administrator, etc. Zabludowski returned in the afternoon from his camp tour.

*May 10, 1941*—In the morning I was informed by Scherer that he would be replaced by Knoll.[16] Knoll inquired why G[ancwajch] and St[ernfeld] are trying to oust me from the Council, adding that they are quite a pair, to which I retorted that that was indeed the case. Knoll then commented that the Community Authority would disintegrate in 10 days if they took it over. In turn I delivered to Mende and Kra[a]tz a graphic compilation of the mortality rate among the Jews for 1939, [19]40, and the first months of 1941. In addition, I submitted a report on the catastrophic conditions in the refugee centers and on the general economic conditions of the quarter.

16. SS-2d Lieut. Walter Knoll served under SS-1st Lieut. Kurt Nicolaus in KdS/ IV-A-1.

Later I was received by *Kommandeur* Müller.[17] He proceeded to tell me that the Jews in Falenty are working in an exemplary manner and that they look healthy. I described to him the conditions in the camps. He mentioned that he saw the Governor in this matter. There will be a Jewish militia in the camps and perhaps one German. He gave instructions that all the *Berichte* [reports] be submitted to him directly or through his adjutant. I was visited by some Jewish social activists, etc., pleading that 30% of the bread ration cards be taken away from the rich for distribution among the poor.

And Dr. Auerswald became the *Kommissar* for Jewish Affairs.

An announcement, signed by me on May 7, on air raid precautionary measures, was posted.

Zabludowski, Wielikowski, with the *Lagerschutz* commander Capt. Meissner, visited the camps in the Kampinos cluster: Roztoki, Narty, Piekło. Later on, Szymanow, near Żyrardów, Miedniewice on the river Sucha and 2 camps near Łowicz, Kapituła, and Maleszyce. Food is dreadfully inadequate. The workers were to receive 6½ ounces of bread, 2.2–2.9 pounds of potatoes, sugar, marmalade, meat, coffee, etc. There are no potatoes and they receive 4–5½ ounces of bread. There is no fat whatsoever. Juske Co., 23 [Three] Crosses Square, in effect reducing the value of the wage by a half, by charging double prices for rations. The camp huts have spoiled straw to sleep on and wind is blowing through the walls. The workers are shivering at night. There are no showers and rest rooms. The workers' boots were ruined in wet sand and clay. There are no drugs or bandages. Treatment of the workers by the *Lagerschutz* in many localities is bad. Meissner did issue orders forbidding the beatings of the workers. Wages were not paid. In general the workers represent potentially good human material; but everything depends on nutrition.

*May 11, 1941*—In the morning at the Community. In the afternoon the first lecture in our paramedical course (Dr. Stein on life and death).

There appeared one Jehuda Warszawiak who had a job in the "13," but would like to be put in charge of a department of Culture and Arts in the Community.

17. SS-Major Johannes Müller succeeded Meisinger as *Kommandeur* of Security Police (KdS), Warsaw district, in April 1941.

*May 12, 1941*—In the morning at the Community. Gancwajch held another "tea party" yesterday with Fuerstenberg and Haendel among the guests. Today H[aendel] is "ill"; it must have been the "tea." Gancwajch attacked the Community again. One Galazka in an alcoholic stupor declared that everybody in the Community Authority lies down on the job. Jewry could be saved by Gancwajch, Sternfeld, and Kon.

I went to see Auerswald who informed me that he and Bischof [18] (director of the *Transferstelle)* are going to be installed in office. It appears that I will be invited as well. He asked for a table of organization of the Council's officials, who will be responsible to me. I am to receive powers of a mayor. He announced that his attitude to the Council was objective and matter of fact, without animosity.

In the courtyard of Brühl Palace I was ordered again to take off my hat.

I received a delegation from the hospitals headed by Skonieczny [19] (the trustee). They informed me that Dr. Hagen is unable to help them—there is no food. I issued instructions for drafting a memorandum to the authorities which I will deliver myself.

A disciplinary decision dated Feb. 10, 1941.

On October 2, 1940, the hospital grounds were toured in a hearse—which held the body of a newly born baby—by Przygoda who was in the driver's seat, urging the horses to go faster, and Rotleder and Trauman on the horses.

Punishment: Rotleder suspended for 6 weeks, the 2 remaining rascals 2 months' suspension each.

Today in the Community offices Mende and his aides began the interrogation of the Jews summoned to the Gestapo. At the same time in the archives he opened a chest which was sent to the Community from Gdansk of East Prussia. He found there antique silver objects used in rituals.

18. Max Bischof took over from Palfinger as director of the *Transferstelle* on May 15.
19. Dr. Waclaw Skonieczny was trustee administrator of Berson and Bauman Children's Hospital.

*May 13, 1941*—In the morning at the Community. Rozen has just informed us that Hoffmann is preparing a threatening move. I proceeded with Rozen to Paemeler and with Ziegler [20] we went to the office of Hoffmann who told us that he had been summoned to the Governor on the matter of the camps. Schoen had remarked at a conference that he would use other methods. Since H[offmann] was threatening the impressment of camp labor by other agencies, the Jew[ish] Order Service will have to supply 1,000 workers for the camps by tomorrow.

I went to Leszno Street to the food office in the matter of the sugar supply for industry. There is a definite need for the reorganization of the Financial-Budgetary Commission. The Community financial director should be named. It is not a good idea that, because of the small number of efficient councilors, some of them have 2 or 3 conflicting work areas.

A news items in the papers today about Hess.[21]

On the streets they are snatching handbags and stealing bread. The Order Service warns that in the near future the transport of bread from the bakeries might no longer be safe. The old women who carry bread have their baskets protected with wire nets at the top.

*May 14, 1941*—In the morning at the Community. Mohns has informed us that the Governor named me the mayor of the Jewish Quarter.

Yesterday the Service delivered about 1,000 workers for the camps while nine railway cars arrived with goods for the workshops.

Today the *Krakauerka* [22] had a communiqué on Hess.

*May 15, 1941*—In the morning at the Community, later with Auerswald. He told me that the Governor postponed the installation for a week. Later I delivered to Kamlah a memorandum about the camps, on the condition of the refugees, and some data on mortality.

One of the citizens summoned by Gancwajch escaped the doubtful pleasure of being associated with him by sending him a doctor's

20. Friedrich Ziegler, probably a German official working with Peemöller.
21. A reference to Nazi party leader Rudolf Hess's sensational jump from an aircraft into Scotland.
22. *Krakauerka* = *Krakauer Zeitung*, principal German-language daily in *Generalgouvernement*.

certificate to the effect that he is suffering from a chronic heart condition making it impossible for him to be active in social work.

When I was walking up the staircase in the Community building today, somebody attempted to knock off my hat. Rozen is being blackmailed because he allegedly made offensive remarks about someone.

*May 16, 1941*—In the morning at the Community. Gingold, a protégé of the Order Service, has been caught in the street and transported to a camp in Krosno. His sister has just appeared, threatening to make a telephone call. I called a meeting of the Council to discuss a proposal of the JHK (that 30,000 well-to-do people be deprived of cards [for rations] in order that [the food] might be distributed among the poor). A committee was chosen to prepare a program of assistance.

Rumkowski telephoned that he will visit the Community tomorrow.

*May 17, 1941*—Last night I was reading Rumkowski's newspaper.[23] My eye was caught by his pronunciamento to "My People." His main concern is that "his people" do not bother him in the streets by handing him propositions and petitions. Instead, he suggests a letter box citing the street and number of the building where it is located. Then follows a tale about his visit to a prison which is under his authority. The better part of those imprisoned are Community officials.

This morning I went to see Mende, Knoll, and Brandt. I showed Mende the horrifying photographs of children in shelters. He kept these. Knoll inquired about some 120,000 [zlotys] in connection with Fuerstenberg. It looks like a new denunciation. While talking about Kon and Heller[24] I remarked that one cannot keep on granting concessions without end to one enterprise. (In this firm the first fiddle is Galazka whom I "got to know" in Kompensata.[25])

Brandt took me and Szerynski to the new chief of his section.

23. Rumkowski's newspaper was the *Geto Tseitung*, published in the ghetto of Łódź.
24. Moritz Kon (or Kohn) and Zelig Heller had German concessions for horse-drawn buses, etc. These entrepreneurs, believed backed by the Gestapo, were suspect in the eyes of the Jews, See entries for May 17 and 19, 1941, February 7, 1942. Both were killed by the Germans in August 1942 during the deportations.
25. Kompensata = Zahan, the organization in which Czerniakow worked before the war.

Later we were directed to Roeller or Koeller,[26] a new expert in camp matters. He had visited one of the camps and appears willing to clear the atmosphere in them.

In the Community Rumkowski was recounting his activities in Łódź. The individual does not exist for him. He uses a *Sonderkommando* [27] for the purpose of requisitioning. He has been collecting diamonds and furs. There are no paupers on the streets. It was pointed out to him that 150,000 [sic] people ran away from Łódź to Warsaw where the conditions are worse; that his mortality rate is 1,000 a month,[28] that the number of births is going down. Much annoyed he replied that he was not suggesting that the living conditions in Łódź are good. There are many people with T.B. in Łódź. He called upon us to make peace with Ganzwajch, but he was against Merin. He believes that the shops in Warsaw should not be closed, but, on the other hand, he mentions that no [new] licenses should be granted. How to reconcile these two positions was not explained. He is replete with self-praise, a conceited and witless man. A dangerous man too, since he keeps telling the authorities that all is well in his preserve. Dr. Milejkowski had to explain all this to Dr. Hagen today.

Kamlah telephoned to inquire about the number of deaths in May. Nossig had been thrown out yesterday from *Transfer* (Steyert). He made a complaint about it to the proper authorities, and the reaction followed today. While listening to Rumkowski's perorations I recalled unwittingly the late attorney Swierzewski (a well known wit). He said once: What would have happened if the accused who was sentenced to death had not been defended by attorney Sterling!

*May 18, 1941*—In the morning at the Community. On the whole a quiet day.

*May 19, 1941*—An eventful day. In the morning at the Gestapo I informed Müller that 1,700 Jewish men and women had died between May 1 and May 15. I explained that this was due to the

26. Possibly Hugo Koehler, an SS noncommissioned officer.
27. Rumkowski's *Sonderkommando* was a special detachment in the Łódź Jewish police. The designation was copied from SS usage.
28. The mortality rates in the Łódź and Warsaw ghettos were approximately equal. The Warsaw ghetto death toll for May 1941 was 3,821.

insufficient food allocation (13 groszy, on the average, per day for a Jew—35 groszy for a Pole). I requested additional food contingents for the police and the Community staff. Müller promised to call the *Ernaehrungsamt* [Food Office]. Later with Brandt and Kra[a]tz. The former asked if Kon and Heller belong to the "13." We told Kra[a]tz about the "activities" of this group. Szerynski was with me.

On my return to the Community I was summoned to Governor Fischer. Unfortunately the car was being used for another errand and I was late for the appointment. On the staircase I ran across Müller, his assistants, and Leist. Standing all by himself was Schoen. Leist asked how many community kitchens we had. Müller mentioned that he had just seen the Governor. Auerswald took me to his office and informed me that I am to report to the Governor on Wednesday. He added that we must organize community kitchens, which is imperative because of *"der Zug der Zeit"* [the trend of the times].

In the afternoon I had a visit from Dr. Wielikowski who told me that he had seen Auerswald who is pleased that I invited A. to the Council. Tomorrow at 8 in the morning he will be leaving with Rozen, Auerswald, and Hoffmann for a tour of the camps. Dr. Auerswald said that I was named the mayor. Together with the King of Croatia.[29]

*May 20, 1941*—Today for the first time in May it is a little warmer. In the morning at the Community. Two men turned up demanding to be shown how we organize a money collection. Zabludowski attempted to explain this but was pushed aside. He then called Brandt who asked the guests to the telephone. Later they insisted that I must talk to them. I ushered them into my own office and proceeded very patiently to explain the incident, pointing out that Zabludowski was just an old man. They are apparently from Łódź; they asked questions about Rumkowski. The latter again summoned a meeting in the JDC calling for an *"entente cordiale"* with Gancwajch. Palfinger is demanding the closing of the Kon and Heller business. It appears that they have written a letter to *Transfer* with a complaint against the Community Authority. Tomorrow I am to see the Governor.

29. Croatia was a new puppet state formed after the occupation of Yugoslavia by Germans and Italians in April 1941. The Italian attempt to name a king of the state turned out to be unsuccessful.

*May 21, 1941*—In the morning at the Community. A call from Rozen. They visited Lekno and one other camp. The conditions are horrendous. Nobody can stand it for a month. The firms which supply the food are stealing it from the workers. The beatings of the workers is to cease. The efficiency of the work, admittedly hard, is low.

At 9:30 Wielikowski and I reported to Auerswald. We were [then] received by Governor Fischer. At the very beginning he contended that starving the Jews was not his objective. There is a possiblity that the food rations would be increased and that there will be work or orders for the workers. He pointed out that the corpses lying in the streets create a very bad impression. Indeed, the corpses do lie unattended (with their faces covered by newspaper and brick). The corpses, he said, must be cleared away quickly. He added that it is possible that we may receive additional food contingents for the police and the Community staff.

The Governor turned out to be a relatively young man, dressed in civilian clothes, but wearing high boots with spurs. His manner was polite. He completed his remarks by saying that he expects compliance, or else. . . .

In answer to a question as to whether we could receive a loan before the budget was approved, he said yes.

At 3 P.M. I was visited in the Community by Dr. Auerswald and Bischof. They were asking questions about procurement of food and production. In between the lines I sensed a certain displeasure with *Transfer* and the boundaries of the ghetto. I started talking about the ghetto, adding that in Kraków a large part of the population has passes and shops outside the Jewish quarter. Auerswald retorted that Kraków is different from Warsaw and that we must carry out the orders of our immediate superiors. He is not pleased with the boundary configuration of the ghetto. When I asked him if we would be permitted to submit our proposal for changes he said we could, adding that every change in the boundaries goes through his office anyway.

Bischof agrees with the view that the Council should represent a separate entity from Provisioning and Production.[30] Outside the

30. Provisioning, originally a division of the Council, was to become the independent Provisioning Authority. Its purpose was the distribution of officially imported food in the ghetto. The Council's Production Division was transformed in August 1941 into Jüdische Produktion GmbH, a corporation with private Jewish capitalization for the manufacture and sale of goods to German and Polish customers.

ghetto a merchants association will be organized for the supply of goods to the ghetto. He inquired if we had any financial experts on the Council.

They want to give us 500 tons of oats to be made into cereal. Unfortunately, we do not have any mills. There is a mill outside the ghetto on Bialostocka Street in Praga. One pound of oats yields six tenths of a pound of cereal. It would be possible to make 6 portions out of that amount.

We had a visit by some functionaries from the propaganda department who informed us that Krakow is against the Warsaw Jewish Community's publishing a paper. Dr. Auerswald is for it.

*May 22, 1941*—In the morning at the Community. A letter from Wielikowski to Schiper,[31] according to which I hugged him [W.] with delight when he joined the Council. Apart from this, Auerswald wants him to replace Rozen as a chairman of the Battalion. Schiper showed this letter to Rozen. Hence a big quarrel.

*May 23, 1941*—In the morning Palfinger telephoned inquiring how things are in his old bailiwick. At 2 P.M. I went with Sztolcman and Wielikowski to see Auerswald. Schneider from the *Ernaehrungsamt* [Food Office] and Legband [?] from *Transfer* were also present.

Certain calculations were made about the oat cereal. Lunch quotas were set for the Order Service, the Community staff, Zytos,[32] and the workers in the shops. I am to post announcements about lunches. Part of these lunches will be distributed without charge. The JHK role here will be limited to the preparation of food (logistics). The Community's welfare department is to distribute vouchers for these lunches.

Auerswald ordered others to leave and informed me that the different bureaus of the Community Authority must be centralized in 6 departments. Wielikowski is to be put in charge of *Fürsorge* [Welfare] and be made the fifth member of the board of the JHK. Furthermore, Auerswald stated that we are not sending men in good health to the camps. They will correct the shortcomings, but if the Council continues to shirk its responsibility we will be sorry.

31. Dr. Izak (or Ignacy) Schiper (spelled also Sziper or Schipper), former member of Polish parliament, an historian and a Zionist. Reportedly he refused a seat on the Council.
32. Zytos = TOZ, a Jewish welfare organization.

The Community Authority has a poor public image and it must be restored to health. I replied that cancers are devouring the community; themselves demoralized, they spread demoralization. He invited me for 2 P.M. tomorrow.

[Extract from *Gazeta Zydowska,* May 23, 1941]

## THE NEW STATUTE FOR THE JEWISH QUARTER

The Chief of the Warsaw district [Fischer] issued the following decree relating to the new statute of the Jewish Quarter.

(a)  The *Kommissar* for the Jewish Quarter

(1)  On the basis of paragraph one of the decree on the Jewish Quarter in Warsaw, dated April 19, 1941, I have appointed as the *Kommissar* of the Jewish Quarter in Warsaw Attorney Auerswald.

(2)  The *Kommissar* of the Jewish Quarter will be receiving orders directly from me.

(3)  The *Kommissar* of the Jewish Quarter will also be involved in working out problems involving Jews in the whole Warsaw district.

(4)  This decree goes into effect on May 15, 1941.

(b)  Chairman of the Jewish Council

On the basis of paragraphs 1–5 of the decree on the Jewish Quarter in Warsaw, dated April 19, 1941, I proclaim

(1)  The tasks and jurisdiction of the *Bürgermeister* in the Jewish Quarter in Warsaw will be performed by the Chairman of the Jewish Council in Warsaw.

(2)  The delineation of tasks and jurisdiction of the Chairman of the Jewish Council from the tasks and jurisdiction of the *Bürgermeister* of the city of Warsaw will be determined by the *Kommissar* of the Jewish Quarter in Warsaw in consultation with the Plenipotentiary of the Chief of the Warsaw district in Warsaw.

(3)  This decree goes into effect on May 15, 1941.

*May 24, 1941*—In the morning at the Gestapo, Mende informed me that they will stop the practice of sending urns [to next of kin]. The deceased in the camps will be buried (after cremation) at the state's expense. Kra[a]tz asked for a report on our preparation for air defense.[33] In the courtyard of my apartment house a sign has been placed at the entrance to the shelter and an air defense group has been organized. In general, there are not enough shelters in the ghetto to accommodate the population. A number of beggars (simulating disabilities, etc.) were arrested on the streets yesterday and sent to special centers. Between 2 and 5 I was with Auerswald. A more intimate discussion. There was a meeting today devoted to vocational schools. I asked Auerswald for a release from the camps of the sick workers after they have been examined by the Jewish doctors, for more piece work, and for extra food rations to feed prospective workers before their departure for the camps. Auerswald proposes that the heads of the 6 or 7 departments and I should receive a salary. I replied that so long as there was no money for the staff, neither I nor the other councilors could accept pay.

*May 25, 1941*—In the morning at the Community. There was as an official ceremony marking the opening of the first field kitchen which will be distributing coffee, bread, etc. I and Niunia both spoke on this occasion. Later we visited the headquarters of the Jewish Police. They used to have a little garden, but several days ago it was taken away from them by the law of the jungle and separated by a 13-foot wall in spite of the fact that this property was within the boundaries of the ghetto.

*May 26, 1941*—In the morning at the Community. At 10 o'clock in the *Ordnungspolizei* [German Order Police] with the *Kommandeur* Petsch [34] and his chief of staff Schaefer. I submitted the data on population and mortality. Later with Kamlah. He is not going to return the garden to the militia since he was told that Asko [?] is expanding construction of an army facility there. Petsch informed me that in a few days there is going to be a trial blackout of the city. Kamlah remarked that the army is on the move.

At 3 P.M. I visited Auerswald on some current matters. The staff of the Community Authority is in an uproar because of the exorbitant cost of food. White bread costs 24 zlotys this morning. At 6 P.M. black bread was 23 zlotys, white bread 31 zlotys,[35] an onion 1 zloty, and a roll 2.50 zlotys.

33. Air defense: the attack on USSR followed on June 22. See also Kamlah's remark, entry for May 26,
34. Lt. Col. of Order Police, Joachim Petsch, was *Kommandeur der Schutzpolizei* (Protective Police: city component of Order Police) in Warsaw.
35. Bread prices on the black market, per kilogram (2.2 pounds).

Toward evening I feel extremely tired. I am going to read *The Life of the Animals* by Brehm. I hope that I will get some rest.

*May 27, 1941*—In the morning at the Community. There has been some looting of the bakeries. The Community Authority staff is rebelling because of the high prices. I received their delegation and promised them 100,000 zlotys from a possible loan tomorrow. I went to see Auerswald with Wielikowski. W[ielikowski] reported on the matter of the kitchens and was rudely castigated for using some inaccurate data. After W[ielikowski] had departed I reviewed the text of a special appeal. W. [sic] rejected my draft on the grounds that it antagonizes property owners. I proposed Balaban as an editor of the newspaper. I asked for permission to return home.

*May 28, 1941*—In the morning at the Community. Later with Bischof and Palfinger. It turns out that we are not going to receive 500 tons of oats but 250 tons of oats and 125 tons of flour. Could this be the work of our Jews who keep visiting *Transfer?* Bischof mentions a loan in connection with *Transfer*'s proposal that we give up Grochów. I noted the need for clearing the air. He instructed me to talk to Steyert about the automobile and the telephones. Steyert ran into the corridor (after a conference with Schoen) yelling to Lichtenbaum, Haendel, and Fuerstenberg, "What are you Jews doing here?" To this, some German police officers who were talking with the Jews responded *"Wir sind keine Juden"* [We are no Jews]. Steyert continued to shout his insults threatening that he himself would "deal with the Jews." At this very point Sternfeld put his head in the door—"Get out," screamed Steyert, "out of the corridor, into the street." And then, turning to me: "Did you want to talk to me?" "Not today, tomorrow." I should have settled the matter of the automobile a long time ago. I went to see Auerswald but he was out. I had a chat with his secretary who comes from Riga and speaks Russian. She is Auerswald's wife. In the Community I gave 100,000 zlotys to the staff for disbursement among them. In our workshops the workers are fainting from hunger. I am asking the authorities for permission to buy food in the free market.

*May 29, 1941*—In the morning at the Community. Auerswald is not receiving today; he instructed me to drop in tomorrow with a report on the communal kitchens. He added that he will also issue instructions for the "13." Palfinger remarked that he will try to process the oats in 3 mills. Part of the flour (10 tons) was delivered to the Provisioning Authority, 5 tons of which I ordered to be given to workers in Production.

Bischof said in a telephone conversation, *"Ich pfeife auf Auf-stellung"* [To hell with the inventory]. It had to do with my promise to draw up a memorandum on the kitchens. According to Haendel, Steyert does not wish me to see him. It is my impression that he told Bischof that the wall construction workers do not want to exert themselves. It is indeed true that we owe the contractors large sums of money and that the workers' wages are low. I promised that I will raise the wages.

Our police have conducted the investigation of our kitchens rather ineptly. In the afternoon I was in conference with Wieli-kowski, Alpern, and Rotenberg.[36] We drafted the guidelines for the memorandum to Auerswald.

*May 30, 1941*—In the morning at the Community. Preparing our report on the kitchens. At 3 P.M. with Auerswald. I submitted the draft of an appeal about providing the extra food for the public at large and the summary of the questionnaire response about the kitchens. A[uerswald] [said] that the "13" is going to be subordi-nated to the Council. Gancwajch must be admitted to the Commu-nity Authority. To a question as to whether I am to take him into the Council he replied this would not be necessary, suggesting that he could perhaps be made our legal counsel. Gancwajch sent us a letter today with a request for admission.

*May 31, 1941*—In the morning at the Gestapo with a memoran-dum on economic conditions in the quarter and the exorbitant cost of living. Later on, in the *Transferstelle*, but Palfinger, Steyert, and their secretary were absent. I visited Bischof; the loan seems to be beyond reach. I kept explaining that we have no means to pay the contractors and the work is grinding to a halt.

Later I went with Wielikowski to Auerswald. We reported on controls of the kitchens. I introduced Szerynski. Auerswald kept wondering about "my title," reaching the conclusion that I should imprint on the forms and letters *"Verwaltung des Juedischen Wohn-bezirks"* [Administration of the Jewish District]. There is a sugges-

36. Zwi Rotenberg, Provisioning.

tion for instituting the Rabbinate and the Chief Rabbi. I gave him my impression of Steyert and Palfinger, adding that I expect integrity in the *Transferstelle*.

A trial blackout in the city this evening. In the meantime, Gancwajch waited for me in the Community, to no avail.

*June 1, 1941*—In the morning at the Community. At 9:30 in the Synagogue on Tlomackie Street. I carried the Torah twice around the synagogue. Toward the end of the service (Shavuot) a cantor had a dizzy spell (paralysis). He had to be transported to the hospital. After the synagogue I visited the Provisioning Authority. Discussion of future tactics *re Transfer*. [Czerniakow inserted his synagogue admission card with the dates June 1–Sep. 13, 1941 imprinted on it. The later date was crossed out.]

Niunia's birthday. A mass of flowers.

*June 2, 1941*—In the morning at the Community. A holiday— Shavuot. Preparations for the blackout of Warsaw. Gancwajch has appeared, suggesting that he would like a position "without port-folio." He insists that he is to report our conversation to Bonifer. I gave instructions to Szerynski, in accordance with the *Kommissar*'s order, to make arrangements for the taking over of the *Ueber-wachungsstelle*. [Control Office—the "13"].

The night duty clerk in the Community Authority announces that in the past he was starving during the day. Now he knows what it means to be starving at night.

*June 3, 1941*—In the morning at the Community Authority. Piekło and Narty, the worst of the camps, had been done away with because the firms supplying food could not obtain it. The same happened to Roztoka, Wola Miedniewicka, Zimnawoda, and Ruda. Part of the work force was transferred to other camps.

I went to see Palfinger. He insisted on adoption of his plan for flour distribution. After a few stormy exchanges he telephoned Auerswald who gave instructions for continuation of his own plan. And that was my scheme, communicated to Auerswald beforehand. Bischof came in. I mentioned the subject of purchasing, with the possible permission of *E. u. L.* [*Ernährungs und Landwirtschaft*— Food and Agriculture] potatoes, etc. in the free market. He agreed provisionally to let us approach *E. u. L.* After a momentary pause he asked Palfinger's opinion. The latter responded that it would amount to an "insult to authority."

The intention behind my plan was to curtail smuggling and reduce prices; [but] Bischof withdrew his consent. In the same vein, Palfinger was asked by Bischof to express an opinion on another proposal of mine (which Bischof had previously accepted), that only specified counselors communicate with *Transfer*. Palfinger again expresses his opposition.

Steyert nourishes an idea of cutting off the little ghetto from the rest at Chlodna Street. They have printed a panegyric about me in the *Gazeta Zydowska* [*Jewish Gazette*].

*June 4, 1941*—In the morning at the Community. At 9 o'clock I mentioned to Palfinger a new kitchen problem—perhaps we should exchange our rye flour for wheat flour, for instead of a soup we are obtaining glue. What a climate in *Transfer* with Bischof as its supervisor. I asked A[uerswald] if he has obtained his personnel; there is no answer from him to our numerous letters. I inspected 4 kitchens. The rye flour soup, provided one adds to it some fat and greens, is not too bad, as they have been telling me. In the Community treasury there were 90 groszy this morning. The typhus is spreading on the Aryan side. Hagen et al. claiming that its source is the ghetto and they are urging that the whole ghetto population be bathed. It is my opinion that typhus spreads because of dire poverty and malnutrition.

*June 5, 1941*—In the morning at the Community. At 4:30 with Auerswald. He promised the Krasinski Park [37] and an enlargement of the ghetto. On the subject of the *Ueberwachungsstelle* [the "13"] he stated that Szerynski should subordinate its staff as ordinary militiamen—Auerswald himself will deal with Gancwajch if he causes any trouble. He is willing to give us three passes exempting the bearers from the armband requirement. He agreed to exchange the rye flour for other produce.

*June 6, 1941*—In the morning at the Community. Major Przymusinski of the Polish police appeared and informed us that 10

37. Czerniakow did not get Krasinski Park.

policemen in the VII Precinct contracted typhus.[38] In view of this development we are to organize a Jewish detention facility for 100–150 arrestees.

I went to see Auerswald. I received Gancwajch in the presence of Zundelewicz and Szerynski. He informed me that he was going to report to his authorities that the "13" personnel are to be incorporated into the Order Service, not as a unit, but dispersed, with a special section in the headquarters, and the enforcement of the price control regulations decentralized in the precincts.

*June 7, 1941*—In the morning at the Gestapo. Kra[a]tz broke his arm. An official ceremony at Ceglana Street marking the presentation of an ambulance to the hospital. Later in the Community a meeting of the patrons of our [symphony] orchestra. Niunia chaired the occasion.

*June 8, 1941*—In the morning at the Community. A meeting of councilors, delegates to the [German] authorities, to decide on courses of action.[39]

*June 9, 1941*—In the morning at the Community. At 3 P.M. at Auerswald's. He promised to supply our communal kitchens, every three months, with 5,000 metric tons of sugar and 10 tons of meat. In addition, he will give us some turnip oil. I introduced Milejkowski. A problem with grinding oats in the ghetto.

In the afternoon I was working at home—with interruptions of the moans of beggars under the window—"Bread, bread! I am hungry, hungry!"

*June 10, 1941*—In the morning at the Community. At 5:30 at Auerswald's. He announced that Gancwajch is to be treated as a *Beauftragte* [plenipotentiary] in the Community Authority and is to be allowed to acquaint himself with all of our departments. I inspected several mills in connection with our oats grinding problem.

38. The implication of Major Przymusinski's statement is that Polish police were infected by Jewish detainees. The VII Precinct had its headquarters on 56 Krochmalna Street. Franciszek Przymusinki became commander of the Polish police in Warsaw, March 1943.
39. Probably a meeting of men delegated to deal with German offices directly.

On June 9, 1941, 42,625 lunches were served to adults and 25,372 to children. All together 65,997.[40] A Jewish detention facility has been set up with Lewkowicz in charge.

*June 11, 1941*—In the morning at the Community. It has been raining. Fortunately for us this does not entail any costs to the Community.

Repeated threats from Gancwajch. He was to see the *Kommissar* today. I went with Szerynski to the Gestapo. Brandt called Levetzow [41] for a conference. L. told him that he is not Gancwajch's protector. Bratenschweis (?) reproached Sztolcman because of the color of his shirt.

*June 12, 1941*—It has been pouring cats and dogs in the morning. In the Community Authority. A headache. Gancwajch had a meeting with his cabal and is mouthing his threats again. Yesterday they were requisitioning watches.

I went to see Bischof and he told me an amnesty decree was going to be issued for currency crimes. He instructed me to organize a cooperative bank and to write a letter requesting cancellation of Haendel's and Fuerstenberg's passes. They will be forbidden to visit *Transfer*.

*June 13, 1941*—In the morning at the Community. At 4:00 with Auerswald. He let me know his displeasure that I dealt with the Gancwajch affair myself, adding that he himself had spoken with him in the presence of a subordinate. He indicated that so far as smuggling is concerned the authorities are looking the other way but that they will take the sternest measures against people leaving the ghetto. The reason—the epidemic. In fact, the epidemic is spreading fast. On June 5, '41 there were 229 confirmed [new] cases and 24 suspected ones. On June 12, '41 278 and 42 respectively.

*June 14, 1941*—In the morning at the Gestapo with Szerynski. I wanted to see the *Kommandeur*—on the subject of obtaining additional food supplies for the population. During Rozen's visit at

40. Lunches: 42,625 + 25,372 = 67,997 (not 65,997).
41. SS-1st Lieut. Alfred Levetzow, Security Service. Levetzow may have lied.

Auerswald's today some letters on Jewish matters were brought in. [While opening the correspondence] Mrs. Auerswald spotted a little creature. Horrified, they immediately sent the "louse" to Lambrecht for tests. A[uerswald] declared that he would not accept any letters from me in the future. No matter that these letters did not come from the Community Authority but from *Transfer.*

In the Warsaw district camps the workers' legs are swelling. In Kraków and in the Lublin district the camps are bearable.

*June 15, 1941*—In the morning at the Community. In the afternoon Schipper, Frydman,[42] and Muszkat came in to announce that they were giving up their [volunteer] work for the Community. They submitted a memorandum which I passed on to Jaszunski, who is going to have a session with them.

*June 16, 1941*—In the morning at the Community. At 9 with Auerswald. There was no louse in *our* letters. I submitted a project for placing Production and Provisioning on a commercial basis. At the same time, Orlean,[43] quite needlessly, delivered this plan to Bischof, who has reservations that are incomprehensible to me. I requested the expediting of the loan and of the Krasinski Park.

*June 17, 1941*—In the morning at the Community. Later with the *Kommandeur* of the Gestapo.[44] He called Brandt and inquired about the "13." He gave orders for summoning Gancwajch, Sternfeld, and Lewin. Bischof telephoned instructing me to call a meeting of the Economic Council, not in the Community Authority but in the Provisioning Authority. I am to participate as a guest. The older Lichtenbaum [45] and First tendered their resignations.

*June 18, 1941*—In the morning at the Community. At 11:30 Auerswald informed me that Gancwajch is to be made an inspector in the Council. I went to see Bischof to inform him that I would not be present at the meeting of the Economic Council.

Our loan is more and more problematic. Grochów [farm] (as-

42. Zysze Frydman, prewar secretary general of Agudath Israel (Orthodox Party).
43. Mieczyslaw Orlean, incorporator and co-manager of Jüdische Produktion GmbH as of August 1941.
44. *Kommandeur* of Gestapo should be *Kommandeur* of Security Police and Security Service.
45. Lichtenbaum Sr. was Marek Lichtenbaum, Czerniakow's deputy and successor. His son, Mieczyslaw Lichtenbaum, was active in ghetto administration as construction official.

suredly) is *eingezogen* [confiscated], that is to say *sichergestellt* [secured]. We are to deal with Krakow in the matter of the buildings. The best solution for us would be to ask the municipality for 300,000 zlotys monthly, based on what they owe us (our share of the city revenues). The costs (270,000 zlotys) of renovating the post office building in the Kramy Nalewkowskie will be paid out of the *Haushalt* [budget].

At 3:00 P.M. Bischof and Rathje [46] arrived at the Community. Bischof informed us that he wanted to attend the meeting at Leszno Street. I directed him there. The conference of the Economic Council lasted from 3:30 to 7 o'clock. The subject: placing the Provisioning Authority and Production on a commercial basis and making them independent of the Community.

*June 19, 1941*—In the morning at the Community. There is a strike in the ZSS. A threat to our kitchen operations. Yesterday 103,000 meals were served. At 9:30 with Auerswald who informed me that for the time being I was not to give Gancwajch any answer. Gancwajch appeared in the Community Authority at 11 o'clock.

I had lunch in the headquarters of the Order Service. The soup (one half a liter) with beans, a tiny bit of meat, and dumplings— good. It is being served from a field kitchen. At 9 A.M. a trial air raid alarm. We closed all the windows—darkened with a black paper.

*June 20, 1941*—In the morning at the Community. I summoned Sagan, Kirszenbaum,[47] and Szereszewki about the strike in the ZSS and informed them that the kitchens must not be struck. I promised to obtain larger rations for the employees of the ZSS.

At 3 P.M. Auerswald informed me that the "13" had been definitively disbanded to come under the command of Szerynski. If there is going to be a criminal division in the Order Service, Gancwajch will take charge of it. About 102,000 lunches were served yesterday.

A Rabbi Kanal has come to see me and requested that if there was going to be an office of the Chief Rabbi he would like to be named.

In the ghetto there appeared a significant quantity of rhubarb. This is the ghetto's manna. Gancwajch speaks as if he were

46. Dr. Hans Ulrich Rathje, the new deputy director of the *Transferstelle*.
47. Szachne Sagan was a Labor Zionist, leftist faction; Menachem Kirszenbaum, a General Zionist, a more conservative faction.

straining every word through his dirty saliva and washing it in his mouth before uttering it.

Haendel has completely lost his head. He is asking for a leave of absence.

A band stopped in front of the Pinkiert [funeral] establishment in Grzybowska Street and proceeded to play some lively pieces.

*June 21, 1941*—In the morning at the Gestapo. Müller,[48] whom I paid a visit with Szerynski, declared that Gancwajch could live off the *Liegenschaften* [real estate]; he will in no way be connected with the Community Authority. The Order Service will receive the Aryan rations.[49]

*June 22, 1941*—In the morning at the Community. It is Sunday. A meeting of the councilors to map out the tactics for the immediate future: the struggle with typhus, lunches, the statutes for the Provisioning Authority and Production workshops. At 1 P.M. the opening of a kitchen for the staff of the central office.

A newspaper special on the war with the Soviets.[50] It will be necessary now to work all day, and perhaps they will not let one sleep at night.

*June 23, 1941*—In the morning at the Community. Later at Auerswald's I learned that the Order Service's Aryan food contingents are to be squeezed out of the general ghetto contingent.

In the afternoon the first air raids on Warsaw. In the evening at 11 a second alarm—we went down to the shelter. Conflicting news reports; Brest Litovsk, and Bialystok are said to have been taken. The loudspeakers are silent.

*June 24, 1941*—In the morning at the Community. Later with Auerswald. Yesterday Szerynski compelled the shopkeepers and bakers to open their establishments. The black market, very strong in the morning, collapsed. The governor called for a report on our lunch distribution. I myself am eating soup every day in the Community.

48. Müller, in this case, was probably the SS-2d Lieut. in the Gestapo (Kds–IV).
49. "Aryan" rations refer to official allocations to the Polish (non-Jewish) population. The official ghetto rations were much lower.
50. Germany attacked the USSR that morning.

One of the supplicants is asking for a grant to pay his rent, adding that he may die of hunger but that he does not want to die in the gutter. In *Nowy Kurier Warszawski* an article about black marketeers [in Polish Warsaw]. And believe it or not, not a word about the Jews. Could there be black marketeers where there are no Jews?

*June 25, 1941*—In the morning at the Community. Later with Auerswald about the food rations for the staff of the Community, the JSS and the Order Service. These and all the other matters are not moving ahead.

*June 26, 1941*—In the morning at the Community. At 3 o'clock with Gepner and Sztolcman I visited Dr. Rodeck, Lehband,[51] and Auerswald. It was decided that the Provisioning Authority should continue to be subordinated to the Council. Auerswald keeps insisting on the resignation of Dr. Milejkowski. I set his mind at ease by promising to mobilize the whole population for the struggle against the epidemic. At midnight an explosion caused by an air raid.

One of the petitioners writes that her deceased father "is now without a job."

*June 27, 1941*—In the morning at the Community. Later with Auerswald who ordered the registration of the foreign Jews in the ghetto. To Fribolin [52] (the mayor of Karlsruhe) on the subject of the ghetto budget. I found him to be a polite and nervous man. Later with Kulski, whom I asked to get in touch with Iwanka on the matter of the city and ghetto budgets.

Auerswald gave me and Sztolcman exemptions from wearing the armbands. Finally he told me to discipline Milejkowski, and it was with difficulty that I convinced him that Milejkowski should be given an assistant with dictatorial powers to help him fight the epidemic.

I summoned a conference on the subject of combating the epidemic. I proposed to make the house committee, the house

51. *Assessor* Ansbert Rodeck, in Auerswald's office, a retired civil servant. Legband (Czerniakow also writes "Lehband"), not identified.
52. Dr. Hermann Fribolin, *Dezernent* in charge of Finance, Health, and Education in German city administration. Killed during Polish uprising, August 1944.

administrators, and the caretakers answerable for hiding the sick, not reporting lice infestation, etc.

I received as a gift from a young art student several of my sonnets with her illustrations.

*June 28, 1941*—In the morning at the Gestapo. Later Auerswald. He gave me the city budget to help me prepare ours. I submitted to him the charter of the Provisioning Authority.

On the grounds of the former Hospital of the Holy Spirit, I saw incubators in which delightful little chickens are hatching.

*June 29, 1941*—In the morning at the Community. Glücksberg bought a box of headache powders for me. A boy snatched the box from his hands in the street and started to eat the powder.[53] We set up baths for 1,000 people a day at Prosta Street.

*June 30, 1941*—In the morning at the Community. Rumors that Lwów has been taken. The June 30 communiqué speaks of the capture of 40,000 Russians, 600 guns, 2,233 tanks, the destruction in 7 days of 4,107 planes with own losses of 150 planes. Grodno was taken on June 23, Brest-Litovsk, Vilna, and Kovno on June 24 and Dvinsk on June 26. East of Bialystok there remains a pocket of 2 Soviet armies with the German troops tightening their grip around it.

*July 1, 1941*—In the morning at the Community. Later at Kulski's with Rozenstadt, Iwanka, and the deputy mayor. A conference on the Council's budget. We are working on a draft. The number of distributed lunches exceeded 118,000. Not many workers in the shops (only 2,100). More death. With a corpse in the entrance of an apartment house, the lice spread through the entire building. Only today have I noticed that the 10-zloty notes bear a sketch of Chopin's monument on the Avenue.[54]

Niunia is very upset.[55]

Lately a series of proclamations and decrees have been posted on

---

53. On occasion, starvation drove people to snatch food from passers-by on the street.
54. The Germans had blown up Chopin's monument.
55. Mrs. (Niunia) Czerniakow may have been worrying about her son Jas, who had been living in Lwów.

the subject of food allocation, registration of aliens, and appeals for quiet and order.

*July 2, 1941*—In the morning at the Community. Later Kra[a]tz and Mende with Szerynski. Brandt is leaving for the east a period of 4–5 weeks. I called a meeting of the Council in the Community Authority on the subject of increasing the price of bread. I argued against this move. In the end it was decided that only the price of the bread cards would go up.

The rabbis are in an uproar because Ettinger,[56] who was engaged as criminal counsel, is a baptized Jew.

*July 3, 1941*—In the morning at the Community. Later I inspected the Jewish house of detention at Gesia Street. It is better equipped than Pawiak prison. Then with Auerswald and Rodeck. The former stated that a detention facility should not be called in German *Gefängnis* [prison] but *Arrestanstalt* [house of detention]. The latter intervened in the matter of oats [flour] which were not delivered to our kitchens by Janicki's mill. Then he read a denunciation of the Provisioning Authority, adding that the *Gazeta Żydowska* also writes about it unfavorably. According to him the charter of the Provisioning Authority has been poorly drafted. A first-year student would do a better job. Bischof and Auerswald share this opinion.

*July 4, 1941*—In the morning at the Community. Later I visited the *Umschlagplatz*.[57] A vast area, huge warehouses, numerous personnel. The magazines are full of supplies for our production enterprises.

Apropos of the commercial transactions—A droshky bulging with radishes just drove in. I visited the production workshops at Prosta Street. A hopeless situation. Out of 29,000 workers only 1,500 are on the job. A meeting of the Economic Council was held to discuss Production, etc. The prices of goods are falling.

*July 5, 1941*—Morning. Mende, in his civilian clothes, is not seeing anybody. He sent me to Knoll who informed me that he will

---

56. Dr. Adam Ettinger, a former professor of criminology at Warsaw Free University.
57. *Umschlagplatz:* (loading place), the location of warehouses and railway siding; site of deportations in 1942.

get back at Palfinger for his financial dealings with the Community. The other day I was asked to submit receipts for the supplies. A Leica camera was listed as costing the Community Authority 600 zlotys. The *Transferstelle* listed it 200 zlotys. Knoll claims that in Berlin a Leica costs 250 *Reichsmarks*.

I went with Szerynski to *Kommandeur* Mueller. He stated that he would help the Order Service to receive Aryan rations, that already 2 weeks earlier he had discussed this matter with the Governor, acquainting him with the general food situation [in the ghetto], that the Governor is appreciative of his intervention, that because the army has moved forward and no longer buys up the food produce, the situation will improve. I asked for his assistance in obtaining [higher] allocations for the workers in our production enterprises and the staff of the Community Authority. He promised to help. He read me the menu from Falenty [camp]. It was so rich that I made a joke that I would give up my post and become a worker there myself. He added that the workers are lazy and he threatened to replace them with others.

He told me that 20,000 Bolsheviks surrendered after killing their commissars. The army is now way beyond Minsk.

I mentioned the subject of requisitions in the ghetto. He told me to report such cases to him or to Stamm.[58] He said that he was leaving for Białystok, but would be commuting to Warsaw. In his absence Dr. Kah will be in charge. He further stated that an officer had been arrested for requisitioning on his own, so was somebody of lower rank in Hohensalza [Inowrocław] who was guilty of the same offense.

We visited Kamlah, asking for intervention in respect of a garden taken away from the police and the food rations for the workers who work in groups in different parts of the city. The number of lunches distributed on July 4, '41 was 117,481.

I went to see Auerswald. He did not have much time for me, but I asked him for a letter on the subject of the "13," especially since Müller was asking whether this matter has been settled.

Bischof and Rodeck criticized the character of the Provisioning Authority, denying that our lawyers have any competence or talent. After the furniture, etc., they are requisitioning our intelligence.

58. SS-Captain Walter Stamm, head of Gestapo section under the KdS.

*July 6, 1941*—In the morning at the Community. As usual a meeting of the Executive Committee of the Council, etc. Today is our 28th wedding anniversary, without Jas.

*July 7, 1941*—In the morning at the Community. Later with Auerswald, Schlosser,[59] and Grassler [60] on current business. Fogel [61] was beaten up in the courtyard today while taking letters to the *Kommissar*.

Outside Zelazna Brama Square some Polish teenagers are trapping Jewish teenagers smuggling rhubarb.

Auerswald announced that the Jews may be allotted the Polish rations by August.

*July 8, 1941*—In the morning at the Community. At 10 o'clock with Rozen at Auerswald's. He informed me that several score of workers escaped from the Dębica camp. If they are fleeing beyond the borders of the GG [*Generalgouvernement*] it matters little, but if they are roaming about in the GG, appropriate measures would be taken. The Jews, according to A[uerswald] should show good will by volunteering for labor. Otherwise the ghetto would be surrounded by barbed wire. There is plenty of it, the spoils of war captured in Russia. The ring will be tightened more and more and the whole population will slowly die out.

In the streets the workers are being impressed for labor outside the ghetto, since there are few volunteers for a job which pays only 2.80 zlotys and provides no food. I went to Kamlah to obtain food for them. So far no results. Considering their dire predicament, the Jewish masses are quiet and composed. As a rule the Jews make noise only when things are going well for them. When Galileo invented the telescope some monk would not look at the skies lest he catch sight of some star not foreseen by the Holy Scriptures. The same is true with the wage voucher of 2.80 zlotys. It is asserted that there is no such thing as inflation, only high prices. Nobody wants to consider the fact that the worker cannot survive on 2.80 zlotys.

*July 9, 1941*—In the morning at the Community. A typical working day. For several days they have been sniping at people

---

59. Schlosser was chief of Warsaw district Economy Division.
60. Dr. Franz Grassler was Auerswald's deputy.
61. Fogel worked in the ghetto housing office.

taking walks after 9 P.M. Today the same is happening in broad daylight.

*July 10, 1941*—In the morning at the Community. Usual work. I went to see Podwinski [62] about the budget. Pawel's wife brought a letter from her husband which she accidentally opened in the post office. It came in an unsealed envelope and was addressed to me at "13 Leszno Street"(?).

Last night I spotted a louse in my nightshirt. A white, many-footed, revolting louse.

*July 11, 1941*—In the morning at the Community. At 10:30 with Rozen to Auerswald. He announced a change in the ghetto boundaries. He will send us an inquiry about population statistics for specific blocks. He advises us not to worry that these particular blocks will be lost. He promised the construction of barracks to enlarge the ghetto, asking if we have carpenters. He reviewed the matter of the Dębica camp.

*July 12, 1941*—In the morning at the Gestapo. Later in the Community. I had planned to go with Gepner to Otwock tomorrow. Because he is indisposed I am not going.

At home in the evening a sort of cabaret. I was depicted as raising a high "C" of responsibility, writing a tract entitled "Sisyphean Labors," and inviting the residents of our building to take trips to Czerniakow.[63]

*July 13, 1941*—In the morning at the Community. For several days it has been extraordinarily hot.

*July 14, 1941*—In the morning at the Community. I tried to see Auerswald twice but he could not receive me. At his behest I went to see Steyert. The latter asked for population statistics for the following streets: (1) Sienna—Panska, (2) Panska—Grzybowska, (3) Grzybowska—Chlodna. What is involved here is the separation of the so-called small ghetto from the [rest of] the ghetto.

62. Stanislaw Podwinski was Kulski's deputy.
63. "Czerniakow": a play on words. There was a section of Warsaw outside the walls by that name.

*July 15, 1941*—In the morning at Auerswald's. Krasinski Park will at last be opened to the Jews. I am to discuss with Steyert the technical aspects of this undertaking (the walls—their cost 50,000 zlotys). We drafted the ghetto budget. I am going to submit it to Auerswald tomorrow.

*July 16, 1941*—In the morning at the Community. Kamlah arrived with his adjutant Dr. Meyer and inspected our vocational school and kitchens. Later they went to Denis to have their pictures taken. We cannot get Krasinski Park since it is used for walks by the wounded soldiers.

*July 17, 1941*—In the morning to Auerswald. He announced that he will give us a letter about the "13." He enjoys the sights in the Old City.

*July 18, 1941*—In the morning at the Community. A delegation of about 30 persons arrived from the hospital. I agreed to receive 3 delegates. Instead of complying they became raucous in the adjoining conference room. They had to be removed by the orderlies. Later I received the troika and explained that I was trying to obtain a loan for the purpose of increasing the pay of employees. They left calmed down. Shortly afterwards I received a letter from Milejkowski from the hospital informing me that he had been kept captive there, and would not be released until the employees receive their back pay.

Stein, Mrs. Braude-Heller,[64] et al. came to make me pay the arrears, though nobody knows out of what funds. I replied that I would not do it under duress. Fliederbaum, Horensztajn,[65] Remba,[66] and First went to the hospital and somehow appeased the mass meeting there. Tomorrow, however, we will have to pay out over 100,000 zlotys.

*July 19, 1941*—In the morning with Mende. He is going on leave. Later with Kra[a]tz. Then with Auerswald who is also leaving on a holiday for Ciechocinek (Hermannsbad). Yesterday I summoned a lady author of a letter to Auerswald, who writes that she is a true

64. Dr. A. Braude-Heller was director of children's hospital at Sliska Street.
65. Szmul Horensztejn was secretariat of the Council.
66. Nahum Remba worked for the ghetto education department.

*BDM*,[67] that one can get a job in the Community Authority with a bribe, etc. I gave instructions for this case to be given to the prosecutor. The more so since she was arrogant. She told me that the Kon and Heller firm takes one thousand zlotys for a job on the [horse-drawn] bus[line].

I gave instructions for the disbursement of 120,000 zlotys to the hospital personnel (a loan from the Labor Battalion and the Provisioning Authority.)

*July 20, 1941*—In the morning at the Community. It is Sunday. I am not feeling well. Yesterday we had an official ceremony marking the opening of the kitchen for the children of the camp workers.

An interesting inscription in a certain institution:

| | |
|---|---|
| *Die über Nacht sich umgestellt* | Those who will change themselves overnight |
| *Die sich zu jedem Staat bekennen* | Those who follow every camp |
| *Das sind die Praktiker der Welt* | These are the men with practical sight |
| *Man koennte sie auch Lumpen nennen.* | One may also call them tramp |

*July 21, 1941*—Yesterday in bed from 3 P.M. Today I will go to the office at 10 o'clock. I worked on part of my chores at home.

In the Community I received a letter from the *Kommissar* on the Gancwajch bureau. Has his career come to an end? *Tempi di guerra tempi di carriera* [In war's gloom, careers bloom].

[Translated from the German]

Copy

File Number: K-1000
Diary: 149/41

To the Control Office for Combating the Black Market and Profiteering in the Jewish District of Warsaw

    att. A. Gancwajch
    13 Leszno Street
    Warsaw

67. "B.D.M.," German initials for "Federation [Bund] of German girls," not "blond German girls." Possibly a Czerniakow joke.

The Control Office for Combating the Black Market and Profiteering in the Jewish District of Warsaw is hereby dissolved. Members of the Control Office are forbidden to engage any further in activities for which the office was responsible.

Property of the Control office is to devolve on the Chairman of the Jewish Council in Warsaw—Administration of the Jewish District.

Official books and all records are to be delivered to the Chairman of the Jewish Council.

Identification cards made out to employees of the office and items of equipment issued to them (caps, etc.) are to be confiscated and likewise delivered to the Chairman of the Jewish Council.

Members of the Control Office will be transferred, as suited, to the Jewish Order Service. The assignment of leading employees is reserved.

Signed   Auerswald                                     July 17, 1941

*July 22, 1941*—In the morning Dr. Grassler handed me the charter of the Provisioning Authority. Gancwajch informed the Executive Committee of the Council that Dr. Kah suspended the dissolution of his bureau.

Today there was another requisitioning of furniture at 11 Elektoralna Street.

*July 23, 1941*—In the morning with Grassler. He had communicated with Kah who told him to come tomorrow in the matter of Gancwajch.

Niunia has been crying all day. There has been no news of Jas.

*July 24, 1941*—In the morning at the Community. Grassler informed me that the municipality will give the Community a credit of 1,000,000 zlotys pending a subsidy. We will now be heading for some really complicated dealings with *Transferstelle.*

On the subject of 13 Leszno Street, Dr. Kah told Grassler that the group is being disbanded, except for the inventory, the disposition of which will be decided after the return of the *Kommissar.* I attended to the matter of a woman cooking instructor in connection with the suggestions I made during a Council meeting to (1) improve the quality of lunches, (2) to set up some procedures to assure that the soup is distributed to the most needy people.

I returned a visit to Reverend Poplawski who called on me at one time on the subject of assistance to the Christians of Jewish origins. He proceeded to tell me that he sees God's hand in being placed in the ghetto, that after the war he would leave as much of an anti-Semite as he was when he arrived there, and that the Jewish beggars (children) have considerable acting talent, even playing dead in the streets.

Who is Miss Ghetto? Naturally Mrs. Judt!

*July 25, 1941*—In the morning at the Community. The matter of the subsidy of 1,000,000 zlotys. (Bischof reviewed with me the logistics. We will be able to draw the required amounts from a bank account. *Transfer*'s fee is 20,000 zlotys.)

[Document translated from the Polish]

Copy

Jewish Council in Warsaw
Headquarters of the Order Service

The Inspectorate
No. In. 366/41

Excerpt from the inspection report In. 366/41, dated July 22, 1941

During an outdoor inspection on July 22, 1941, I ascertained the following:

In front of 16 Krochmalna Street I was stopped by a commander of a military sanitary column and shown the corpse of a child in an advanced stage of decay. According to information obtained on the site, the corpse, already decomposed, was abandoned there yesterday. On the basis of subsequent investigation it was established that the body was left behind by its own mother, Chudesa Borensztajn, residing at 14 Krochmalna Street, apartment 67, and that the child's name was Moszek, age 6. In the same apartment there was the body of Malka Ruda, age 43, in which rigor mortis had not yet set in, and in the courtyard of the same house lay the body of Chindel Gersztenzang, from apartment 66. The sanitary column stopped a passing funeral cart belonging to the funeral firm "Eternity" and ordered the removal of the remains. We were also instructed to furnish the funeral society employees with the necessary certificates including the names of the dead. The sanitary column proceeded to engage in a superficial inspection of the buildings at 14, 16, and 18 Krochmalna Street. They found the most unhealthy conditions everywhere. In the house at 18 (an Aryan building—Administrator Krzyzanowski) the public toilet had not been disinfected and the stench was so strong that the soldiers hesitated to enter. Complete lack of lysol, lime, etc. The column ordered the notification of the lst Precinct and to have instructions issued for the elimination of the unsanitary conditions in the above houses, threatening that they will seal all of Krochmalna Street for 14 days. He adds that the child's mother Chudesa Borensztajn testified in the presence of the commander of the sanitary column that she had abandoned the corpse because the Community Authority refuses to bury anyone without payment, and that the child had died and she will soon die precisely because she had no money. It was ascertained that the child had indeed died of hunger and the mother's extremities are swollen from starvation.

Signed:
The Supervisor of Inspection
Seweryn Zylbersztajn
Patrolman

Beggars are the plague of the street. Among them are many professionals and children who keep on moaning monotonously, making it difficult for anybody to work. To curb this the Order Service posted sentries. Yesterday in the afternoon I observed how a patrolman resolved the problem. In a matter-of-fact fashion he wards them off, away from my window, with handouts. No policeman of any other nationality would act in this way.

*July 26, 1941*—In the morning with Szerynski at the Gestapo, first with Kra[a]tz, then with Kramer.[68] Mueller has been dismissed. In his place a new official from Berlin. My wife attended Pulman's [69] concert. Nossig—another task.

*July 27, 1941*—In the morning at the Community. From 10 to 2:30 a fruitless meeting of the Council. The main topic was the

68. Kramer, could refer to Erich Kramer, office of the KdS.
69. Szymon Pulman, Warsaw conservatory, was conductor of ghetto symphony orchestra.

question of whether the Community Authority should hire baptized Jews: among others, the lawyer Ettinger. After some stormy exchanges, nothing was decided.

*July 28, 1941*—In the morning at the Community. At 3 o'clock with Auerswald. The rations for the Jews will not be increased next month. We are experiencing difficulties with lunches because the little mills in the ghetto are not very efficient.

*July 29, 1941*—In the morning at the Community. I visited the Public Health Department and a depot storing the disinfectants. I would like to have some publicity in the city about the struggle against typhus, etc. Yesterday there were 70 new typhus cases.

A delightful baby in the courtyard to her grandfather: "Grand-daddy, come to me." And after he came close: "Go to 'hojei' [hell]."

Rumors that Schoen was made governor of Białystok.

In our courtyard the same view every evening. Dozens of tenants come down for a walk along Stawki Street. There are no gardens. Babies are pushed in their carriages to a "little garden" on the site of the former Hospital of the Holy Spirit. They sit there among the ruins of the bombed-out hospital.

*July 30, 1941*—In the morning at the Community. At 11 o'clock with Auerswald. He has been scolding my aides because of the reduction in the number of lunches distributed. He handed me a letter on this subject as well as one about telephone service in the ghetto.

Kulski sent me a letter about the advance of 1,000,000 zlotys.[70]

*July 31, 1941*—In the morning at the Community. Kamlah arrived at 8:30 [for an inspection]. I requested Mrs. Judt not to accompany us. We visited the police headquarters, a precinct, and the Jewish detention facility. Everywhere we found neatness and cleanliness. The prisoners are complaining about the lack of bread. They receive 4½ ounces a day instead of 14 as in other prisons. We must organize a group of patrons. Zundelewicz was supposed to have worked on that. Unfortunately, this has been going on for several weeks.

70. The advance: possibly rebated taxes.

*August 1, 1941*—In the morning at the Community. There is suspicion that bran is being sold for fodder independently of the Provisioning Authority. The productivity of the mills: one 4 t., the second one 1 ton.[71] And we need 5 tons a day. At 3:30 I saw Auerswald. I mentioned the requisitions which of late are occurring again; the working conditions of our laborers in Drewnica; Krasinski Park; a loan to fight the epidemic; a project of demolishing [war damaged] buildings; concessions for tobacco and liquor.

*August 2, 1941*—On Saturday, as usual in Szuch Avenue with Szerynski. We found nobody there. *Kommandeur* Müller has been transferred to Lublin. In his place Maj. Dr. Hahn (previously an attaché in Bulgaria) [72] was named.

Of the million zlotys I want to give 300,000–350,000 to the staff. Today the Executive Committee of the Council worked out the guidelines.

*August 3, 1941*—At the Community.

*August 4, 1941*—At the Community. I received the following letter from Auerswald on the subject of the "13." Aug. 4, 1941 *G.G. Distrikt Warschau*. [Letter in notebook is a copy written July 17 to Gancwajch.]

Copy

To the
Control Office for Combatting the Black Market
and Profiteering in the Jewish District of Warsaw

att. A. Gancwajch
    Warsaw
    13 Leszno St.

---

71. Productivity of the mills: Czerniakow means output per week.
72. SS-Major and *Regierungsrat* (civil service rank) Dr. Ludwig Hahn, an attorney, succeeded Johannes Müller as KdS. Promoted in November 1941 to SS-Lt. Col. and in December to *Oberregierungsrat*. After the war, he was employed in the insurance and investment business. He was tried in a West German court in 1971; sentenced to twelve years in 1973; ordered into prison, 1975.

File No. K-1100
Diary: 149/41

The "Control Office for Combatting the Black Market and Profiteering in the Jewish District of Warsaw" is hereby dissolved. Members of the "Control Office" are forbidden to engage in any further activity within the sphere of jurisdiction heretofore exercised by the "Control Office."

The property of the "Control Office" devolves upon the Chairman of the Jewish Council in Warsaw—Administration of the Jewish District.

The books and all of the records are to be transferred to the Chairman of the Jewish Council.

Service papers made out to "Control Office" employees and equipment issued to them (such as caps) are to be collected and delivered to the Chairman of the Jewish Council.

Members of the "Control Office" will be taken over as suited by the Jewish Order Service. Decision is reserved for the utilization of leading employees.

Sgd. Auerswald

*August 5, 1941*—In the morning at the Community. Later a conference with the *Kommissar* and Inspector Altman [73] about the budget.

The disbanding of the "13" took place as stated in the enclosed protocol.

[Translated from the German]
On August 5, 1941 at 11:15 A.M. the representatives of the Jewish Council in Warsaw, Councilors Benjamin Zabludowski and Dr. Henryk Glücksberg, as well as the Director of the Jewish Order Service Jozef Szerynski, appeared at the headquarters of the "Control Office for Combating the Black Market and Profiteering in the Jewish District of Warsaw" and were received by the representatives of the "Control Office," Abraham Gancwajch, Dawid Sternfeld, and Ignacy Lewin. In the presence

73. Altman = Altmann: specialist in Interior Division of German Warsaw district administration.

of SS-First Lieutenant Lewetzow (Security Police) and Dr. Grassler as deputy of the Kommissar for the Jewish District, the following was decided with regard to the dissolution of the "Control Office":

1. Operations of the "Control Office" will cease as of today, August 5, 1941.
2. The assets of the "Control Office," insofar as they are not private property, will be made available to "Jewish Relief Assistance in the Jewish District."
3. All the files, except for personnel and disciplinary records, will be destroyed. The personnel and disciplinary material will be secured by the German Security Police in Warsaw. The personnel roster will be made available to the Director of the Jewish Order Service until the transfer of "Control Office" members has been completed. This roster is to be handed over by the Director of the Jewish Order Service to Division II of the Security Police upon conclusion of the transfer work.
4. Members of the "Control Office" will be taken over by the "Jewish Order Service" on the basis of current stipulations and regulations.

Applications from members of the "Control Office" for possible transfer to the "Jewish Order Service" should include

   a. The request
   b. Biography
   c. A binding declaration to perform one's service without compensation in accordance with current practices [?] of the Jewish Order Service.
   d. Questionnaire

Rank in the "Control Office" will not be considered in any possible transfer.

5. Official identification papers, with the exception of numbers 1, 2, and 13, service numbers and armbands have to be handed in to the Director of the Jewish Order Service by August 7, 1941.

August 5, 1941
Signed by

Representatives of the Control Office
A. Gancwajch

D. Sternfeld
I. Lewin
Representatives of the Jewish Council
B. Zabludowski
Dr. H. Glücksberg
Director of the Order Service
J. Szerynski

*August 6, 1941*—In the morning at the Community. Today I watched our little dog Kiki. Animals are children arrested in their development.

*August 7, 1941*—In the morning Auerswald. He announces that drafted workers will be clearing the rubble and razing the ruins if only for 3 portions of soup a day. Yesterday out of the 1 million zloty loan I distributed 355,000 zlotys to the staff, etc.

*August 8, 1941*—In the morning at the Community. Later with Auerswald. He promises a very small number of the telephones. The Construction Bureau prepared an estimate of the costs of dismantling the buildings (in the ghetto north of Chlodna Street as per instructions of the *Kommissar*). The first sentence begins with "And therefore it is necessary. . . ." Why the "therefore" will remain the secret of the bricklayers conversing with me [sic]. One of my lady acquaintances exclaimed today at the sight of another, "What a monster!" It is late evening. They are to deliver to me from the Community Authority a copy of a draft of the budget which I am to submit to the *Kommissar* tomorrow.

*August 9, 1941*—In the morning with Szerynski to Kra[a]tz and Mende. Later at the Community.

*August 10, 1941*—In the morning at the Community. Later, working at home as usual.

*August 11, 1941*—In the morning Auerswald, later Altman[n] on the budget. In the afternoon a fiscal official attached liens to the contents of our apartment for income taxes for 1938 which I paid long ago.

*August 12, 1941*—In the morning at the Community. Later in the Revenue Department. Auerswald is leaving for Kraków. At 8:30 two cars stopped in front of an apartment building at Elektoralna Street.[74] It was Auerswald with some guests from Kraków. What took place was an impromptu conference on the street. They were asking questions about Public Assistance, etc.

*August 13, and 14, 1941*—Work as usual in the Community.

*August 15, 1941*—In the morning at the Community. Later I inspected several facilities for the refugees. In one of these (run by Zytos) I discovered the corpse of a child. The mother, who was brought to me, appeared to be demented. Then I visited the vocational school in Stawki Street. A breath of fresh air after a nightmare in the refugee quarters.

*August 16, 1941*—In the morning with Szerynski to Mende and Levetzow. The "13" spawned a new host of patrolmen. Levetzow takes the view that we should recognize only 228 and get rid of another hundred. Apart from that, there is no need for their "officers"—all kinds of lawyers *minorum gentium.*

I issued intructions for the Council members to tour the refugee compounds regularly.

*August 17, 1941*—In the morning at the Community. Normal preoccupations.

*August 18, 1941*—In the morning at the Community. Szerynski and I were to be received by Hahn today. For several days we have been getting refugees from Nowy Dwór [75] (up to 4,000).

*August 19, 1941*—In the morning at the Community. At 2 o'clock at Auerswald's with a letter on the subject of the epidemic. I propose summoning a conference with Dr. Hagen, our own doctors, and Dr. Hirschfeld. I delivered Hirschfeld's [76] memorandum about decentralizing the struggle against the epidemic.

---

74. Czerniakow lived on Elektoralna Street at that time.
75. Nowy Dwór was located outside *Generalgouvernement* in Polish territory incorporated into the Reich.
76. Dr. Ludwik Hirszfeld was a prominent bacteriologist and a convert to Christianity. He survived.

Auerswald declares that Kraków is also inclined not to starve out the ghetto Jews. However, the rations cannot be increased at this point because the newly captured territories absorb a lot of food. Our budget was supposed to have been approved in Kraków with some changes.

*August 20, 1941*—In the morning at the Community. A meeting of the grocers about the reserves for the winter, food substitutes, etc.

One of the Poles has commented that there has been a change in the official policy toward the Jews. Permission was granted to manufacture slippers (an allocation of the leather scraps).

# Notebook Seven

*August 21, 1941*—In the morning at the Community. For several days they have been looking for J[as].[1] In the afternoon with Auerswald. He handed me a draft of the agreements with the gas and electricity works. We will be responsible for current as well as past payments.

*August 22, 1941*—In the morning at the Community. I submitted to Auerswald a critique of the projected agreements with the gas and electric works. He informed me that there was a possibility that the southern part of the ghetto could be severed from the rest. He suggested that I should start looking for a new location for the Community Authority.[2] He pointed out that we should not build a market on the corner of Gesia and Lubecki Streets since he plans to have some barracks there for reducing the density in the ghetto. With reference to the South I pointed to the typhus and the destruction of human life. He said that he was touring the ghetto today with a higher SS officer. He reached the conclusion that the ghetto is not properly sealed.

1. J. (Jas), Czerniakow's son, had been living in Lvov before it was captured by the Germans from the Soviets at the end of June. It is unclear when or how Jas had left Lvov or where he might have stayed in the interior of the Soviet Union. Also unclear is who was looking for Jas in Lwów. The Jewish Historical Institute in Warsaw believes that Jas died in the Kirghiz SSR on July 18, 1942, at the age of 28. Adam Czerniakow killed himself on July 23, 1942.
2. Grzybowska Street, headquarters of the Jewish Community, was located in the southern part of the ghetto.

*August 23, 1941*—I write verse occasionally. A vivid imagination is needed for that, but never did I have the imagination to refer to the soup that we are doling out to the public as lunch.

In the morning with Mende. He gave me a list of the deceased (Auschwitz and Buchenwald groups).

*August 24, 1941*—In the morning at the Community. Normal activities.

*August 25, 1941*—In the morning at the Community. Later at the [municipal] electric works. The agreement with the gas and electric works, which I drafted in accordance with instructions of the authorities, was approved. We will be paying through the nose. I went to see Altman[n] who agrees with me. Also Bischof who suggested that I should refuse [to sign the agreement]. And if necessary he will help. Auerswald was not in his office today—he is ill.

Yesterday engineer Luft [3] was shot on the street. His family brought me his German [Iron] Cross and several Austrian decorations marked with swords.

*August 26, 1941*—In the morning at the Community. Normal activities. I went with Altberg to see Director Zoepel in the gasworks. In his presence Tülpe (?) remarked that only the Jews are stealing gas.

*August 27, 1941*—In the morning at the Community. Later with Szerynski to Lewetzow. He stated that the rumors which have been causing much anxiety in the ghetto about expelling part of the Jewish population from Warsaw have not originated with the Germans. To his questions as to what I think of a certain individual I replied that he would be a Gancwajch if he were given power.

Mende informed me that Dr. Morgenstern [4] was going to be severely punished for using HIAS stationery in his foreign correspondence. I showed Luft's decorations to Auerswald, Mende, and Brandt.

3. Luft: a Jewish World War I veteran, Austrian army.
4. Dr. Morgenstern was an official of HIAS, Hebrew Sheltering and Immigrant Aid Society of America.

*August 28, 1941*—In the morning at the Community. Later with Auerswald (4 P.M.). He said that rumors about the resettlement include not only the Jews but also the Poles.

Auerswald informed me that the agreements on gas and electricity will not burden us with a liability for periodic lump sum payments. We will be merely acting as collectors for these city departments. We would be permitted to raise the prices. I handed him a list of school facilities for 4,300 children; a memo about a new allocation of cabbage for the staff. I asked for a one million zloty advance from the city and 250,000 for fighting the epidemic. He expressed the opinion that organizing a roulette game would burden our conscience in these trying times. I told him about recent requisitions (Szerynski had a painting taken, other tenants lost their furniture). I requested an increase in the number of telephones for our commercial and industrial undertakings (250) and no more. In the beginning he told me that I talk too much and asked me to come to the point. I replied that I am not *ein redseliger Herr* [a talkative man]. When he contradicted me, I said that since he would not grant tobacco and liquor concessions for the ghetto, he should at least grant that I am not loquacious.

*August 29, 1941*—In the morning at the Community. A meeting of the Council with the participation of Giterman [5] (on the agenda a matter pertaining to the doings of the financial subcommittee of the Resettlement Commission)—apparently the Commission has been too rigorous in its methods with recalcitrant contributors. In addition it was voted to exact a loan from the consumers (a levy on bread and sugar) for winter reserves.

Today the German, Polish, and Jewish police sealed Krochmalna Street and escorted 8,000 people to public baths. Unfortunately, the neighborhood scum used this opportunity to steal many articles from the residents.

*August 30, 1941*—In the morning Auerswald. Schools will be permitted on Monday, that is day after tomorrow. The Order Police 2,000 strong. Gdansk has offered assistance to Jews who were formerly residents there. I am preparing a list. I delivered a

5. Izak Giterman, a Jew of Lithuanian origin, headed the JDC staff in Poland. Killed by Germans, January 1943. He had been associated with the underground.

memorandum on the subject of the 1,000,000 advance on our budget. At Mende's behest the post office was instructed not to permit any correspondence in Yiddish and Hebrew of letters requesting food from the Reich.

I requested Auerswald to permit our tailors to work outside the ghetto. He promised to authorize 100 passes. I asked for his intervention in the matter of Morgenstern.

I took part in the opening of the graphic arts show at Sienna Street. I authorized a gift of 50 zlotys per student to be distributed to several score of the best boys and girls.

*August 31, 1941*—In the morning at the Community. On Saturday, as usual, I received a list of the deceased. I am always tense when I receive that list lest I see an unexpected [familiar] name.

Warsaw, August 31, 1941

## THE CHAIRMAN OF THE JEWISH COUNCIL IN WARSAW
### PROCLAMATION

The Provisioning Authority for the Jewish District intends to provide for the winter so far as possible.

An amount in the millions is required to purchase even modest quantities of food. Capital available to the Provisioning Authority is by far too meager. Consumers must therefore be approached for support which will benefit them. Since also that support will be insufficient, the Provisioning Authority is making an effort in addition to obtain permission for loans from banks.

Consumers will contribute to the creation of capital through surcharges on various products, mainly bread and sugar. The Jewish Council in Warsaw has unanimously agreed to this proposal and it has allowed the Provisioning Authority to raise prices during the next two months, that is September and October 1941, as follows:

Bread—Z1. 0.70 + surcharge Z1. 0.50 = Z1. 1.20 per Kilogram.
Sugar—Z1. 3.00 + surcharge Z1. 3.00 = Z1. 6.00 per Kilogram.

Upon expiration of these two months, the price rise is extinguished and in the following months the surcharge paid by customers will be made good to them in a corresponding effect on bread and sugar prices or on the winter supplies on hand.

The Chairman of the Jewish Council
Eng. A. Czerniakow

*September 1, 1941*—In the morning at the Community. Later an exhibition of the handicrafts of the students in our vocational school on Stawki. I also allocated a number of grants of 50 zlotys a month for a period of 6 months as well as one-shot prizes of 50 zlotys each.

The *Kommissar* called for some maps of the ghetto and the adjoining areas for his meeting with the Governor.

*September 2, 1941*—In the morning at the Community. Later with Gepner and Sztolcman to Auerswald. He approved the loan for our winter reserves. Gepner asked for the inclusion of children in special allocations. On our way out we were ordered to turn back by the guard because we had not shown obeisance.

The police appeared at the post office and requisitioned 6,000 parcels [6] (a loss, plus or minus, of 1,000,000 zlotys and 10,000 in revenue to the post office).

A[uerswald] informed Lichtenbaum yesterday about the directives for rebuilding the ghetto as well as squeezing it through severance of its southern part.

Niunia and I had our first anti-typhus inoculations.

*September 3, 1941*—In the morning with Auerswald on the matter of the post office requisition. I requested that the food that had been seized be assigned to our communal kitchens. I also reminded him about schools, public insurance, etc.

The *Kommissar* still has a mind to sever from the ghetto its southern part from Sienna to Chlodna Streets. The walls are to be erected along the middle of the street, the guard posts are to be reduced and the smuggling of people and commodities is to stop. According to him several thousand Jews are escaping from the ghetto monthly, spreading the typhus.

I told him that I was going to write him a memorandum on this subject. All my verbal arguments have proven fruitless so far.

6. Food parcels came from the provinces and neutral countries.

[Translated from the German]

Warsaw, August 31, 1941

Jewish Council in Warsaw
Division of Assistance Projects

Report
in the matter of the bath and disinfection measures on Krochmalna Street on August 28, and 29, 1941

On August 28, 1941 at 4 A.M. functionaries of the Jewish
Order Service instructed all residents of Krochmalna Street to be
prepared for bathing. The whole of Krochmalna Street from
Ciepla to Rynkowa Streets was to be disinfected and its inhabitants bathed.

Residents of this street unfamiliar with disinfection regulations
initially thought that they were going to be resettled. From each
house all the inhabitants, including janitors, were led outside,
assembled at the former Wielopole Square, and brought from
there in groups to the public baths, mainly the bath on Spokojna
Street. Men and women were separated; ill and crippled persons
were transported in hand-carts and rickshaws. Significant numbers of persons struck by the epidemic were driven to the
hospital. At 7:30 P.M. the groups that had been bathed returned
and by 9 o'clock they were admitted to Krochmalna Street and
assembled in courtyards, entrance halls, and at the gates. Eight
hundred persons who could not be bathed in the course of the day
were gathered under horrible conditions without food or warm
clothes on Wielopole Square. At 8 P.M. these people were fed for
the first time by Jewish Self-Help. Eight hundred portions were
to be supplied, if cauldrons could be found. Also 275 pounds of
bread were delivered. Plates and spoons were collected in the
nearest houses. The [German] First Lieutenant of *Gendarmerie*
[Rural Police] permitted the transfer of the people to the Janasz
Market Hall for the distribution of soup and bread and to keep
them there, closed-off, overnight. Because of bad weather, the
soup was not distributed, but the 275 pounds of bread were
available so that each person obtained a half pound [sic]. As a
consequence of the rain and the lack of warm food, it was a
difficult night. A five-year-old boy was taken dead from the arms

of his mother, and a twenty-year-old girl was found dead in the hall. The women with children in their arms were walking around all night since it was not possible to lie down on the asphalt. The gendarmes permitted ten stalls to be cleaned out for women with babies and small children to the age of two. At four in the morning the distribution of the soup began upon orders of the First Lieutenant. Because of a scarcity of plates the soup was literally received in caps, towels, handkerchiefs, the laps of jackets and coats, and even in one's hands, since these people had been starving for fourteen hours. At six in the morning another portion of soup, which had been guarded through the night by gendarmes at Rynkowa Street 11 near the wall, was handed out. Fifty plates, intended solely for children, were produced. Ten Polish police functionaries had to be called to disperse the crowd which wanted to tear the meal from the hands of the children. At 6:30 the people were brought, again in groups, from Wielopole Square to the bath. Drinking water was delivered from 3 Rynkowa Street through a rubber hose and 30 bottles. Corpses which could not be identified were transported away. Preparations for distributing soup in the blockaded street began at eight in the morning. The distribution lasted to 1 P.M.—3,000 [soup] tickets were handed out. This number was insufficient, since the blockaded street contains 15–18,000 inhabitants, mainly poor people. For such important proceedings, which may require instant attention at any time, a special group of employees has to be formed for purposes of liaison between the various technical and welfare organizations.[7]

For the Director of the Division
The Deputy
(Signature)

*September 4, 1941*—In the morning at the Community. A visit from Przymusinski. At the post office it was announced that parcels would be arriving again. It turned out later that Bischof visited the exhibit of graphic arts and our school in Stawki Street.

*September 5, 1941*—In the morning at the Community. I am not getting any answers to a number of my letters [to the authorities].

---

7. Sanitation problems on Krochmalna Street were mentioned in a report of the Jewish Council as early as the beginning of July, 1940.

Among other requests I submitted one for authorization of Children's Month. At last permission was given today for opening the elementary schools. I summoned a commission at once and we held a meeting. I received an order from the *Kommissar* for the arrest of one Sirota from the so-called "ambulance service." [8]

I had planned to take some time off, starting at noon. Unfortunately, I must stay because the *Kommissar* wants me to show him the exhibitions.

*September 6, 1941*—In the morning with Szerynski to Mende and Brandt.

*September 7, 1941*—To "Brijus" in Otwock. In the evening return home.

*September 8, 1941*—In the morning at the Community. News about the death of 51 workers in a camp. A meeting of the School Commission. Election of the Curriculum and Financial Committee [s].

*September 9, 1941*—In the morning at the Community. A functionary from Hagen, Starke, appeared with Skoneczny.[9] He announced that Ganc [10] is to be given 200 Order Servicemen with whom he will fight the epidemic. I am to pay these men 6 zlotys a day.

I submitted to A[uerswald] reports about the 51 [dead] in a camp, about the abuses of the disinfection columns. I received permission for Children's Month, and for a 3-million-zloty loan for the Provisioning Authority.

*September 10, 1941*—In the morning at the Community. I forgot that it is Wednesday today. What has happened to yesterday's Tuesday?

Kikus off to Otwock to stay with Roma. A strange dog—he runs away at the sight of a bitch and is confused by humans. Man is the worst demoralizer of animals.

8. Sirota, son of a well-known cantor, and a protégé of Gancwajch, was in charge of pseudo-philanthropic *Rettungshilfe* (ambulance service).
9. Skoneczny = Skonieczny. See note for May 12, 1941.
10. Dr. Tadeusz Ganc, formerly a Major, Polish army medical corps, became administrative chief of Council's Health Division, in charge of anti-epidemic measures in the ghetto. He was a director of a state hospital after the war; died 1972.

*September 11, 1941*—In the morning at the Community. Jaszunski together with a draftsman is preparing a memorandum for Auerswald on the boundaries of the ghetto in order to save its southern part up to Chlodna Street. The proposal is to erect walls on both sides of Chlodna Street, to construct an overpass across Zelazna Brama Place and either an overpass or crossing gates at Chlodna Street near the intersection with Zelazna Street. Furthermore, walls along Okopowa Street with an overpass across Okopowa Street to the [Jewish] cemetery. The last idea will have to be changed, however, since it will not be possible to carry the dead over the pass.

*September 12, 1941*—In the morning at the Community. In the afternoon with Auerswald. We are receiving another 1,000,000 zlotys, but the 250,000 to fight the epidemic is uncertain. I telephoned Iwanka, municipal director of finances, who promised to talk about this matter with Fribolin. I visited Stawki Street. I inspected a building for the refugees, presently unoccupied. The [previous] residents (Aryans) had dismantled the stoves and kitchens. There are no sewers. And we were to bring to the 66 apartments our refugees from Elektoralna Street and from the Chinuch building [11] where we had planned to locate our schools.

On that very street [Stawki] a poor maker of gaiters and his wife (well advanced in years) have a workroom in a little shop. Through this shop people cross to Niska Street. Even the corpses are carried through here.

*September 13, 1941*—In the morning at Brandt's. A scene with Eljasz. It is impossible to save Morgenstern. I asked for the release of Rabbi Wajnberg.[12] An interesting personality and an interesting attitude. His outlook was so different from all the other Jews.

In the afternoon Auerswald demanded that the Order Service ascertain through a questionnaire, by 3 P.M. on September 15, how many residents under 14 and over that age live in the southern part of the ghetto below the [dividing] line.

It is a question of plus or minus 100 apartment houses. I have no idea whether this is for the purpose of expulsion or resettlement.

11. The Chinuch building was site of former Jewish high school.
12. Rabbi Abraham Wajnberg devoted all his time to religious studies. He was deported to Treblinka, August 1942.

When queried by me Auerswald did not give me a clear answer.
At 3 P.M. I left for the "Brijus."

*September 14, 1941*—In Otwock. The air, the woods, breathing.

*September 15, 1941*—In the morning at 7:30 at the Community.
At 10 with Milejkowski and Skonieczny at Dr. Hagen's. He asked
for the dismissal of Mrs. Syrkin-Birenstein [13] and ordered the
reorganization of our setup for the fight against the epidemic. I
proposed Dr. Hirschfeld for one of the top positions under Milejkowski. Later with Dr. Fribolin on the matter of a new million.
Then with Director Iwanka on the same errand. Last at Auerswald's. The matter of the southern ghetto looks bad. Not even I am
secure on Elektoralna Street.

Yesterday, with Szerynski and Czaplicki [14] in the SD.[15] At the
corner of Chlodna Street we were stopped by a guard who ordered
us out of the car and proceeded to search the car and our briefcases.
He swore the Jews are.... Having found a stick in Cz[aplicki]'s
briefcase he made an issue of it.

In the evening my wife was visited by Mrs. Werfel and later by
Anka Lew. They both managed to upset my wife in no time,
speculating about the fate of the children. Mrs. Lew was treating
my teeth, and she had come for that purpose. Having realized what
chagrin she was causing my wife, she began to console her. She
stated that she herself was in the same predicament (in fact, her
situation was somewhat better than ours). Early in the morning I
was informed that at 3 A.M. she had jumped out of a 4th floor
window.

*September 16, 1941*—In the morning at the Community. Attend-
ing to current problems. At 2 o'clock there was Mrs. Lew's funeral.
Tomorrow I will see Auerswald to arrange for an audience with the
Governor on the subject of [the southern part of] the ghetto.

*September 17, 1941*—In the morning at the Community. Vexa-
tions with Production (cronyism in the workshops). Rumors about

13. Mrs. Syrkin-Birenstein, Ghetto Health department.
14. Czaplicki = Marceli Czaplinski, Szerynski's adjutant. Wounded in assassination attempt
by Jewish underground, October 1942.
15. SD = *Sicherheitsdienst,* German Security Service.

the little ghetto. People are sitting on suitcases. The municipality (housing department) received an order to resettle by October 10 all Polish residents of the area (Wolnosc Street, etc.) adjoining the western boundary of the ghetto. There is room there for 30,000 people. The southern part of the ghetto has 95,000. In addition they are to exclude from the ghetto an area around Bonifraterska Street.

I was summoned for 9 o'clock tomorrow to Stabenow.[16]

*September 18, 1941*—In the morning at the Community. I was called by Dr. Stabenow who together with Levetzow led me to the Deputy *Kommandeur* Dr. Kah. Here I was informed that the *Rettungshilfe* [Ambulance Service] has been endeavoring for a long time to be taken over by the Council and asked why I had not done so. I replied that we do, after all, have the JHK which provides that. I was instructed to submit a written explanation.

I took advantage of the occasion to mention food rations, the fight against the epidemic, smuggling. I stated that [only] 5% of the smuggling passes through the walls, hence the new walls will not curtail this activity. On the other hand there has been a growing anxiety among the population which has a depressing effect, disrupting and slowing economic activity and contributing to many cases of mental depression. Later I went to see Kamlah and requested him to intervene in the matter of the proposed resettlement of the population. On my return to the office I found a letter from the *Kommissar* releasing Dr. Sirota.

Gancwajch came to the Community and informed me that he has been discussing the ghetto with Dr. Kah. He added that he had withdrawn from public life and is now engaged in commerce, dealing in mattresses, blankets, and the like.

*September 19, 1941*—In the morning at the Community. Then with Stabenow delivering the requested memorandum drafted by the Order Service together with Zundelewicz and Szereszewski. He declared that the *Rettungshilfe.* should be disbanded because it is not needed. I handed a copy of the report to Mende.

I am visited again by Gancwajch who passed the word around that somebody somewhere is plotting against the ghetto.

16. SS-2d Lieut. Dr. Gerhard Stabenow, served in III-D under Kah (see note for September 18, 1941).

Auerswald returned from Kraków this morning and his first question was whether the walls were being built. Lichtenbaum replied in the negative adding that there were no instructions to do so. In the meantime behind the scenes the debate goes on. There are some people who are against the walls. There are signs that tensions may be lessening.

Today I distributed vast sums of money for the various activities of the Council and Welfare. The municipality (housing department) instructed the house administrators west of the ghetto that tenants there have until October 10 to find alternate accommodations.

*September 20, 1941*—In the morning Auerswald. Probst [17] asked Lichtenbaum and Haendel for a sensible proposal about the overpasses, etc., possibly without the exclusion of the southern ghetto. In answer to my question, Auerswald stated that the plans for reducing the size of the ghetto have not been discarded. I asked for an audience with the Governor and he promised to arrange it. He gave permission for services on the New Year holy days and on the Day of Atonement in the Jewish detention facility. I asked for *Sukkoth* as well, but did not press the point in order to get the first 3 days.

I barely made it to the 12:30 opening ceremonies of the Child[ren]'s Month. The gathering took place in the movie theater "Femina" and was very well attended. After my opening remarks there were addresses by Berman,[18] Niunia, Neustadt, Przedborski,[19] Giterman, etc. I announced 100,000 zlotys for assistance to children. Judging by the applause Niunia won the laurels.

A[uerswald] made a trip to Kraków, where general policy matters were discussed, among others the epidemic. A decision was made to establish ghettos in a number of cities.

*September 21 and 22, 1941*—In the morning at the Community. Later in the "Brijus" [in Otwock]. The New Year.

*September 23, 1941*—The New Year. I returned in the morning to Warsaw. I worked in the Community.

17. Hermann Probst: an employee in Auerswald's office.
18. Berman = Dr. Adolf Bermann, member of the board of Centos, an organization assisting orphans. He survived and moved to Israel.
19. Dr. Jan Przedborski, a pediatrician associated with Centos. He died in Auschwitz.

I went to see Kulski. The municipality is submitting a memorandum to the authorities with a negative reaction to the new boundaries.

*September 24, 1941*—In the morning at the Community. Later with Auerswald. He informed me that Sienna Street on the odd-numbered side is to be excluded from the ghetto. This very week. As for the rest of the ghetto, the issue has not yet been resolved. A piecemeal approach will be used. The furniture will be moved by the rickshaw requisitioned for that purpose. It will be our responsibility that the residents do not take the doors and windows with them. Special loans (?) or subsidies to cover the cost of moving will be granted. Those who will have moved by Oct. 5, 1941, will be allowed to take all their possessions with them.

I received a letter from Auerswald on the subject of one Bronislaw Poborca, instructing me to let him investigate the coal supply. It is possible that A[uerswald] will order us to employ this man in the Provisioning Authority or the Community, after having received his report on the coal situation. Poborca has presented himself and stated that he was a Jew, emphasizing this several times. Last year there was a telephone call in support of him from one Nowakowski who was allegedly speaking on behalf of Krwala suggesting—and quite emphatically—that Poborca be given a position on our staff.

*September 25, 1941*—In the morning with Mende who had summoned me and Szerynski, because he is leaving. Later with Levetzow and Stabenow on the ghetto [boundaries]. They informed me that Kah was going to see the Governor on this matter. Later with Bischof who is preparing a memorandum to the *Kommissar* on the basis of the recommendations of the Economic Council. At 3 P.M. there is to be a meeting of the [different] German authorities for an exchange of views.

The *Komendatura* [20] wrote to the Governor General in Kraków and was informed that the matter has been under discussion. I saw Auerswald for a moment. He is supposed to be going to Otwock today to procure timber for the barbed wire posts.

The Criminal Police telephoned that the young Sachsenhaus—the

---

20. *Komendantura*—Polish expression for German military *Oberfeldkommandantur.*

son of the famous father [21] was arrested. The young S[achsenhaus] headed a gang of robbers.

Photographs of A[uerswald].

*September 26, 1941*—In the morning at the Community. Yesterday's session in the Palais Brühl eventuated in a decision to exclude from the ghetto its southern part. At 5 o'clock I went to see A[uerswald]. He asked how the keys of the residents on the odd-numbered side of Sienna Street should be handed over. It was decided that the [building] administrators should turn them over to the police stations. He instructed me to ascertain the number of rooms in each building, the factories, etc., as well as the number of inhabitants. He is going to Berlin for a few days. I asked Probst where to relocate the expellees. He replied that he is depending on our organizational talents.

News about J[as] that he had left.

*September 27, 1941*—In the morning at the Community. We received two letters from Auerswald. In the first he ordered that the Jews—residing on the odd-numbered side of Sienna Street, as well as the Jews from Twarda, Sosnowa, and Wielka Streets, south of Sienna Street—be resettled by October 5, 1941, in the northern part of the ghetto, above Chlodna Street. The second letter refers to the statistics on the little ghetto.

I dispatched a circular to the House Committees on this matter with a warning against speculating with apartments. Panic in the city.

The Technical Building Department has prepared a plan of solving this ghetto problem in another manner through the exchange of apartments between 15,000 Jews and 15,000 Poles. The plan also includes the construction of some overpasses and crossing gates.

Haendel and Lichtenbaum left for Otwock to bring in some posts for the barbed wire. The barbed wire itself is supposed to be available locally.

*September 28, 1941*—In the morning at the Community. A meeting of the Housing Commission. The police are demanding a building at Dzika Street.

21. Sachsenhaus's father was a German Jew and agent of Gestapo. See diary entry of November 4, 1940.

Work! Work! Anyway, don't I belong to those hard-working people who toil from boredom?

*September 29, 1941*—In the morning at the Community. A meeting of the Council on resettlement. A plan was worked out to deal with the problem in segments. Some socially minded people have shown up asking to be permitted to help: their offer was accepted. Haendel and Lichtenbaum learned from Probst that Jesuiter [22] likes the proposal prepared by the Technical Bureau according to which only 15,000 Jews would be resettled.

Rozen introduced the issue of compulsory labor, since it has been impossible to obtain 2,000 persons in Warsaw.

*September 30, 1941*—In the morning at the Community. In the afternoon to Otwock.

*October 1, 1941*—Otwock. Today is the Day of Atonement. I was to return to Warsaw in the evening, but the car broke down. I stayed [for the night].

*October 2, 1941*—In the morning at the Community. Probst presented our plan to Auerswald. In addition we prepared statistics on the Zelazna–Chlodna Street area and delivered them to A[uerswald].

*October 3, 1941*—In the morning at the Community. At 3 P.M. with Auerswald, who informed me that tomorrow there is going to be a conference with the Governor on the ghetto [boundaries]. When I asked if he liked our recently presented plan he said that he did. He added that all the difficulties connected with the removal of the [Polish] inhabitants of the area bordering the west of the ghetto have been overcome. Nevertheless he wants to have a clear conscience. After all, what is involved here is the south of the ghetto. I ended the conversation with the words *"Wir verlassen uns auf Ihre Weisheit"* [We are relying on your wisdom]. He ordered us to confiscate the merchandise of the street peddlers south of Twarda Street tomorrow morning. I mentioned that tomorrow is Saturday, to which he retorted that the rabbis will praise him [for this action].

---

22. SS-Major (later Lt. Col.) Max Jesuiter, in the office of the SS and Police Leader, Warsaw district.

*October 4, 1941*—In the morning with Szerynski to Brandt and Levetzow.

At 10 o'clock a meeting at the Governor's on the subject of the little ghetto. We are receiving unconfirmed tidings that the little ghetto has been saved. Bischof disclosed yesterday that Warsaw is merely a temporary haven for the Jews.

The roundup of the peddlers accomplished very little.

*October 5, 1941*—In the morning at the Community. Today the first meeting took place under my chairmanship in connection with Children's Month. Guidelines were agreed upon. I opposed the pessimistic target of the drive, 500,000 zlotys, since the subsidy from the Council and the Provisioning Authority would account for 3/5 of the sum and the police would use "persuasion" to distribute window stickers for part of the remaining 2/5. When then does the public come in?

During the meeting Dr. Schipper again behaved foolishly. Since he contrasted those present with the "true mentors of the people" I asked him where these "mentors" were? Should we not look for them among those who have fled or among those who tried to leave but did not succeed. (He himself had a passport in his pocket.) He replied that those people would be punished. His own actions were entirely honorable.

Moszek Wajsmehl, a 15 year-old youth, was substituting for his parcel-carrier father. He was shot at Elektoralna Street. In spite of a wound, with his intestines spilling out and his spinal cord hit, he crawled to a house on Elektoralna Street and rang the bell of a stranger on the second floor asking for the parcels to be turned over to a policeman.

*October 6, 1941*—In the morning at the Community. Later with Auerswald. The southern part of the ghetto has been saved. On the other hand, the Jews are to leave many apartment buildings west of Zelazna Street. In the middle of Zelazna Street there will be a wall. The streets east of Bonifraterska Street (18,000 people) are also to be vacated. On top of this we are to lose a synagogue and the odd-numbered houses on Elektoralna Street. The plan also includes overpasses. I pointed out to Auerswald that some 60,000 Jews will be involved in the resettlement. He replied that the number would be 50,000, adding that I myself may stay at Elektoralna Street. I responded that I would not. He forbade me to discuss this plan.

Probst summoned Lichtenbaum and instructed him to begin the construction of the wall and the plans of the overpass. It will be necessary now to fight for space inch by inch. In the meantime, the odd-numbered side of Sienna Street has been resettled. The overcrowding in the apartments defies imagination. The doctors and self-employed people generally have no room to work. We did call upon the the so-called "socially minded people" to assist us, but help us they did not. They came, as they stated, to "supervise" the Community's staff.

*October 7, 1941*—In the morning at the Community. It is *Sukkoth*. At 4:30 I was called to the office again. Auerswald has arrived with visitors headed by the court president [?]. I had to brief them on the ghetto. I pointedly mentioned the mortality rates and the typhus.

There is grave apprehension in the city on account of the new reductions in the size of the ghetto. I calculated that the area we are to lose contains 43,530 residents; we are getting space for 8,100.

*October 8, 1941*—In the morning at the Community. Later with Auerswald. I asked him whether, in view of the large number of the Jews to be resettled, some relief could not be granted. He replied in the negative. I talked with Probst, informing him that we were going to submit proposals on the parts of the ghetto we were about to lose.

Just before I entered A[uerswald]'s office a guard took away my permanent pass to Brühl Palace.

Bischof telephoned about the parcels requisitioned at the post office. During September 15,000 parcels, with an estimated value of several million zloty, were requisitioned. They requisition parcels over 6 pounds if they contain leather, flour, fats; under 4 pounds if there are several parcels for one addressee. Bischof made an accusation that "like all Jews I am not accurate" and that as representative of 500,000 Jews I have been doing nothing in this matter. I replied that I raised this issue many times with the *Kommissar*. They say that these parcels go to Meinl's chain store.[23]

*October 9, 1941*—In the morning at the Community. It was suggested to Auerswald that Chlodna Street should be blocked with

23. The firm Julius Meinl, a grocery chain, acted as middle-man in distribution of confiscated food to canteens and other favored German users. A few months later, the food went directly to Order Police Battalion 61.

wire on both sides. In this manner there would be no need to lose a block on the western side of the ghetto.²⁴ For the time being A[uerswald] is requesting plans for an overpass at Chlodna Street. He has been informed that there were some technical difficulties having to do with extensive underground cables. He again ordered us to prepare plans for the overpass at Chlodna Street.

Auerswald inquired with a German electrical firm about conducting current by wire. He received a reply that it would take 14 months to install a new setup and that it would cost a fortune. Bischof intervened with Mikulecki to assist us in obtaining telephones. I am sending Rozenstadt to him.

*October 10, 1941*—In the morning at the Community. Later in the workshops at Prosta Street. A conversation with the contractor Tevens [Többens] ²⁵ and Dr. Lautz. ²⁶ Tevens is in charge of the workshops; he has introduced discipline. Both of them would like the Jewish Council to take responsibility for [the welfare] of the Jewish workers (food, coal, shoes, boots, baths, etc.), since the wage vouchers do not suffice to cover the workers' needs.

Later with Bischof. We discussed food rations, telephones for the Council, community kitchens. He suggested going to Wigand.²⁷ Later with Mikulecki.

In the evening in our apartment the lights went off. I thought that Dürrfeld cut off the current for the Jewish quarter, in accordance with his earlier threats. Fortunately it turned out to be merely a brief citywide breakdown.

*October 11, 1941*—In the morning with Szerynski to Levetzow, Kra[a]tz, and Brandt. I presented to them the issue of the boundary changes in the ghetto in its several aspects. They asked me for a memorandum in writing. I have prepared this document today and will deliver it on Monday. A little child said today: "I do not yet wear the armband, but when I grow up I will wear one." A fine portent.

Auerswald gave out the contract for the construction of the walls

24. Czerniakow is referring to the bulge west of Zelazna Street on both sides of Chlodna Street.
25. Tevens = Walter C. Többens was a German manufacturer in the ghetto.
26. Dr. Lautz was one of the German managers of a brush factory.
27. SS-*Oberführer* (a rank between Colonel and Brigadier General) Arpad Wigand, SS and Police Leader, Warsaw district.

in Okopowa and Wolnosc Streets to an Aryan firm. How we shall be able to get to the cemetery we do not know.[28]

*October 12, 1941*—In the morning at the Community. A heavy snowfall during the night. Perhaps this will bring the construction of the walls to a halt.

Last night I wrote a memorandum, challenging the new ghetto boundaries. Tomorrow (since it is Sunday today) I will deliver it to the proper authorities. The snow has melted during the day and now it is muddy.

*October 13, 1941*—In the morning at the Community. Later with Levetzow and Brandt submitting materials on the subject of the ghetto boundaries and community kitchens. Later at Auerswald's. He has no time as he is preparing a report to the authorities for the 15th.

Haendel introduced to me the Aryan contractor who will build the walls. At 3 P.M. a meeting in the Community Authority on the subject of Production. A resolution to strengthen the administration with new persons was voted upon. The old management failed to live up to expectations.

*October 14, 1941*—In the morning at the Community. Later I inspected the hospitals. Corpses in the corridors and three patients in each bed. I visited in turn all the wards, typhus, scarlet fever, surgery, etc. In one of the sickrooms I gave some assistance [29] to a policeman Jakub Katz whose head was clubbed by some smugglers.

While leaving the hospital I was stopped by staff members with complaints (partly justified) to the Council about their pay, coal, etc. After the car was put into reverse, it started moving forward with difficulty. Auerswald telephoned for statistical materials relating to the feeding of the population. These were submitted to him today.

Bischof asked for photographs of our workshops in operation. The Industrial-Commercial Department prepared a series of them.

*October 15, 1941*—In the morning at the Community. In Brühl Palace the *"Regierungssitzung mit Dr. Frank in Warschau"* [Gov-

---

28. A stretch of Okopowa Street, separating the inhabited ghetto from the cemetery, was to be walled off.
29. Assistance to policemen was probably a sum of money.

ernment Session with Dr. Frank in Warsaw] according to the following.

[Czerniakow includes a clipping from *Krakauer Zeitung* containing report dated October 18, 1941, on conference chaired by *Generalgouverneur* Frank in Palais Brühl. An excerpt dealing with Jewish affairs is reproduced below; it was marked by Czerniakow himself.]

## The Question of the Jewish Districts

The presence of more than 600,000 Jews in the District of Warsaw gave rise to wide-ranging discussions. About 116,000 of these Jews live in the eastern zones of the District, and around 500,000 are lodged in the Jewish Quarter of Warsaw itself. The District is free of Jews in the western zones.

Altogether, the formation of the District's Jewish quarters was decided upon in order to prevent Jewry's asocial behavior from disturbing the German economic and administrative effort and—inasmuch as the Jewish population was recognized as harboring the most dangerous disease—to check the latent danger of epidemics. At the same time, the Jewish quarters were to make possible the employment of the Jews in productive labor. Experience with the Jewish quarters to date has confirmed their necessity, for they were the means (for example in Warsaw) whereby typhus, carried primarily by Jews, was kept at a distance from the rest of the population. Stricter supervision of traffic between the Jewish Quarter and the remaining city areas should reduce the health danger, caused by the presence of a half-million Jews in the midst of a German and Polish population of a million, to a minimum. A decree issued by *Generalgouverneur* Dr. Frank in Warsaw about the leaving of closed districts should support these measures.

For the rest, the Jews were given broad freedoms within their quarter. *The Jewish self-administration, whose chairman was accorded the powers of a mayor, has not given rise to complaint.* [Czerniakow's emphasis.] Through the work of the *Transferstelle*, the economic potential of the Jewish Quarter was also used to a larger extent. The *Transferstelle* has now worked out its direction of economic relations in the Jewish Quarter.

Naturally, the problems faced by the German city administration of Warsaw are strongly influenced by the creation of the Jewish Quarter. Despite large demands on municipal finances, produced by the continuing removal of war damage in all areas as well as the sudden emergence of new tasks, it has been possible so far to balance the budget at last year's level of 160,000,000 zlotys, a sign that management has been most circumspect and frugal. . . .

*October 16, 1941*—In the morning at the Community. A continuation of the governmental conference in Brühl Palace. In the office I began a winter season. The winter this year started early. Yesterday I was chilled to the bone in the office. As a result I returned home sick and suffered liver pains during the night. Today I moved my desk farther away from the window and gave instructions for a fire to be set in the stove. The typhus continues to spread. The whole staff of the Funeral Department, with its chairman Kaminer and his wife, are sick.

*October 17, 1941*—In the morning at the Community. At 3:30 with Auerswald. The bread rations (1 kilogram) are still a problem.[30] On the other hand, *Nutzarbeiten* [useful labor] will be introduced for both men and women. During yesterday's and earlier [top-level] meetings, the police line toward the Jews has been reaffirmed. At last I engaged a director of finances for the Jewish Council.

Odessa has been captured.

*October 18, 1941*—In the morning with Szerynski to Mende and Levetzow. Kra[a]tz claims that there will be no resettlement. Levetzow [said] that Wigand listens to Szuch Avenue. On Tuesday the answer about the resettlement will be given.

Kaminer died.

*October 19, 1941*—In the morning at the Community. Kaminer's funeral at 3 o'clock. I delivered the oration. Later proceeded to the synagogue for the memorial service. In our building Belmont [31] has passed away.

30. Bread rations at the end of 1941 were approximately 20 ounces per week.
31. "Belmont" was the pen name for Leopold Blumenthal, a convert and a writer. See also entry of November 18, 1941.

*October 20, 1941*—In the morning at the Community. Later a tour of the sites where the workers were to demolish buildings and dig pits. Only a handful of the workers turned up. Wages are 6.40 zlotys plus a bowl of soup.

Two building contractors have been arrested. One Lehrt, a tailor at 66 Marszalkowska Street, took from Stefa her paintings, and from Zosia her fur and tuxedo.

I was visited by Hirszhorn, Gawze, and Chilinowicz. They declared their willingness to work on a paper to be published by the Jewish Council.[32]

*October 21, 1941*—In the morning at the Community. I received from Auerswald a letter about further resettlement. By October 26 the following are to vacate their apartments: (1) the residents of the area west of Zelazna Street on Ogrodowa, Chlodna and Krochmalna Streets; (2) the residents of the northern side of Krochmalna Street between Walicow and Ciepla Streets.

I immediately communicated with Auerswald, asking for an extension of the deadline. He refused, explaining that there is no other way of resettling the Poles. I suggested that I would come next day to ask for relief. Then I issued the necessary instructions. Where will we find room for more than ten thousand people?

The Order Service is restless because it is not being paid.

I had a visit from Dr. Lautz and Tevens. They asked for an allocation of food for the workers. Then they went to Gepner who promised them various food items for their kitchens.

I telephoned Levetzow who was to give us an answer today about the resettlement. He is ill in the hospital. Everything seems to conspire to reduce the ghetto.

*October 22, 1941*—In the morning at the Community. Lautz is again clamoring for sugar "for his workshops." I went to see Auerswald. I obtained an extension of the deadline for resettlement from Oct. 26 to Oct. 30, for a block east of Zelazna Street. He indicated that he was forced to give us short notice, because the Aryan residents who are to be resettled cannot move into the apartments on Sienna Street, since they are too large [sic] for them.

---

32. Samuel Hirszhorn was an editor of the prewar Yiddish daily *Hajnt;* A. Gawze was a journalist associated with *Hajnt;* and Ben-Zion Chilinowicz was a journalist with the prewar Jewish daily *Moment.* German permission was never obtained for any newspaper other than the officially sponsored *Gazeta Zydowska.*

He also stated that Aryans are to leave their residences by November 15, the rest of the Jews (thus also those on Elektoralna Street) by November 30. The project of extending the ghetto is no longer feasible since the whole plan was already signed by the Governor General. He announced a visit in the Community from *Rundfunk* [the radio station] tomorrow. For several days Warsaw has been in darkness. Dürrfeld has been cutting electricity, allegedly because of the lack of coal.

*October 23, 1941*—In the morning at the Community. Several members of the Order Service beat up the supervisor of our Housing Office, Fogel, while they were in the process of arranging accommodations for themselves. At 3 P.M. with Professor Hirschfeld, Dr. Milejkowski, Dr. Ganc, Korman, Lambrecht, Auerswald, and Grassler at Prof. Kudicke's[33] After some discussion of the problem of fighting the epidemic it was concluded that the typhus is caused by lice infestation. I remarked that those present are simplifying the problem thinking that $F = f(V)$, when F stands for typhus [34] and V for *Verlausung,* a condition of lice infestation. In my opinion the formula is more complex: F depends on the density of the population and food rations. Warsaw, this accursed city, in which a Jew receives 13 groszy worth of food. I described under what conditions we have to work. Ideas do not have hands and feet, but people do. One cannot exact efficiency from a bureaucracy which is not receiving its salaries.

*October 24, 1941*—In the morning at the Community. Aggravations not of my own making. The squeezing of more people into the apartments is progressing with difficulty. On the streets one sees people pulling little carts loaded with their belongings. In view of the fact that Jews are not allowed on Szuch Avenue now I wonder whether I should proceed there tomorrow with Szerynski in response to Mende's summons.

Auerswald ordered the requisitioning of the rickshaws for transporting bricks (?). The investigation of Loebl and *Transfer* is being conducted by a Dr. Pohl. Some of Haendel's orders for merchandise, etc. are involved.

33. Kudicke was the German director of a prewar Polish state medical institute.
34. $F = Fleckfieber = $ typhus.

*October 25, 1941*—In the morning with Szerynski to Mende. We received an official notification of Dr. Morgenstern's death. Later with Wielikowski, Giterman, Wyszewianski,[35] Szereszewski, Rotenberg at Auerswald's. A discussion took place on the subject of the JHK (kitchens, assistance to children, etc.).

In conference of *Bevoelkerungswesen* [Population Division of the German administration] in Kraków, there was a feeling that plans exist which go beyond the mere reduction of the ghetto area (could it be resettlement?).

*October 26, 1941*—In the morning at the Community. At 4 P.M. Auerswald arrived with his wife in front of my apartment, asked why the peddlers were permitted in the streets, and gave instructions for workers engaged in building demolition to work in two shifts.

*October 27, 1941*—In the morning at the Community. Mende permitted a monthly subsidy to Morgenstern's family. According to Miss Ghetto one of the vaccines ended up in the wrong hands.

At dusk, a Jewish boy grabbed a parcel with a paraffin candle from Bella's hands and started to eat it. When she took it away from him, he noticed her doctor's [arm]band and, crying, apologized saying that he did it because he was hungry.

Alarming rumors about the fate of the Jews in Warsaw next spring. I received the following proposal from the rabbis: "Because the epidemic raging in our city is spreading from day to day, we propose to organize at public expense as a propitiating religious rite at the cemetery, a marriage ceremony between a bachelor and a spinster, both of them poor people, immediately after the approaching Day of Atonement. This rite has been studied and tested, and with God's help will certainly be effective in arresting the epidemic." This resolution was agreed upon at the meeting of the Rabbis' Council on September 28, 1941.

*October 28, 1941*—In the morning at the Community. Normal problems.

---

35. Dr. Szymon Wyszewianski, a Łódź manufacturer, was on the board of the JHK.

*October 29, 1941*—In the morning at the Community. Probst, Roeder,[36] Münsterman[n] [37] and an *Oberleutnant* of the *Schutzpolizei* [German city police] showed up for the purpose of requisitioning 200 horse carts to carry the bricks to the wall sites. At their order I gave them 70 policemen from O[*rdnungs*] D[*ienst*] [Order Service.]

Auerswald, queried on the telephone, replied that he had no time to get in touch with Fribolin in the matter of another million for the Council. A rumor that Auerswald is leaving. His position is to be filled by St[abenow].

The typhus is raging. A new theory: not only the louse itself contaminates but also her secretions floating in the air.

On the streets adjoining Bonifraterska Street some chiselers are collecting funds from the residents to save them from resettlement. A rumor that this scheme is being masterminded by the notorious G[ancwajch].

*October 30, 1941*—In the morning at the Community. Regular worries. Not a penny in the coffers. The daily appeals for money are in vain.

*October 31, 1941*—In the morning at the Community. Auerswald drove in with Probst *et al.* on the business of brick transportation. He is of the opinion that this could be done by the rickshawmen. The problem was resolved in that he ordered Szerynski to requisition handcarts and horsedrawn carts for the purpose of carrying the bricks. Otherwise, he claims, he has no need for Jewish administration of the district. I toured the new streets which are to be incorporated in the ghetto. What shabby buildings and streets.

*November 1, 1941*—In the morning with Szerynski at Mende's. Later alone with Auerswald. He gave me the text of his proclamation on resettlement of Aryans by November 20, 1941. He asked me whether he should set a new deadline for Jewish resettlement now.[38] I replied that it would be better to wait a while. He stated

---

36. SS-Captain Roeder supervised wall construction. He was under the jurisdiction of the Order Police.
37. Münstermann was the owner of the construction company Schmidt & Münstermann, which built the wall.
38. On new deadline: see entry of October 22, 1941.

that he was going to throw young Lichtenbaum in prison for laziness. It was finally concluded that Engineer Pozaryk would substitute for him [Lichtenbaum, Jr.] in the construction work. The problem is that, although enough bricks are taken from the ruined buildings, there are not enough horsecarts. The Aryan horsecarts, which Auerswald himself was to make arrangements for, did not materialize. The Jewish drivers do not consider this job to be worth their while. Auerswald maintains that a worker should labor at extracting bricks from the ruins all day for a bowl of soup. I remarked that he could also have a wife and children. Auerswald retorted that 2 bowls of soup might be made available. And how is he going to have his shoes repaired? As for myself, although I could afford it, I purchased only one pair of late. I then permitted myself to observe that as a recently married man Auerswald could not understand what it means to have a family. I added that, although in his mind I am just a *Spiessbürger* [bourgeois], I nevertheless have a strong conviction that people should be paid for working.

I mentioned for the *nth* time that the Order Service receives no pay. I also commented that when it came to the worst I could explain to the Order Service functionary that Dr. Fribolin has not given us any money. He [the functionary] will understand, but a [cart]horse which is not given any fodder will not.

All this toil, as I see it, bears no fruit. My head spins and my thinking is getting muddled. Not one single positive achievement. The food rations were to be increased. The mountain gave birth to a mouse. The population will reportedly receive, per person, 10½ ounces of sugar per month, 3½ ounces of marmalade a month, 1 egg per month, 220 pounds of potatoes per year. The bread ration is to remain as before: not a chance of increasing it.

*November 2, 1941*—In the morning at the Community. Seventeen horsecart drivers have been arrested, because they could not be found at home at night by the Order Service (bribery?). A parley has begun. They are ready now to supply a certain number of wagons.

A benefit concert in "Melody Palace" took place in support of the Child[ren]'s Month fund. I addressed the gathering and so did Niunia. After her appeal several donors contributed several thousand zlotys.

*November 3, 1941*—In the morning at the Community. The 17 arrested drivers were released yesterday after signing a pledge that they would report for work today. Nine of them actually appeared; some of those absent submitted excuses.

Heavy snow and cold in the streets. It is uncertain whether it will be possible to continue wall building much longer.

The guard posts have been strengthened today. [At each gate] there are several German policemen and air force men [?]. Orders have been given to place under arrest in the Jewish detention facility one Galazka, a well-known conniver. He has been complaining that he was assigned a chore of cleaning the lavatories. In the past he used to scheme in the "Europa" and in "Kompensata," most recently in well-known ghetto circles.

*November 4, 1941*—In the morning at the Community. Twenty-two horsecarts arrived for the demolitions. Yesterday 35,000 bricks were transported. Fifty thousand more are ready to be moved. A[uerswald] toured the [wall] construction sites. Apartments on the streets which are to be incorporated into the ghetto are already being traded for money.

*November 5, 1941*—In the morning at the Community. Later with Auerswald, who had summoned me to inform me that the [most efficient] workers (the Stakhanovites) [39] engaged in the dismantling of buildings will receive bread bonuses. Of course, from our own Provisioning Authority.

*November 6, 1941*—In the morning at the Community. No money. Our indebtedness to the staff is growing.

Mrs. Zofia Feigenbaum died of typhus. Here was a human being who could laugh.

Auerswald issued a proclamation about the death penalty for Jews leaving the ghetto. A wall is being erected at Zelazna Street. The one at Okopowa Street has now been completed. I am engaged in a fight to save the Synagogue and the Judaic Library.

Zofia's death affected Niunia very much; she does not stop crying. Unwittingly I thought of a story of a dying man who spoke

39. Stakhanovites: the hardest workers, named for Stakhanov, a Soviet miner before the war who far exceeded his quota.

thus to his lamenting family: Somebody would think that it is you who are dying and not me.

*November 7, 1941*—In the morning at the Community. I issued a proclamation forbidding the renting of apartments in the recently added streets without the permission of the Housing Office.

*November 8, 1941*—In the morning with Szerynski to Mende and Stabenow. I submitted a memorandum about conditions in the ghetto. I queried St[abenow] whether the rumors about changes in the *Kommissar*'s office were true. He replied that he had heard rumors concerning himself, but knows nothing that would confirm them. Auerswald summoned me for Monday.

At 12 o'clock a meeting of the Central Committee of Assistance to Children. It transpires that the collection will bring ca. 700,000 zlotys. The JDC is adding 250,000 zlotys, which means that the public has contributed from 60 to 85,000 zlotys.[40] It was decided to continue the mandatory subsidy for the benefit of the children by the Jewish Council and the Provisioning Authority.

*November 9, 1941*—In the morning at the Community. At 12 a funeral for Mrs. Feigenbaum. Niunia delivered a eulogy.

A report of the Order Service about cases of graves being dug up by some gang to extract gold teeth from the dead.

*November 10, 1941*—In the morning at the Community. I learned of a decree that the Jews who left the ghetto would be shot in the Jewish detention facility by the Polish police.

I named as directors of the Funeral Department Ekerman [41] and Horowicz.

*November 11, 1941*—In the morning at the Community. There is much stealing of doors, windows, oven tops, etc. [from the vacated houses].

I went to see Fribolin. He promised an advance of 1,000,000 zlotys. I pointed out to him that we asked for 7 million zloty as the municipality's share in our expenses instead of the 4.5 million that

40. On the collection of money, see the original plan, entry of October 5, 1941.
41. I. A. Ekerman, a Council member, Orthodox faction.

the city allocated to us. He asked me why I do not take my problems to the *Kommissar*.[42] I visited Kulski on the matter of the "Skra" for the cemetery.[43] I received a delegation of the hospital's staff. I promised them 200,000 zlotys.

Minc, a manipulator in the funeral business, was detained in the Jewish prison. Some boards were stolen last night from Münsterman[n], the wall building contractor. He is claiming that the *Judenrat* should be held responsible for this. I telephoned Auerswald stressing the point that M[ünstermann] wants me to be his nursemaid. A contractor must protect his own boards. To which I received a reply that I was talking *Unsinn* [nonsense]. The Order Service has a duty to guard Münsterman[n['s boards. J[as] visited Mrs. Klaften [44] in 1939. Since that time she has seen no reason to be interested in his fate. She belongs to that breed which loves mankind but forgets that mankind consists of individual persons.

*November 12, 1941*—In the morning at the Community. We have received unofficial news that those caught leaving the ghetto would be shot in the Jewish detention facility the day after tomorrow. Among them are some women. It is not known who will carry out the execution: the Polish police or the Jewish Order Service. One prisoner escaped yesterday from the Jewish detention facility. Haendel was summoned today to Kraków as a witness [in an investigation].

Niunia has received a 2-day pass to look over our new apartment.[45] A difficult day as usual.

*November 13, 1941*—In the morning at the Community. As yet we have not received offical notification about the execution. A new batch of the arrested. It is cold, 21°F, as a result of which there is no

---

42. According to Ivanka's memoirs, the city paid 5,224,000 zlotys to the Jewish community for the benefit of the JSS during 1941–42, as the Jewish share of a routine allocation for welfare purposes of revenues derived from municipal charges for electricity, gas, water, and sewerage. Ivanka makes clear that the authorization for the transfer of these funds to the ghetto had to be given in the first instance by Fribolin.

43. Czerniakow probably wanted to acquire the Skra soccer field, adjacent to the Jewish cemetery, for additional burial space.

44. Mrs. Klaften was a former associate of Czerniakow's in vocational education, and lived in Lvov.

45. Czerniakow's old apartment on Elektoralna Street was in a section about to be detached from the ghetto. His new accommodations, on Chlodna Street, were in an apartment block which was to be incorporated into the ghetto.

work on the walls. One part of the ghetto has walls, another one barbed wire. Niunia has seen our new apartment.

An air raid on Warsaw.

*November 14, 1941*—In the morning at the Community. I telephoned Auerswald to ask him for permission to send a telegram to Frank from families of the condemned men in the Jewish detention facility. He told me that at any rate the decision rests with Frank.

Zacharjasz [46] has appeared in the Community Authority with a letter from St[abenow] on the subject of an apartment.

*November 15, 1941*—In the morning with Szerynski at Mende's and later alone with Stabenow. St[abenow] informs me that he has an idea for the Jewish quarter to be governed by a body consisting of several men. He did discuss the matter of the food rations with the *Ernaehrungsamt* [Food Office]. He does not agree that the O[rdnungs] D[ienst] has been assigned an improper role [in the execution of people].

Szerynski has learned that the execution would take place at 6:30 in the morning next Monday (today is Saturday) and that it would be carried out by the Polish police. Yesterday the families of the condemned sent telegrams asking for a pardon. The supreme authority chose not to grant it.

*November 16, 1941*—In the morning at the Community. A conference with Gepner and the Provisioning Authority on the subject of money for the Council. I stated that it is impossible for me, as it has always been, to conduct the business of the Council without a significant participation of the economic institutions: the Provisioning Authority, the pharmacies, and the like.

At 12 a ceremony marking the end of the Children's Month activities. Both of us, Niunia and I, addressed the gathering. Over 1,000,000 zlotys had been collected. The voluntary contributions amounted to about 80,000 zlotys. I stressed this point in my speech.

Przymusinski and Szerynski looked at the prison today.

*November 17, 1941*—In the morning at the Community. At 7:30 the execution was carried out in the prison yard. Those present

---

46. Zacharjasz was a member of the "Thirteen."

were: the prosecutor, Schoen, Szerynski, Przymusinski, 32 Polish policemen. Karczmarek (?) gave the order. Szerynski was standing by. Auerswald drove in after the execution. Lichtenbaum prepared a timber [back] wall. A bungling rabbi.

*November 18, 1941*—In the morning at the Community. The car is skidding. A thaw. My car overturned a rickshaw and nearly ran into a streetcar. It has warmed up. They are building the walls again. I visited Auerswald and brought up current business in a strictly matter-of-fact way. The hospital staff, although I borrowed 100,000 zlotys for them yesterday, are threatening to strike today.

The Council had to pay the Protestant Community for the grave of Leo Belmont, a Polish writer.

Nossig started a row with me in the presence of Rozen.

*November 19, 1941*—In the morning at the Community. Rumors about threats to the southern part of the ghetto. Several days ago I submitted a petition to save Elektoralna Street, the Synagogue, and the Judaic Library.

Kra[a]tz arrived in the Community offices with two colleagues (one of them supposedly his successor). They closeted themselves with Nossig. They were shown our vocational school.

In the public assistance shelters, mothers are hiding dead children under the beds for 8 days in order to receive a larger food ration. A young child was brought to the Community yesterday (the parents were detained), and today we had a baby (the father is dead, mother detained). I am bringing together all social services under the Community's supervision.

*November 20, 1941*—In the morning at the Community. Continuous complaints that there is nothing to bury the dead in. They have to be left naked in holes dug in the ground. There isn't even any paper which could be used as a substitute for linen shrouds.

Today I visited our school of chemistry. It looks like a garbage dump. Another surprise. They are going to exclude from the ghetto part of Dzika Street, etc. above Parysowski Square. Not so long ago (one month) the expellees from Sienna Street moved into the houses on Dzika Street.

*November 21, 1941*—In the morning at the Community. In the afternoon with Szerynski to Kamlah about the most recent occurrence and to request his intercession. Sz[erynski] spoke of the influence one of his military commanders had on his life. K[amlah] responded that since the establishment of civilian authority he cannot have any influence on events. He promised, however, to do what he could.

At 4:30 I went to see the *Kommissar* and talked with him until 7 P.M. I mentioned his historical role and responsibility. About Hudson Lowe.[47] About the tragic mood of the population and about the rationality of the official measures. About the causes: small food rations and lack of work. About the lack of constructive work and about all the unproductive labor. In the end, I asked for an audience with the Governor. He replied that the governor would not receive me! He agreed that perhaps telegrams from families [of condemned men] should be sent to the G.G.

He mentioned that the population would be divided into three categories: A, B, and C, and that the first one will be receiving 6.6 pounds [of bread?], the second one 4.4 pounds, and the third one 1.1 pounds.[48] I replied that I will come with telegrams for a conference with him on Monday. I added that the right kind of psychological climate will be more effective than fear in reducing the escapes from the ghetto.

The Synagogue cannot be saved.[49]

*November 22, 1941*—In the morning with Szerynski to Mende. Later on with Stabenow who informed me that it is possible that the SD would take over the administration of the ghetto.

*November 23, 1941*—In the morning, in the inner courtyard of the Community building, a special ceremony to honor the members of the Order Service who died in performance of their duty. Szerynski, I myself, and the officer in charge of the Polish police, Reszczynski, addressed those present. At the very end of the ceremony I announced that I would earmark 100,000 zlotys for the Service on this occasion.

Later attending to the current business of the Council. At 1:30 a funeral of an educator, Mrs. Oderfeld. I delivered the oration. The typhus has abated somewhat, but it is more virulent than ever. Mrs.

---

47. Hudson Lowe was the governor of St. Helena at the time of Napoleon's exile there.
48. These probably were weekly rations.
49. The large synagogue on Tlomackie Street was about to be detached from the ghetto.

Oderfeld died of typhus; our staffer Brüll, one of the many, also died of typhus yesterday.

The problem with the Synagogue. Should we leave the furnishings and the candelabra? The Committee wants to do so, since others may want to use the Synagogue as a concert hall. My attitude on this is skeptical indeed.

*November 24, 1941*—In the morning at the Community. At 4 o'clock to Auerswald with Gepner and Sztolcman. We have been discussing the matter of dividing the food according to categories.

*November 25, 1941*—Princess Zaslawska (a Jewish woman) died in the ghetto of tuberculosis. She left 2 children: one, a 12-year-old girl and the other, a tiny baby.

*November 26, 1941*—In the morning in the Community. Later with Auerswald and Rodeck (a financial expert) on the subject of the budget.

The Poles are moving out of Chlodna Street. Not so from Zelazna Street. Apparently, the deadline has been extended until November 30.

*November 27, 1941*—In the morning at the Community. Agnieszka at A[uerswald]. Yesterday a police captain arrived with Probst in the headquarters of the Order Service and ordered them to move out immediately. They managed to obtain an extension, perhaps until Saturday. Nossig called a meeting on the subject of the repertoire of the Jewish theaters in the ghetto.

*November 28, 1941*—In the morning at the Community. The *Kommissar* summoned First. An order to supply furniture for 50 bedrooms and 4 offices. Otherwise it will be requisitioned.

A visit by Mühlenberg in the matter of a bill for the *Sonderdienst* [German Special Service in Auerswald's office].

*November 29, 1941*—In the morning with Szerynski to Mende, Brandt, Levetzow, Kra[a]tz, and Stabenow. They informed us that for the time being they are not taking over the administration of the [Jewish] quarter. In the Community the councilors honored me today on the occasion of my birthday tomorrow. Gepner and Prof.

Balaban spoke. They offered me 2 valuable books (one of them a bible). In the evening the Housing Commission gave a reception at Zabludowski's.

*November 30, 1941*—In the morning at the Community. Delegations from the staff. Receiving the best wishes all day long. I would not care to be born a second time. How tiring all this is!

# *Notebook Eight*

*December 1, 1941*—In the morning at the Community. Current business.

*December 2, 1941*—In the morning with the *Kommissar.* He received me with *Assessor* Rodeck. They instructed me to prepare, for the fourth time, the Council's budget, with the proviso that for the period from April 1 to December 31, 1941, the actual expenses be included; and for the period from January 1, 1941, to March 31, 1942, the anticipated expenses. I suggested in the course of the discussion that it is not we who should be paying for the cost of the walls, but those who are thus being protected from our epidemic. When someone buys medicine in a pharmacy, it is not the pharmacist who foots the bill.

A[uerswald] replied that I could make that point at an international conference some time, but not now. At the end he informed me that some newspaperman wanted to sit in on a meeting of the Jewish Council. However, after giving some thought to it, he [Auerswald] decided that it would be better to just leave him with me.

In Siedlce the burying of the dead has been assigned to an Aryan firm. In Warsaw it is difficult even to reach the cemetery.

*December 3, 1941*—In the morning at the Community. An order to furnish 50 bedrooms, 4 offices, etc. First discussed [this matter] with *Hauptsturmführer* [SS Captain] Krueger.[1] We will place the necessary orders. Perhaps the House Committees will pay part of the expenses.

Kamlah telephoned Auerswald that some Jew in a German uniform was waiting in the *Komandatura* [Headquarters of the local German Army Commander]. Lustberg [2] proceeded there with some civilian clothes. It turned out that one Gedalia Szafir (from the Baltic coast area) has been in the army for over a year. He was to be given the civilian clothes and then transferred to the ghetto. He was given a certificate by K[amlah] to the effect that he had been a driver of a *"Panjewagen."* [3]

*December 4, 1941*—In the morning at the Community. The ghetto budget has been prepared for the fourth time. In the evening I drafted a report on conditions in the ghetto. Typhus is raging. Friends and acquaintances are dying all around me—all of them members of the intelligentsia.

*December 5, 1941*—In the Community. Current business.

*December 6, 1941*—In the morning with Szerynski at Mende's. Later to Levetzow. I pointed out to him that we received legally 1,800,000 zlotys' worth of food in the ghetto monthly, and illegally 70 to 80,000,000 zlotys' worth.[4] The first figure refers to the provisions through the *Transferstelle* and some Aryan suppliers, who make up only a small fraction of the imports. In the ghetto, one might reckon, there are 10,000 capitalists, plus or minus 250,000 who earn their living by work, and 150,000 who have to rely on public assistance.

Levetzow indicated that eventually the policy line advanced by his office will prevail.

*December 7, 1941*—In the morning at the Community. At 12 I spoke at the ceremony marking the opening of the courses for

---

1. SS-Captain Christian Krüger was probably stationed in the office of the SS and Police Leader.
2. Mieczyslaw Lustberg: administrative chief in Division of Public Welfare.
3. *"Panjewagen"*: a horsedrawn cart used by the German army on the eastern front.
4. The 1.8 million zlotys' worth was at controlled prices and 70–80 million zlotys at black market rates.

pharmacists. At 1 o'clock I delivered an address at the official function of the "Winter Assistance."

*December 8, 1941*—In the morning at the Community. At 11 with the *Kommissar*. He informed me about the deadlines for the resettlement, 15–21 [Dec.]. I brought to his and Rodeck's attention the matter of the balance of payments of the ghetto: 1.8 million zlotys' worth of legal imports, 30–40 times as much more in smuggled provisions.[5] How is the ghetto paying 80 million zlotys each month? He was astounded by these figures. And the walls were to curb the smuggling. Councilor Berman died.

*December 9, 1941*—In the morning at the Community. At 1 o'clock, Berman's funeral. At 4 p.m. to the *Kommissar* and Rodeck with a bookkeeper and a financial officer in the matter of the budget.

*December 10, 1941*—In the morning at the Community. In our apartment they are getting ready to move. In the "Zofiowka" in Otwock a coffeehouse [Café Variété] was set up to provide additional income.

"Important" matters in these times.

*The Jewish Gazette,* Dec. 10, 1941. Stanislawów. (J.M.)

The Provisioning Section of the Economic Department of the Jewish Council in Stanislawow arranged, during the period December 1–7, for a distribution of beef and veal, in the quantity of 4 ounces per person. The distribution was carried out by the meat centers at 38, 101, and 113 Belwederska Street. The [Community] personnel received an additional 4 ounces. Between December 1–7, each staff member received 1 kilogram of meat.

The permanent staff is receiving at 47 Kollontaj Street the first installment of potatoes in the amount of 22 pounds per person. In addition, arrangements are being made for the distribution of

---

5. Comparing official purchases with imports smuggled through the wall, Czerniakow implies that 30 or 40 times as much money was spent for illegally acquired goods. Even allowing, however, for major discrepancies in the two price structures, the statistics did not seem altogether believable.

milk to children under 3 years of age and those certified sick by a doctor at the rate of a half-pint per person.

*December 11, 1941*—In the morning at the Community. I inspected with Szerynski the [new] headquarters [of the Order Service] at Chlodna Street. They are erecting walls at Chlodna Street. There is no access to Elektoralna Street. And at Zelazna Street there is a bottleneck.[6] From time to time the police allow throngs of people to cross. I have been trying to get permission to dismantle part of the wall at Elektoralna Street for the period of resettlement; otherwise the carts with furniture will not be able to cross into the ghetto.

*December 12, 1941*—In the morning at the Community. At 1 o'clock the *Kommissar* arrived with his wife to examine the furniture supplied by the Messing firm. I am busy getting ready to move to our new apartment tomorrow.

*December 13, 1941*—In the morning with Szerynski to Mende. Later at Brandt's and one floor up (Kra[a]tz's deputy). I was commenting on the impossibility of maintaining the balance of payments of the ghetto.
I moved to an apartment at 20 Chlodna Street.

*December 14, 1941*—A very difficult night. I am alone with my family, in the whole apartment house, without light and water (a pipe burst).
Tomorrow there is to be an execution in the Jewish detention center of 17 people caught outside the ghetto. They are going to be shot in 3 batches.

*December 15, 1941*—In the morning at the Community. Fifteen persons were shot today in 2 batches (out of the 17 mentioned yesterday, one woman died, another has been taken ill).

*December 16, 1941*—In the morning at the Community. Today, for the fifth time, the Council budget with new supplements was submitted to *Assessor* Rodeck.

6. The bottleneck near Zelazna Street was in the vicinity of the overpass then under construction. The pass, over Chlodna Street, was to connect the large and little ghettos.

*December 17, 1941*—In the morning at the Community. Later with Iwanka on the contribution from the municipality. We agreed to ask Kunze for the money on Monday. I discussed our budget with Auerswald and Rodeck. The *Kommissar* demanded 880 pounds of bread for the Aryan workers of the Münsterman[n] firm (it appears that this is a bonus or some special holiday distribution). The bread is to come from the contingent of the Jewish quarter. A photographer brought me a number of photographs of me. One should never look at one's own portraits. A man always has a different notion about his own appearance. I have always believed that I look younger than I appear in the photographs.

*December 18, 1941*—Current business.

*December 19, 1941*—Current business.

*December 20, 1941*—Current business.

*December 21, 1941*—In the morning at the Community. At 12:30 an official ceremony honoring the Community schools. Niunia and I spoke, as well as representatives of the former educational organizations.

It is rumored in the ghetto again that eight points were read to me about patches, etc. [sic]. A councilor from Slonim visited me.

*December 22, 1941*—In the morning at the Community. A possible deportation of 120,000 Jews from Warsaw. The Provisioning Authority submitted a proposal for increasing the price of bread, since the present price is economically unfeasible. I called a meeting of the Council, which voted the increase by a majority.

I received the following letter from the Jewish detention center. [The letter is missing from the diary.]

*December 23, 1941*—In the morning to Auerswald. I would like to go to Otwock with Niunia for a day or two. I drew his attention to the rumors circulating in the ghetto about some 8 points for the Jews. He asked: What points? I replied that I was interested in only one: the prohibition of marriages. I got the impression that something is in the offing. I added that it might be the time for a change of attitude toward the Jews. I reminded him of Bismarck's dictum.

*December 24, 1941*—I left by car, in terrible weather, with my wife and Szerynski for "Zofiowka." To make things worse, I have a cold. In the evening I became sick. Nausea and vomiting. I received a message from Warsaw that—according to an edict—we must surrender all the furs—both men's and women's. I am to be personally responsible. The deadline has been set for December 28, 1941.

*December 25, 1941*—At 8 in the morning I left for Warsaw. In the Community building, in the large conference room, and at 27 Grzybowska Street a collection of furs. At 1 o'clock Auerswald appeared. I asked him for an exemption from the requisition for the members of the Order Service and the doctors. He promised to give me his answer tomorrow. I am still sick.

*December 26, 1941*—In the morning I got up aching. At the Community building, etc., the collection. By 12:30, 1,100 fur coats and fur pieces had been gathered.

At 1:30 Auerswald and Jesuiter came. Auerswald signed a letter authorizing electricity for the Community Authority building, since it is difficult to work without it. He informed me that the requisition edict applies not only to the Jews of the G.G.[7] but also to the "foreign" Jews. The only exception is the Jewish citizens of neutral countries, such as Sweden and Switzerland.

*December 27, 1941*—There are enormous lines in front of the 7 fur collection points. By noon 8,870 receipts were issued. In Radom they do not have to surrender the lining or the top cover. In Kraków, also, only the furs themselves. But, in addition, it was announced there that new unused underwear and high and Zakopane-type boots must also be surrendered. Jews were forbidden to leave their apartments. In Lublin also the pelts only. It is anticipated that woolens as well will be requisitioned. Each family will be required to contribute to the quota.

A. Szpinak died in Otwock [see footnote for Dec. 2, 1939].

*December 28, 1941*—An immense line of people with furs in front of the Community Authority and at 27 Grzybowska Street. Auers-

---

7. Jews of the *GG*—Jews resident in the now five districts of the *Generalgouvernement.*

wald visited the Community. In our large conference room huge piles of furs. All normal work in the offices has stopped. Everybody is busy with fur collection. I managed to bring back Niunia and Roma from Otwock. Their trip to Warsaw is a story in itself.

*December 29, 1941*—In the morning at the Community. Auerswald and Jesuiter arrived, complaining furiously that by 9 in the morning they had not received a report on the collection. It has been explained to them that it has been impossible to sort and count the huge piles that would fill perhaps 6 large boxcars. They ordered us to have the inventory ready by 3 P.M. (This was said at 12 noon.) The staff in all the departments was drafted for counting the furs. At 3 P.M. it was ascertained that by 6 P.M., December 28, the collection yielded 690 men's fur coats, 2,541 ladies' fur coats, 4,441 men's fur linings, 4,020 ladies' fur linings, 222 silver fox pelts, 258 blue fox pelts, 872 red fox pelts, 5,118 fur handwarmers, 39,556 fur collars, 7,205 assorted pelts, 2,201 sheepskin coats; and 25,569 receipts were issued.

Wiesenberg [8] and Popower were summoned to Rodeck at Brühl Palace, for 3 P.M., on the subject of the budget. Wiesenberg was stopped at one of the guard posts for wearing two jackets (in place of his fur coat that was taken away). They barely let him go.

|  | *Funerals* | | |
|---|---|---|---|
|  | *1941* | *1940* | *1938* |
| October | 4,716 | 457 | 379 |
| November | 4,801 | 445 | 413 |
| December |  | 581 | 437 |

|  | *New Cases of Typhus* | |
|---|---|---|
|  | *1941* | *1940* |
| October | 3,438 | 16 |
| November | 2,156 | 23 |
| December |  | 17 |

*December 30, 1941*—Yesterday the inhabitants of the ghetto have surrendered: 23 men's fur coats, 113 ladies' fur coats, 358 men's coats, fur linings, 287 ladies' coats fur linings, 14 silver fox pelts, 7

---

8. Wiesenberg was a Jewish Council official.

blue fox pelts, 144 red fox pelts, 553 handwarmers, 4,972 fur collars, 485 assorted pelts, 281 sheepskin coats; 2,834 receipts [sic] were issued.

I telephoned A[uerswald] at his apartment at 8:30 A.M. He has not yet returned home.

I saw Dr. Rathje in the Provisioning Authority. I mentioned to him that the walls were constructed without any previous examination of the Community balance of payments. He retorted that somebody must be responsible.

Detainees in the Jewish prison staged some skits. I received one of their couplets. [Rumors are being spread that they are checking receipts] of those who did not surrender any furs.

*December 31, 1941*—In the morning at the Community. I telephoned Auerswald suggesting that the collected furs be moved to the *Umschlagplatz* for sorting before their delivery to the authorities. I am seriously worried about theft. Yesterday, while some furs were being transported from 27 to 26/28 Grzybowska Street, some of the parcels were thrown aside for "friends."

At 10 o'clock the *Kommissar* announced that tomorrow, January 1, 1942, there will be a holiday for the Community. At 3 P.M. we received a letter from him postponing "for the last time" the deadline for the surrender of furs until January 3 and ordering us to announce this through the loudspeakers.

New Year's eve gathering at Zabludowski's in which I took part. I addressed myself to the occasion briefly, which moved one of those present so much that he gave me 10,000 zlotys (ten thousand) for charities.

*January 1, 1942*—In the morning at the Community. The collection of furs continues. In the afternoon many well-disposed people with New Year's wishes.

*January 2, 1942*—In the morning at the Community. An official communication from the *Kommissar* arrived yesterday on the subject of allocating bread rations according to privileged and non-privileged categories of the population. In addition, he has instructed us to impose a tax on bread, sugar, etc. In this way 1 kilogram of bread will cost 90 gr. [.9 zloty].

Auerswald gave us permission to remove the linings and top

covers from the fur coats. We are earmarking those for public assistance.

Today is the first day of severe cold, $-4°F$ to $-5°F$.

*January 3, 1942*—At 8 in the morning [one of the] Zabludowski[s] sent a message that Councilor Benjamin Zabludowski died at 3 P.M.

At 9 I went with Szerynski to see Mende. Niunia is sick with bronchitis.

*January 4, 1942*—In the morning at the Community. The weather has relented. Work on the walls will again be resumed. At 1 P.M. Zabludowski's funeral. I delivered a eulogy at the coffin in the apartment of the deceased. The funeral procession reached the cemetery through a gatepost using passes issued by the Community.

*January 5, 1942*—In the morning at the Community. The collecting of furs was completed yesterday. Then the furs were moved by the SS trucks to the *Umschlagplatz* for sorting. Jesuiter and Auerswald were present. Each truck was escorted by guards on motorcycles armed with rifles. We are worrying about the possibility of theft. The furs were packed in paper bags.

I spoke to Auerswald about compensation. He believes that he might be able, perhaps, to give us an extra food allocation. I have an idea of my own. I will present it to Auerswald this Wednesday. Somebody reported to the authorities what went on at our school ceremony. The work of a well-known scoundrel.

*January 6, 1942*—In the morning at the Community. I increased by 10,000 the number of vouchers exempting their holders from the requirement of the bread tax. These [exemptions] now number 150,000. I discussed with a delegation from the House Committees the arrests by the Order Service of the chairmen of these committees for not carrying out instructions aimed at helping the poverty-stricken tenants. Once more, I enjoined the Order Service not to make these arrests without my [specific] authorization.

*January 7, 1942*—In the morning at the Community. Later with Auerswald. I submitted my proposal requesting him to petition his superiors for the release of the condemned men (in the Jewish prison). This would be our compensation for the furs that we have delivered. I stressed that I had been asking previously for an additional food contingent, but I would be willing to forego this food, since the saving of lives of so many people is at stake. I added that the official channels do lead, after all, from the *Kommissar* to the Governor to the Governor-General. The *Kommissar* replied that the release of the prisoners is solely in the hands of the Governor. This being so, I implored him, in the name of humanity, to submit the appropriate plea to the Governor. After a lengthy discussion he promised to raise the issue earnestly with the Governor.

\* \* \*

I read in "Popioly" [9] by Zeromski: "Don't I, indeed, have under my command all manner of thugs, cutthroats, and murderers, and yet I spare them and prize them; for it is they that know best. . . . They are the very ones that will lead you safely out of an ambush." These are the words of Captain Wyganowski.

\* \* \*

In the afternoon, 3 functionaries from the *Schutzpolizei* [German Street Police] with a Lieutenant from the *Ghettowache* [Ghetto guard], all armed with loaded submachine guns, appeared in the office asking whether I telephoned them about an alleged attack by the Poles on the Jews of the ghetto. I informed them that I knew nothing about it.

It is impossible to buy a calendar of any kind either in the ghetto or outside the ghetto. I had to devise my own.

*January 8, 1942*—In the morning at the Community. Once more, plus or minus 4,000 inhabitants of the ghetto (from the vicinity of the Tobacco Monopoly Authority) are to lose the roof over their heads. At home, in the afternoon, a meeting of the executive committee of the Association of the Friends of the Prisoners in the Jewish Detention House, with the prison superintendent participating. Certain procedures within the framework of regulations were agreed upon. I passed on to them the 10,000 zlotys donated during the New Year's Eve gathering for the families of the prisoners.

*January 9, 1942*—In the morning with Szerynski to Mende. Later to Iwanka. Fribolin is opposing any new subsidies to the Council.

9. "Popioly," a Polish epic about the Napoleonic wars.

He is of the opinion that they should be replaced with funds from payments by the Jews for water, gas, and electricity.

While I was talking to Iwanka, I was summoned to Auerswald. He informed me that the Governor was willing, in accordance with my proposal, to release the condemned prisoners and also those who are about to be condemned, if we supply 1,500 sheepskin coats within a week. I immediately set the appropriate machinery in. motion to cope with the task. At this moment there are 40 condemned men, as well as 800 persons detained in prison.

*January 10, 1942*—In the morning at the Community. Later on, at the opening of an orphanage *Dobra Wola* [Good Will] at 61 Dzielna Street. I addressed the gathering.

*January 11, 1942*—In the morning at the Community. A meeting on the budget of the JHK (lunches). Later, a special benefit performance for the hospital fund. I gave a speech. Return to the Community.

For several days we have had extremely cold weather, the more difficult to endure since the people lost their fur coats. Niunia wears Jas's topcoat. It seems that everybody has a cold. At Chlodna Street they are building a wooden overpass for the ghetto pedestrians.

*January 12, 1942*—In the morning at the Community. In the afternoon with Auerswald. He summoned me in the matter of the budget. Rodeck, his financial expert, is "familiarizing" himself with the data to prepare the budget.

*January 13, 1942*—I called a meeting of the Council and of the rabbis for 9 A.M. I formed a committee to coordinate the collection with two subcommittees: a financial one and one to purchase the sheepskin coats.

I managed to obtain passes to the Warsaw District for four of our buyers, experts in the trade, for the purpose of procuring the sheepskin coats. I received Auerswald's permission to supply just the sheepskins in place of the complete coats.

In the afternoon, with Szereszewski and Wielikowski at Auerswald's on the JHK budget. I informed Rodeck in their presence of the burden on the population (in the price of bread) in connection with building the wall. A[uerswald] retorted that he would deduct

250,000 zlotys from the 500,000 zlotys (import taxes on the food products) for the cost of the walls. As a result, we do not have as much as we need for lunches.[10]

*January 14, 1942*—In the morning in the Brühl Palace. A[uerswald] was not in his office. Supposedly, yesterday was the Russian Christmas.[11] I wanted to ask him about the prisoners who have not yet been sentenced. In the Community Authority they have been collecting money from the public for the [sheepskin] project. The results today were meager. I, myself, borrowed 250,000 zlotys from the Provisioning Authority. By Friday the suppliers are to deliver 350 sheepskin coats and enough sheepskins for 150 coats. Subsequently, they will furnish 100 per day.

This morning fire erupted at the *Umschlagplatz* in the fur decontamination chamber (the furs in question were not collected from the Jews). Most likely, the faulty servicing of the furnace was responsible. There were many suspicions and much excitement.

*January 15, 1942*—In the morning at the Community. Later with the *Kommissar*. I requested that the amnesty should include the other categories of prisoners in addition to those already sentenced or about to be sentenced to death, with the exception of [common] criminals. A[uerswald] instructed me to prepare a list of all the prisoners for tomorrow; I passed on this order to the prison superintendent. I asked A[uerswald] for an additional food contingent for the ghetto population. In the Community Authority a large traffic of people and much bargaining in connection with the sheepskin fund collection; the money is to be used to release the condemned men. Some members of the families of those imprisoned are unwilling to make any contribution, in anticipation that the Community Authority itself will ransom the prisoners. Others claim that they have already given to the *machers* [organizers] considerable sums of money for this purpose. Yesterday, out of the 700 who were summoned, only 170 reported. I issued instructions for the rest of them to be forcibly brought in.

10. Apparently, Czerniakow had been counting on a rebate of the entire 500,000 zlotys (paid in food import taxes) to finance free distribution of midday meals.
11. Russian Orthodox Christmas (actually, New Year's). It is not clear whether the Auerswalds were celebrating Russian Orthodox holidays.

*January 16, 1942—*In the morning at the Community. I inspected the furrier workshop at Gesia Street (sheepskin coats to save the lives of so many people!). It is freezing cold in the shabby little room. The craftsmen have been busy all through the night. Unfortunately, only 120 coats have been finished, 300 are being worked on.

I telephoned the *Kommissar* and arranged to submit to him at 3:30 the list of the prisoners and a report on the progress of our efforts. It is now 3:20 and the list is not ready yet. One must have my nerves to withstand these pressures, or rather to pretend that one is withstanding them. Today, the collection is proceeding quite well. By 1 P.M., 60,000 zlotys were scraped together. I do not know whether it is compassion or coercion that plays the greater role here. It is not very comforting if I admit that more likely it is the latter.

*January 17, 1942—*In the morning with Szerynski to Mende and Stabenow. I asked if it were true that the guarding of the ghetto was to be taken over by the Lithuanians (the *szaulisi*). They denied it. I queried the *Kommissar* on the same matter and he replied that "he knew nothing about it." I told him that—according to my informants—the *szaulisi* have already moved into Ksiazeca Street. Again, he said that he knew nothing about it. In regard to commuting the death sentences, the *Kommissar* informed me that the Governor (1) extended the deadline for the delivery of the 1,500 sheepskin coats, (2) approved the submitted design, (3) would commute the death sentences of women, (4) would release the children, (5) ordered that the remaining prisoners, with the exception of the common criminals and smugglers, be examined by a medical commission (5 Jewish doctors and 1 SS doctor). Those fit for work would be sent to a camp in Treblinka.[12]

Then he discussed with Szerynski the problem of smuggling in Krochmalna Street. Yesterday he requisitioned the rickshaws (selling soda water, etc.). Szerynski explained that the rickshaws are needed for the delivery of coal, etc., to the population. The Order Service would see to it that the rickshaws would be used only for this purpose. The *Kommissar* ordered the liquidation of a street

12. Czerniakow's first mention of the Treblinka camp, which at that time was still being used for forced laborers, mainly Poles. Subsequently it was enlarged to accommodate gas chambers. Gassings began with the first Warsaw ghetto transports in July 1942.

market "Piekielko" on Krochmalna Street. In the "Piekielko" before the war, the pimps were openly selling women.

*January 18, 1942*—In the morning at the Community. At 12 noon the memorial service for the 7 deceased members of the Council in Nozyk's synagogue. The collection of funds for the sheepskins continues. It has been freezing. The overpass at Zelazna Street is almost completed.

*January 19, 1942*—Freezing. In the morning at the Community. The Community workshop (15 furriers), making sheepskin coats in connection with the possible release of the prisoners from the Jewish prison, is very busy.

At the orders of the *Kommissar,* a medical commission (7 specialists) examined, in the Jewish jail, the prisoners under the jurisdiction of the *Sondergericht* [Special Court] who were arrested for leaving the ghetto. This group is estimated to include 443 males (of whom 121 are boys). There are 213 minors of both sexes (including the 121 boys); in respect of these 213, applications for release have been given to Auerswald by the prison superintendent for submission to the prosecutor's office. Two hundred and fifty adults were given medical examinations; 54 were found fit for work. As some of them suffered from scabies we were given orders that they be cured by January 23. On that day they will be taken away. We must provide the necessary clothing for them.

I have heard that Auerswald had been summoned to Berlin. I cannot shake off the fearful suspicion that the Jews of Warsaw may be threatened by mass resettlement.[13]

*January 20, 1942*—In the morning at the Community. Five hundred sheepskin coats are ready. Because of the meager contributions, I decided to invite the richest Jews to my office and to make a personal appeal to their generosity.

I inspected 4 types of our primary schools. Where the teachers are idealists, the conditions from the educational point of view are pretty satisfactory. On the other hand, in general, the classrooms,

---

13. In Berlin, on January 20, 1942, high-ranking civil servants met to discuss the "final solution of the Jewish question" in all Europe. The *Generalgouvernement* was represented at that conference by *Staatssekretär* Dr. Bühler (Frank's deputy). Auerswald was not a participant at that crucial meeting, but may have traveled to Berlin for information or briefings.

corridors, and staircases are very dirty. I reprimanded the administration.

*January 21, 1942*—In the morning at the Community. The drive for the sheepskin fund has not been completed. We are short of the goal by 500,000 zlotys. The house committees led by incompetent men failed us utterly. I asked their representatives to see me today.

Yesterday, another 600 parcels were confiscated at our post office.

*January 22, 1942*—In the morning at the Community. Later in the Provisioning Authority to discuss fats and sugar for the school children (2,700 are involved).

I sent Wielikowski to one of the newly rich, who in any case has a reputation for generosity. He obtained a loan for 200,000 zlotys for the sheepskins. I also summoned the first batch of the citizenry, demanding an additional contribution for the sheepskin fund. In one hour I received well over 20,000 zlotys.

The *Kommissar* has returned from Kraków [14] but did not go to his office until later in the afternoon. In spite of several calls, I didn't manage to get in touch with him, so I do not know what he has up his sleeve.

Haendel returned yesterday evening from the provinces bringing with him several dozen sheepskin coats. They are larger in size and cheaper, as a result of which the price of sheepskin coats fell in Warsaw, and it appears that we will save over 200,000 zlotys.

*January 23, 1942*—In the morning at the Community. I went to see Auerswald and asked him whether he had received any new instructions from Berlin. He answered that his trip to Berlin was private.

At 2 P.M. I received a group of Jews whose contributions to the fund for the release of the prisoners were either small or nonexistent. Two liars among them pretended to be poverty-stricken; I gave orders for their detention. One Obremski, a manufacturer of footwear, was arrogant. On top of it, he did not give a single penny.

---

14. Czerniakow states on January 19 and again on the 23d that Auerswald's destination was Berlin. Auerswald may have traveled to Krakow (capital of the *Generalgouvernement*) on his way back.

In the evening Haendel returned from Węgrów. He managed to purchase a sufficient quantity of sheepskin coats more cheaply than in Warsaw.

*January 24, 1942*—In the morning with Szerynski to Mende. Mende summoned Lindenfeld [15] in the matter of Tine and Anders, who had been arrested for extorting funds from various Jews, for alleged release from the prison. Later, I watched a "satire" at the Provisioning Authority.

*January 25, 1942*—In the morning at the Community. A nocturnal fantasy: I was born on Zimna Street and want to die on Chlodna Street.[16]

*January 26, 1942*—In the morning at the Community. The sheepskin fund drive is approaching its target. To date, the public has contributed 600,000 zlotys. I managed to borrow a similar amount. In the morning Auerswald arrived at the Community with some SS men who kept asking questions about the ghetto.

At 8:30 in the morning I was stopped on the street by Probst near the wooden overpass at Chlodna-Zelazna Streets (now *Eisgrubenstrasse* and *Eisenstrasse*), who ordered the guards to open the overpass to the public. I asked him not to introduce tolls for the users (Auerswald is planning to charge a fee).

*January 27, 1942*—In the morning at the Community. 3°F. The police have been dismantling a wooden fence at the corner of Grzybowska and Zelazna Streets for firewood. Now they are taking posts to keep warm.

We already have 1,500 sheepskin coats. Yesterday I did something heroic—I took a bath in a tub (lukewarm water, freezing temperature in the apartment).

*January 28, 1942*—In the morning at the Community. 0°F. Löbig from the Gestapo appeared in the matter of a Jewish American

15. Dr. Ludwik Lindenfeld, a former Polish judge and a convert to Christianity. In the Order Service, superintendent of the Jewish detention facility. Killed August 1942.
16. In Polish, Zimna = Cold Street, Chlodna = Cool Street. Czerniakow's new address was on Chlodna Street.

citizen, Fanny Rapaport, 51/8 Leszno Street, ordering us to return to her all the articles requisitioned from her for our hospital services, because she is an alien. We were also forbidden to collect any taxes from her. The articles in question were returned.

I had a visit from the Jewish actors, who perform in Polish, asking me for assistance. I instructed them to communicate with [other] Jewish artists and prepare a joint statement.

Fixing k____ [indecipherable word] in the ghetto.

*January 29, 1942*—In the morning at the Community. Disturbing news from "Zofiowka."

Fribolin has blocked the payment to us of 500,000 zlotys. He informed Iwanka that the whole question of the subsidy to the Community Authority is under scrutiny.

I have received a request from the Moriah synagogue for a grant for its staff and for necessary repairs. The Jews are incapable of supporting even the three synagogues which we were permitted to open. It is reported that a non-Jew financed the roof repairs in one of the synagogues.

*January 30, 1942*—In the morning at the Community. 18°F. Later with Grassler and Auerswald. A[uerswald] is to communicate with the Governor on the sheepskin coats. So far he has not informed us where they are to be delivered. Apart from this, as usual, he had no time for numerous other matters.

*January 31, 1942*—In the morning at the Community. 18°F. With Szerynski to Mende. Later at Brandt's. They telephoned the *Kommissar* on the subject [of the disposition] of the sheepskin coats. Apparently, the Germans will collect them themselves on Monday and Tuesday.

I participated in the ceremony marking the opening of a new orphanage at 29 Ogrodowa Street. In my address I emphasized my firm resolution to apply severe sanctions against the rich who refuse to contribute their share to help the poor. The orphanage cares for 50 street children. Some of them are talented.

Probst informed me today, in connection with a certain official speech, that the future looks grim for the Jews.

This is the final result of the fur requisition:

| | | |
|---|---:|---|
| men's furs | 5,347 | |
| women's furs | 14,672 | |
| sheepskin coats | 6,053 | |
| pelts | 7,755 | |
| silver fox collars | 271 | |
| blue fox collars | 175 | |
| red fox collars | 1,600 | |
| fur collars | 134,975 | |
| fur hand warmers and caps | 10,940 | |
| total: fur items | 181,788 | |

scraps: about 200 sacks
minimum value: 50,000,000 zlotys

| | |
|---|---:|
| contributions to the sheepskin coat fund | 564,860.45 zl. |
| pledges | 98,006.30 zl. |
| Total | 662,866.75 zl. |

For the rest we will have to tear our guts out.

*February 1, 1942*—In the morning at the Community. Auerswald came up with a new idea which involves surrendering the buildings of the police at Ciepla Street in exchange for No. 5 Przejazd Street. The entire office personnel of the Labor Battalion is passing time with trivial errands for their chief. Tine, a well-known scoundrel, died yesterday.

*February 2, 1942*—In the morning at the Community. 16°F. The Economic Council met yesterday. A policy, which I am preparing, of exacting contributions from the rich to support the poor came under a barrage of criticism. To top it all, I was visited today by a delegation from the welfare shelters stating that over twenty per cent of their charges died of starvation.

In the "Azazel" they sing a couplet alleging that the funds collected during Child[ren's] Month were poured down the drain. I ordered an investigation to find out the names of the author, the singer, and the director of the theater.

Tine was buried in a regular plot (regrettably) in the cemetery.

Placards were posted with my proclamation that the consumers would be reimbursed 1,500,000 zlotys, that is, their loan for preparing the winter food supplies would be returned through free distribution of rationed bread and sugar.[17]

*February 3, 1942*—In the morning at the Community. In the afternoon an inspection of the 1,500 sheepskin coats by a commission (Probst, etc.). In the evening a special ceremony in the Centos to honor the late Zabludowski.

Auerswald was too busy to see me. He visited the ghetto and for a while watched the traffic from the overpass.

*February 4, 1942*—In the morning at the Community. The commission will complete the inspection of the sheepskin coats tomorrow morning.

An artist, Sliwniak, has just completed my commission for the stained-glass windows in the office of the Council's chairman. Some biblical scenes. They turned out to be quite beautiful.

The *Kommissar* demanded 100,000 zlotys today, probably for the overpass. Just outside my office door, seemingly endless bickering goes on about money contributions by the citizenry toward the cost of the sheepskin coats. I went to see Auerswald. He informed me about having had some difficulties in his attempt to obtain the release of the prisoners, but they have now been overcome. To be released are women, children, adult males, with the exception of 54 of the latter who will be sent to the Treblinka camp. I pleaded for good treatment for them in the camp and for the *Kommissar's* protection of them.

I also mentioned the matter of the several buildings for the Order Police, etc., at Ciepla Street, corner of Grzybowska Street.

*February 5, 1942*—10°F. In the morning at the Community. Today we are expecting the commission that will inspect the sheepskins. Should we not forget geographic considerations in running our educational system? Centos is looking for staff for its boarding school, but insists on those who have already had typhus. One of the applicants wrote that although he had not yet gone through that experience, he was willing to do so. We now get

17. See the proclamation of Provisioning Authority, diary entry of August 31, 1941.

electricity during the daylight hours, but every few days the lights go out.

*February 6, 1942*—In the morning at the Community. 9°F. At the *Kommissar's* office, the staff in a bad mood. I paid a visit to Iwanka. Fribolin failed to get positive results on further transfers of funds to the Community. The situation is fluid. On the corner of Grzybowska Street I encountered Auerswald with Probst. They might have been inspecting the overpass. At home the light is out again and the candles are very expensive. They have installed a telephone [in my apartment]. Watching some people I come to the conclusion that life is too short to enable them to reveal the whole gamut of their stupidity and malice.

*February 7, 1942*—In the morning with Szerynski to Mende. Later at Brandt's. He called the *Kommissar* to ask for a cancellation of the order specifying separate routes for the horsedrawn streetcars in the south and north of the ghetto.[18] Auerswald refused the request. *Kommissar* [sic] Boehm [19] advised me to raise this matter personally with Auerswald. The latter informed me that he has reasons of his own for not assisting Kohn and Heller.

Up to this point the sheepskin coats have not been collected by the German authorities.

*February 8, 1942*—In the morning 16°F. It is Sunday. At 1 P.M., a meeting to wind up "Child[ren's] Month."

In the afternoon a memorial ceremony for the late poet Braun. Niunia addressed the gathering.

*February 9, 1942*—In the morning at the Community. A conference with the Provisioning Authority and with Community staff on their food allocations (a very grave situation). The Orthodox faction demands expansion of the prerogatives of the Religious Commission and matzos for the holidays. (The Provisioning Authority has already taken steps to obtain the wheat flour.)

The sheepskin coats remain uncollected.

A Jewish youth—Szymek—is Auerswald's majordomo. He claims

18. Auerswald did not want these cars on Chlodna Street.
19. SS-1st Lieut. Johannes Boehm, KdS/IV-A (Gestapo).

that since there has been a man in the household he has been left in peace [sic].

*February 10, 1942*—In the morning at the Community. The artist, Sliwniak, has now completed the stained-glass windows for my office. I am ordering some also for the conference room in the Community Authority building. Sliwniak and Reingewirc submitted a project for opening a ceramics workshop. I directed them to Rechthand [20] (Lieferungsgesellschaft).[21]

Auerswald visited the Community Authority and later the jail.

*February 11, 1942*—In the morning at the Community. 23°F. I inspected the Council's Institute of Chemistry and Bacteriology and offered them 5,000 zlotys for the purchase of equipment. I will order a collection of chemistry books for the Institute.

A women's home delegation pleads for an increase of assistance. They have been receiving from 70 to 100 zlotys a month. I allocated 20,000 zlotys for them today. I am trying very hard to obtain [additional] food for the Council's personnel.

*February 12, 1942*—In the morning at the Community. 18°F. A nice day. The sun glistens beautifully through the stained-glass windows in my office. Several days ago the *Kommissar* received our proposed budget for the period April 4, '41–March 31, '42 (expenditures, 38,029,100; receipts, 26,446,002; deficit, 11,583,098).

The recently arrested swindler, Albeck, confessed that together with some functionary in the billeting office he made arrangements for housing (bribery).

I was inoculated yesterday for the second time against typhus. The blood test showed a negative reaction, which indicates that I could contract the disease. Several months ago the rabbis proposed that a marriage ceremony be performed in a cemetery. This is supposed to bring about the end of the epidemic. The scientists who do the blood testing and at the same time declare that neither a positive nor a negative reaction is conclusive are as helpful as the abovementioned rabbis.

---

20. Kazimierz Rechthand, in ghetto office for space allocation, with responsibility for commerce and industry, also member of the ghetto's Economic Council.
21. "Lieferungsgesellschaft" = Lieferungsgesellschaft des jüdischen Gewerbes, a Jewish ghetto firm.

*February 13, 1942*—In the morning at the Community. 23°F. I miss the Pekinese "Kikus." The little fellow has disappeared. Lord only knows in whose hands he is now.

And where is Jas, my only child?

With the *Kommissar* I raised the matter of the prisoners. He issued instructions for preparing separate dossiers for each prisoner, which was done. I suggested that the smugglers should also be released after paying an appropriate fine. He agreed to have a list of the smugglers prepared and the amount of fines they might be allowed to pay.

A fellow named Szwajcer, on the instructions of the *Transferstelle,* is to be the middleman in all the deliveries of the vegetables, marmalade, etc. for the Provisioning Authority. His commission is to be 10%. In this matter, Dr. Rathje is to intercede with higher authority. I am also supposed to make an inquiry with the appropriate authorities about this.

Julek Poznanski tells the story of how he came to Andrzej Rotwand, many years ago, asking for a pension for his mother (Poznanski's father worked in Rotwand's bank for 35 years). Rotwand did not give him a penny, claiming that the bank was too poor. Julek kept on sending his mother money by check until her death, never revealing the fact that he himself was footing the bill. She continued to believe that the bank was paying her a pension.

*February 14, 1942*—In the morning at the Community. 27°F. With Szerynski to Brandt. The jailed Hepry is accusing Goldstat, a thoroughly decent man, and Glücksberg. Today, at the jail, a confrontation of the acting head of the Housing Department, Fogel, and Albeck, who claims that the two of them were accomplices. The Perkowicz girl and Kinowicz have also been summoned. The latter did not turn up because of illness.

Today I saw the priest Trzeciak [22] from a distance; I do not know him personally.

*February 15, 1942*—In the morning at the Community. 27°F. The *Kommissar* had issued an order forbidding any assistance to the Jewish prisoners in Pawiak and Danilowiczowska Street for which we had petitioned.

---

22. Trzeciak: a well-known anti-Semite.

Yesterday, Brandt said that all manner of good-for-nothing Jews who are blackmailing the populace would be arrested. I retorted that the Jewish commanding generals in that same sphere of activity are free to ply their trade as before. Brandt replied that their time will come too.

I issued orders forbidding entry to the offices of the Community Authority and the Provisioning Authority to that repulsive witch popularly known as "Miss Ghetto" [also known as Miss Regina Judt]. I also gave instructions for the cancellation of her franchises. This despicable woman has been making the rounds of councilors and other officials pressuring them for jobs and concessions. Worse yet, she is supposed to have been taking money from relatives of arrested persons for their alleged release from prison.

Mister Goldfeil, an official in the Labor Department, is claiming that all the applicants for new positions in the Authority should first be approved by the *Arbeitsamt-Nebenstelle* [Local German Labor Office], which means probably on his (Goldfeil's) own recommendation or with his approval. This clearly amounts to undermining the authority of the Council and diminishing its prerogatives. According to the opinion of our Legal Department there is no basis for this position in law.

*February 16, 1942*—In the morning at the Community. 27°F. At 2 P.M. a meeting of the Council on the baking of matzos for the holidays. Becher and associates in connection with unsuccessful money collection.

On the streets teenagers are snatching parcels from people's hands and hats from their heads.

Today the *Kommissar* received from us the individual dossiers of those arrested. In reply to my report the *Kommissar* forbade any assistance in feeding the prisoners in Pawiak and Danilowiczowska Street. Disturbing rumors are multiplying in the population about expulsions, resettlement, etc.

I issued a directive to the Education Department to maintain or introduce some balance as to the types of elementary schools. We are in the midst of preparations to open special teacher-training courses.

*February 17, 1942*—In the morning in the Community. 14°F. Dr. Grassler, in response to a query, informs us that he will empty the prison by Thursday. He has been in communication in this matter with the *Staatsanwalt* [prosecutor], who is to produce a list of the prisoners. At my request, the prisoners at Pawiak and Danilowiczowska Street will also be considered.

Gepner, talking with some staffers: Do you know how to count? Yes, we do. Then don't count on me.

*February 18, 1942*—In the morning at the Community. 19°F. For several days a concerted effort has been going on to clean the inner courtyards of the buildings of the avalanches of excrement. I put a tax of 50 groszy on bread cards for this purpose.

I received a delegation on lunches. The whole undertaking will come to a halt unless I contribute another subsidy to it. And I am permitted to contribute 310,000 zlotys. What is needed is 800,000 zlotys.

Arranging for the window curtains, etc., in Lublin.[23]

*February 19, 1942*—In the morning at the Community. 25°F. I went to Auerswald. He inspected the prison yesterday. As a result 50 people were directed to a camp, probably Treblinka. Today he informed me that the *Staatsanwalt* failed to provide the documentation on those to be released. He has the Governor's authorization and could order the release of these prisoners, but this would produce chaos in the files of the *Staatsanwalt*. Anyway the matter is still pending. I raised the issue of smugglers, again requesting that they should be punished by a fine. A list of such people is being prepared. Lastly, I mentioned the issue of the lunches, asking for the increase of the subsidy from 310,000 zlotys, which the Council was to contribute, to 410,000 zlotys. I used the argument that the Council owes 700,000 zlotys for the lunches. This influenced him to give me a positive decision for the 410,000 zlotys.

I called a meeting of the Council for 2 P.M. today. The problem of subsidizing the lunch program during the next few months was discussed. The month of February has already been taken care of. With reference to March and April, a committee has been chosen to work out a plan.

*February 20, 1942*—In the morning at the Community. 23°F. Yesterday there was an official inspection of the shelter on Stawki Street. Dr. Wielikowski, who was our guide, carried away by

23. Window curtains: perhaps for the fifty rooms to be furnished for the Germans.

oratorical fervor, was describing the miraculous improvements in the cultural life of these quarantines. At a particularly interesting moment of this fascinating discourse, when the speaker seemed truly overcome by his words, a large round rear end was stuck out of one of the windows. The shocked bystanders asked Wielikowski whether he was the *Artz* [doctor]. Apparently he was mistaken for Dr. Milejkowski.

On February 19th, on orders of the *Kommissar*, 59 persons (prisoners) were taken from the Jewish detention facility and transported to the Western Station under an escort of the German police; one might guess they were directed to Treblinka. Each prisoner was given a pound of bread for the trip. The *Kommissar* needed some construction workers.

At this very moment (11:33) Colonel Szerynski, the chief of the Order Service, has reported a case of cannibalism in the Jewish Quarter. Mother–child. Here is the report:

*D. Szwizgold, patrol leader 1845. The report refers to a case of cannibalism.* At the request of the supervisor of IV sector of the Z.O.S. [24] [Jewish Social Welfare], Nirenberg, I proceeded to No. 18 Krochmalna Street, apt. 20, where I found, lying on a bunk, the 30-year-old Urman, Rywka, who stated in the presence of the witnesses, Mrs. Zajdman, Niuta, the secretary of the House Committee, and Murawa, Jankiel, that she was guilty of cannibalism, involving her own 12-year-old son, Berk Urman, who had died the previous day, by cutting out a piece of his buttock.

> Signed D. Szwizgold, patrol leader 1845
> Patrolman M. Grossman 393
> J. Murawa, Chairman
> February 19, 1942

In the morning the *Kommissar* came to the Community with a senior SS officer and some Swiss national (a doctor?) who was asking questions about the ghetto and the typhus. Before he arrived, Auerswald forbade me to make any mention of the mortality rates. In January the mortality was 5,123 persons. He who is unhappy with his own house becomes a social activist.

24. ZOS *(Zydowska Opieka Spoleczna)*, another way of referring to JSS.

*February 21, 1942*—18°F. In the morning with Szerynski to Mende (Brandt and Stabenow). They just received a situational report on the Quarter (the case of cannibalism). Stabenow lauds the *Rettungshilfe* [Ambulance Service].

I submitted to the *Kommissar*'s office a report on the case of cannibalism and told Rodeck and Grassler what I myself think about this tragedy and what conditions lead to such a crime. Rodeck informed me that I misheard the words of the *Kommissar* on the business of the 410,000 zlotys for the lunch program. They have authorized only 300,000 zlotys. I retorted that I clearly emphasized the sum of 410,000 zlotys and that the *Kommissar* accepted this information approvingly. Anyway I owe the JHK 700,000 for the lunches. Moreover, I have already notified the JHK and the Council that I was going to pay them the 410,000-zloty subsidy for February.

*February 22, 1942*—In the morning at the Community. 18°F. At 3 P.M. 32°F. At 12, a funeral ceremony for the precinct commander, attorney Maksymiljan Schoenbach.[25] I spoke. I wrote the obituary.

*February 23, 1942*—In the morning at the Community. 27°F. Beautiful weather. Are we approaching spring? One fellow asks another: What is the news from the front? I have no idea, my apartment is at the back, was the reply. The widow of the bandit Tine, on the instructions of the police, returned the possessions of her husband with the exception of the cap pistol, which the *Sicherheitspolizei* [German Security Police] people wanted to be delivered to them. The matter of releasing the prisoners from the central Jewish detention facility is not moving forward. I am spitting blood from my ceaseless efforts, unfortunately to no avail.

Yesterday evening a conference took place in my apartment: Weichert, Gepner, Jaszunski, Giterman, Wielikowski on the topic of social welfare. What is involved is the centralization of the program. A committee was chosen to draft a proposal to be submitted to me.

A conversation with a caretaker who has been scolded for the filth in his building: "What do you think I am, a janitor?"

25. Maksymiljan Schoenbach, a specialist in corporate law, helped organize the Order Service.

*February 24, 1942*—With the *Kommissar*. He promised to attend to the prisoners' release himself; all the other formalities have been taken care of.

The apartment buildings are filthy beyond description. I issued instructions for an energetic removal of garbage. I added two loudmouthed fellows, Usman and Pozaryk, to the garbage section.

*February 25, 1942*—In the morning at the Community. 32°F. At 12 o'clock at the Stawki Street hospital. Professor Hirszfeld gave a lecture about blood and race. Subsequently Dr. Stein performed an autopsy on a 30-year-old woman, mother of 5 children (plus 5 miscarriages) who had died of starvation.

I had a visit in my office from Gancwajch with pleas of a personal nature. What a despicable, ugly creature.

Jewish inventiveness in the ghetto: contraceptives made of baby pacifiers, carbide lamps made from the metal "Mewa" cigarette boxes.

*February 26, 1942*—19°F. In the morning at the Community. Later with Auerswald in the matter of the prisoners. At last I received a list which I must supplement with additional information. And then they will be released. Auerswald told me that had he known how complicated the whole business was, he would not have undertaken it. I told him to listen to the voice of his conscience [26] above all.

At 12:30 I was waiting for the second time for Auerswald in the Housing Office at Nowolipie Street. As he was getting out of the car, a parcel, thrown from behind the ghetto wall, passed over his head. Auerswald slapped the patrolman and took away his armband.

At 2 P.M. I was at the Provisioning Authority. I discussed the requisitioned [smuggled] flour and designated one truckful for the Council staff. Three consignments went to the community kitchens.

*February 27, 1942*—19°F. In the morning at the Community. The first meeting of the supervisory board of the new vocational secondary school took place yesterday. The principal, Buchweitz,

---

26. "Conscience": Czerniakow writes *Bog* (God).

together with his colleagues, was given the task of preparing the program of instruction.

In the morning at the Community. Later I delivered to Auerswald a list of 150 prisoners for release. One Adam Zurawin [27] came with a letter requesting permission for opening a photographic studio for the *Kennkarten* [identity cards]. When I told him that we were not authorized to grant concessions to Aryans he replied that behind him there is a Jew, one Wolf Szymonowicz.

*February 28, 1942*—23°F. Frost. In the morning at the Community. Mende informed me and Szerynski that he would be leaving for Germany for a retraining course. He will be back in 8 weeks. Brandt claims that he (Mende) will not return to his post in Warsaw.

Judge Lindenfeld submitted in my name 3 lists of prisoners to Auerswald. I made a call to Auerswald who told me that there is no reason to hurry since the release of the prisoners would take place in 2 or 3 days. Mende gave orders for notifying one Ellie Bibula that her husband Zygmunt died in Sachsenhausen.

*March 1, 1942*—In the morning at the Community. Attending to current problems. An idea that because of the condition of the houses the owners of the buildings should assume responsibility.

*March 2, 1942*—37°F. In the morning at the Community. The *Kommissar* wrote us to dismiss 10% to 20% of the personnel. Some Jewish woman appeared with a letter from Probst to the effect that she should be given 20 tons of sugar monthly. She threatens that, in the case of refusal, the *Leutnant* will come and put things right. I telephoned Auerswald who ordered me to pass the matter to the Provisioning Authority, adding that we must not take action against the woman.

*March 3, 1942*—21°F. In the morning at the Community. Today is *Purim*. A letter from Auerswald ordering the emptying of the [Great] Synagogue and the neighboring buildings by March 20. The key to the [Great] Synagogue with the Order Service.

27. Zurawin: See entries of March 4 and May 24, 1942.

*March 4, 1942*—25°F. For several days we are again without electricity. In the morning at the Community. Later with Brandt and Stabenow in the matter of Zurawin, who received a letter signed by Stabenow and Mueller [28] requesting a concession to take photographs for the identity cards. Zurawin represents one Wolf Szymonowicz, allegedly a nephew of Gancwajch. I explained to Stabenow that he burdens the population unnecessarily for the benefit of Zurawin and Co. He promised to reconsider.

I also raised the issue of the Jewish woman who is demanding 20 tons of sugar on the strength of a letter from Probst. Probst, when questioned, replied that his letter was written out of courtesy and that he does not insist that we must allocate sugar for this ugly black-market operator. Auerswald confirms the above.

Auerswald wants to change the boundaries of the ghetto again. Several thousand Jews will lose the roof over their heads. We are preparing a statistical presentation to defend them. Auerswald equivocates about the prisoners. I have no idea when he will release them. I received from the *Kommissar* the *Aufenthaltbeschränkungen im jüdischen Wohnbezirk in Warschau* [Residence Restrictions in the Jewish District of Warsaw].

*March 5, 1942*—21°F. In the morning at the Community. Later with Iwanka and Kulski on the question of obtaining money from the municipal treasury. We discussed the formation of a commission to clear accounts between the Council and the city.

*March 6, 1942*—0°F. In the morning at the Community. Attending to current problems. The *Kommissar* ordered payment to the *Abt. Ehrnährung und Landwirtschaft, Unterabt. Wasserwirtschaft* [Food and Agriculture Division, Subdivision Water Resources] of 60,000 zlotys for the *Lagerschutz* [camp guard] in the camp.[29]

*March 7, 1942*—In the morning with Szerynski to Brandt. Dog-catchers Hepry and Luboszynski offered to disclose something.

I went to see Auerswald. He refuses to authorize a regulation requiring the released Jews who are better off to contribute money for those who are being sent to the camps. When I interposed that

28. SS-2d Lieut. Mueller of the Gestapo.
29. Subdivision Water Resources maintained a number of camps in several areas of the Warsaw district.

this was being done for the last two years, he retorted that it will be done differently for the next five.

*March 8, 1942*—16°F. By 6 P.M. 28°F. In the morning at the Community. Yesterday evening they brought a doctor to me. He gave me two injections (a heart attack?), following trying personal experiences.

A conference took place in the Community on centralizing public welfare. The Central Commission will remain attached to me. Subordinate to it will be the KOM,[30] the public assistance committee at the Council, and the Provisioning Authority. All suggestions will be submitted to the Commission. It will make the money allocations for public welfare.

It is very cold and there is no coal. Hutzinger, who is the fuel czar, does not allow Jews near him, leaving the Fuel Commission with no one to talk to.

*March 9, 1942*—28°F. In the morning at the Community. The inaugural meeting of the Religious Commission with the rabbinate. I spoke about the spirit of and need for religion. Rabbi Kanal [31] and the Chairman of the Commission, Mr. Frydman, responded.

I was examined by Dr. Hochsinger. Enlargement of the heart and aorta.

*March 10, 1942*—In the morning at the Community. An order was issued yesterday evening for 5 writing clerks to leave for Treblinka at 9 A.M. today.

I visited the pharmacies. At 3 P.M. Auerswald informed me that 151 prisoners are going to be released. He instructed me to discharge them by March 11. I stated that I want to take care of them, especially the younger ones. I summoned to my apartment Szerynski, Lindenfeld, First, Wielikowski, and my wife to discuss the matter.

---

30. KOM: Polish abbreviation for welfare organization apparently identical to JHK (Jewish Relief Committee).
31. Rabbi Yitzhak Meier Kanal, 82 years old, vice-chairman of the Congregation of Rabbis in Poland. He was killed during the deportations in August 1942.

# Notebook Nine

*March 11, 1942*—Yesterday Dr. Wielikowski submitted to Auerswald a list of 28 candidates for consultants [1] who will be permitted to practice law in the Polish courts with the same rights as Polish lawyers.

At 3 P.M. I released from the Jewish prison 151 people. Among them 5 were dead, 7 are being hospitalized. I placed more than 30 of them in the shelter; the rest went home. I addressed the prisoners; everyone was deeply moved. A crowd of people gathered in the street to wait for the released.

*March 12, 1942*—30°F. In the afternoon 18°F. In the morning at the Community. The artists brought the stained-glass windows for the auditorium in the Community building.

*March 13, 1942*—10°F, 7°F. In the morning at the Community. Yesterday Auerswald called at 6:30 with instructions that the Lichtenbaums should contact Münsterman[n] about the renovation of the market stalls at Nalewki Street. The *Zollfahndungsstelle* [Office of Customs Investigation and Enforcement] is to be located there. The ZOS is now without a home. They have been evicted from the Judaic Library and their efforts to get new accommodations from the Community have been in vain. Responding to our

---

1. *"Consultants"*: German designation for Jewish attorneys.

complaints, Probst told us to compare the situation of the Jews in Warsaw with what is going on in the east, etc.

*March 14, 1942*—In the morning at the Community. 19°F. Toebens (Jahn?) called Krol,[2] the engineer yesterday, on behalf of one Jungermann, asking that Jungermann be exempted from taxes because he works for them as hatmaker.

*March 15, 1942*—In the morning at the Community. 16°F. I went to "Brijus" in Otwock. In the evening I returned to Warsaw.

*March 16, 1942*—19°F. In the morning at the Community. Orders from Krüger for some goods. I visited with Auerswald various houses to check on the garbage [disposal] situation. At 2 P.M. a meeting of the delegation of the community workers (Orzech, Sagan, Kirszenbaum, Frydman, etc.) about the supervisory body to coordinate welfare. I am asking that this body should be attached to the KOM.

While the meeting was in progress, Jesuiter (SS) turned up with a Gestapo general from Berlin (?) and his entourage and ordered me to present a report on the Council.

*March 17, 1942*—32°F. In the morning at the Community. At 10:30 opening ceremony at the Jewish technical school. I spoke twice. Jaszunski and Buchweitz also addressed the gathering. I received some photographs of the release of the detainees from the Jewish prison. One can sense in these photographs the joy of the waiting crowd. It is the first time I see the Ghetto smile. A smile on the face of the released prisoner. I am trying to save the [Great] Synagogue, so far without success.

*March 18, 1942*—32°F. In the morning at the Community. The artists have completed their work on the stained-glass windows in the Community building auditorium. Alarming news [3] from Lwów (expulsion of 30,000 people), Mielec and Lublin. Nossig drew my

2. Michal Krol, "general secretary" of the Community (ranking administrative assistant). See entries of June and June 17, 1942.
3. A reference to first reports of mass deportations. Most of the victims were sent to the Bełżec death camp.

attention to one of the stained-glass windows, in his opinion inappropriate.

*March 19, 1942*—27°F. In the morning at the Community. I feel miserable—rheumatic pains, headache, cough. With great effort I barely managed to climb the four flights of stairs at the Brühl Palace. I told Auerswald that the Jews are not suited for heavy manual work, digging with shovels outdoors. They should be utilized in workshops. As for social welfare, which has been virtually reduced to the state of anarchy, Auerswald suggests that we should set up a special committee. I said that the appropriate efforts are being made in this direction.

In Szerynski's presence I asked A[uerswald] why Probst was complaining about Sz[erynski]. Several days ago Probst informed us through Lichtenbaum junior that Sz[erynski] is incapable of catching 3 thieves, former patrolmen, because the police is corrupt. Auerswald replied that he does not blame Sz[erynski]. There is corruption in the rank and file because wages are insufficient for survival.

Asked about further release of prisoners, Auerswald said that this matter is within his authority and that the decision will be made in a few days. I went to Probst and suggested that Sz[erynski] should explain the situation. Probst greeted Szerynski with sarcastic remarks. He said that those under suspicion spend hours at Lours [4] and that he would have to catch them himself before Sz[erynski] will do anything about it. In the afternoon Probst called that 2,000 Jews from the district will be resettled in Warsaw, April 1–4. We must make the necessary arrangements.

I went to bed with a temperature of 100°.

*March 20, 1942*—16°F. Because of illness I am working on Community business at home.

*March 21, 1942*—16°F. Sick at home (inflammation of the trachea). I wrote a poem entitled "The Manifesto" for some ceremony at the Community.

*March 22, 1942*—16°F. Ill at home. Two prisoners guarded by the Polish police escaped from the Czyste Hospital. One of them,

4. Lours, an elegant coffeehouse in the Europejski Hotel outside the ghetto.

Gomolinski (filed the iron bars). Every day two detainees die in the Jewish prison. Corpses lie there for 8 and more days because of unsettled formalities. On March 10, 1942, there were 1,261 prisoners and 22 corpses in the detention facility. The capacity of these two buildings is 350 persons.

The [Great] Synagogue could not be saved. I tried to get in touch with Kulski about Mostkowski Palace, from which the municipal technical offices could be moved so that we might get the building for the Judaic Library. Unfortunately, in view of the planned eviction of a [Polish] hospital from the Merchants Club, it is not known whether this will be possible (Podwinski's information).

*Further resettlements:*
A block of buildings at Dzielna and Pawia Sts. 4,700 residents, by Apr. 20, 42. Szczesliwa and Dzika Sts. (2,500 residents), by May 1, 42. Zoliborska Ave.: Bonifraterska–Muranowska–Sierakowska Sts. = 7,600 residents, no deadline set.

*March 23, 1942*—39°F. In the morning at home. I am ill. I telephoned Auerswald. I am to see him with a certain Mrs. Grossman, the *Gazeta Zyd[owska]* editor, who had [just] paid me a visit at home.

Lindenfeld calls and informs me that he saw Auerswald on Saturday about the list of prisoners which he had to alter. It looks—I believe—that in a few days 260 will be released. At the same time I issued instructions for the preparation of a list of detainees (in the category qualifying for release) from the Pawiak and Daniloowiczowska Street [prison], etc. Besides, a list of prisoners in the Jewish jail, who have not so far been put on the lists although they were qualified.

*March 24, 1942*—32°F. In the morning at the Community. At 10 with Auerswald. Admonitions on account of the nonpayment of some debt to Tworki [Warsaw's insane asylum]. I went to Auerswald with Mrs. Grossman (a disgusting woman). In the afternoon I received a letter from A[uerswald] on the emptying of the houses in the vicinity of the Tobacco Monopoly Building. I reminded A[uerswald] about further release of prisoners. He promised to speed matters.

*March 25, 1942*—37°F. In the morning at the Community. Current business. A transport of 500 expellees is about to arrive, nobody knows from where. At 3 p.m. I learned that the first batch of them came from Pustelnik, Radzymin, and Marki. About 400 persons all together were placed in the quarantine facility at 109 Leszno Street [outside the ghetto] because the streetcars dumped them at the ghetto gates and the guards did not let them in.

*March 26, 1942*—37°F. In the morning at the Community. Trouble with the Provisioning Authority (their own social welfare).

*March 27, 1942*—34°F. In the morning at the Community. Gepner arrived with his friends. We discussed the holiday assistance program. The Community receives from the Provisioning Authority 100,000 zlotys for relief etc. and 50,000 zlotys for the expellees. The [Community] staff receives parcels from the allocation of food left at my disposal by the *Kommissar*. From the flour, matzos will be baked for them.

In the evening several functionaries told us that the Provisioning Authority changed its mind and would not bake the matzos. I went to see the *Kommissar* to discuss our finances. He cannot help me. On the matter of coal supply—Rodeck is to make the arrangements for the ghetto. The *Kommissar* states that any larger camps are not being planned.

Yesterday at 9:35, 2 noncommissioned officers from the *Sonderdienst* came to the detention facility with young auxiliaries and patrolmen from the *Schutzpolizei* and proceeded to take 16 people away to be put at the disposal of the SS and *Polizeifuehrer*. Moving the prisoners took 5–7 minutes. They did not have enough time to take their belongings. The whole operation lasted 15 minutes. Reportedly they have been sent at 10 a.m. from the Eastern Railroad Station to Treblinka.

*March 28, 1942*—In the morning with Szerynski to Brandt. In the afternoon the chess tournament was concluded (six prizes).

*March 29, 1942*—In the morning at the Community. An unpleasant incident with the Provisioning Authority. Our staff was promised to have matzos baked from the flour requisitioned by the authorities. Today they were refused the matzos on the pretext that there will not be enough for the population from the regular allocation, and the staff may have bread. Our office workers refused to accept it.

In the afternoon Szerynski called from Otwock. A[uerswald] telephoned him and said that he observed Jews who were moving out of the houses on Stojerska Street taking floors etc. with them. He stated that the Order Service men who were passively standing by would be sent to Treblinka and the Community would pay for the damage.

*March 30, 1942*—37°F. In the morning at the Community. Current business. At night, air raid alerts.

*March 31, 1942*—In the morning at the Community. Later with Lindenfeld to Auerswald. He promised to release 260 prisoners tomorrow. We submitted to him a list of prisoners who thus far have not been covered by the amnesty. He promised to return to this matter after making sure that it is within his authority to do so. He gave permission for prayers in prison. I asked for the return of the 200,000 zlotys from his discretionary fund (a loan from us). So far he has not settled it.

*April 1, 1942*—(The Seder night.) In the morning at the Community. Tomorrow Passover.

News from Lublin. Ninety per cent of the Jews are to leave Lublin within the next few days. The 16 Council members together with the chairman, Becker, were reportedly arrested. Relatives of the other councilors, aside from their wives and children, must also leave Lublin.[5]

The *Kommissar* telephoned to say that a transport of 1,000–2,000 Jews from Berlin will arrive at 11:30 P.M. and that we must be ready to receive them. As of midnight we had no idea at which railroad station they would arrive and at what time. At 12 o'clock A[uerswald] notified us that they would be in Warsaw in half an hour. There will be a thousand of them. I decided to put them in the quarantine facility just outside the ghetto at 109 Leszno Street. In the morning hours about 1,000 expellees from Hannover, Gelsenkirchen, etc. were sent over. They were put in the quarantine at 109 Leszno Street. At 10 A.M. I witnessed the distribution of food. The expellees had brought only small packages with them. Those

5. Bełżec's gas chambers went into operation in March; Sobibor's in April; Treblinka's were still being readied. Both Bełżec and Sobibor were located in the Lublin district, Treblinka in the Warsaw district.

over 68 years of age had been allowed to stay in Germany. Older people, many women, small children.

*April 2, 1942*—In the morning at the Community. Later with Auerswald. Some Swiss officers were with him, listening to a report on the ghetto. I went to see the expellees from Germany in the quarantine at 109 Leszno Street.

*April 3, 1942*—32°. Today German *Karfreitag* [Good Friday]. Offices are closed. I was at the Community since early morning (offices closed—the second day of Passover). Is another swarm of refugees going to descend upon our shoulders?

*April 4, 1942*—In the morning with Szerynski to Brandt. Today at 7 P.M. 642 people deported from Germany are to arrive. I issued appropriate instructions. We have no housing and no money.

*April 5, 1942*—The *Umschlagplatz,* 4 A.M. At 8 A.M., 1,025 expellees from Berlin came in. All together there will be 2,019 persons in the quarantine. We cleared the way and led them to the 109/111 Leszno Street facility. The Order Service in front, the German police on the sides. Trailing behind a dozen carts with baggage and a few more with the sick. One of the sick has his leg in a cast (he was taken from a hospital). Mainly older people, partly intelligentsia. Many women.

There are 30 Lublin people at the Community.[6] The guards sent them over to remain at the disposal of the Council. As the noncommissioned officers did not object. . . . [sentence not completed]

*April 6, 1942*—In the morning at the Community. At 12 with Gepner and Sztolcman to Auerswald. He discussed the economic situation of the ghetto. I suggested that a special facility should be set up on the Aryan side, in which the Jewish craftsmen could be in touch with their Polish buyers. Auerswald proposed the market stalls at Nalewki Street for that purpose.

*April 7, 1942*—41°F. In the morning at the Community. Current business. The well-known good-for-nothing Rosner is supposed to

---

6. The 30 Lublin residents apparently were escapees from death transports.

have come to Warsaw for a few days. He is the *Obmann* [Chairman of the Council] at Rowne.

*April 8, 1942*—In the morning at the Community. Jewish Passover holiday. Once again I requested Auerswald to release the prisoners. He promised *unverbindlich* [without committing himself] to settle this matter today. Besides, he admonished us for not clearing the rubble in the streets. I replied that [my] *Arbeitsdienst* [Labor Service] proposal is gathering dust in his office, and that it could bring revenue. A[uerswald] retorted that there is no need whatsoever for money. He added that we have also failed in our tax collecting for the [municipal] Revenue Department. I said in turn that it is difficult to exact taxes from people who had everything taken away from them. As usual the conversation came to nothing. I went to the Leszno Street quarantine to see the expellees from Berlin, Frankfurt, Hannover, Gelsenkirchen, etc. I distributed some candy to the children. I addressed the youth and found them responsive.

In the afternoon several SS men turned up with a demand that the Berlin and Frankfurt Jews hand over all their gold. There was not much of it.

*April 9, 1942*—50°F. In the morning at the Community. Auerswald ordered 160 young German Jews from the quarantine to be taken to Treblinka. A smugglers' truck which could be seen in the ghetto for months bearing markings of the gasworks was stopped at the gate.

Auerswald sent a letter authorizing the release of about 260 prisoners.

*April 10, 1942*—41°F. In the morning at the Community. At 11 o'clock I released 260 prisoners from the detention facility after a speech fitting the occasion.

At 10 in the morning a transport of the German Jews, 17 to 35 years old, left for Treblinka from the quarantine at 109/111 Leszno Street.

Auerswald is demanding that we evacuate several apartment buildings in the ghetto and assign them to the remaining German Jews.

*April 11, 1942*—In the morning with Szerynski to Brandt. Later to Auerswald about the orchestra. The *Kommissar* sent me a letter yesterday suspending performances of the orchestra for 2 months for having played the works of Aryan composers. When I tried to explain, I was told that the Propaganda and Culture Department has a list of [the] Jewish composers. Today's concert will, nevertheless, take place just as before. The authorities learned about the concert programs from the *Gazeta Zydowska*. I will raise the issue with Auerswald once more on Monday.

Today 3 priests are coming to the Jewish prison (to hear detainees' confessions).[7]

*April 12, 1942*—In the morning at the Community. Current business.

*April 13, 1942*—In the morning at the Community. Current business.

*April 14, 1942*—In the morning at the Community. Later to Auerswald. I requested that numbers 29 and 31 Bonifraterska Street not be taken away from the Quarter. Instead they should be given to the German Jews. The stores and workshops should remain there. The *Kommissar* ordered me to discuss this matter with Kulski, since he (Auerswald) wants to acquire an apartment building on Przebieg Street which now houses beggars (?) for the purpose of placing some of the German Jews there.

I had a conference with Kulski and his deputy Podwinski. They are not hopeful about the Przebieg Street building.[8] They added, however, that there are prospects for acquiring the state-owned Staszyc building. Then, they would cede to us the Mostkowski Palace.[9]

They say that a thousand Jews will arrive from Germany tomorrow night.

*April 15, 1942*—In the morning with Szerynski to Brandt. Later with the *Kommissar*. I requested him to obtain the Staszyc building

7. Priests heard confessions of Christians of Jewish origin.
8. The Przebieg Street building, on a small street just outside the ghetto, contained a convalescent home and way-station for vagrants. A long correspondence within the German bureaucracy was occasioned by this building, as *Stadtdirektor* Becher opposed its incorporation into the ghetto and Probst finally agreed with him.
9. Czerniakow never obtained the Mostkowski Palace.

for the municipality in order that we may occupy Mostkowski Palace.

Allegedly a German policeman had an argument with a youth from the auxiliary who is no longer among the living. The policeman is supposed to have been wounded. The incident took place in the cellars of the ruined Treasury building.

Brandt and Auerswald informed us that a transport will arrive from Magdeburg and Potsdam at 6 o'clock tomorrow morning.

*April 16, 1942*—39°. At 4:30 A.M. at the *Umschlagplatz.* The train with the newcomers from Germany arrived at 6 A.M. It seems there are about 1,000 people. I led the transport to the Judaic Library.

I invited over 200 people for tea after 4 o'clock to report to them on the prisoner release operation.

This took the form of a public meeting of the Council. In addition to the 24 councilors some 200 persons representing different social strata attended. The auditorium was decorated with the curtains from the holy ark. The stained-glass windows, made by our artists under the direction of Sliwniak, added to the atmosphere. I described the course of our laborious efforts which led to the release of some 500 prisoners. Rechthand reported on his assignment of purchasing the sheepskin coats and Rozenstadt on the financial aspects of the operation. Gepner, Prof. Balaban and Frydman also addressed the gathering. Rabbi Kanal offered his best wishes.

*April 17, 1942*—43°F. In the morning at the Community. Brandt summoned Czaplinski [10] and Lejkin [11] of the Order Service for twelve o'clock noon. He ordered them to provide a 20-man Order Service detachment that evening for the purpose of checking on our night establishments.

In the afternoon panic erupted in the ghetto. Stores are being closed. People are crowding in the streets in front of their apartment buildings. To calm the population I took a stroll through several streets.

The Order Service detachment was to report at 9:30 P.M. in front of the Pawiak [prison]. It is now 10:30 and I am waiting for a

10. *April 17, 1942*—Marceli Czaplinski, one of Szerynski's deputies.
11. Jakob Lejkin, a lawyer, received prewar reserve officer's training in Polish infantry. He became the acting chief of the Order Service upon Szerynski's arrest in May 1942. He was killed at the age of 34 by the Jewish underground in October 1942.

report from the Order Service headquarters on what has transpired. It arrived at 7 A.M. Fifty-one persons had been shot.[12]

*April 18, 1942*—In the morning a conference with Hagen on the disposal of garbage. A certain Dr. Biskup, who represents Fleming, stated that the Jewish garbage disposal division is asking 30% more than prices on the Aryan side. I replied that they do not even receive 30% less. After lengthy arguments Hagen agreed with me and wrote to Fleming ordering him to pay [us] 270,000 zlotys and that the Aryan owners of the buildings should also [be made to] pay their share.

I went to see Auerswald about the expellees from Germany. I requested a building behind the Synagogue for the new transport on April 20 (some 1,000 persons). He gave me a list containing 78 names from the last transport; these people are to be sent to Treblinka. Besides he gave me two letters from the workers who are already there. One is asking for phonograph records, the other for tools.

I raised the subject of the last night's events. He knows what had happened. He is of the opinion that this was a special action. I pointed out that panic is spreading and that economic life will wither as a result of psychic breakdown. I added that I was going to try to get more information from the Gestapo. He asked me to inform him about the outcome.

I called Brandt, who told me that I must reassure the population and that people should return to their usual activities. Those who do just that will be left alone. I issued instructions to the Order Service to convey this assurance to the population through the house committees.

*April 19, 1942*—In the morning at the Community. Gepner, Sztolcman, Graf,[13] and Kobryner came in. Apropos recent occurrences, they claim that underground papers may bring about untold harm to the Jewish population.

Dr. Wielikowski returned: Kraków issued a directive to the district governors that in case of expulsions the last ones to leave the

12. The shootings were probably conducted by Brandt: 51 or 52 Bund members, underground pamphleteers, and others were pulled out of their apartments and shot in the back of the neck on the street.

13. Graf: cf. entry of April 15, 1940, appointed by Czerniakow as head of textile merchants. A Council member.

ghetto are to be the members of the JHK [*Jüdisches Hilfskomitee*— the Jewish Relief Committee].

*April 20, 1942*—50°F. In the morning at the Community. Later I went to the Gestapo to obtain details about the night of the 18/19th. I did not find anyone. I then went to Auerswald who told me that that night had nothing to do with the murder of a *Sonderdienst* man who had probably fallen from a bullet of a "Polish" smuggler. A[uerswald] added that if a Jew were responsible a thousand Jews would pay the price.

Yesterday I instructed the Order Service to raid the stores which display luxury foodstuffs. Sardines, chocolate, bacon fat, cakes, etc., were confiscated. The cakes were distributed among the children in the streets. The rest will be given to the orphanages. A pastor among the German refugees has asked for permission to conduct services for forty Protestants in their midst. Somewhere in the provinces, as I was told, another pastor was in the habit of soliciting aid from both a priest and the [Jewish] Community. When asked why he was turning to the Community, he replied that in the present hard times relying on one God is not enough.

*April 21, 1942*—In the morning with Brandt. He informed me that it was the underground papers appearing in the ghetto that brought about the repressive measures that night, and that more severe means will be employed if the papers continue to appear. He authorized me to inform the public that this was a special action and that the population can return to work without fear. He informed me that Council member Winter [14] had also been included in the list, but that he made inquiries and learned that the accusations were groundless. I asked him about young Fuerstenberg [15] (the elder one escaped death) and whether I could tell him that B[randt] is not interested in him. (F.[uerstenberg] had asked me to find out.) Brandt agreed with a proviso that "for the time being" he is not interested.

14. Samuel Winter, corn merchant from Włocławek, member of the Council and board member of the Provisioning Authority, reportedly connected with Ringelblum's effort to collect archival ghetto material.
15. Czerniakow was making inquiries on behalf of the young Fürstenberg, who was in the Order Service. Cf. note of September 2, 1940.

In the afternoon I was notified that Gorka, the cripple, and his mother were executed.

Refugees from Germany were supposed to arrive today. At the last moment I was informed that they would come around the 24th of the month.

Above Brandt and his chief, Böhm, there is Nehman.[16] Brandt drew my attention to the fact that on Panska Street. . . . [sentence unfinished]

*April 22, 1942*—In the morning with Szerynski to Brandt. B[randt] told us that the authorities discovered a [secret] organization in the ghetto. It is headed by foreign Jews.

He stated that Fuerstenberg is to stay in the Order Service. They brought to the Jewish prison 10 Gypsies,[17] men and women, with their "king" Kwiek. The Gypsies are refusing to eat at the Jewish prison.

I went to Auerswald. He admonished me, because Jewish officials stand too close to him when they talk to him, a practice that—in his opinion—creates a bad impression with his subordinates. Soup transported in trucks from Pawiak to the Jewish prison is often spilled on the way.

Yesterday a pedestrian was killed on Leszno Street by a bullet fired from a passing car.

*April 23, 1942*—In the morning at the Community. A certain Sliwniak, 19 years old, and 2 women, apparently middle-class, have been killed.

A new batch of Gypsies was brought to the Jewish prison. Tomorrow we are to receive a larger group. Tomorrow we are [also] expecting a transport of German Jews.

*April 24, 1942*—52°F. In the morning at the Community. I am thinking of approaching the Berlin Jews for assistance for those deported to Warsaw.

I visited the detention facility today. The young detainees engage in physical exercises and sing. I entered the Gypsy cell. We talked.

At 3 P.M. I was at the *Umschlagplatz* waiting for the transport of

16. Nehmann = SS-Capt. Gottlieb Höhmann, deputy chief of Gestapo in the office of the KdS.
17. Gypsies were the only ethnic group other than Jews subject to indiscriminate gassing.

1,000 Jews from Germany. At 5 P.M. the *Kommissar* called that they would arrive at 6. Later on it was announced that the transport had been directed to Łódź.

I went on an inspection tour of the ghetto today. One can see no white bread or delicacies in the store windows. The outcome of the recent raid of the Order Service. Also, after my latest instructions there is not much garbage in the streets.

*April 25, 1942*—In the morning with Szerynski to Brandt. There was no one in the whole section. A letter came from Auerswald ordering that Gypsies and Polish beggars brought into the Jewish prison should be deloused and then set free in the ghetto; he included a suggestion that it would be best to organize a shelter for them.

*April 26, 1942*—In the morning at the Community. At 1 P.M. a meeting of the Centos. Topic: the winding up of Children's Month. A report of the Auditing Commission (Szereszewski, the engineer) was rejected as exceptionally inane and instructions were given to prepare it anew.

An unpleasant exchange between Gepner and Szereszewski, then between Gepner and Giterman.

N[iunia] concludes that the newly rich brushmakers do as they please, disregarding all values and taking no notice of intelligentsia or experts. She added that one must prepare for death with dignity.

*April 27, 1942*—In the morning at the Community. A transport of 1,000 people arrived from Bohemia today. They were unloaded at 6 A.M. Later they were assembled in the [Great] Synagogue. I addressed the gathering.

I went to Auerswald. As a result of my entreaties he relieved me of the Aryan beggars who were to be dumped in the ghetto.

*April 28, 1942*—In the morning at the Community. Current business.

*April 29, 1942*—In the morning with Szerynski to Brandt. I raised the issue of the closing of the Great Synagogue. He went on to say that there is a continuation of unrest in the ghetto. I had the impression that further repressive measures might be taken.

Auerswald requested by Saturday population statistics according to streets and apartment buildings. Probst followed with a demand for 10 maps of the ghetto. Is a decision in the offing?

Yesterday Auerswald came to the prison with ___[illegible]. He ordered that an office be prepared for a German court (?). Could this be an indication of speeding up the process of releasing the prisoners? It has been cold for several days. 37°F in the morning.

It appears from the newspapers that Lübeck, Rostock, and Cologne have been bombed. In retaliation English cities were bombed. The municipality refuses to vacate the poorhouse on Przebieg Street. Some 8,000 Jews from the Muranow area are threatened with eviction.

*April 30, 1942*—In the morning at the Community. Haendel turned up with the news that Brandt in the company of 8 officers, in uniforms that looked neither like the Army nor the Gestapo, went to Auerswald's offices. From my office window I noticed these guests driving in a car. They were apparently making a tour of the ghetto. They were said to be seen in Brühl Palace in the afternoon.

I had a report that Chairman [Jozef] Diamand [of the Jewish Council] of Radom had been arrested and reportedly deported.

*May 1, 1942*—37°F. Before 8 in the morning, a call from the *Kommissar* ordering me to report at 8 A.M. at Brühl Palace. In view of yesterday's panic I thought some evil development was in store. It turned out that some Propaganda functionaries had arrived. The *Kommissar* told me to give them a briefing on the ghetto, which I proceeded to do. They are going to film the activities of the Council and life in the Quarter. From my office they left for the prison. At the *Kommissar's* request they inspected a company of the Order Service in prison. They also watched as the Service was dispersing vendors at Lubecki Street.

Szerynski was summoned by the *Kripo (Kriminalpolizei)* to Danilowiczowska Street for 8 A.M. We were told: "*Er kommt nicht wieder*" [He will not return]. I made a call to Brandt. He gave me the same message. He agreed to see me in this matter tomorrow morning at 8. Auerswald, to whom I sent First on the same errand, also stated that Szerynski would not be released. He is going to intervene tomorrow.

*May 2, 1942*—At 8 in the morning I went to Brandt about Szerynski. He told me that Szerynski was arrested on account of the furs which he had left for safekeeping with a Polish police officer who had also been arrested. A certain Jew who bore a grudge against the Polish officer had his hand in that.

The Gestapo chief is, according to Brandt, indignant at Szerynski and the Jews. A few unpleasant words were aimed at me. I asked him to apply for the release of Szerynski once more, which he promised to do, without, however, giving me much hope. Then I returned to the Community (today is a German holiday postponed from May 1). I then conferred with Haendel and the rest of the staff of the Order Service. I am trying to avoid the loosening of discipline. For the time being Lejkin is likely to be the acting commander. At the moment he outranks everybody else.

The German propaganda people are in the ghetto; they visited the prison and the refugee shelter at Tlomackie Street, filming.

*May 3, 1942*—In the morning at the Community. At 10 the film crew from the Propaganda Office arrived and proceeded to take pictures in my office. A scene was enacted of petitioners and rabbis entering my office, etc. Then all paintings and charts were taken down. A nine-armed candlestick with all candles lit was placed on my desk.

Szerynski is to be moved to the Jewish prison today or tomorrow. The *Transferstelle* has demanded a list of all those who work in the Quarter, including the Community Authority staff. It seems to me that what is involved could be the deportation of the unproductive elements from Warsaw.

*May 4, 1942*—In the morning with Lejkin to Brandt. I suggested Lejkin for the post of *Sachbearbeiter*.[18] Brandt told him that he was too short. In the end Brandt accepted him. I again requested that Szerynski not be moved to the Pawiak prison but to our own. Brandt appeared to agree. He promised to present the matter of S[zerynski] to the *"Kommandeur"* once more.

At 3 P.M. Brandt called me to announce that Lejkin is too short

18. *"Sachbearbeiter"* in German civil service denoted expert working in a particular functional area. Czerniakow probably intended to convey the role of caretaker of the police.

and to suggest that Szerynski's job should temporarily go to Nadel, the Commander of the 3rd precinct. Haendel turned up and informed me that at 3 he was in Brandt's office with Kon, who suggested Nadel. Haendel then expressed his willingness to influence Kon in such a way that Nadel's candidacy would be withdrawn. I told Haendel in strong terms not to intervene.

I had the impression that Haendel is scheming, the more so since he grumbled about Nadel, saying that Nadel shared a profitable little racket with the police and was friendly with Kon.

Nadel added that they want to get rid also of Czaplinski, the adjutant. Tomorrow morning I am going with Nadel to B[randt].

Auerswald was not in his office; he is ill with periostitis. In the afternoon a higher official from Krakow came to my apartment with director Iwanka and started asking questions about the Council's budget. He stated that he had never been shown our budget, but that, in any case, those decisions belong to Warsaw. He knew nothing about the ghetto's administrative setup, about the *Kommissar*, or the *Transferstelle*.

*May 5, 1942*—In the morning with Brandt. Lejkin was named the acting commander of the O[rder] S[ervice]. During a briefing of the officers of the O[rder] S[ervice] I informed them of this decision and urged them to remain calm and disciplined under the command of their new chief. Brandt promised to talk with the *"Kommandeur"* about Szerynski today.

Auerswald is still ill with periostitis. Today [is the] Jewish children's holiday: *Lag B'Omer*. I was at the "Femina" to watch a performance by the children from the Council's schools.

The film crew is still much in evidence. They are filming both extreme poverty and the luxury (coffeehouses). The positive achievements are of no interest to them.

Disturbing rumors about deportations persist in the city. A police order was issued forbidding the Poles to enter Saski Gardens as of May 1.

*May 6, 1942*—In the morning at the Community. It is still cold. A Polish policeman escorted the hollow-cheeked and unshaven Szerynski through the ghetto streets to the Pawiak prison.

At 2:30, at the Polish Police Headquarters, I introduced Lejkin as acting commander of the O[rder] S[ervice] to Colonel

Every Jew was required to wear
an armband bearing the Star of
David. A child offers them for sale.

Street vending was the only
occupation possible for many.

The misery of starving
mothers and children
in the streets.

Children were sometimes able to smuggle food into the ghetto.

Famine claimed victims hourly. The starving collapsed and died in the streets.

A prayer service.

Jewish ghetto police, the "Order Service," on duty.

Everyday sight on Muranowski Square.

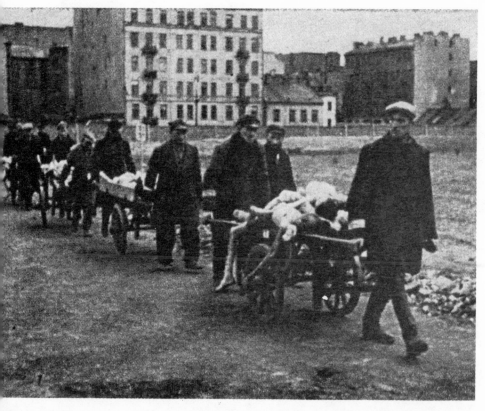

Abraham Gepner (Courtesy of Yivo Institute from the catalogue *Jewish Life in Poland,* in preparation.)

Janusz Korczak

Czerniakow's grave.

Jews being marched to the *Umschlagplatz*. This photo was probably taken after Czerniakow's death.

Rzeszczynski, Major Przymusinski, and Captain Schreiber (?).

In the city alarming rumors about deportations continue. The *Kommissar* told us to get in touch with the filmmakers. We are to make civilian clothes for them, which they apparently need for work.

*May 7, 1942*—In the morning at the Community. I was supposed to see Auerswald. The conference was canceled because Auerswald's son was being born. I inspected the workshops on Smocza Street (toy-making, galvanizing, weaving, assembling of calculators).

I held a conference with Gepner, Weichert, and Jaszunski concerning an interdepartmental loan. I also decided to appoint Dr. Wielikowski to succeed Szereszewski who resigned as Chairman of the KOM.

Jews were being filmed in the streets.

*May 8, 1942*—In the morning at the Community. At 3:30 with the *Kommissar*. He promised to talk to the *Kommandeur* about Szerynski. I introduced Lejkin.

He [Auerswald] asked me whether he should give permission for a satirical show in which I am being caricatured. I told him that I had no objections. Just as I do not mind their singing in the streets: *"Czerniakow hot a grojssen boch. Er esst Klop und trinkt joch* [Czerniakow's belly is big and round. Gulps broth and meatballs by the pound]." In spite of this he did not settle the matter favorably, and postponed the decision.

I raised the subject of prisoners in the Jewish detention facility. He said that the prison supervisor should discuss the matter with the appropriate judicial office.

With reference to the Gypsies (Hungarian, Roumanian, and Bulgarian citizens), he mentioned that he had no desire to become a Gypsy king. Auerswald blocked the payment of Szerynski's salary but permitted us to help Mrs. Szerynski out of the social welfare funds. He gave consent for setting up workshops in prison. He refused our request for establishing a special body of night watchmen. He also announced that he was going to prohibit the use of sugar in the coffeehouses.

I appointed 3 representatives, headed by attorney Altberg, to the Municipal Advisory Budget Commission, chaired by one Kubala.

*May 9, 1942*—In the morning with Lejkin to Brandt. I brought up the subject of Szerynski and requested an audience with the *Kommandeur*. Brandt replied that he had not yet received the Szerynski file. The *Kommandeur* receives no one but his own experts; thus he will not see me.

The head of the Economic Department, First, was summoned to the *Kriminalpolizei* and committed to the Jewish prison.

*May 10, 1942*—In the morning at the Community. I inspected the work being done in the little square in front of the Community building, where a playground is to be prepared. Working there are 30 German Jews, only recently deported from the Reich, a teacher, a factory owner, a cattle dealer, etc. I had cigarettes distributed among them. They receive 6.40 zlotys plus half a loaf of bread per day. They are satisfied with the work and the way they are being treated. In their efficiency, attitude to work, and, *last not least* [original English], their appreciation of our modest efforts to ease their lot, they could serve as an example for our Jews.

Not long ago Kapota [19] summoned Councilor Rozenstadt, stating that he would be charged with fraud, etc. The reason, as it turned out, being that he had granted an apartment to someone on an order from the authorities. R[ozenstadt] did not lose his composure and went to the police who quietly listened to his story for which he had documentary evidence.

*May 11, 1942*—In the morning at the Community. At 11 with the *Kommissar*. I asked him to call Ogorek and inquire about First. Auerswald telephoned but Ogorek was not there. Promised to call him again at 2 o'clock.

He called Hoehenmann [Höhmann], Brandt's chief, about Szerynski. They do not have Szerynski's file. First was released at noon, after interrogation. Michalski, arrested in connection with the Szerynski affair, was released from prison.

*May 12, 1942*—In the morning at the Community. Avril [20] arrived with the filmmakers and announced that they would shoot a

19. "Jossel Kapota" = Jozef Ehrlich, a young man of about 30 at the time, who wore a caftan *(Kapota)* from the prewar days when he was a student in a religious academy. Now suspected of working for German police. Killed by the Germans in 1943.
20. SS-Sergeant Franz Avril, KdS/III-B-4.

scene at the ritual baths on Dzielna Street. They need 20 Orthodox Jews with earlocks and 20 upper class women. In addition a demonstration of circumcision. This is to be arranged on orders by Dr. Milejkowski. Since the actor weighs 4.4 pounds there is danger that he may not last that long.

*May 13, 1942*—54°F–64°F. In the morning with Lejkin to Brandt. Brandt replied to my question that the *Kommandeur* refused to release Szerynski. He will be transferred to the Jewish detention facility. He concluded our conversation by saying that should Szerynski be released he would not resume the command of the Service but would at best become a *Berater* [advisor].

Yesterday they were shooting a scene at the ritual baths. We had to replace the women originally assigned. One of them refused to undress. They insisted that the circumcision be performed in a private apartment instead of a hospital.

I brought up the matter of the filmmaking with B[randt] and the *Kommissar*. I posed a question to them as to why our schools etc. were not being filmed.

*May 14, 1942*—57°F. In the morning at the Community. A children's playground is taking shape in front of the Community building at Grzybowska Street. I am planning several such playgrounds in different parts of the ghetto. I would like music once a week at the playground at Grzybowska Street.

At 4 o'clock, on my return home, I found uniformed filmmakers, etc.

Romcia [Roma] is ill in bed. Niunia, as usual of late, was not feeling well.

According to the papers, an offensive has started on Kerch; 40,000 Russians were taken prisoner.[21]

*May 15, 1942*—57°F. In the morning at the Community. At 8:30 A.M. I am waiting at home for the film crew. I requested that a couple be engaged to be actors. The movie men arrived at 8:45 and were shooting until 12:30. They placed a sign on the door with something written on it. Two women and a male "star" were

---

21. Kerch offensive on Crimean peninsula, start of major German drive into Caucasus and towards Stalingrad.

brought to the apartment. Then, an old Jew. They started shooting.

The city is full of rumors about deportations. Tens of thousands are being mentioned. Purposeful work under such conditions is worthy of admiration. And [yet] we are doing it every day. Tears will not help us. I must repeat Dickens' words once more: "You cannot wind your watch with your tears."

Haendel turned up about Lejkin's three stars.[22] The authorities decided to promote him.

In the afternoon the filmmakers were busy in the bedroom of Zabludowski's neighbors. They brought with them a woman who was seen applying lipstick in front of a mirror.

At my apartment, they were full of admiration for a little statue of Confucius and for a piece of sculpture, "Motherhood," by Ostrzega. One of them asked whether my Watteau on the wall was an original. I replied that the original was in a Berlin museum. My painting, I added, was a poor copy.

I am seeing Auerswald tomorrow morning about sanitation week, the settling of accounts with the municipality, and the possible taking over by the Council of the registration offices, which until now were staffed by Polish functionaries. It was Auerswald's idea that we do the latter [registration]. Delingowski [Kulski's deputy] insists that he will not surrender these offices unless he receives such orders from the *Stadthauptmann* [Leist]. In the meantime the offices are closed since our staff receives no passes.

During the movie-making an old Jew with a Vandyke beard was seized in the street. He sat in my apartment for hours, but his photogenic qualities were not utilized. I can imagine what happened when he returned home and tried to tell his wife that he had earned nothing, waiting for three hours to be a "star." I wonder whether I will ever meet you, my professional colleague. Didn't we two miss our destiny. Anyway when he happens to watch a movie some time, he will remark sarcastically: "As though I couldn't do it myself."

*May 16, 1942*—In the morning with Auerswald. I reported on yesterday's developments. In the end I casually mentioned the [Order] Service orchestra and asked permission for it to play outdoors. I would like the band to play in the children's playgrounds we are planning.

---

22. Three stars denoted rank of Deputy Chief of the Order Service. The Chief had four.

Life's thread caught on canvas [23] for G[epner?]—a Baroque paint-ing. For a long time I myself was pestered by U., the painter, to sit for him. When I yielded, the result was a disaster. Finally I had the idea of giving him a position [with the Community]. Since then he is gone from sight.

*May 17, 1942*—In the morning at the Community. Current business.

*May 18, 1942*—In the morning with Boehm and Brandt about Szerynski. Böhm promised to talk to the *Kommandeur*. Brandt stated that Szerynski's file was at the *Kommandeur*'s and that it may even be sent higher up. I asked whether it would not be advisable to appeal to Wiegand [Wigand] through the *Kommissar*. He did not think it would. On several occasions recently he stressed that if it came to me or Szerynski, he would not be able to decide anything by himself and would have to turn to his superiors. The case might even be sent up to the Governor-General. I was visited at the Community by Auerswald and some German dignitary from Minsk, to whom I had to explain the organizational structure of the Community. He asked me how Poland could have dared to chal-lenge German might.

Besides all this, persistent rumors about deportations. It appears that they are not without foundation.

Lederman and Capt. Fleiszman from the Order Service are involved in some scheme with Gancwajch. It has to do with filling the position of the Order Service Commander. Fleiszman has set his mind on it. Czerwinski, a rather dull Council official, died of a heart attack.

*May 19, 1942*—In the morning at the Community. The film-makers came to a Jewish restaurant. They ordered that food be served. Chance customers devoured everything with an enormous appetite, several thousand zlotys worth. Somebody telephoned the Council that the Community should foot the bill for the alleged costs. Czerwinski's funeral took place at 4 P.M. It was filmed. The cemetery was visited by a provincial governor. First served as guide.

On their way home the motorcade stopped at the abovemen-

23. Life's thread: meaning unclear. Possibly G. (Gepner?) sat for a portrait. Conceivably Czerniakow alludes to Velazquez painting *The Spinners*.

tioned restaurant. The governor was astonished at the food which he found there.

The movie people ordered a party to be arranged tomorrow in a private apartment. The "ladies" are to wear evening dresses.

*May 20, 1942*—In the morning with Böhm in the matter of Szerynski. He promised to talk with the *Kommandeur*. Later with Auerswald. Trifling matters like that of the armbands for the [Order] Service; should they be worn on the left or the right arm? Two bands or one? Not a word about finances. From Rozen, he demanded 400 craftsmen for some camp (rumor has it that it is Minsk).[24] Workers were to be sent there with their families. In the end they dropped the idea. The functionaries from the *Transferstelle* asked me if it was true that my apartment was turned into a movie set.

Gepner visited me yesterday at home. I discussed the sanitary conditions in the Provisioning Authority facilities and the issue of subordinating the fuel division to the Provisioning Authority.

*May 21, 1942*—In the morning at the Community. At 10 an air raid drill. We all hurried to the Archives Building [shelter]. Auerswald suggested that perhaps some German and Czech Jews be included in the camp contingent of the 400.

There are prospects for the release [from prison] of several hundred youngsters,[25] up to the age of 17, and several hundred elderly people as well. I am doing my best to bring this about. Avril came and sharply reprimanded First for the alleged shortcomings in connection with the filmmaking. The Order Service again raided the restaurants and confiscated luxury foodstuffs. They will be distributed to the orphanages and refugee shelters.

In the afternoon a hall was prepared for the filmmakers, where a ball with champagne, etc., is to take place tomorrow at 8:30. A messenger arrived with instructions from Avril that I am to play the role of host of the ball. I [let Avril know] that at 8:30 I am supposed to be with Lejkin, the chief of the [Order] Service, at Brandt's, to which he said that he would get Brandt's approval for the postpone-ment of the appointment so that I can be used by the movie-makers.

24. On Minsk: See entry and note for May 30, 1942.
25. The children in the Jewish detention facility on Gesia Street had been caught crossing the wall in search of food.

I called Auerswald who told me: "I am forbidding you to perform." He added that I should be at the Community at 7:30, for something might change yet. This suggests that the matter has not been settled. Will I have the strength to acquit myself honorably in this affair?

The Chairman and the members of the Personnel Commission have submitted their resignations as a result of the stand I had taken in their squabble with the Labor Department. They were not motivated by general welfare; they could not rise above their own selfish aspirations.

Later in the day I looked out of my window and saw a hearse full of flowers which were being taken from the cemetery to the ballroom.

*May 22, 1942*—55°. It is 5:30 in the morning. I will be leaving for the Community at 7. I am waiting for Auerswald's telephone call about the filming.

Before 8 A.M. Dr. Grassler called summoning me to the Brühl Palace on an "urgent matter." I came but was told I must wait a while without going out in the street. Auerswald, with whom I soon got in touch, had had a telephone conversation with Brandt. Brandt shares Auerswald's opinion about yesterday's proposal. I reported with Lejkin to Brandt. He informed me that he understood that Avril had summoned me to the "ball" as a technical consultant. Brandt will have a word about the incident with Avril.

I asked Dr. Stabenow whether A[vril] was subordinated to him; he denied it. On hearing what had transpired, A[uerswald] instructed me not to go to the filming and to refer any questions to him. First was also excused from offering a toast at the ball, for he does not speak Yiddish. He was replaced by a professional comedian, Norski-Nozyca.

I had a session with Galuba.[26] He told me that he was an orator and that he was able to hold 20,000 people spellbound for hours. He is full of sensational stories. He insists that Einstein is a swindler and that Liebermann stole the formula for the synthesis of alizarin from Graebe. On the basis of his personal experience he claims that the Jews deprived him of a large fortune.

26. Hans Galuba, in Auerswald's office.

I ordered requisitioning of luxury foods from the restaurants. The proceeds were distributed among the children in the orphanages.

*May 23, 1942*—In the morning at the Community. Probst and the *Kommissar* arrived at Tlomackie Street. Thirty Jews have been sent to Treblinka.

*May 24, 1942*—In the morning at the Community. At noon a concert of the Order Service orchestra under the baton of Kataszek. Jewish compositions were played and sung. The auditorium was full. A very good performance. The following died yesterday: Lewin (a well-known scoundrel from the Gancwajch pack), Mandel Gurwicz or Gurewicz and one Szymanowicz (reportedly, Gancwajch's nephew).[27] [The latter] came to me once with one Adam Zurawin, trying to use blackmail to get a concession for taking identity card photos. The gang leader himself, Gancwajch, is said to be away from Warsaw. The other boss, Sternfeld, fled. One Zachariasz was also out of town they say.

When I think of the activities of certain social activists, I see that the attitude of the public toward them has no relation whatsoever to their work. People are usually loved more for their vices than for their virtues.

*May 25, 1942*—In the morning at the Community. Christian Pentecost. [German] offices closed.

*May 26, 1942*—In the morning with Auerswald. He issued an order (to be posted) that no armbands except [those with] the Star of David are to be worn. Only the members of the Order Service are entitled to wear two bands, one of them being part of their uniform.

Once again I raised the subject of release of some 700 detainees in the Jewish and other prisons; many of them are minors.

*May 27, 1942*—In the morning with Lejkin to Brandt. Brandt declared that if any Jewish family hides Gancwajch, Sternfeld, Zachariasz, and one Zelman (name unknown to us), it will suffer the consequences. At noon I went with Rozenstadt to Dr. Cytner

27. When Czerniakow refers to the deaths of men associated with Gancwajch, he means that the Germans shot them.

who was with Fleming. Cytner informed us that he would with-draw the 4% of the rent receipts, unless the Council carries out its obligations more effectively. The Council has been receiving a little over 6,000 zlotys a month from the trusteeship administration of real property, whereas the office expenses exceed 10,000 zlotys. Moreover, I expended 100,000 zlotys for refuse collection and lent the contractor 90,000 zlotys.

At 5 P.M. the Order Service Headquarters called that 600 Jews are about to arrive from Radzymin. It was, however, ringing the dinner bell after the meal, since they arrived earlier and were already housed at 109 Leszno Street.

It is said that Lejkin (who is short) started his exercise of authority by abolishing visor caps. The reason: the visor interfered with his raised knees when marching.

Mende returned to Warsaw. Haendel left for Otwock on ac-count of his child's illness.

*May 28, 1942*—64°F. In the morning at the Community. At 11 with Lejkin to Auerswald. He discussed the matter of 500 patrol-men who are to be paid 10 zlotys per day. They are to guard the walls and to be responsible (with their lives) for any holes made in them. I mentioned that the holes were being dug from the Aryan side. Auerswald retorted that the militiamen are privileged. They are not being sent to the camps, to Russia, etc., so they should do their duty well.

Israel Platek (from Germany), a janitor at 29 Leszno Street, fired for theft and filth in his building, appealed to *Kommissar* Auerswald. Platek claimed that although himself a Jew he knew little about the Jews until his eyes were opened as a result of reading a certain tome. And although he is only a janitor he now knows how to manage Jewish real estate and how to carry on the struggle against the Jews until their total destruction. He requested an appointment with A[uerswald]. He reportedly received a pass for May 26 and 27. When questioned by us, Auerswald said that he knew nothing about this. Grassler asked my opinion about a Berlin proposal that Warsaw Jews wear the same badge as the one worn by the German Jews. I replied that, one, there is little cloth, and, again, they spend their time within the ghetto walls, few of them venturing outside. Why, then, the armbands at all, and by the same token why the change?

*May 29, 1942*—In the morning at the Community. The *Kommissar* ordered us to provide a contingent of 900 people who are to leave tomorrow for an unknown camp. A roundup was carried out in the streets. In addition 240 prisoners between 15 and 18 years of age and 4 of those pardoned by the Governor-General are also leaving for the same camp.

A[uerswald] spent several hours today in the Jewish detention facility. He summoned me for 4 P.M. in connection with the state of sanitation in the ghetto. I have been devoting much time to this problem myself, for neither the Sanitation Department nor the Order Service can be relied upon.

I have been going through the streets with Brodt issuing reprimands or dispensing money awards to the janitors. Considering the level of civilization in this community, the ghetto cannot be kept clean. People, unfortunately, behave like pigs. Centuries of slovenliness bear their fruit. And this is compounded by the utter misery and dire poverty.

Director Meyer [28] from the municipality paid me a farewell visit today. I asked him to leave the garbage bins and carts, since, beginning June 1, we are taking over the collection of waste. Meyer's chief, Schulten [29], is to make a decision in this matter tomorrow.

*May 30, 1942*—In the morning with Lejkin to Brandt. Later with Mende, who has resumed his regular duties. I raised the subject of Szerynski for the *n*th time. Brandt announced that he would see to it that Szerynski is allowed to receive parcels. The fate of Szerynski is in the hands of the *Kommandeur*. I hear from other quarters that the *Kommandeur* is taking a two-week leave. Last night 914 were taken away (including 150 youngsters between 15 and 18 years of age). The transport left for Bobruisk [30] (?) in the morning. At the very last minute 300 pairs of boots and several hundred shirts for the youngest deportees were handed over to the German escort. The curfew hour was extended to midnight yesterday to make possible

28. Kazimierz Meyer, director of Warsaw city sanitation department, dismissed by the Germans.
29. Schulten apparently was Meyer's German supervisor.
30. Bobruisk, southeast of Minsk, in the occupied USSR under German military administration. A transport of 912 Jewish workers, including 500 arrested on the street, were dispatched to the Higher SS and Police Leader in Russia Center, an area which included Bobruisk.

the delivery of parcels to the deportees. Auerswald was present until late at night and in the morning.

Last night more than ten persons died.[31]

*May 31, 1942*—In the morning at the Community. Several meetings. At noon, I took part in a conference of instructors of advanced courses.

Schulten took away all the garbage bins and carts and tomorrow we are taking over the garbage collection and cleaning of the streets. Meyer, who paid me a farewell visit, assured me that he had no need for any trash cans and carts, but he had to wait for Schulten's order. Grassler telephoned Sch[ulten], as far as I can see, in vain.

In one of the letters to the *Kommissar* submitted to me for signature, I found the following passage. "Those who are ill with infectious diseases should be taken out of the towns. The Bible." Some feat it would be if by quoting the Bible I brought about the deportation of the Jews from Warsaw. This convinces me that— unfortunately—I must read all my correspondence.

At 7 P.M. a conference on placing all the ghetto cleaning operations under a single management. At 8 o'clock a meeting on the Children's Home.

And now I am thinking what tomorrow will bring. *Penser, c'est le moyen de souffrir* [To think is to suffer], (Flaubert, *"Première lettre d'amour à Louise Colet,"* 4 August 1846).

*June 1, 1942*—In the morning at the Community. The film-makers had ordered that up to a hundred men and women, half of them from the higher strata, be made available and then they filmed them in the Community auditorium.

From 9:30 to 11:30 I was with Auerswald. I asked for the extension of the curfew hour. I reported on the subject of sanitation in the ghetto. I inspected the square on the corner of Gesia and Nalewki Streets and another one at Nowolipki Street where the children's playgrounds are planned.

Auerswald called at 3 P.M. asking for several hundred more people for Treblinka.

*June 2, 1942*—In the morning at the Community. At 10 o'clock I was again filmed in my office. An idea—taking away the bread cards

31. More than ten persons were killed in continuation of German shootings.

from those who are better off and distributing them to the children in the streets.

Eljasz the upholsterer passed away today. Zachariasz's daughter is a hostage.

*June 3, 1942*—In the morning with Lejkin to Mende. Later Lejkin was left alone with M[ende]. I spoke to Brandt about Szerynski.

I issued instructions to the [Order] Service for the arrest of the notorious blackmailer Judt. Lately, she has been swindling all kinds of people again, taking thousands of zloty for the purported releases. I went to see A[uerswald] to get his approval for a religious evening. He said that this was a matter for the SD and the Gestapo. Yet Brandt said that it was up to Auerswald to decide.

I saw Nikolaus [32] about emigration. He informed me that foreign Jews will be allowed to leave, to be exchanged, provided their foreign documents are in order.[33] If need be they can complete their papers at the Swiss legation in Berlin. The Swiss legation represents American republics. A conference of the GG [*Generalgouvernement*] governors was held in Warsaw.

Auerswald said that the population would be allowed to import small quantities of potatoes. I suggested that the Provisioning Authority should be designated a *Werkküche* [factory kitchen] as defined in Governor Fischer's announcement. We could then purchase supplies for the population at the *Landwirtschaftliche Zentrale* [Agricultural Distribution Center].

*June 4, 1942*—In the morning at the Community. Current business. We are to receive from the *"Finanzinspektor"* 300,000 zlotys from the sum of about 420,000 that is due to us. The *Kommissar* earmarked the remainder for his discretionary fund.

*Gazeta Zydowska*, June 3, 1942
From Krakow

Changes have occurred in the administration of the Jewish Residential Quarter in Krakow. The former administration has been

---

32. SS-1st Lieut. *Kriminalkommissar* Kurt Nicolaus, Chief, KdS/IV-A (Gestapo).
33. Jews who were citizens of Great Britain and Western Hemisphere countries at war with Germany were pulled out of the ghetto to be exchanged for German citizens.

dismissed [34] and Mr. David Gutter from Tarnow has been appointed the new head. A Council of 7 has been named to assist him. The new Administration of the Community is of a predominantly economic nature. It conforms to the new composition of the Jewish population.

*June 5, 1942*—In the morning at the Community. Auerswald, Grassler, and Probst arrived at 1 P.M. They had a look at the 2 new carriages (two-wheelers) purchased by the Council. They did not come to see me.

A rusted rifle and a few shells were found in the building of the vocational school. The precinct commander of the Order Service, Guzina, informed the Polish Police about the fact.

*June 6, 1942*—In the morning with Lejkin to Brandt and Mende. I raised the subject of Szerynski with them and their chief Böhm. They told me that my conscience should be clear since I have done everything in my power to help him. Unfortunately, so far, my efforts were in vain. When the despicable bitch, Mrs. Judt, was about to be arrested she pretended to have a fever of 103°. Now she has disappeared. Thus the blackmailer who has robbed so many unfortunates is still free.

I was at a concert of a quartet and singers at the "Femina." For quite a while I have been actively supporting the idea of having an opera staged. It could be "Zydowka" [*La Juive*], "Carmen," or "The Tales of Hoffman." [35]

*June 7, 1942*—In the morning at the Community. At 9:30 an opening ceremony at the playground at 21 Grzybowska Street. The orchestra played under the direction of Kataszek, choirs sang, and the children from the Council schools danced and performed calisthenics. The playground was handed over to the [younger] children by the [older] children. Three delegates, two men and a woman, did the announcing in Polish, Yiddish, and Hebrew. I

---

34. The Kraków ghetto Jewish Council was dismissed for inefficiency in readying deportees for transport. Its chairman (together with several thousand ghetto inmates) was deported a few days later.
35. Halevy: composer of *La Juive*, and Offenbach, composer of *Tales of Hoffmann*, were Jews. Not so Bizet, who composed *Carmen*.

spoke twice. The ceremony made a great impression on those present. Balm for the wounds. The street is smiling!

At 1 P.M. I arranged lunch for the workers deported from Germany. After my welcoming speech, Dr. Wielikowski delivered an address. Two representatives responded. Lunch: soup, meat—8 zlotys—we ordered it at a nearby restaurant. Moreover, everyone received a packet of cigarettes and some candy.

I distributed chocolate to the children present.

*June 8, 1942*—In the morning at the Community. Auerswald has been absent from his office for several days. Haendel tells funny stories about Haberbusch. People of the ghetto earn their living in many ways. A eulogizer pays me a visit from time to time bringing illustrated poems in my praise. A few days ago several gentlemen visited *Docent* Sterling [university lecturer in medicine] and offered him an honorary diploma for being a great man, a savior, etc. Later they solicited a donation for the impoverished merchants. S[terling] refused saying the merchants do not aid the impoverished physicians. On hearing this, they bowed but also requested the return of the parchment, thus depriving him of a claim to immortality.

*June 9, 1942*—In the morning at the Community. Last night more than 10 people died; smugglers, etc. Also a movie director Szaro [36] and his father-in-law Goldman. I went to see Auerswald. I submitted a petition for an extension of the curfew hour until 10 o'clock and an application of the Provisioning Authority for food purchases on the free market. I requested the release of the minors from prison, because of overcrowding (1,650 detainees, capacity 500). Recently a transport of 60 Gypsies arrived from Lowicz; they are demoralizing the prison.

I visited the anti-typhus exhibit organized by the Health Department.

*June 10, 1942*—In the morning with Lejkin to Brandt and Mende. Mende will not do much for Szerynski. The deputy precinct commander Ehrlich threatens the Czaplinskis.[37] A conference in the Community about the lunches, which have to be cut

36. Henryk Szaro (Szapiro) and father-in-law Goldman (president of prewar insurance company).
37. Marceli Czaplinski (Szerynski's adjutant) and his brother, both in the Order Service.

down considerably because of lack of money. I am going to see Auerswald tomorrow to ask him to increase the allocation for Social Welfare from 15% to 20%. Thus we may find our way out of the difficulty.

A[uerswald] arrived at the Community at 3:30 and tried out the 3 carts which we have ordered. He did not bother to see me. Yesterday afternoon several people were shot. The perpetrators—some barefooted civilians with armbands.

Today *Junacy* [an informal designation of uniformed youth groups, mainly ethnic German] searched the cellars of the house at 20 Chlodna Street, allegedly looking for hidden leather.

At the Gestapo I raised the question of the "Frankenstein" who keeps shooting at people every day at one of the gates.

In the afternoon, Ehrlich sent Haendel and First to my apartment (he himself was waiting in the street) to inform me that he feared my "displeasure." Step by step, various scoundrels are beginning to tremble, especially since the liquidation of the Gancwajch gang.

*June 11, 1942*—In the morning at the Community. Before I left, I saw *Junacy* with whips guarding Jews (among others Mitelberg, the merchant, who was seized on the street) in the courtyard of the building at 20 Chlodna Street. The Jews were ordered to carry armfuls of leather from the secret tannery (?) in the cellar to a large wagon.

At 1 P.M. Auerswald arrived with some visitors whom I was ordered to brief on the ghetto. Deputy Precinct Commander Jozef Ehrlich came to report to me; I refused to see him.

Fogel, a functionary in the health insurance bursar's office, was released. There is restlessness in the ghetto because of the daily shootings of smugglers as well as of law-abiding pedestrians by elements not readily identifiable.

I saw a portrait of myself at Kramsztyk's. A very good pose in a beautiful setting, but the face is very old and tired and bitter. Kramsztyk claims that the face is not finished. I could not sit for him as the light was not right. Tomorrow morning at 9 they will deliver 34 Gypsies from Lowicz to the Jewish prison.

*June 12, 1942*—In the morning at the Community. A conference with the Inspectorate and the Order Service to verify credentials. I decided to dismiss nearly two hundred functionaries.

At 6 P.M. I went to the "Eldorado" Theater to watch a play by Kobryn. A certain Revenue Department functionary sealed an apartment together with the tenants inside for the nonpayment of the less than one hundred zlotys in taxes.

*June 13, 1942*—In the morning with Brandt and Mende. I raised the problem of deaths in the Quarter and informed them that some unknown civilians are shooting not only at smugglers but also at innocent passersby. I requested that they get in touch with Auerswald in order to put an end to the situation.

More Gypsies were crammed into the detention facility. The number of prisoners now exceeds 1,800. People faint; every day deaths occur because of overcrowding. I discussed this problem with Dr. Grassler who advised me to talk it over with Auerswald. Unfortunately, he was not in.

Mende took me to *Kommissar* Nikolaus, who proposed to the Council an exchange of Jews for Germans in the United States and South America, with the exception of Chile and Argentina. Palestine also enters into the picture. The wives of husbands who are in Palestine will be allowed to join their spouses there.[38]

They ordered me to issue to the Gypsies armbands with a letter Z.[39]

*June 14, 1942*—Cloudy. Today is Sunday. I am not sure whether the orchestra could perform in the playground. It turned out that it did play in spite of a light rain. I issued instructions for the children from a precinct detention room, organized by the Order Service, to be brought to the playground. They are living skeletons from the ranks of the street beggars. Some of them came to my office. They talked with me like grown-ups—those eight-year-old citizens. I am ashamed to admit it, but I wept as I have not wept for a long time. I gave a chocolate bar to each of them. They all received soup as well. Damned be those of us who have enough to eat and drink and forget about these children.

*June 15, 1942*—At 8 in the morning 500 Order Service men paraded for Auerswald in the courtyard at 40 Grzybowska Street.

38. Palestinian nationals and their spouses were considered enemy aliens, eligible for exchange. Germans in Palestine, then a British mandate, were subject to internment.
39. "Z": an abbreviation for *Zigeuner,* German word for "Gypsy."

At 1 o'clock the *Oberleutnant* [First Lieutenant] in charge of the guard [at the ghetto gates] came to see me. I presented to him the problem of haphazard shootings in the ghetto by unauthorized personnel. He promised to straighten things out.

At 4 P.M. I went to see Auerswald. I discussed with him the matter of taking away bread allocations from privileged groups to help the children in the streets. This is supposed to be a one-month proposition. For afterwards I am counting on a voluntary renunciation of bread cards for the benefit of the poorest. I raised the subject of extending the curfew hour. Then I presented the problem of "conditions à la Mexico." A[uerswald] told me that he was waiting for the Gestapo to declare its position in this matter.

*June 16, 1942*—In the morning at the Community. At 2 P.M. Auerswald arrived with 18 journalists whom I had to brief on the administration of the Quarter. This morning the Secretary of the Council, Engineer Michal Krol had died (from typhus).

Following an order from the authorites today I released 190 Gypsies from prison and instructed them to wear white armbands with a red letter Z. They all turned up at the police station and asked for the armbands because they do not know where to go. To be humane, I have to take care of them, especially their women and children.

*June 17, 1942*—In the morning with Brandt. I raised the matter of B[randt]'s visit in the Provisioning Authority in connection with Gepner and Tenenbaum. The answer was that no one objects to G[epner]. On the other hand, various Jews keep on sending slanderous letters about Gepner, myself, etc. and this leads to investigations.

I took the attorney Lubinger, from our Legal Department, to Nikolaus. A text of an announcement through the house committees was decided upon concerning emigration to the USA, South America (except Argentina and Chile), and Palestine (wives to husbands, children to parents, parents to children). At 11 A.M. Gepner, Altberg, and some contractors about various finished products for which the Quarter may obtain food or perhaps some other relief.

At noon I spoke at the cemetery at Krol's funeral. Besides me, Professor Balaban and Mr. Fliederbaum made speeches in the name of the staff.

It is reported that the Gypsies are to be deported from the ghetto. Thus I will not be an emperor of Ethiopians any more.

*June 18, 1942*—In the morning at the Community. A suggestion for the Provisioning Authority or perhaps the Production Company by one Dr. Schmied.[40] He claims that he had discussed this matter with Dr. Kah and he is about to have a meeting with Brandt. In view of this I asked B[randt] what it was all about and was told that as soon as Schmied comes to him, Brandt will ask Kah to summon me on this matter.

In the afternoon Schmied or his representative called saying that he would like to barter; for 500 boots, etc., he would offer us some merchandise.

[There is no entry for *June 19, 1942*.]

*June 20, 1942*—In the morning with Lejkin to Brandt. Szerynski's case is in bad shape. A "collector" of scrap metal, Nass, was seeing Brandt. He has been visiting factories, reportedly designating good machinery as junk. It is easy, however, to make him change his mind. I went to see Auerswald about bread for the children in the streets, the *Arbeitsdienst*—public works, etc.

In the afternoon I took part in a reception given by the student welfare association of the Teachers College. I spoke. In my reply (to Dr. Szyper) I made reference to the deer (a swift-footed animal) on the stained-glass windows in the Community auditorium—a symbol of those who run away.

*June 21, 1942*—In the morning at the Community. At noon a concert on behalf of the prisoners aid committee. My wife gave an address in the name of the committee.

Tobruk and Bardia fell. Sevastopol is still holding out.[41]

*June 22, 1942*—In the morning with Sztolcman to Auerswald. We discussed the issue of bread allocation. The decision on the street children was postponed until Wednesday. Auerswald cannot

---

40. Schmied (from Berlin), not further identified. See diary entry for July 16, 1942.
41. Tobruk and Bardia, major German victories over the British in Libya. Sevastopol, Russian-held fortress under siege in Crimea.

make up his mind about the project of reducing bread allocations for the privileged for distribution to the street children.

Problems of exports and employment were discussed. I made three suggestions: export premiums, compensation in goods, an improved turnover.

A[uerswald] ordered me to be at home after 5 P.M. for he had something to communicate to me. Later he left for a conference at the Governor's at which it is said a high SS dignitary participated. At 5 P.M. Auerswald's secretary called, saying that she had nothing to tell me. I suppose it is a question of a larger contingent to be sent to camps.

Managers from (E. Gerlach and Pulst) factory paid me a visit today stating that they must get 800 workers (grinders, etc.). They will train them if we cover 50% of the cost (50,000 zlotys). I remarked that the difficulty of finding applicants is the result of low wages, which are not sufficient to keep a man alive. One of the managers retorted that he himself used to work for the Jews, and that the Horowitz Company did not mind paying as little as 2 *RM* for work on a woman's suit which took 4 days to make.

Jewish optimism: "Two Jews standing in the shadow of the gallows. The situation is not hopeless, says one of them, they have no bullets."

*June 23, 1942*—In the morning at the Community. Auerswald arrived with some visiting dignitary and his retinue. I had to brief them on the Quarter. At 12:30 with Iwanka. The municipality recognized as indisputable a debt they owe to the Council (the rest is in dispute) and were reprimanded for their action. The payment of over 1 million zlotys is up to Dr. Fribolin. The well-known hypocrite Orzech (a citizen of Honduras) provoked a scene on the street. It came to blows and finally the Order Service placed him in the detention facility at Gesia Street.

Auerswald summoned me at 7 o'clock and handed me a written order according to which the residents of the Pokorna, Muranowska, Bonifraterska, and Zoliborska Streets are to be notified tomorrow at 6 A.M. that they are to vacate their apartments by 8 P.M.

*June 24 1942*—In the morning at the Community. I inspected work on the playgrounds at the corner of Franciszkanska and Nalewki Streets and at Nowolipki Street, also a garden on the grounds of the prison. At 4 o'clock tomorrow morning 80 persons are to leave the prison for a camp. They are now in a wooden building adjoining the prison. When they recognized me there was wailing and shouting, until I reached the gate. Several hundred other prisoners are to follow.

Mister Orzech, who was taken to the police station yesterday, was very sorry today for what he had done, promised to apologize to the officers whom he had insulted in public and to make a donation to the precinct detention room.

*June 25, 1942*—In the morning at the Community. A[uerswald] was present when 80 condemned and 150 other prisoners left for camps. The German and Protectorate [of Bohemia and Moravia] refugees are to leave the Synagogue and the Judaic Library.

I received Auerswald's permission to use 36 tons of flour from the general allocation for lunches. In this way it will be possible to feed some of our charges. A permit to hold religious evenings was obtained.

Auerswald demanded documentation concerning Tebens' [Toebbens] debt [to us] which amounts to 550,000 zlotys. T.[oebbens] reportedly claimed that somebody fired at his car in May (!) and hence demanded 2,000,000 zlotys as a bond to guarantee the safety of his family. He decided then to keep the 550,000 zlotys.

*June 26, 1942*—In the morning at the Community. Later with Auerswald. At 11 A.M. he arrived at the Community with some visitors whom, as usual, I had to brief on our affairs.

Someone named Zawadzki came to the Housing Department with Usenka and Dr. Dobrin about a building adminstrator who was to be arrested for breaking the Department seals. Under threats attorneys Baumberg [Head of the Housing Department] and Adler [42] promised that the administrator would not be arrested. We will have to do something about this.

I am preparing a public Council meeting on Sunday, at which individual councilors will report on their work.

*June 27, 1942*—In the morning with Brandt. He had seen Szerynski. I asked Brandt to intercede on Szerynski's behalf. Yes-

---

42. Ignacy Baumberg and Stanislaw Adler, ghetto housing office.

terday near the Eastern Railroad Station the Jewish workers were involved in a brawl with Polish railway men. As a result one Polish worker is dead, 2 Jewish workers have been stoned to death, and many Jews are injured.

In the afternoon I spoke at a ceremony marking the opening of the detention room at the Order Service precinct at Chlodna Street.

*June 28, 1942*—In the morning at the Community. At noon the second public meeting of the Council. Brandt came to see the auditorium in which the meeting and reception took place. The hall was overflowing. The following reports were made: Engineer Sztolcman on the Provisioning Authority, Attorney Altberg in the name of the Economic Council on the economic situation in the Quarter, Councilor Rozen on the activities of the Labor Department and camps. The latter made an appeal calling for more productive work. Finally I said a few words of tribute about Gepner on the occasion of his seventieth birthday and unveiled his photograph in the Council Room. Anticipating my remarks, Gepner, in an earlier speech, thanked me for my attitude toward him and offered those assembled his best wishes.[43]

*June 29, 1942*—In the morning at the Community. I gave instructions for the removal of rubble from Chlodna Street in the "Aryan" part between the walls. I want to avoid the breaking of window panes in the Jewish houses by Polish teenagers, and not only teenagers.

Following a decision by the municipality we were to receive 1,275,000 zlotys as a payment of an acknowledged debt. The supervising authorities disallowed the payment, stating that we, on our part, should take responsibility for arrears owed by individual Jews. Thus, if Mister Auerswald fails to protect the Quarter, we will probably receive 500,000 zlotys.

We have drafted the bread distribution plan for the population. I will present it to the *Kommissar* at 8 A.M. tomorrow.

*June 30, 1942*—At 8 in the morning with Sztolcman and Wielikowski to Auerswald. Flour distribution was discussed. I insisted

43. Ludwik Hirszfeld, who wrote his memoirs in 1943, describes this meeting in some detail. According to Hirszfeld, Czerniakow actually read excerpts from his diary to the audience.

that the 15% of the total allocation is not enough for welfare needs. Thus the discrepancy has to be filled from the proceeds of requisitions [confiscated food]. Auerswald retorted that Jews always come up with unrealistic projects. I drew his attention to the fact that out of his windows he could see a whole street that had been built on the basis of "unrealistic" Jewish projects.

Earlier a conference was held with A[uerswald], Dr. Grassler, and Major Przymusinski. Asked whether I would be able to place in correctional centers 20 children arrested daily by the Polish police, I answered that to save them from prison, etc. I had no choice.

I was summoned to Auerswald for 4:45 P.M. to receive a text for a poster to be printed. On my arrival he handed me a written order announcing that 100 Jews and 10 Order Service men would be executed for having physically opposed orders of German policemen. Later in the afternoon I telephoned Auerswald that—not to mention the others—the 10 patrolmen were guilty of no crime. Some of them were seized in the street.

I sent First and Lejkin to A[uerswald]; they returned at 10:30 reporting that A[uerswald] has invited me for 8 o'clock tomorrow morning on the matter of the execution. Perhaps there is still some hope! In the meantime the courtyard has become black [with people]. Panic in the whole Quarter.

The cemetery has been ordered to stop work on a large grave. The gravediggers are to report with their spades at 1 P.M. tomorrow to the *Schutzpolizei* [German City Police].

*July 1, 1942*—In the morning, at 8 o'clock, with Lejkin to the *Kommissar*. I submitted to him a petition for the release of 10 functionaries of the Order Service (sentenced to death). Auerswald informed me that he would pass on my petition to the German police.

I argued that 3 of those involved were taken from the street as hostages in place of others who were summoned but who had disappeared. Moreover, there are names on the list [of the ten] who had nothing to do with smuggling. A[uerswald] ordered me to hold up the printing of his poster announcing the execution of the 100 prisoners and 10 functionaries, adding that he was going to alter its contents.

In the afternoon he came to the detention facility with Galuba. Later he informed me that I was mistaken, since the police had proven to him that all the arrested functionaries were guilty. First was told to call Auerswald at 7:30 tomorrow morning about the possible printing of the announcement. I suppose the execution will be carried out tonight or tomorrow morning.

I submitted my own report on the workers' altercation at the Eastern Railroad Station, presenting the incident in a different light. I also spoke to Brandt about the impending execution. He promised no help. I talked with his chief Böhm on the matter of Szerynski. He promised to ask for a pardon.

There was a roundup of Jews for work in the streets today. There are very few volunteers. Panic in the Quarter. Both yesterday and today rumors about deportation of 70,000 Jews. The rumors are groundless (so far).

They say that 3 smugglers died tonight. The wives would not leave the bodies.

*July 2, 1942*—In the morning at the Community. In 3 convoys the 110 persons were driven out of the detention facility between 4 and 6 in the morning. The *Kommissar* amended the text of the announcement.[44] Later in the afternoon 300 copies of his orders were posted. I requested the *Kommissar* to issue an order about extending the curfew hour until 10 o'clock at night. He telephoned Brandt and told me that the matter would be taken care of.

Nikolaus, the SD *Kommissar,* arrived at the Community on the matter of 3 children who are to be brought to Pawiak [prison] with small suitcases and enough food for 5 days. An exchange is to take place. Their parents are said to be already abroad.

I received a letter from the Commission on Religious Affairs to the effect that during the traditional weeks of mourning there should be no parties or musical and singing performances. I said to Ekerman, who was supporting this position, what I often repeat, that "one cannot wind one's watch with tears" (Dickens). To which he replied that it is precisely with tears that a Jewish watch can be wound. He did not edify me with these words.

In the evening the [Order] Service was stopping pedestrians and

---

44. According to Auerswald's announcement, the ten Order Service men were shot for bribery and other acts of malfeasance; the 100 civilians (90 men and 10 women taken from the detention facility) were killed in reprisal for an alleged incident involving resistance to German police orders and even attacks on German police personnel. Work details guarded by German police were still being employed outside the ghetto.

directing all of them not to go along Zelazna Street but through Ogrodowa Street and across the overpass, in order to avoid Burchard's [a sadistic guard] abuse on the corner of Zelazna and Chlodna Streets.

*July 3, 1942*—In the morning at the Community. Later at the Children's Home at Wolnosc Street. During the night a bag of smuggled goods was thrown over the wall. When the police arrived, the night janitor fled. The police took the name of the headmistress, Mrs. Polman. I issued instructions for enlarging the walls separating the Children's Home from other buildings and for nailing up the door leading through the courtyard to another street. I inspected our new playgrounds under construction at Nowolipki Street and at the corner of Franciszkanska and Nalewki Streets.

*July 4, 1942*—In the morning with Lejkin to Brandt and Mende. At my request Brandt released the 64-year-old Heller, the *Obmann* [Chairman of the Jewish Council] from Stoczek. Encouraging hints about the Szerynski case.

I was summoned by Nikolaus, the head of the Emigration Section. Nikolaus was concerned that Jozef Ehrlich interfered several days ago with an order to bring 3 children to the Pawiak [prison] (the children were to be sent abroad to their parents for exchange). Ehrlich had told the escort to bring the children to his apartment. Nikolaus informed me that Ehrlich has been rendering certain services, but not with regard to emigration.

Brandt told me that he had gotten in touch with Auerswald on the issue of an extended curfew hour. I sent First to A[uerswald] to get the text of the announcement. A[uerswald] said that he was preparing it for Monday.

*July 5, 1942*—In the morning at the Community. The Order Service band played at the playground. A program was offered by 600 boys and girls from elementary schools. From among the performers I invited to sit at the stand with me a little girl who was made up as Chaplin (great applause). The religionists are opposed to merrymaking with music and singing during the current 3 weeks (a period of mourning).

*July 6, 1942*—In the morning at the Community. We are to provide 500 workers for Lublin. A roundup for 1,000 people. In the afternoon a conference with Dr. Milejkowski. The findings of scientific research on hunger. Papers were given by Dr. Apfelbaum, Dr. Stein, Dr. Fliderbaum, and Dr. Drein (?).[45]

Auerswald ordered women to be registered for work.

Today is our 29th wedding anniversary.

*July 7, 1942*—In the morning at the Community. A delegation from the Order Service arrived (Niunia was present) and presented 32,900 zlotys, the proceeds of the charity concert to aid the prisoners. I discussed the question of a welfare council with Gepner and Sztolcman. G[epner] suggested a permanent body which could be of value also after the war. I expressed the viewpoint that a nucleus of 7 to 9 persons should be formed with 10 or more advisors around it.

I asked G[epner] to speed up the deliberations of the Children's Aid Committee (reformatories, etc.); the children will be sent over by the Polish police from the Aryan side.

The *Kommissar* is sick today. (The problem of the extended curfew hour still unsettled.) I borrowed 300,000 zlotys in town.

The Gypsies who are involuntary residents of the ghetto submit to me their "humble and loyal" petitions. Lately, some of the Gypsies, who claim they were born in Hamburg and have lived there for centuries, came to me on the matter of their return to Germany. They are the Weiss family. One of them fought in the Great War [World War I] and received numerous decorations for valor. They added that several of their close relatives were at that very moment serving in the German Army.

*July 8, 1942*—In the morning with Lejkin to Brandt and Mende. B[randt] claims that he had done his best with the *Kommandeur* on the subject of extending the curfew hour. The rest depends on Auerswald. For tactical reasons he does not feel that he should intercede on behalf of Szerynski. Mende asked for *Die Grundlagen des XIX Jahrhunderts,* [The Foundations of the 19th Century] by Chamberlain.[46]

I proceeded to the *Kommissar*. Speaking of the curfew, he told me that he had to refer to legal sources. (Although not asked, I sent

45. Dr. Emil Apfelbaum was a cardiologist; Dr. Jozef Stein, an anatomist and pathologist; Dr. Julian Fliderbaum, an internist. All of them were involved in starvation studies.
46. Houston Stewart Chamberlain, racist author of British origin, son-in-law of Richard Wagner.

him his legal sources in the afternoon.) I raised the subject of the homeless children. I added that if he signs the decree on the basis of which those employed would be paying a tax for their exemption from [camp] labor—I would be in possession of funds for rebuilding the ruined houses. In this way we will have enough accommodations for at least 5,000 children. Another solution to the problem: setting up several children's correction homes outside the ghetto. Auerswald replied that he could not publish a decree yet. When asked what his reasons were, he replied that they had to do with need for workers in the East. Discussions of this matter are continuing.

He incidentally raised the subject of women. He had indeed issued instructions to the *Arbeitsamt* to register all women who were working. I asked whether housewives fall into this category. Would the volunteers in social work be registered? I did not get a clear answer. As usual, I perceived a lack of sympathy for this class of people.

He added that the definition of export would be revised. Exportation for its own sake, that is to balance the imports, should stop. Exportation profitable to the authorities should remain. Mirrors, etc. are unnecessary.

Concerning finances, it turns out that he again appropriated 700,000 zlotys. He is to give us 300,000 zlotys of it. Today he ordered that several hundred thousand zlotys are to be transferred from the discretionary fund to the reserve fund. The purpose of the latter is unclear. For a dire emergency? A long time ago (several weeks) he ordered the checking of credentials of all the members of the Order Service. The list was submitted to him. He asked me today whether we have received it back. Unfortunately, we have not. He promised to talk (. . .) to Fribolin about our funds. I do not expect much from this conversation.

Mende has prohibited answering letters arriving in Warsaw in which questions are asked about the Jews.

About 11 at night some 700 people (many of them women and children) from Rawa, etc., were brought to the Community building. The residents of Grzybowska Street helped with tea, etc. A hundred loaves of bread were distributed to the deportees.

Many people hold a grudge against me for organizing play activity for the children, for arranging festive openings of playgrounds, for the music, etc. I am reminded of a film: a ship is sinking and the captain, to raise the spirits of the passengers, orders the orchestra to play a jazz piece. I had made up my mind to emulate the captain.

*July 9, 1942*—In the morning at the Community. I sent the *Kommissar* the legal references as grounds for his announcement about the curfew. It is now up to him alone to contrive a few lines and sign. A *Trägheitsmoment* [a moment of inertia].

I invited Gepner, Sztolcman, Jaszunski, and Altberg, and proposed a shift of exports to commodities most in demand [by the Germans]. I reported on my recent conversations and the thinking of the decision-making authorities. I informed my guests that I would spare no efforts to get in touch with the highest authorities responsible for the Jewish question.

At 8 in the morning I went to the little square at Ceglana Street to see about 800 deportees from Rawa Mazowiecka and surroundings, who were brought there during the night. Small children, babies, women. The sight would break my heart, had it not been hardened by 3 years of misery.

In the afternoon Polish urchins [keep] throwing stones over the little wall to Chlodna Street. Ever since we removed the bricks and stones from the middle of Chlodna Street, they have not got much ammunition left.

I have often asked myself the question whether Poland is Mickiewicz and Slowacki [47] or whether it is that urchin. The truth lies in the middle. I was informed in the evening that someone had hidden a fur coat, a shabby one at that, in a cellar. In view of the possible consequences I instructed the Order Service to turn the fur coat over to the Polish police.

Brandt turned up at the prison and wanted to be shown Mrs. Judt. Out of sheer curiosity, I think.

*July 10, 1942*—In the morning at the Community. I toured a ceramics studio and workshop, accompanied by Heyman, etc., who used to own a ceramics factory at Włocławek. I have suggested that bowls and cups be produced there. So far, to no avail. I visited the playgrounds at Nalewki and Nowolipki Streets. They will be ready by Sunday. At 2 P.M. I inaugurated an [in-service] training course for teachers in the Community auditorium. Besides me, Mrs. Wolf

47. Adam Mickiewicz and Juliusz Slowacki, Polish Romantic poets of the nineteenth century.

and Brandszteter [48] addressed the gathering. The room was over-flowing.

The *Arbeitsamt* is supposed to have received a letter stating that the SS is going to take over the Labor Office function of processing workers for the labor camps.

*July 11, 1942*—In the morning with Lejkin to Brandt and Mende. I asked B[randt] whether it would be possible for him to talk over the question of the Quarter with the *Kommandeur* or the SS in Brühl [Palace].

No progress in the Szerynski case. Mende repeated his order forbidding supplying information about individual Jews in the ghetto. I went to see Rodeck. He informed me that he would allocate to the Council part of the tax money he received from the *Finanzinspektor*. I drew his attention to the fact that the sums I receive are insignificant in relation to our needs. I pointed to the necessity of rebuilding the orphanage, etc., to move children out of the streets. Also I am supposed to set up the fire department.

I raised the issue of social insurance which does nothing for the Quarter but which at any time can call upon me to make huge payments. It transpired that they are planning to open a *Nebenstelle* [branch office] in the Quarter. In the course of the conversation I mentioned the rumors: resettlement, directing tens of thousands to the East. I received the answer that these matters are under discussion. An order may be issued any day.

On my way out I encountered Auerswald. He asked me to postpone our conversation until Monday. He has not yet settled the matter of the curfew hour.

The economic situation in the Quarter is as follows: In January 1942, 1,268 men and 165 women obtained jobs through the *Arbeitsamt;* in June, 9,250 men and 1,802 women. All together [for 1942] 24,357 men and 5,739 women.

At the end of April the number of those gainfully employed was 79,000 (not counting those persons whose employment we are not allowed to control). As of now, 95,000 people work (without the 2nd group); of these 4,500 outside the Quarter, 50,000 in industry, crafts, and as self-employed.

In December 1941 our exports amounted to 2 million zlotys; in June, 12 million zlotys.

48. Michal Brandszteter, Jewish educator.

*July 12, 1942*—In the morning at the Community. At 9:30 the opening of a playground at the corner of Franciszkanska and Nalewki Streets for schoolchildren. Crowds of people: in the streets, on the roofs, on the chimneys, on the balconies. Orchestra, choirs, ballet. I addressed the children. In the street the children gave me an ovation. At noon the opening of workshops at the prison. I spoke. The first anniversary of the Jewish detention facility.

*July 13, 1942*—In the morning at the Community. After a heat wave, there has been a significant drop of temperature in the last few days. Rains. Several days ago the guards [at the gates] were replaced by the military police but not for long. An incident with Wundheiler.

Kon arrived yesterday and reported that there was chaos in the Provisioning Authority. I summoned Gepner and we came to the conclusion that Kon might be right.

Auerswald withdrew the armband exemption from Rechthand and Graf; also from Haendel to whom he had granted this right himself and which he had extended not so long ago.

*July 14, 1942*—In the morning at the Community. Later with the *Kommissar*. I want to introduce the raising of rabbits in the ghetto. A[uerswald] retorted that we would not be given oats.

He told me that the question of burying Protestants in the Jewish cemetery should be postponed until Grassler's return. He agreed that the children in the detention facility could be placed in orphanages until the children's reformatory is ready to receive them.

I made a request for the release for the condemned, present and future, in the same way as it had already been done once. He refused. I suggested then a labor camp right in prison. He agreed, provided that Toebbens, Schultze or the brushmakers [49] set up the workshops. I summoned Gepner, Rechthand, Wielikowski, Lejkin, Lichtenbaum, and Lindenfeld for a meeting. I asked Lindenfeld to make up a list of prisoners. I ordered Lichtenbaum to prepare an estimate for construction of barracks on the prison grounds, or for

49. Fritz Emil Schultz was a German entrepreneur. The brushmakers were employed by German army.

the conversion of a Community-owned building at Ceglana Street (baths). Rechthand is to talk to the brushmakers, etc.

*July 15, 1942*—In the morning with Lejkin to Brandt and Mende. Later with Mueller [50] about Schmied who had come from Berlin to arrange a barter involving a variety of goods from us for something that is still unspecified. The *Kommissar* called and ordered that we take away the German Jews from the quarantine at 109/11 Leszno Street since he wanted to use the premises as an assembly area for the workers on their way to camps (next transport 620 people). I issued instructions for the Housing Department to find accommodations for the German Jews. I visited a commercial establishment at 31 Nalewki Street. In a sort of a coffeehouse I found more than 50 young people playing dominoes and cards. I will use the premises for the children from the detention facility (a reformatory). On my way I stopped to visit the playground at the corner of Franciszkanska Street (full of children). Nikolaus arrived at the Community and issued orders for (over 80) foreign Jews to be brought to Pawiak [prison] on Friday morning from where they are to be sent abroad. Schmied came. The problem of delivery of goods was discussed. He declared that prisoners would be released in exchange.

It does not seem that the Jews will be able to take advantage of Fischer's decree permitting certain food purchases even though Fischer did not exclude Jews from his enactment. Neither shall we obtain the buildings outside the ghetto for industrial workshops. I made arrangements for a conference on this matter tomorrow at 9 A.M. Auerswald's announcement extending the curfew hour to 10 P.M. was posted today throughout the Quarter.

*July 16, 1942*—In the morning at the Community. Later with the *Kommissar*. He instructed me to meet with Schmied. When I asked who S[chmied] was, Auerswald answered that he could not tell me. I decided to seek advice for tomorrow's session with Schmied from Gepner, Sztolcman, Rechthand, etc.

I went to see Galuba and arranged a meeting with him for 9 tomorrow morning. He will inspect the premises (reformatory) for the children from the detention facility and will probably release the children.

50. SS-2d Lieut. Müller, Security Police.

I gave instructions for the transfer of German refugees from 109/ 11 Leszno Street to make room for the camp assembly area.

Rumors about the deportation of Jews from the Quarter, with 120,000 to be left behind. We have drafted a short memorandum about our economic situation, about Jewish production in the Quarter, and delivered copies of it to the several authorities on whom our fate depends.

In the evening our welfare building at Ogrodowa Street was forcibly occupied by someone from Toebens' Co. for German-Jewish employees evicted from 109 Leszno Street. I asked Wielikowski to call the *Kommissar*.

Evening (the second day of the extended curfew hour), rickshaws were being stopped and not allowed to cross under the overpass at the corner of Chlodna and Zelazna Streets.

*July 17, 1942*—At 7 o'clock in the morning, a list of condemned prisoners, etc., was brought to my apartment for discussions with Schmied.

In the morning at the Community. Miss Glass [51] from the *Kommissar's* office telephoned saying that today we must empty the Synagogue of the refugees. The building is to be at the disposal of the SS. I dispatched First to Brühl Palace in this matter. The day has started badly. Fortunately it turned out that the Synagogue is needed for foreign Jews. I must empty it today to make room for the emigrants to America, etc.

Two Germans came at 11 A.M. and offered a barter transaction: if we supply shoes, etc., we will be permitted to purchase rye flour and some prisoners will be released. In a conference with Gepner, Sztolcman, Rechtman, and Altberg, the main points were agreed upon. Maybe on Monday the matter will be definitely settled. I will make an appointment with the *Kommissar* tomorrow. The evacuation of 1,700 of the German Jews from 109 Leszno Street took place in an orderly manner. Sixty or more apartments were taken for that purpose.

*July 18, 1942*—In the morning with Lejkin to Brandt and Mende. A day full of foreboding. Rumors that the deportations will start on Monday evening (All?!) I asked the *Kommissar* whether he knew anything about it. He replied that he did not and that he did not

---

51. Traute Glass, from Auerswald's office.

believe the rumors. In the meantime panic in the Quarter; some speak of deportations, others of a pogrom. Today and tomorrow we are to empty the Synagogue for the foreign Jews to move in.

When I was sitting in Mende's office a Polish girl, 16 or 18 years old, came in and reported that a converted Jewish woman has been living in her house.


*July 19, 1942*—In the morning at the Community. Incredible panic in the city. Kohn, Heller, and Ehrlich are spreading terrifying rumors, creating the impression that it is all false propaganda. I wish it were so. On the other hand, there is talk of about 40 railroad cars ready and waiting. It transpired that 20 of them have been prepared on SS orders for 720 workers leaving tomorrow for a camp.

Kohn claims that the deportation is to commence tomorrow at 8 P.M. with 3,000 Jews from the Little Ghetto (Sliska Street?). He himself and his family slipped away to Otwock. Others did the same.

A Czerniakow, allegedly a relative of mine, is a "fixer" [a small scale influence peddler] in the Labor Department where he used to work for a long while. I ordered that he be put in prison.

Because of the panic I drove through the streets of the entire Quarter. I visited 3 playgrounds. I do not know whether I managed to calm the population, but I did my best. I try to hearten the delegations which come to see me. What it costs me they do not see. Today I took 2 headache powders, another pain reliever, and a sedative, but my head is still splitting. I am trying not to let the smile leave my face.


*July 20, 1942*—In the morning at 7:30 at the Gestapo. I asked Mende how much truth there was in the rumors. He replied that he had heard nothing. I turned to Brandt; he also knew nothing. When asked whether it *could* happen, he replied that he knew of no such scheme. Uncertain, I left his office. I proceeded to his chief, *Kommissar* Böhm. He told me that this was not his department but Hoeheman [Höhmann] might say something about the rumors. I mentioned that according to rumor, the deportation is to start tonight at 7:30. He replied that he would be bound to know something if it were about to happen. Not seeing any other way out,

I went to the deputy chief of Section III, Scherer.[52] He expressed his surprise hearing the rumor and informed me that he too knew nothing about it. Finally, I asked whether I could tell the population that their fears were groundless. He replied that I could and that all the talk was *Quatsch* and *Unsinn* [utter nonsense].

I ordered Lejkin to make the public announcement through the precinct police stations. I drove to Auerswald. He informed me that he reported everything to the SS *Polizeiführer*. Meanwhile, First went to see Jesuiter and Schlederer,[53] who expressed their indignation that the rumors were being spread and promised an investigation.

I returned to the Community and found Dr. Schmied. The barter deal, shoes, etc., for rye is being concluded (1,250,000 zlotys).

Today I discussed with the *Kommissar* the problem of children in the detention center. He ordered me to write him a letter for their release, on the condition that they be placed in reformatories and that a guarantee would be given that they would not escape. I suggested that the prisoners' aid committee be charged with the care of the children. The *Kommissar* demanded a person be designated who would be responsible for guarding them. It is to be someone from the Order Service.

I talked this over with Kaczka, the manager of a transit center on Dzika Street. Some of the children would be placed there. I am also planning to complete alterations in a building at Ceglana Street (the baths) to provide additional accommodations. It appears that about 2,000 children will qualify for reformatories.

*July 21, 1942*—In the morning at the Community. Just before noon officers of the S.P.[54] ordered me to detain in my office those Councilors who were present in the Community building. Besides, they asked for a list of the remaining councilors. Soon the members of the Council in my office were arrested in groups. At the same time the senior officials of the Provisioning Authority, with Gepner heading the list, were also seized. I wanted to leave with those

52. Czerniakow spoke to several relatively low-ranking members of the Warsaw Gestapo: SS-Capt. Höhmann, deputy chief, Office IV (Gestapo); SS-1st Lieut. Boehm, IV–A; SS-1st Lieut. Scheerer, IV–B (Jews); SS-2d Lieut. Brandt, IV–B (Jews); SS-Sgt. Mende, IV–B (Jews).
53. SS-Major Jesuiter and SS-1st Lieut. Josef Schlederer in the office of the SS and Police Leader. Schlederer specialized in Jewish matters.
54. S.P.: probably *Sicherheitspolizei* (Security Police).

arrested but was instructed to stay in the office. In the meantime others reached my apartment looking for my wife. They were told that she was at the Children's Home at Wolnosc Street. They left only to return to the apartment with an order that my wife should be home by 3 P.M. Some of the Council members were freed today.

I contacted Brandt who told me that everyone would be released tomorrow or the day after tomorrow. I interceded with Auerswald on behalf of Gepner and his colleagues of the Provisioning Authority. He promised to see to it tomorrow morning and asked who exactly was involved. I had the impression that he hesitated about Gepner. I stressed that Gepner was the heart and soul of the Provisioning Authority.

I decided to stay at the Community until 6 P.M., having brought my wife there earlier. The evening was quiet. During the night, deaths.

*July 22, 1940* [sic]—In the morning at 7:30 at the Community. The borders of the Small Ghetto surrounded by a special unit in addition to the regular one.

*Sturmbannführer* Höfle [55] and associates came at 10 o'clock. We disconnected the telephone. Children were moved from the playground opposite the Community building.

We were told that all the Jews irrespective of sex and age, with certain exceptions, will be deported to the East. By 4 P.M. today a contingent of 6,000 people must be provided. And this (at the minimum) will be the daily quota.

We were ordered to vacate a building at 103 Zelazna Street for the German personnel who will be carrying out the deportation. The furniture was kept where it was. As the Council staff with their wives and children are exempted from deportation, I asked that the JSS personnel, crafts-men, and garbage collectors, etc. also be excluded. This was granted.

I requested the release of Gepner, Rozen, Sztolcman, Drybinski, Winter, Kobryner, which was approved. By 3:45 P.M. everyone but Rozen is already back in the ghetto.

In the afternoon Lejkin sent a message that a piece of glass had

55. SS-Major Herman Höfle headed a 20-man *Aussiedlungsstab*. [Resettlemant Staff]. Although subordinated to SS and Police Leader Globocnik of the Lublin district, Höfle's detachment handled roundups and loadings in several *Generalgouvernement* districts.

allegedly been thrown at a police car. They warned us that if this were to happen again our hostages would be shot.

The most tragic dilemma is the problem of children in orphanages, etc. I raised this issue—perhaps something can be done.

At 5:30 one of the officials Forwort (?) drove in and demanded that Jozef Ehrlich should be named Lejkin's deputy. Ehrlich is already wearing 3 stars.

*Sturmbannfuehrer* Höfle (*Beauftragter* [plenipotentiary] in charge of deportation) asked me into his office and informed me that for the time being my wife was free, but if the deportation were impeded in any way, she would be the first one to be shot as a hostage.

*July 23, 1942*—In the morning at the Community. Worthoff [56] from the deportation staff came and we discussed several problems. He exempted the vocational school students from deportation. The husbands of working women as well. He told me to take up the matter of orphans with Höfle. The same with reference to craftsmen. When I asked for the number of days per week in which the operation would be carried on, the answer was 7 days a week.

Throughout the town a great rush to start new workshops. A sewing machine can save a life.

It is 3 o'clock. So far 4,000 are ready to go. The orders are that there must be 9,000 by 4 o'clock. Some officials came to the post office and issued instructions that all incoming letters and parcels be diverted to the Pawiak [prison].

56. SS-1st Lieut. (later Capt.) Hermann Worthoff, on Höfle's staff.

# Documentary Appendix

EXEMPTIONS FROM FORCED LABOR

YAD VASHEM Microfilm Roll JM 1113
YIVO Institute Microfilm Roll MKY 77

COPY

THE CHAIRMAN OF THE JEWISH COUNCIL
WITH THE JEWISH COMMUNITY
IN WARSAW

MR 4761

To the

Plenipotentiary of the District Chief
for the City of Warsaw
in Warsaw

May 21, 1940

In connection with the compulsory labor imposed on the Jewish population, I am supplying various employers with ca. 9,000 persons daily [handwritten note in the margin: "Based on statistics: ca. 8,000"]. As a consequence of the labor requirements of the City Sanitation Department this figure is yet to be increased.

Considering that I dispose of a limited supply of people I am trying to solve the tasks imposed on me in such a way as to induct all men between 17 and 55 for work. Thereby those that are called may theoretically give up every third one of their number for the cause of forced labor.

A whole series of employers, however, demand the allocation always of the same workers in order to carry out an accurate check of the work force. I am consequently compelled to employ a major number of workers for wages.

Since I possess no means whatever for covering the costs arising in connection with this matter, I am forced to release a certain number of persons against payment of a fee, the amount of which is dependent on the financial circumstances of the petitioner concerned. Basically, these fees are set at 60 to 100 zlotys monthly, whereby individual reductions are granted to persons who are socially active or who work over a period of time to support a family and who are without means.

Those who are paying this fee or who are excused for illness receive identity cards, a sample of which is enclosed. The cards certify that the bearer has fulfilled his duty with regard to forced labor for the month concerned. The population can be encouraged to obtain these identity cards only if they are honored by the authorities. The reduction of the current financial problems of the Labor Battalion is thus in large measure dependent upon a favorable attitude on the part of the authorities toward these identity cards.

Taking account of the above, I ask you kindly to consider my request and to issue the appropriate indispensable directives.

The Chairman of the Jewish Council
with the Jewish Community in Warsaw

signed Eng. Adam Czerniakow

1 enclosure
[not in the microfilm]

## 2. A NEED FOR NEW REVENUES

YAD VASHEM Microfilm Roll JM 1113
YIVO Institute Microfilm Roll MKY 77

THE CHAIRMAN OF THE
JEWISH COUNCIL
and President of the Council of Elders
of the Jewish Community
    in Warsaw
Grzybowska 26/28

[Handwritten
notat,on indicating
letter was read by
*SA-Oberführer*
Leist]

To the

Office of the Chief of the Warsaw District
—Resettlement Division—*Transferstelle*
    in Warsaw
Brühl Palace

January 8, 1941

Constrained by circumstances, I have on various occasions portrayed the very bad financial state of the Jewish Council to the authorities and asked them to look into these conditions. I have constantly asked also for the creation of the kind of situation that would enable the Jewish Council to balance its expenses with its income and generally to conduct its work on the basis of a realistically constructed budgetary plan which, despite mounting difficulties, is within reach. I would not be fulfilling my duty if I did not indicate that the financial situation that has currently arisen exceeds by far any of the difficulties which the Jewish Council has had to confront to date.

As illustration, I permit myself to cite the following figures:

The cash balance as of January 6, 1941, was 132 zl.
The cash balance as of January 7, 1941, was 517 zl.

This is happening at a time when the daily expenditures of the Jewish Council amount to ca. 40–50,000 zlotys, while receipts average ca. 10–20,000 zlotys.

Anticipating this state of affairs, mindful of the difficult tasks and directives imparted to the Jewish Council, and considering the Council's responsibilities vis-à-vis 400,000 people in its care, I have—as pointed out above—already referred to the existing state of affairs repeatedly, stepping forth with radical projects for the relief of the poor financial state of the community, and also a minimal program which would make possible at least partially a rational and planned implementation of the budget.

Without touching at this time on a maximum program for restructuring community finances, which as I understand is being weighed by the authorities also and for which I am presently preparing proposals, I will now confine myself to a fragmentary conception of this matter. I am therefore going to summarize briefly the projects with which I have approached the authorities for the resolution of the Community's finances.

Thus, towards the end of May 1940, I have first of all requested the approval of a statute on taxes for the benefit of the Jewish Council in Warsaw, above all the permanent tax which would be collected in the form of a surcharge, say at the rate of one zloty monthly, in the course of the food ration card distribution. Second, I have handed in a project on June 24, 1940, for doubling existing commercial license fees, and third I have proposed, also on June 24, a draft of a tax on the immobile property of the Jews to amount to 4% of the taxable base.

Considering the deplorable financial condition of the Jewish social service institutions, I have, fourth, advanced the idea that the city administration make available to the Jewish Council appropriate subventions from sums raised for the benefit of social welfare, that is to say from the additional charges for street car tickets, electricity, and gas, as well as residence fees. [Handwritten comment in the margin: "no!" initialed L (Leist)]

Fifth, I have finally approached the authorities with the request—for the alleviation of the Jewish Council's transitional difficulties—to permit me to take out a loan of a least 300,000 zlotys at the Warsaw Bank.

Of all these projects, the first measure was approved. In this manner, the treasury of the Jewish Council is being supported to the extent of more than 300,000 zlotys monthly from the distribution of the food ration cards. This relatively considerable amount has enabled me to maintain the budget at an appropriate level. The chronic deficit of the Jewish Council—resulting from the fact that receipts never covered expenditures, in that every single month expenses foreseen in preliminary budget plans were expanded considerably by totally unforeseen payments in pursuance of unexpected directives issued almost daily—was thereby measurably improved.

Last month, the money from this source flowed in as usual, but could not serve to cover the normal needs of the Jewish Council, inasmuch as very large sums had to be spent for the walls and fences as well as for the furnishings of the *Transferstelle*. The amount expended for these purposes was almost 300,000 zlotys. This expenditure has caused a deficiency in the financial situation of the Jewish Council and enlarged its debt vis-à-vis suppliers, employees, laborers, etc. Total indebtedness has reached ca. 2,000,000 zlotys.

The second project, respecting a surcharge of 100% on commercial tax cards, was sanctioned through your ordinance of December 5, 1940. Its implementation, however, did not follow and this—so far as I know—because the city administration has not received an appropriate directive from the Plenipotentiary of the District Chief for the City of Warsaw. [Words following the second dash underlined by Leist with notation, question mark, and initial in the margin. Leist was the Plenipotentiary.] Since the commerce tax is being paid during the current month and no additional payment for the Jewish Council is being demanded from Jews who are renewing their licenses, it is to be feared that after the renewal of the commercial tax cards the collection of the fee for the benefit of the Jewish Council will be very difficult.

The project with regard to burdening Jewish real estate has not been approved until now. To be sure, the administration of Jewish real estate in the Jewish Residence District [ghetto] has in the meantime been maintained. The stipulations, however, which incidentally have nothing to do with the tax project, but which bear on the administration of the property, are such that rather than count on any income whatever, one may contend with a superfluous burden involving various expenses.

Although the fourth project respecting subventions for the benefit of social welfare has been received with understanding by the key welfare officials, it has not been formally instituted with regard to Jews.

In this manner, Jewish social welfare is battling with unheard-of difficulties. I could not vouch for my conscience and would not carry out the duties transferred to me by the authorities if at this point I did not call attention to the frightening situation of the welfare institutions. The reports and inspections of orphanages, shelters, etc., the thousands of poor people at the gates of the community and its facilities as well as at the welfare organizations, testify daily to the absolute necessity for finding means to alleviate this situation. Proceeding from a realistic basis, I have always sought and will go on seeking sources of income from the Jewish community. All my requests have burdened only this population. In the name of justice I was—and am—striving to place the burden rather on the well-to-do than the poor. This is the direction also of the second and third of the above-mentioned projects. To mitigate the first project in regard to food ration cards, I have ordered that 70,000 persons be freed from the obligation of paying a surcharge for the cards.

Summarizing the above, I ask with a view to the prevention of the threatening financial collapse of the Jewish Council, as well as the possibility of covering the most necessary expenses, for kind consideration and possible directives in the following:

1. Establishment of the principle that the Jewish Council has to work in accordance with a fixed budget, i.e. that expenses be balanced by income.
2. The matter of surcharges on the commercial tax cards in the amount of 100% for the benefit of the Jewish Council: I ask you to approach the Plenipotentiary of the District Chief for the City of Warsaw in this matter for appropriate instructions to the city administration. As I allowed myself to point out above, this matter is especially urgent.
3. Confirmation of the ordinance for a surcharge on the real estate tax, in the amount of 4% of gross income, for the benefit of the Jewish Council.
4. Award to the Jewish Council of an appropriate percentage of the amounts raised by the city administration for the benefit of social welfare from the residence fee as well as surcharges on the prices of street car tickets, the rates for electricity, and gas. [Question mark in margin]
5. A bank loan for 300,000 zlotys. I ask you kindly to turn to the

Bank Surpervisory Agency so that it may agree to this loan from the Warsaw banks.

In connection with the above, I have the honor to point out that in searching for other income sources, I have ordered that for the obligatory shields on the doors of Jewish apartments a fee of 0.50, respectively 1.00 zloty, be raised monthly. Similarly, I have ordered that for the needs of the Health Department, i.e. for fighting the epidemic, 0.50 zloty per room be raised monthly. Beyond that, upon instigation by the authorities, the introduction of Jewish identity cards is envisaged. These documents could be presented to well-to-do persons for a fee. In this manner an amount could be obtained which would be sufficient for a portion of the current needs of the Jewish Council as well as for coverage of a portion of the debts. Thus far, however, I have not received a directive of this kind.

Finally, after the Jewish Council has taken over the post office in the Jewish district, income could be derived from the sale (to stamp collectors, among others) of special postal marks. For the sake of correctness I permit myself to point out that the postal administration, as in the past, does not incline positively to this idea.

In conclusion I permit myself to add that a resolution of the relationship between the Jewish Council and the Trusteeship Administration of Jewish Real Property would be highly desirable. On the basis of your letter of November 26, 1940, I was entitled to assume that the major efforts of the Jewish Council in this area would be honored correspondingly. Past practice as well as the tariffs proposed by the Trusteeship Administration collide with your directive of November 26, 1940 ["your directive" and date underlined by hand] and provide the Jewish Council with no appropriate income whatever.

The Chairman of the Jewish Council
with the Jewish Community in Warsaw

[signed]
Eng. Adam Czerniakow

ACz/Po/MR

## 3. SOAP MUST BE DELIVERED

YAD VASHEM Microfilm Roll JM 1113
YIVO Institute Microfilm Roll MKY 77

Record
of the discussion of February 3, 1941, in the office of division Chief
Schön *re.* various matters pertaining to the Jewish district.

Present:  *SA-Oberführer* Leist    Division Chief Schön
          Director Becher          Specialist Mohns
          Director Makowski        2 Experts
          Hanika, Civ. Eng.

1. *Collection of municipal taxes and fees through the Jewish Council:*

   Considering the obstacles in the traffic between the Jewish Council and the rest of the city, there are difficulties in the collection of municipal taxes; the inflow leaves something to be desired. *Oberführer* Leist intends to charge the Jewish council with the collection, so that the tax administration and public works will not have anything to do with individual tax- and rate-payers. The Jewish council should be compensated for this task.

   Beyond that, it would be most expedient to consider the Jewish district as an administratively independent municipality, with all of the appropriate duties and liabilities, but also rights and revenues. To establish the necessary basis for that development, B[echer] should work out a charter for the Jewish district on behalf of the city of Warsaw.

   Division chief Schön agrees with this concept.

2. Passes for entering the Jewish district should be prepared, as of March 1, 1941, exclusively by the *Transferstelle.*

3. Jewish labor columns may move about in the Aryan part of the city only when led by a guard detail. Needless to say, guard details may be furnished not only by the Armed Forces or the SS, but also by the police.

4. It was agreed that only the police confiscate goods. On the other hand, anyone who suspects a punishable act may "se-

cure" the merchandise, so long as he immediately notifies the police which proceeds with the confiscation. However, the disposal of confiscated items is the concern of the trusteeship branch office.

5. The gates to the Jewish district have to be equipped in such a way that control officials may actually exercise control. To be avoided is the situation of a guard no longer being able to see in a crowd whether someone is going in or out, or who is going where. One will have to aim at setting up block houses for guards, as well as turnstiles through which only one person at a time can pass. The construction office should try to obtain the required timber. Division chief Schön will also attend to the timber allocation.

6. Pending the charter provisions envisaged in Par. 1, the Polish Police should continue to maintain the lists of persons in unrecognized religious communities.

7. The supply of foodstuffs to the Jews is the subject of precise agreement with the Food and Agriculture Division. The Resettlement Division is not interested in the complaints of the Jewish council in this regard. The delivery of soap, however, must be carried out, lest the Jewish council can rightfully maintain that German offices are increasing its difficulties in carrying out hygienic directives.

[initialed by Makowski]

## 4. GHETTO HOUSES WITHOUT MUNICIPAL SEWERS

YAD VASHEM Microfilm Roll JM 1113
YIVO Institute Microfilm Roll MKY 77

THE CHAIRMAN OF THE JEWISH COUNCIL
  PRESIDENT OF THE COUNCIL OF
    ELDERS OF THE
JEWISH COMMUNITY IN WARSAW

N/321/41

February 12, 1941
Grzybowska Street 26/28

To the

Office of the Chief of the Warsaw District
*Transferstelle*
in Warsaw

Re: Emptying of Excremental Pits from real
     property without canalization

As a consequence of the creation of the Jewish district a question has arisen about the emptying of excremental pits in those houses which have not yet been connected to the municipal sewer system. Before the Jewish district was closed off, the removal had been taken care of by rural people from the vicinity of Warsaw who had been buying their fertilizers from the owners of the houses. The interested parties have now turned to the municipal purification plant, but were told that, because of insufficient transport, the plant could not take over the work.

Inasmuch as the failure to remove the waste will entail grim consequences for the spring and summer, it has become urgently necessary, either to permit entry into the Jewish district of the country people who have declared themselves ready to take away the waste, or to charge the municipal purification plant with the task. I ask you kindly for an appropriate directive.

The chairman of the Jewish Council
[signed]

Eng. A. Czerniakow

[Handwritten in the margin:] Feces Removal!

## 5. AUERSWALD'S SUMMATION

YAD VASHEM Microfilm Roll JM 1112
YIVO Institute Microfilm Roll MKY 77

[Excerpt]

September 26, 1941

File No. K-0100-

## Biennial Report

The Office of the Commissioner for the Jewish District in Warsaw was established by the Ordinance of the Governor-General of April 19, 1941 (*Official Gazette of the General Government*, p. 211). A report on the activities of this office may therefore begin only from this date. The following, however, should briefly describe the development of the Jewish District in Warsaw.

In view of the large number of Jews, the German administration of Warsaw necessarily thought from the very beginning of concentrating them in a Jewish district. A major consideration was the wish, in the first instance, of separating the Jews from the Aryan world on general political and ideological grounds. In practical terms, there were weighty sanitary, economic, and other imperatives.

The first concentration of the Jews—albeit without a resettlement of the Poles—was brought about in a "quarantine" which was located in large part on the site of the present Jewish District (see appendix 1 [not included in microfilm]). After lengthy deliberations as to whether a closed Jewish district should be created and which city district might be used for that purpose (among others, Praga as well as two ghettos east and west at the edge of the city were examined as possibilities), the final decision was made in August 1940 to create a Jewish district on the site of the existing quarantine.

At last, October 7, 1940, the Order of the District Chief No. 50/40 was issued for the formation of a Jewish district in the City of Warsaw. The resettlement, encompassing 700 ethnic Germans, 113,000 Poles, and 138,000 Jews, was carried out at once; 11,567 non-Jewish apartments in the Jewish district and some 13,800 Jewish apartments in the rest of the city were surrendered. The whole move was completed in not quite six weeks, and police pressure had to be applied only to a residue of especially stubborn persons.

At this point the Jewish district is situated on 403 ha. [1.55 square miles]. The population is ca. 450–500,000 Jews. Density in the Jewish District is comparatively high: 110,800 persons per square kilometer [0.386 square miles] compared to 38,000 per square kilometer of inhabited space in the City of Warsaw.

The Jewish District was closed off by means of walling in streets and gaps with the use of existing fire and separation walls. The present borders, as illustrated on the map—appendix 2 [not in microfilm]—resulted from the fact that on the one hand the Jewish District had to be blocked off most rapidly and that on the other hand all requests [by Poles and Germans] to spare houses or groups of houses [from the ghetto] were honored so far as possible. A single look suffices to reveal the difficulties of guarding these borders which run mainly through rear courtyards. . . .

Generally, the Jewish District in Warsaw has never given rise to concern. The outbreak of war with Russia and the introduction of blackouts have changed nothing in that respect.

The three most important problems which the Jewish District has posed are food, health, and the economy.

Food and health are closely interlinked. The quantum jump in the death rate during May of this year showed that the shortage of food had already grown into hunger. The food supply was consequently the most urgent task. In the first instance the attempt was made to raise the output of the community kitchens, both as to nutrition and quantity. This increase has already come about in considerable measure, as may be seen from the following statistics: The daily portions handed out by Jewish Social Self-Help, at first fewer than 30,000, were raised to ca. 50,000 by the end of May of this year and to ca. 115,000 in June, and being held at ca. 120,000 in July and August. These figures were reached with the help of special allocations amounting to ca. 170 tons of oats, 125 tons of rye flour, 2,000 dozen sugar [tablets], 100,000 kilograms [220,000 pounds] of bread, 10,000 kilograms of meat, and some other items.

All the same, the quantity of legal deliveries is insufficient by far to stem the tide of hunger in the Jewish District. Although the foodstuffs smuggled into the Jewish District are not insignificant, they benefit because of their high prices only the well to-do Jews. If there is to be a larger utilization of Jewish labor, substantial increases of food deliveries will be necessary.

From the outbreak of the war, the Jews have been sinking into misery to such an extent that the higher food imports could not prevent a rising death rate. The following figures provide an impressive picture of the deaths:

| | |
|---|---|
| January 1941 | 898 |
| February 1941 | 1023 |
| March 1941 | 1608 |

| | |
|---|---|
| April 1941 | 2061 |
| May 1941 | 3821 |
| June 1941 | 4290 |
| July 1941 | 5550 |
| August 1941 | 5560 |

... A second reason for the increasing death rate is the spread of typhus.

Under the leadership of the *Transferstelle* Warsaw, the economy has soared.... The increase of employment may be seen in the following numbers:

Unemployed Jewish men in the age group 14–60:

| | |
|---|---|
| June | 76,102 (first count) |
| July | 70,894 |
| August | 69,862 |

The figure of employed at the end of August was

36,198

including labor in

| | |
|---|---|
| Outside camps | 2,359 |
| Agriculture | 768 |
| Details with [German] offices and Aryan firms | 5,372 |
| Industrial shops of Employment Program | 3,029 |

Quite distinct is the increase in the workshops of the employment procurement program:

| | |
|---|---|
| Early May | 220 |
| Early June | 1,377 |

| Early July | 2,134 |
| Early August | 2,424 |
| Early September | 3,055 |

Sgd. Auerswald
Certified, Dr. Grassler

## 6. QUESTION AND ANSWERS

YAD VASHEM Microfilm Roll JM 1112
YIVO Institute Microfilm Roll MKY 76

Plenipotentiary of the *Generalgouverneur*
November 7, 1941

[Polish address crossed out and Berlin,
Standarten St. 41 listed instead]

No. I/657841        vM/Er

*THE DEPUTY*

To Chief of Staff Dr. Hummel
*Warsaw*
Brühl Palace

[Dear Dr. Hummel:]

I am terribly sorry that you did not look me up on the occasion of your last visit here. Now I have a request. Would you be good enough to send me a short summary report about Jewish self-administration in the Jewish District of Warsaw? I am specially interested in the "economy" of the Jews, which must, after all, still be around in some form. How do they make their living? Specifically, what are the tasks of the *Transferstelle?* How does it function and what kind of achievements does it have? How have the Jews managed with it (examples)? What kind of experiences have been gained with this district as a precedent for the future?

Should you, dear Party Comrade Hummel, find no time for these ca. 4 typewritten pages—which would really be a shame—then please pass on my request to the *Kommissar* for the Jewish District or the Director of the *Transferstelle*. If the material can be used, I will take care of an honorarium for any contribution.

In any case, do you have photos of the Jewish District (prototypes, living conditions, misery, sealing of walls, street crossings, etc)? I would be equally grateful for a loan of such materials.

Inasmuch as this matter is very, very [the second "very" handwritten in text] urgent, I ask you to let me know if you could deliver the compilation by the 20th of this month. Since you are on the scene, you should not have all that much trouble with this matter.

Heil Hitler<br>
Your<br>
[signed]<br>
(Dr. von Medeazza)

November 24, 1941

To the
Deputy of the Plenipotentiary
of the *Generalgouverneur*
Dr. von Medeazza
Berlin W [?] 35
Standarten St. 14

File No. K - 0100
Register 1090/41

Re:  Your letter—1/6578/41 vM/Er—to the Chief
of Staff on Nov. 7.

Dr. Hummel has passed on to me your letter. . . . The following are short answers to your questions.

*What about the "economy" of the Jews?* Most Jewish industrial firms [in the city of Warsaw] have been placed under trusteeship. . . . Inside the Jewish district, the only enterprises still in Jewish hands are relatively unimportant firms serving the local needs of the district.

Jewish economic resources of any remaining importance are

primarily in the artisan field. Before the war, some 50% of all artisan enterprises in Warsaw were in Jewish hands. In some occupations, the Jewish share was even higher. Naturally the productive capacity of these artisans exceeds the needs of the Jewish district, and for this reason the attempt was made in the first instance to mobilize this Jewish labor for exports from the district.

Shortly after the erection of the district, Jewish communal work-shops were instituted. Since in the long run the *Transferstelle* could not assume the economic risks for these shops, German firms have been introduced to direct the shops and obtain orders for them. . . .

*How do the Jews live?* The Jewish population, like other parts of the population, is allotted specific rations for food and other necessities. Upon allocation by the appropriate supply offices, these goods are purchased by the Jewish Provisioning Authority and distributed in the district. The "Provisioning Authority for the Jewish District" functions under a charter granted by me. It employs only Jews and uses customary procedures for distributions. Permission is granted for the operation of certain bakeries and retail outlets, food ration cards are handed out, etc., etc.

Aside from these official satisfactions of demand, the Jews naturally attempt even today to cover their additional needs through smuggling. As the Jewish district is increasingly sealed, this source of supply is losing importance and one may count on a complete elimination of this route in the foreseeable future.

*What are the specific tasks of the Transferstelle?* According to its charter, it regulates and furthers trade between the Jewish district and the outer world. . . .

The *Transferstelle* Warsaw grants entry and exit passes. Further, it grants permits for commodity and monetary transactions. . . . At the same time it functions as a middle man in all questions pertaining to the supply of needs in order to reduce the difficulties which in the nature of things the Jews encounter with German offices, Aryan enterprises, etc.

The *Transferstelle* Warsaw is a corporation of public law. The charter is granted by the *Gouverneur* of Warsaw. It has an apparatus of ca. 70 employees, mainly Germans.

*How have the Jews managed with the situation?* The general mood is not bad. The Jews are waiting for the end of the war and in the meantime conduct themselves quietly. There has been no sign of any resistance spirit to date.

The principle that in my view has turned out most advantageously was to allow the Jews maximum freedom to regulate their own affairs inside the district. The entire communal administration lies in their hands. The Chairman of the Jewish Council—obviously recognizing the true situation—has worked loyally. When deficiencies occur, the Jews direct their resentment against the Jewish administration and not against the German supervisors. Added to that is the widest freedom accorded to the Jews until now in so-called cultural activities. They have theaters, variety shows, coffee houses, etc. The Jews have opened public schools and to a considerable extent developed the trade school system.

All these measures have produced a certain reassurance which is necessary if their economic capacity is to be exploited for our purposes.

*Experiences?* Despite all these relatively favorable circumstances, the existence of a Jewish district inside a large city is naturally a perpetual source of uneasiness. The danger of a spread of epidemics can never be eliminated one hundred per cent, and there are always various other difficulties as well. Hence the best solution would apparently still be the removal of the Jews to some other place.

So long, however, as Jews are still present here, the course of action adopted in Warsaw would seem to be the most appropriate: to seal off the Jews as much as possible from their surroundings, to exploit their labor according to plan, and to allow them the widest latitude in regulating their own affairs.

I hope that the above will in some measure be sufficient. The photos you have asked for have been ordered, but unfortunately I have not yet received them. I will send them on to you as fast as possible.

Heil Hitler
a [signed initial]
(Auerswald)

## 7. CONTRIBUTIONS AND THE CAPITAL MARKET

YAD VASHEM Microfilm Roll JM 1112
YIVO Institute Microfilm Roll MKY 76

Warsaw, March 4, 1942

The Chairman of the Jewish Council—Czerniakow—reports the following:

The Director of the *Transferstelle*, Mr. Bischof, announced to representatives of the Jewish Provisioning Authority, Gepner or Stolcman, his disapproval of the chairman's conduct in collecting fees, contributions, and the like; when Czerniakow arrested Jews to force payment, he was ruining the capital market. He, Bischof, was going to have a meeting with the board of the Jewish Provisioning Authority, invite Czerniakow there, and induce him to change his methods.

Gepner—or Stolcman—passed on this recent utterance to Czerniakow with the comment that even the German side regarded his procedures as too harsh.

Czerniakow expressed the fear that such utterances by the Director of the *Transferstelle* undermined the chairman's authority among the Jews, necessarily undermining the implementation of directives handed to the chairman by the Germans.

[initialed Auersw.]

[file note]

## 8. BILLS FOR THE WALL

Zentrale Stelle der Landesjustizverwaltungen in Ludwigsburg (Akten Auerswald) Polen 365d, pp. 302-303.

IV.  Statement of Balance

for:  the <u>Kommissar</u> for the Jewish District, Warsaw

from:  Schmidt & Münstermann, Tiefbaugesellschaft, Inc.

Account:  Emmissicnsbank in Polen          Warsaw, January 7, 1942

Postal Account:                            Mars Street 8 - 3

| Running Number | Running number of cost addition | Time during which work was performed | Number | Subject | Amount per unit Zl. Gr. | Amount total Zl. Gr. |
|---|---|---|---|---|---|---|
| | | | | We bill you for work completed to this date in accordance with summary calculation below | | |
| 1. | | | 3061.23 | Cubic meters of erected wall | 150.00 | 459,184.50 |
| 2. | | | 457.23 | Cubic meters foundation | 140.00 | 64,012.20 |
| 3. | | | 1111 | Pieces of iron supports | 10.00 | 11,110.00 |
| 4. | | | 3059.55 | Linear meters of cement cover | 8.50 | 26,007.03 |
| 5. | | | 12 | Weeks (10/13/41-1/3/42) | 900.00 | 10,800.00 |
| | | | | Total | | 571,113.73 |
| | | | | 1.  Part Payment 10/29/41 100,000.00 | | |
| | | | | 2.  Part Payment 11/28/41  65,000.00 | | |
| | | | | 3.  Part Payment 12/3/    15,000.00 | | |
| | | | | 4.  Part Payment 12/10/    50,000.00 | | |
| | | | | 5.  Part Payment 12/19/    60,000.00 | | 310,000.00 |
| | | | | Balance | | 261,113.73 |

In words:  Zloty two hundred sixty-one thousand, one hundred and thirteen 73/100.

[3061.23 cubic meters = 108,020.81 ft$^3$]
[3059.65 cubic meters = 107,975.05 ft$^3$]

SCHMIDT & MÜNSTERMANN
TIEFBAUGESELLSCHAFT INC.

The <u>Kommissar</u> for the Jewish District, Warsaw

Warsaw, Brühl Palace

STATEMENT OF ACCOUNT

as of July 7, 1942

ZLOTY

|  |  | <u>Debits</u> | <u>Credits</u> |
|---|---|---|---|
| <u>1941</u> | Charges for cessation of work | 1,248.53 | |
| | "  "  calcium chloride | 806.20 | |
| | "  "  equipping construction office | 30,000.— | |
| | Part payment for the bridge: | | 30,000.— |
| | Part payment for ghetto wall: | | |
| | 10/29/41  Zl.  100,000.— | | |
| | 11/28/ "  "  85,000.— | | |
| | 12/3/  "  "  15,000.— | | |
| | 12/10/ "  "  50,000.— | | |
| | 12/19/ "  "  60,000.— | | 310,000.— |
| | 12/31/41  to balance carried forward | 307,945.27 | |
| | | 340,000.— | 340,000.— |
| <u>1942</u> | To balance carried forward | | 307,945.27 |
| 1/10 | Payment | | 100,000.— |
| 1/22 | " | | 100,000.— |
| 1/30 | Charges for the bridge  100,216.— | | |
| | — Payment  30,000.— | 70,216.— | |
| 2/8 | E R Bridge | 16,918.28 | |
| 2/12 | I N R " | 5,647.50 | |
| | Payment | | 100,000.— |
| | II N R | 1,615.65 | |
| 2/13 | III N R | 600.— | |
| 2/28 | Charges for calcium chloride | 806.20 | |
| 4/16 | Payment | | 100,000.— |
| 4/28 | " | | 100,000.— |
| 5/12 | Charges for repair of wall | 37,828.75 | |
| 5/18 | "  "  <u>Transfer</u> building | 113,900.— | |
| 5/26 [?] | Payment | | 100,000.— |
| 5/30 | To R. 24 for bridge Leszno St. | 24,057.68 | |
| | " R 25 for guard post Nalewski St. | 8,550.— | |
| | " R 26 for "  " additions | 3,900.— | |
| 6/4 | Payment | | 100,000.— |
| 6/11 | " | | 50,000.— |
| 7/4 | To charges R 30 -- wall repair | 6,737.18 | |
| | "  " R 31 -- guard post | 11,700.— | |
| | "  " R 32 -- " | 25,050.— | |
| | "  " R 33 -- wall repair | 9,569.62 | |
| | "  " R 34 -- VII on account | 972,462.85 | |
| | Balance carried forward | | 251,614.44 |
| | | 1,309,559.71 | 1,309,559.71 |
| 7/8 | To balance carried forward | 251,614.44 | |

<u>S</u>.<u>E</u>. & <u>O</u>.

SCHMIDT & MÜNSTERMANN
TIEFBAUGESELLSCHAFT INC.

Warsaw, July 8, 1942

Warsaw  Mars St. 8/3
Tel.

## 9. DELIVERIES

YAD VASHEM Microfilm Roll JM 1112
YIVO Institute Microfilm Roll MKY 76

THE CHAIRMAN OF THE
   JEWISH COUNCIL               Warsaw, June 20, 1942
   IN WARSAW                  Grzybowska St. 26/28
ADMINISTRATION OF THE
   JEWISH DISTRICT
   IN WARSAW

Certificate of Delivery No. 220

RE: Delivery of items listed below
Previous: Letter of *Kommissar* for the Jewish District in Warsaw.
    File No. K - 0100 Register 1237/42, of June 19, 1942

1. 1 (one) quilt
2. 1 (one) pillow
3. 2 (two) sheets
4. 2 (two) pillow cases
5. 2 (two) quilt covers
6. 4 (four) hand towels

Director of Economic Division
First
[signed]

[handwritten note in margin
indicating receipt
July 2, signed Makowski]

## 10. THE ELECTION OF A NEW CHAIRMAN

Zentrale Stelle der Landesjustizverwaltungen in Ludwigsburg
(Akten Auerswald) Polen 365 e, pp. 642-43

THE CHAIRMAN OF THE JEWISH COUNCIL
IN WARSAW

# ADMINISTRATION OF THE JEWISH DISTRICT IN WARSAW

No. K/9985

To the *Kommissar* of the Jewish District
in Warsaw

I permit myself hereby to enclose my report of the activities of the Jewish Council in Warsaw for the month of July.

The Chairman of the Jewish Council
in Warsaw
[signed] Marek Lichtenbaum

Enclosure
WXIII—Stat. 483/42
Al/fr

[Stamp of *Kommissar* and
notations in ink]

67th Report
of the Chairman of the Jewish Council in Warsaw for the month
of July 1942

[Excerpt]

The following report about the activities of the Jewish Council is composed of two parts, the first dealing with the period July 1–21, the second with the period July 22–31 from the onset of the resettlement action.

---

The Chairman of the Jewish Council in Warsaw, Adam Czerniakow, died on July 23; during a night meeting on July 23–24, the Jewish Council elected Eng. Marek Lichtenbaum chairman, and Eng. Abram Sztolcman and Dr. Gamsej Wielikowski deputy chairmen.

# Notation on
# Sources

## DOCUMENTS

Almost all the remaining correspondence, whether orders, reports, or conference minutes, pertaining to the Warsaw ghetto, was found in German files at the end of the war. The records now extant are fragments, albeit substantial, of the original collections. The following materials, which have been preserved in various forms, have been used in preparation of this volume:

1. Two Yad Vashem microfilm rolls filled with documents from the offices of Leist, Auerswald, and the *Transferstelle*. Reports by the Jewish Council and letters over Czerniakow's signature are included in these files. Rolls JM 1112 and 1113.
2. Texts of several weekly reports and statistical materials prepared by the Jewish Council in 1940 prior to the establishment of the ghetto, in Szymon Datner, "Dzialalnosc Warszawskiej 'Gminy Wyznaniowej Zydowskiej' dokumentach podziemnego archiwum getta warszawskiego ('Ringelblum II')" [Activities of the Warsaw Jewish Community in the documents of the underground archives of the Warsaw ghetto (Ringelblum II)], *Biuletyn Zydowskiego Instytutu Historycznego,* No. 73 (January-March, 1970), pp. 101-132 and No. 74 (April-June, 1970), pp. 87-136.

3. A Yad Vashem microfilm roll containing situation reports by territorial officials in the *Generalgouvernement,* including Hummel's office. JM 814.
4. The *Akten* Auerswald, in three volumes, at the Zentrale Stelle der Landesjustizverwaltungen in Ludwigsburg. These records overlap somewhat with Yad Vashem's microfilms.
5. Miscellaneous materials in Ludwigsburg drawn from cases prepared against Beutel *(Einsatzgruppe IV)* and Hahn.
6. National Archives microfilm T 175, roll 484, mainly for identification of Security Police personnel in the Warsaw district.
7. Jüdisches Historisches Institut Warschau, *Faschismus—Getto— Massenmord* (Berlin: Rütten & Loening, 2d ed., 1961), a collection of printed documents dealing with Jewry in all of German-occupied Poland, and including important items about Warsaw.
8. The diary of Hans Frank, actually an official log containing minutes of meetings attended by the *Generalgouverneur,* in Nuremberg document PS-2233; excerpts reprinted in International Military Tribunal, *Trial of the Major War Criminals,* Vol. 29 (Nuremberg, 1947–49), pp. 356–724, as well as in other collections.
9. Friedrich Gollert, ed. *Warschau unter deutscher Herrschaft.* Krakow: Burgverlag G.m.b.H. 1942. An official publication sponsored by *Gouverneur* Fischer. Mainly background information (essays, tables, and photographs).

## BOOKS, ARTICLES, AND MANUSCRIPTS

The following list contains firsthand accounts (diaries and memoirs) as well as secondary sources (studies of ghetto institutions or assessments of Czerniakow), all of which shed some light on the contents of Czerniakow's diary. The enumeration, however, is not exhaustive. In particular, it does not include most of the unpublished manuscripts or any of the typewritten transcriptions of oral testimony in various archives and libraries.

Berg, Mary. *Warsaw Ghetto.* New York: L. B. Fischer, 1945. A diary spanning October 1939–July 1942. The author, daughter of an American citizen, was still in her teens when she was repatriated with her mother in 1943. Translated from the Polish. Very detailed.

Donat, Alexander. *The Holocaust Kingdom.* New York: Holt, Rinehart, 1963. Autobiographical account of a middleclass survivor. Only the opening chapters deal with the ghetto before the deportations

Ernest, Stefan. "Trzeci front: o wojnie wielkich Niemiec z Zydami Warszawy 1939–1943." [Third Front: The war of Greater Germany against the Jews of Warsaw 1939-1943]. Memoirs of a Jewish labor official written while in hiding early 1943. He did not survive. Insightful descriptions of Council members and other Council personnel. Unpublished manuscript in the private collection of Dr. Lucjan Dobroszycki.

Friedman, Philip, ed. *Martyrs and Fighters.* New York: Frederick A. Praeger, 1954. Short selections, mostly from memoirs and diaries, ranging from 1939 to 1944. Still valuable.

Goldstein, Bernard. *The Stars Bear Witness.* New York: Viking, 1949. Memoirs of a Bund leader, translated from the Yiddish.

Gutman, Israel. "Adam Czerniakow—The Man and His Diary." In *The Catastrophe of European Jewry,* edited by Israel Gutman and Livia Rothkirchen, pp. 451–89. Jerusalem: Yad Vashem, 1976. Sophisticated analysis of Czerniakow's role and character.

Hirszfeld, Ludwik. *Historia jednego zycia* [The story of a life]. Warsaw: Czytelnik, 1946. The recollection of a scientist who is mentioned in Czerniakow's diary. Hirszfeld wrote them in hiding during 1943.

Ivanka, Aleksander. *Wspomnienia skarbowca* 1927–1945 [Memoirs of a treasurer 1927-1945] Warsaw: Panstwowe Wy-dawnictwo Naukowe, [Warsaw: State Scholarly Publishers], 1964. Memoirs of the chief financial officer in the Polish municipality of Warsaw under German occupation. Revealing glimpses of Czerniakow and German administrators. Informative on financial relations between the municipality and the ghetto.

Kaplan, Chaim. *Scroll of Agony.* Translated and edited by Abraham Katsh. New York: Macmillan, 1965, published in paperback as *The Warsaw Diary of Chaim Kaplan.* Diary, filled with personal reactions and reflections. The twelve months from April

1941 to May 1942 were missing from the hardcover, but were subsequently found and published in the paperback edition. The author was principal of a Hebrew elementary school. Original in Hebrew.

Landau, Ludwik. *Kronika lat wojny i okupacji* [Chronicle of the years of war and occupation] vol. 1. Warsaw: Panstwowe Wydawnictwo naukowe, 1962. Diary of a Jewish economist associated with the Polish underground. The entries cover Polish as well as Jewish affairs. They provide, however, significant detail about Warsaw Jewry. Vol. 1 only to November, 1940; two other volumes from the end of 1942.

Ringelblum, Emanuel. *Notes from the Warsaw Ghetto.* Translated and edited by Jacob Sloan. New York: McGraw-Hill, 1958. Original in Yiddish. Ringelblum was a professional historian. The Sloan edition of his diary is a translation of selections published in Warsaw. Sloan did not have access to the full text, either the original in Warsaw or a copy in Israel.

Trunk, Isaiah. *Judenrat.* New York: Macmillan, 1972; paperback, Stein and Day, 1977. The indispensable book on ghettos in Nazi eastern Europe. A heavy work, very detailed. Contains considerable information about Warsaw.

Turkow, Jonas. *Azoy iz es geven* [That is the way it was]. Buenos Aires: Central Federation of Polish Jews in Argentina, 1948. Turkow was a stage director and actor before the war. In the ghetto he was associated with Jewish Social Self-Help. His memoirs deal, *inter alia,* with the theater, the JSS, and a number of Jewish public figures.

Tushnet, Leonard. *The Pavement of Hell.* New York: St. Martin's Press, 1972. A sensitive study of Rumkowski (Lódź), Gens (Vilna), and Czerniakow.

———. *The Uses of Adversity.* New York: Thomas Yoseloff, 1966. Medical aspects of starvation in the Warsaw ghetto. The author is an American physician.

## NEWSPAPERS, LEGAL GAZETTES

*Gazeta Zydowska*
*Krakauer Zeitung*
*Verordnungsblatt des Generalgouverneurs*

# Index

Names of persons and localities mentioned by Czerniakow only in passing and having no apparent significance in his life or for the fate of the Warsaw Jewish community have been omitted from the index.

# 418 · Index